WITHDRAWN

Slavery, Race,
and
American History

Slavery, Race, and American History

Historical Conflict, Trends, and Method, 1866–1953

John David Smith

M.E. Sharpe
Armonk, New York
London, England

Library of Congress Cataloging-in-Publication Data

Smith, John David, 1949–
Slavery, race, and American history : historical conflict, trends,
and method, 1866–1953 / John David Smith.
p. cm.
Includes bibliographical references and index.
ISBN 0-7656-0377-2 (hardcover : alk, paper)
1. Slavery—United States—Historiography. 2. Afro-Americans—
Historiography. 3. Racism—United States—Historiography.
4. United States—Race relations—Historiography. 5. Historians—
United States—History. I. Title.
E441.S6555 1999
305.896'073—dc21   98-41941
CIP

Printed in the United States of America

The paper used in this publication meets the minimum requirements of
American National Standard for Information Sciences—
Permanence of Paper for Printed Library Materials,
ANSI Z 39.48-1984.

BM (c) 10   9   8   7   6   5   4   3   2   1

For Holman Hamilton, whom I never had a chance to thank

Contents

Preface

This book examines the first generations of historians who studied African American slavery and race and analyzes their importance in establishing those topics as major interpretive questions for modern scholars. The early historiography of slavery, race, and the American South provides a useful window to view conflicts between historians, to highlight interpretive trends, and to chart methodological advances among historians of the South in the century following Appomattox. Though early scholars such as James Ford Rhodes and Ulrich Bonnell Phillips, respectively, revived elements of the old neoabolitionist and proslavery arguments, they nevertheless raised many new and important questions about the history of race relations in America. Their interpretations in turn influenced a cadre of later scholars and, in the case of Phillips, led to a "Phillips school" of state studies on slavery that dominated the historiography of slavery until the early 1950s.

In those years, a broad range of other historians, including George H. Moore, Frederic Bancroft, W.E.B. Du Bois, and Clement Eaton, challenged traditional interpretations and suggested new avenues of inquiry. Central to this book is my belief that contemporary scholars tend to pay insufficient attention to the contributions of their intellectual forebears, especially those with whom they disagree ideologically or in terms of research method. As the essays in this book suggest, however, early historians of slavery and race overcame many obstacles and contributed much to our understanding of these topics. They not only prefigured later scholarship but also reached conclusions of lasting significance, unearthed primary sources, and constructed methodologies adopted by scores of later historians. Significantly, the post–Civil War decades witnessed the "professionalization" of the historian's craft in the United States, the rise of rigid racial segregation in the South, and the first serious challenges to the system of American apartheid by blacks. The essays that comprise this book frame the early scholarship on slavery and race within that intellectual and social context.

Long before the modern civil rights era, slavery and race emerged as major topics of concern for American historians. Not surprisingly, historians disagreed openly and engaged regularly in vituperative public debates over such issues as the institutional origins of slavery, the extent of "Africanisms" within the African American population, the nature of slave life, the domestic slave trade, varieties of slave resistance, slavery's profitability, and "plantation paternalism." The essays contained in Part 1 focus on controversies among historians on these and other issues. Though I emphasize the power of race, class, and sectionalism on the various historians I discuss, students no doubt will recognize the highly *personal* nature of much of the criticism leveled by historians against their peers. Historians of an earlier day, like historians today, were human beings whose historical criticism sometimes masked intensely personal issues as well as professional ones.

Chapter 1 examines the highly partisan controversy sparked by the publication of George H. Moore's obscure *Notes on the History of Slavery in Massachusetts* (1866). Writing in the age of emancipation, Moore used historical evidence to expose what he considered to be a long tradition of hypocrisy over slavery and race among Massachusetts abolitionists, politicians, and historians. Ironically, white southerners cited Moore, a harsh critic of slavery, as an ally in their condemnation of Radical Reconstruction. Later in the century, another scholar, future president Woodrow Wilson, challenged the influential neoabolitionist interpretation of slavery set forth by James Ford Rhodes in the first volume of his well-known *History of the United States from the Compromise of 1850* (1892). The conflict between Wilson, a "scientifically" trained southern intellectual, and Rhodes, a "Brahmin" capitalist and amateur historian, is the focus of chapter 2. Professionally trained historians sympathetic to the South and its most "peculiar institution," slavery, would reign over historical scholarship on race as the sun set on the nineteenth century. They espoused what I have described elsewhere as "An old creed for the new South."[1]

The Georgia-born historian Ulrich Bonnell Phillips led historians of African American slavery during the first half of the new century and, as a result, he is the central figure in this book. Debates over Phillips's scholarship and the importance of his work are the subject of chapters 3, 4, and 5. Phillips's "scientific" historical training, his belief in black inferiority, his condescension toward working-class people in general, and his identification with slaveholders equipped him well to dominate the historiography of slavery during the age of segregation. In many pathbreaking essays and, especially, in his two landmark books—*American Negro Slavery: A Survey of the Supply, Employment and Control of Negro Labor as Determined by the Plantation Régime* (1918) and *Life and Labor in the Old South* (1929)—Phillips analyzed slavery's social and economic history in more depth and with more sophistication than any previous investigator.

His innovative use of primary sources, his analysis of slavery on a cost basis, and his belief that a complex system of paternalism characterized master-slave relations marked Phillips's writings as perceptive and unique. In keeping with the racial thought and "scientific" historical method of the Progressive era, Phillips described slavery as a benevolent "school" that educated savage blacks in the ways of "civilization." Convinced that slavery largely was good for blacks but bad for whites, he concluded that the "peculiar institution" was generally an unprofitable form of investment, "less a business than a life," one that "made fewer fortunes than it made men."[2] Students may note Phillips's subtle influence on E. Merton Coulter's reactionary analysis of emancipated Kentucky slaves in his landmark *The Civil War and Readjustment in Kentucky* (1926), the subject of chapter 10.

Chapters 11, 13, 14, and 15 treat several aspects of Phillips's career, including his surprisingly myopic observations of non-Western plantation societies; his part altruistic, part self-serving efforts to promote the collection and preservation of southern archival materials; and his little-discussed pioneer labors as a documentary editor. For the sake of students interested in the history of historical method, archival history and practice, and documentary publishing, I have grouped chapters 13, 14, and 15 together in Part 3 of this book.

Though Phillips's prosouthern, proslavery interpretation continued to dominate slavery scholarship long after his premature death in 1934, as early as 1913, a host of critics—led by W.E.B. Du Bois, Carter G. Woodson, and Frederic Bancroft—identified serious weaknesses in his historical method and condemned his blatantly antiblack interpretations. Significantly, criticisms of Phillips and his scholarship mirrored challenges by blacks and whites to the Jim Crow system of race relations that Phillips and his white disciples represented and endorsed. The stinging post–World War II denunciations of Phillips by Richard Hofstadter and Kenneth M. Stampp in fact signaled a "new" history of slavery as surely as the 1954 *Brown v. Board of Education* case marked the beginning of segregation's demise. I have chosen to include Clement Eaton's valuable southern travel narratives in this book (see chapter 12) as a counterpoint to Phillips. Eaton epitomized the "liberal" southern white scholar of the 1930s, 1940s, and 1950s and remains an important transitionary figure in the historiography of the South. Though largely ignored today, Eaton's significant scholarly contributions—ranging from insightful analyses of the freedom of thought struggle in the Old South to its cultural history—await thorough analysis.

Part 2 of *Slavery, Race, and American History* examines various earlier revisionist trends that contributed significantly to the historiography of African American slavery and race relations. Chapters 6, 7, 8, and 9 focus on the ideas of a broad range of scholars who initiated fresh inquiries about varied aspects of slavery. Early in the century, Alfred Holt Stone, a Mississippi planter-capitalist and amateur historian, sought answers to fundamental questions about the conditions of slave life and plantation economics that remain central to today's historians of slavery. So too did historian Howell M. Henry, whose 1914 doctoral dissertation on the "police control" of South Carolina slaves remains one of the few extant studies of that important topic.

Scholars also have paid surprisingly little attention to how black intellectuals during the Progressive era and after responded to the works of Phillips and others sympathetic to slavery. My research, summarized in chapter 8, suggests that blacks seriously challenged the new proslavery argument by emphasizing slavery's barbarities and by documenting the blacks' various modes of resistance. Early analyses of black folk expression—music, dance, folk tales, and material culture—are the focus of chapter 9. Not only did this corpus of scholarship present the black man's view of slavery, but it also foreshadowed many of the topics examined and sources employed by later scholars as well. Students might compare the early writings on slave folk culture with such important recent works as Dena J. Epstein's *Sinful Tunes and Spirituals* (1977), Lawrence W. Levine's *Black Culture and Black Consciousness* (1977), Sterling Stuckey's *Slave Culture* (1987), and *Stylin'* (1998) by Shane White and Graham White. My point is that much can be learned about the history of slavery and race by the careful reading of hard-to-find and generally ignored scholarship. Despite the racism of the pioneer white scholars, and the methodological limitations of historians of both races, the historians whose work I analyze in this book still have much to teach us about the history of slavery and race.

I conceptualized this book with the student reader in mind. Though each of the essays has appeared in print previously, my intent is to make them accessible to a broader audience and to make the articles available in one convenient place. Because instructors may assign selected chapters to their classes, I have chosen to reprint the articles largely in their original form. This will allow them either to stand alone or as part of an interrelated whole. Rather than update the bibliographical references in each essay, I have elected to provide a Select Bibliography that brings the articles in line with current scholarship.

While readers will find a degree of unavoidable repetition in some of the articles, especially those on Phillips, my hope is that this in fact will underscore the book's central themes. Phillips's life and labor set the interpretive parameters not only for this book but also for the intellectual history of slavery and race in the first half of the twentieth century. Until the post–World War II era, most mainstream scholars accepted Phillips's proslavery interpretation. The image of the happy slave and benevolent master infiltrated many elements of American popular culture. Phillips's writings unquestionably suggest the strengths and weaknesses of Progressive era historical methodology. And significantly, the determination of early African American scholars to challenge Phillips's views prepared the way for the revisionist writings of such influential historians as John Hope Franklin, John W. Blassingame, and Nathan I. Huggins. While it took almost fifty years to dethrone Phillips as the master of slave historiography, I believe that our understanding of the "peculiar institution" is richer thanks to his pioneer labors. As a new century nears, we can look back calmly and dispassionately to the contributions of those early historians who, during the racially tense era of Jim Crow, recognized the central place of slavery and race to understanding American history. These topics are no less important or timely today.

John David Smith

Acknowledgments

Aside from stylistic changes, minor emendations, and the expansion and standardization of bibliographical citations, the fifteen essays that compose this book appear largely as they did in their original form in thirteen journals and one book in the period 1979 to 1994. They are reprinted here by permission.

"George H. Moore: 'Tormentor of Massachusetts' " appeared in *The Moment of Decision: Biographical Essays on American Character and Regional Identity,* ed. Randall M. Miller and John R. McKivigan (Westport, CT: Greenwood Press, 1994), 211–226. "James Ford Rhodes, Woodrow Wilson, and the Passing of the Amateur Historian of Slavery" appeared in *Mid-America* 64 (October 1982): 17–24. "W.E.B. Du Bois and Ulrich Bonnell Phillips: Symbolic Antagonists of the Progressive Era" appeared in *Centennial Review* 24 (Winter 1980): 88–102. "Historical or Personal Criticism? The Case of Frederic Bancroft Versus Ulrich Bonnell Phillips" appeared in *Washington State University Research Studies* 49 (June 1981): 73–86. "The Historiographic Rise, Fall, and Resurrection of Ulrich Bonnell Phillips" appeared in *Georgia Historical Quarterly* 65 (Summer 1981): 138–153. "Alfred Holt Stone: Mississippi Planter and Archivist/Historian of Slavery" appeared in *Journal of Mississippi History* 45 (November 1983): 262–270. "Neglected but Not Forgotten: Howell M. Henry and the 'Police Control' of Slaves in South Carolina" appeared in *Proceedings of the South Carolina Historical Association* (1980): 94–110. "A Different View of Slavery: Black Historians Attack the New Proslavery Argument, 1890–1920" appeared in *Journal of Negro History* 65 (Fall 1980): 298–311. "The Unveiling of Slave Folk Culture, 1865–1920" appeared in *Journal of Folklore Research* 21 (April 1984): 47–62. "E. Merton Coulter, the 'Dunning School,' and *The Civil War and Readjustment in Kentucky*" appeared in *Register of the Kentucky Historical Society* 86 (Winter 1988): 52–69. "Ulrich Bonnell Phillips's World Tour and the Study of Comparative Plantation Societies" appeared in *Yale University*

Library Gazette 68 (April 1994): 157–168. "A Southern Historian on Tour: Clement Eaton's Travels Through the New South" appeared in *Southern Studies: An Interdisciplinary Journal of the South* 21 (Summer 1982): 163–207 (with Randall M. Miller). "'Keep 'Em in a Fire-Proof Vault'—Pioneer Southern Historians Discover Plantation Records" appeared in *South Atlantic Quarterly* 78 (Summer 1979): 376–391. "The Historian as Archival Advocate: Ulrich Bonnell Phillips and the Records of Georgia and the South" appeared in *American Archivist* 52 (Summer 1989): 320–331. "Ulrich Bonnell Phillips's *Plantation and Frontier Documents: 1649–1863:* The Historian as Documentary Editor" appeared in *Georgia Historical Quarterly* 77 (Spring 1993): 123–143. I am grateful to the various editors and to the Greenwood Publishing Group for their permission to reprint my articles.

Through the years, many colleagues commented on drafts of these essays and assisted me in innumerable ways. I especially wish to thank Thomas H. Appleton, Jr., James C. Klotter, Randall M. Miller, David P. Gilmartin, Charles W. Joyner, Mark E. Neely, Jr., Sylvia Neely, Charles P. Roland, John Cimprich, the late Aubrey C. Land, the late Clement Eaton, John C. Inscoe, Kenneth P. Vickery, Jeffrey J. Crow, the late Howard N. Rabinowitz, Leslie Smith Rousell, and Sylvia A. Smith. Professor Miller graciously has allowed me to reprint "A Southern Historian on Tour: Clement Eaton's Travels Through the New South," an article that we co-authored in 1982. Chris Graham, my graduate research assistant at North Carolina State University, provided yeoman service in verifying the accuracy of texts, checking bibliographical citations, and conducting additional research. As usual, Richard Costello, B.D. Sossomon, and Brett Larson patiently answered my seemingly endless computer questions. Peter Coveney, my editor at M.E. Sharpe, encouraged me to undertake this collection and provided many valuable suggestions. Esther Clark, Eileen Maass, and Steven Martin smoothed out details and saw the book through the publication process.

Many years ago, the late Professor Holman Hamilton of the University of Kentucky piqued my interest in American historians in general and the historiography of slavery, race, and the South in particular. A gifted teacher and literary stylist, Dr. Hamilton set a high scholarly standard and continues to inspire my work in the history of the South and the Civil War. I dedicate this book to him with deep affection and gratitude.

I

Conflicts

1

George H. Moore
"Tormentor of Massachusetts"

A school of "romantic nationalists," according to historian David D. Van Tassel, dominated American historical scholarship in the three decades before the Civil War. Inspired by the European romantics, George Bancroft, Francis Parkman, and Jared Sparks used their histories to evangelize the ideology of American freedom and spread the message of America's rise and progress. As influential as these historians' works were in fostering American nationality, however, the Civil War era gave rise to a new generation of scholars who viewed the work of their forebears with considerable skepticism. Such now-little-known historians as Charles Deane, Edmund B. O'Callaghan, and Nathaniel B. Shurtleff focused largely on local studies to test the findings of their hero-worshipping predecessors. The new "critical" breed of historians scrutinized "often-repeated stories and burrowed into accumulated documents to verify and correct older histories." This transitional group of historians—falling between the romantic and the "scientific" historians who emerged later in the century—contributed significantly to the revisionist tradition in American historiography. According to Van Tassel, they "not only raised the general standard of scholarship but also improved current methods of collecting, evaluating, and editing documents."[1]

New Hampshire native George H. Moore (1823–92) stands as one of the most talented and controversial of the unsung school of critical historians. Joking about his origins, Moore admitted that although he was a New Englander, his "ancestors were not Puritans—but among those who came to 'catch fish.' "[2] His father, Jacob B. Moore, was himself a pioneer historian, antiquarian, and librarian of the historical societies of New Hampshire and New York.[3] The younger Moore earned his bachelor's and master's degrees in 1842 and 1845, respectively, from the University of the City of New York and was awarded an LL.D.

from that institution in 1869. Although he never actually taught, for a decade Moore held a professorship in legal history and literature at the same university. He is best known, however, as librarian first of the New-York Historical Society (1849–76) and then of the Lenox Library (1876–92), which later became the core collection of the New York Public Library. As a librarian, Moore supplied copies of documents, pamphlets, and rare books to some of the most important historians of his day, including Parkman, O'Callaghan, and Justin Winsor.[4] In addition, he corresponded about his own scholarship with several persons who later significantly influenced the course of U.S. history. Most notably, in 1839, while Moore attended Dartmouth College, Captain Robert E. Lee assisted him with his research on Charles Lee, U.S. Attorney General (1795–1801).[5] Moore ultimately wrote nine monographs and many articles and ranked as one of the country's most distinguished historians of colonial and Revolutionary America.[6]

Although a New Englander by birth and education, Moore felt compelled to distance himself intellectually from his region in order to write the section's history fairly, accurately, and critically. He believed in overturning what he called "the myths and traditions" of "the old school" of New England history. For too long, Moore said, Massachusetts had magnified men such as John Winthrop, Increase and Cotton Mather, and John Endicott. Instead, Moore was determined to examine under a microscope Massachusetts's "historical reputation," especially its alleged "early and consistent zeal against slavery."[7] Not surprisingly, he welcomed Brooks Adams's iconoclastic view of Massachusetts's past. It illustrated Moore's "theory of social evolution, which," he said, "likens the inner court of the New England Theocracy, the association of the elders of Massachusetts, to the sacred caste of the Zuni Indians."[8] On another occasion, Moore remarked to historian George Bancroft that Massachusetts natives could view things only through "Mass-spectacles."[9]

Moore's critical spirit transcended his historical work. In 1852, for instance, he judged both Franklin Pierce and Winfield Scott so weak as presidential candidates that he threatened not to vote at all. He informed Daniel Webster's private secretary George J. Abbot:

> Southern treachery and Northern cowardice have opened a new chapter, not only in the history of the Whig Party, but of the Country; what its final record will be, no human being can foresee. For my part, I am so thoroughly sickened of Whig Politics that I am inclined to believe I should vote the Democratic Ticket had they nominated anybody but a N.H. Loco Foco [Pierce].[10]

Nearly forty years later, Moore declared: "Politicians have as much interest in history as hogs and generally about the same amount of knowledge thereof. Perhaps I am doing injustice to the animals, who are said to be very sagacious."[11]

For all his self-professed iconoclasm, however, in his political thought, Moore lined up with the old New England Federalists. He claimed never to have "held any spark of sympathy" for the Antifederalists, because they valued "subserviency to the popular will" over "principle." Had the country followed the Federalism of Washington and Hamilton, Moore said, it would have been spared "the folly and wickedness of those who have perverted their teachings and yielded to . . . 'the madness of the people.' " This attitude spilled over into Moore's view of history as he ridiculed those who believed "that *facts* of history are *not true* and the *opinions* which the majority favor *are* true." Writing to Bancroft, Moore complained that Bancroft had given "*the enemies of the Constitution* too much credit for honesty as well as patriotism. The greatest misfortunes and disgraces of our government have been due, in all its history, to the fact that its administration was so easily transferred to the hands of its enemies."[12]

Despite his admitted Federalist bias, Moore considered himself a member of "the new school of historical criticism" that rejected all partisanship and hero worship. "Much of our earlier history," he informed Charles Deane, "is open to criticism, for errors which I am sorry to admit, have not always been due to ignorance or want of material." Moore argued that it was "high time to expurgate the mythical element from the treatment of a history which is so recent and for which the documents are so abundant as our own." He complained that too few of his fellow historians were "really patient and critical." Also, Moore was shocked by the "ignorance" that passed as history—for example, the uncritical flag-waving nationalism of the 1876 Philadelphia Centennial celebration. "I believe in the truth of history," Moore declared, "and unpleasant as the truth may be—intend to draw all my lines with a single purpose for absolute fidelity to what I regard as the first canon of historical criticism—'above all things—truth.' " According to pioneer African American historian George Washington Williams, Moore's contributions shined "with an energy and perspicuity of style" and "his refined sarcasm, unanswerable logic, and critical accuracy give him undisputed place amongst the ablest writers of our times." Moore's blend of Federalism, skepticism, cynicism, and determination to get the facts straight set him on a collision course with the venerable traditions of Massachusetts.[13]

In 1866 Moore published the controversial book that established his reputation as "the tormentor of Massachusetts."[14] *Notes on the History of Slavery in Massachusetts* merged critical historical methodology with an intense antislavery ideology into a broadside attack on what he deemed Massachusetts's hypocrisy on the slavery question.[15] The irony of condemning the state, long considered the cradle of abolitionism for its gross complicity with the evil of slavery, was not lost on Moore.

Moore's historical views were closely related to his political beliefs. His devotion to Federalism led Moore first to join the Whig party and, after its demise, to become an ardent Republican. Unlike most white Republicans, however, Moore favored the emancipation of blacks early in the Civil War. During that conflict, Moore published a pamphlet that underscored the resistance to the recruitment of blacks as soldiers and their emancipation during the American

Revolution and singled out Massachusetts's persistent "conservative policy" on the question.[16] Four years later, Moore announced that his *Notes on the History of Slavery* contained nothing "to comfort proslavery men anywhere." For almost a century, supporters of Massachusetts had "drawn" the "curtains" on slavery's ignoble history in the state, Moore wrote. Now it was his responsibility as a historian to "let in the light upon them."[17]

In the best tradition of the critical historians at mid-century, Moore reprinted scores of official records from Massachusetts archives as well as extracts, travelers' accounts, inventories, supply bills, newspaper advertisements, church records, and petitions to underscore the "tough black knot" that slavery and racism held on Massachusetts for more than a century. He was determined to rest his argument "on facts rather than opinions," employing the calm judgment of the historian, "without disparagement and without exaggeration." The records of slavery everywhere, he insisted, showed "the same disregard of human rights, the same indifference to suffering, the same contempt for the oppressed races, the same hate for those who are injured." Moore sought to allow the documents themselves to trace the origins of the institution in Massachusetts. As narrator, he stood back and let his arsenal of primary sources indict Massachusetts before the world for greed and hypocrisy. Then, Moore stepped in to conclude that the "stains which slavery has left on the proud escutcheon *even* of Massachusetts, are quite as significant of its hideous character as the satanic defiance of God and Humanity which accompanied the laying of the corner-stone of the Slaveholders' Confederacy."[18]

Colonists in Massachusetts, Moore showed, enslaved Indians during the Pequot War and imported black slaves as early as 1638. Moore charged that, subsequently, the Atlantic slave trade, "since known and branded by all civilized nations as piracy . . . continued to flourish under the auspices of Massachusetts merchants down through the entire colonial period, and long after the boasted Declaration of Rights in 1780 had terminated (?) the legal existence of slavery within the limits of that State." He also cited a 1639 Massachusetts account of "one of the earliest, if not, indeed, the very first attempt at breeding of slaves in America." When narrating a 1644–45 case concerning slave stealing along the African coast, Moore identified "not a trace of anti-slavery opinion or sentiment, still less of anti-slavery legislation; though both have been repeatedly claimed for the honor of the colony." Moore blamed the success of slavery and the slave trade in Massachusetts on the greed and racism of the colony's officials.[19]

Moore argued further that the Bay colony's officials in fact passed the first positive legislation establishing slavery in America, the 1641 *Body of Liberties of the Massachusetts Colony in New-England*. Although guaranteeing the fundamental rights of some persons, Massachusetts leaders protected the institution of slavery "as an existing, substantial fact." In assessing the 1641 code and its revisions, Moore declared that self-righteous defenders of Massachusetts no longer could preach that slavery was forced upon unwilling colonists by England. He was particularly outraged by Senator Charles Sumner's speech of June 28, 1854, which asserted that " 'In all her annals, no person was ever born a slave on the soil of Massachusetts,' and 'If, in point of fact, the issue of slaves was sometimes held in bondage, it was never by sanction of any statute-law of Colony or Commonwealth.' " "Never," Moore complained, "were the demands of a free people eluded by their public servants with more of the contortions as well as wisdom of the serpent." On the contrary, Moore wrote, to Massachusetts's shame, the colony preceded "any and all the other colonies" in sanctioning slavery by law, years ahead of even the most notorious of the southern slaveholding colonies and states.[20]

Massachusetts whites, Moore explained, drew a clear distinction between the legal and social status of Christian (white) indentured servants and the status of Indians and black slaves. Early in the eighteenth century, when Bostonians sought to end black slavery in favor of white servitude, the resulting legislation riveted slavery more firmly on the colony than ever before. A 1703 law requiring security bonds to be posted for all manumitted blacks remained on the books as late as 1807. Other laws restricted slaves in much the same manner as the slave codes of the Old South and the Black Codes of Presidential Reconstruction. Moore noted that Massachusetts slaveholders frequently freed sick or elderly slaves, "to relieve the master from the charge of supporting them," a practice for which abolitionists had commonly attacked southern slaveholders.[21]

Moore argued further that slavery remained an important element in Massachusetts's economic and social fabric until the decade before the American Revolution. Individual blacks filed successful "suits for liberty," but these had no cumulative impact on the institution of slavery in Massachusetts. In discussing one of these suits, Moore challenged the notion that *James v. Lechmere* (1769) declared slavery unlawful in Massachusetts. It, in fact, was settled by the parties in question and, consequently, led to no legal precedents. Although one of the "cherished fancies" of defenders of Massachusetts was the idea that *James v. Lechmere* prefigured *Somerset v. Stewart* (1772), Moore maintained that in the *Somerset* case, Lord Mansfield prohibited only the forced removal of slaves, not the institution of slavery.[22]

Like many later historians, Moore credited the Revolution with unveiling "the inconsistency of maintaining slavery with one hand while pleading or striking for freedom with the other." However, he insisted, even then, that public opinion in Massachusetts was reluctant to emancipate the slaves and favored only gradual change.[23] This was the hypocrisy that so irked Moore. "If there was a prevailing public sentiment against slavery in Massachusetts—as has been constantly claimed of late," Moore argued, "the people of that day, far less demonstrative than their descendants, had an extraordinary way of not showing it." In no way did Massachusetts take the lead in freeing its slaves, even after ties were severed with England. Not until the authority of the U.S. Constitution was established, he said, did an end to the "pernicious commerce" in human flesh come to pass.[24]

To be fair to Massachusetts, Moore commended attempts—albeit unsuccessful ones—by the legislature and by individuals, white and black, to kill slavery in the state during the Revolution. Nevertheless, the failure of the legislature to do so when it was hammering out a state constitution in 1777 resulted from a lack of overall sympathy for blacks and from the growing assumption that abolition would fall under the province of the new national government. Consequently, the Massachusetts Constitution and Form of Government of February 1778 recognized slavery's existence and excluded blacks, Indians, and mulattos from the rights of citizenship.[25]

Moore found not "the slightest trace of positive contemporary evidence" to support the assertion that the first article of the Declaration of Rights of Massachusetts 1780 Constitution was intended to abolish slavery in the state. Rather, that claim was yet another Massachusetts tradition that "will not stand the test of historical criticism." Only lawsuits and "bold judicial constructions" gradually transformed the first clause of the Declaration of Rights into an "instrument of *virtual* abolition" because the Massachusetts legislature had never met "the subject [of abolition] fairly and fully" but operated instead with all the "cupidity" of Massachusetts's "slave-trading merchants." The most tragic and "humiliating" part of the sad story was that Massachusetts even failed to support its indigent former slaves.[26]

Finally, in 1788, Massachusetts passed legislation "directly and positively hostile to slavery," the prohibition of the slave trade to Massachusetts. Moore, ever suspicious of motives of Massachusetts politicians, believed that his cynicism was borne out by another bill passed in 1788 requiring the removal from the state of virtually all blacks who could not prove U.S. citizenship. Although this act allegedly was intended to prevent fugitive slaves from becoming a burden on the state, Moore interpreted it as the racist response of whites to fears of slave revolt and the presence of uncontrolled free blacks. He doubted "if anything . . . can be found which comes nearer branding color as a crime!" Aghast at the subsequent "arbitrary and illegal extension of the statute" to citizens of African American ancestry, Moore wrote that the law disgraced Massachusetts until its repeal in 1834.[27]

By 1834, of course, Massachusetts was conspicuously in the forefront of the abolitionist movement. Although Moore was careful to note that the abolitionists themselves had "little if any historical connection with the existence of Slavery," his overriding message was that despite its meritorious accomplishments in battling slavery and later in fighting to preserve the Union, Massachusetts still had to acknowledge its long identification with slavery. Indeed, because slavery in Massachusetts had been abolished only *virtually,* not formally by legislation, only after the passage of the Thirteenth Amendment in 1865 did slavery come to cease in point of law.[28]

Given the racial, political, and sectional tensions of Presidential Reconstruction, Moore's book attracted controversy like a lightning rod. Critics greeted

Moore's book with mixed reviews. New York's Henry B. Dawson, a biting critic who at one time or another had taken virtually all of the leading contemporary American historians to task, welcomed *Notes on the History of Slavery* with unrestrained praise. In the *Historical Magazine,* critical history's foremost journal,[29] Dawson proclaimed, "No Roundhead ever performed his iconoclastic labors with more zest or more thoroughly" than Moore. "He has labored patiently . . . dispassionately . . . [and] effectively, as is proved by . . . the extreme backwardness of all competent Massachusetts men in the work of disproving" it. Finally, Dawson doubted that "the claimants to superiority, throughout the Bay State, can maintain the elevated position . . . which they have so long and so insolently attempted to occupy."[30]

The Democratic press, as might be expected, also lavished praise upon Moore's book, but not because of any commitment to critical scholarship. Rather, the *New York Herald* cited *Notes on the History of Slavery* as a timely reminder of "the inherent hypocrisy and baseness" of the Republican party. The reviewer held New Englanders accountable for "the worst features of slavery" and added that the Republicans—through the Freedmen's Bureau—were now engaged in a plot to establish "a system of negro servitude infinitely more heartless and grinding than any that has ever been charged to the Southern planter." In his own column, editor James Gordon Bennett also used discussion of Moore's book to attack the Republicans' efforts to guarantee civil rights for the freedmen. Bennett accused the "firebrand agents" of the Freedmen's Bureau with extorting the blacks and "trading in their labor—which is only another kind of slavery." "These modern Pharisees of New England," who first enslaved the blacks, wrote Bennett, "now say they would not have done what their fathers did" and threaten the nation with black revolution and race war. "Truly, they are the children of the old Puritan Pharisees."[31]

The *Springfield Weekly Republican* surprisingly welcomed *Notes on the History of Slavery* with a generous and balanced critique. The newspaper warned readers that although Moore's work "spoils a great deal of our virtuous brag," it would provide for "most a new revelation and to many a mortifying one." Indeed, the reviewer emphasized that because Massachusetts historians and orators had, unlike Moore, failed to consult original records, they had perpetrated the myth that no slaves had ever been born on Massachusetts soil. While accepting Moore's allegations, the reviewer noted that not all Massachusetts slaveholders were wicked men and that they only subscribed to the "prevailing ideas and spirit of the age in which they lived." Still, he declared defensively, Massachusetts not only was the first colony to emancipate its slaves but also led the nation in the abolitionist crusade. "We do not therefore feel the least inclination to be angry with Mr. Moore for having given us the first true account of slavery in Massachusetts," he wrote. "We may not brag henceforth as largely as before, but we shall do it more intelligently and to better purpose." Moore found the *Republican's* review of his book gratifying and remarked to George Bancroft that the reviewer had "met it manfully."[32]

Other friends of Massachusetts, blacks, and the Republican party, however, trained their guns on Moore. The *Nation,* for example, charged that Moore "distorted" his reading of the 1641 *Code of Fundamentals,* which, it said, sanctioned, *not established,* slavery. "His conclusions will, of course, comfort the enemies of emancipation," explained the reviewer, who went on to condemn Moore's "apparent jealousy of New England's preeminence" and his "aversion to Puritanism."[33] The *Independent,* noting Moore's "intrepidity," his "rare degree of courage . . . [and] audacity," predicted, quite correctly, that his book would please the Copperheads. However, the critic said, Moore naively assumed that because black children were held as slaves, they were enslaved legally; rather, they were enslaved by "an ignorant and vicious custom," which "does not affect the fact that they were illegally so entreated." Unlike Moore, the *Independent's* reviewer praised the 1641 *Body of Liberties* because it "limited and restrained" the slavery then current. Never establishing slavery, it proclaimed that those "then held as slaves . . . should be lawfully so held, freeing all other persons by its necessary interpretation."[34]

Some critics leveled personal attacks at Moore. George T. Davis charged him with carelessly accusing an innocent Massachusetts slaveholder of murdering his bondsman and incorrectly reporting the slaveholder's conviction and execution.[35] Charles F. Dunbar, editor of the *Boston Daily Advertiser,* who reportedly spent five months researching his criticism, intimated that Moore wrote his book "to gratify 'the personal resentments of [his] literary friends.' "[36] Dunbar blasted Moore as "a layman, not of conspicuously judicial instincts," who selected his evidence only with an eye toward bolstering his arguments. "There are few parts of his book," Dunbar wrote, in "which . . . it is safe, for the reader to follow the author upon trust." Not only did he accuse Moore of "suppressing inconvenient authorities," but Dunbar also asserted

> That where this process will not avail, he does not lack assurance in coolly setting aside their opinion or statements; and that his assumptions, not few in number nor unimportant in effect, have a single purpose,—to make out a case against this Commonwealth, in a matter better adapted to practice in the criminal courts than to historical discussion.

Specifically, Dunbar denied that Massachusetts authorities encouraged the slave trade and, like other reviewers, argued that because slavery existed in Massachusetts prior to 1641, it was not established by the *Body of Liberties.* Concerning hereditary slavery, Dunbar discredited Moore's "liberal interpretation" of the 1641 law, accusing him of dishonestly suppressing evidence that proved unequivocally that children of slaves were not held as slaves. Finally, Dunbar attacked Moore's allegation that slavery was not abolished by the 1780 Declaration of Rights but remained law until the Thirteenth Amendment.[37]

Moore's contention that the 1780 Massachusetts Convention never intended to abolish slavery remained under debate as late as 1875. Justice Charles Doe of the New Hampshire Supreme Court wrote that although "as, a matter of law, slavery could not exist under that constitution," he assumed that "Moore was right in concluding that neither the convention nor the people understood they were abolishing slavery by adopting the constitution." Doe, hoping "to give practical legal effect to the general declaration of freedom and equality and the right of life, liberty and property," asked to see George Bancroft's evidence to support his claim in Volume 10 of *History of the United States* that the Massachusetts Convention specifically added a clause to abolish slavery. For his part, Moore remained convinced that he, not Bancroft, was right. "I must renew my regrets that you have committed yourself to so serious an error as that respecting the intention in the Mass. Convention to abolish slavery," Moore wrote to Bancroft. "I know you are wrong—and the position cannot be maintained."[38]

Moore enjoyed his controversial reputation as "the Devil's advocate, opposing the canonization of Massachusetts." He warned anyone who challenged Massachusetts's "threads of tradition and history" to expect the "ugly storm of reproaches" that had descended upon him.[39] In responding to his critics, Moore surrendered no ground, defended himself against charges of suppressing and misrepresenting sources, and launched new attacks. He gave Davis's criticisms short shrift, arguing that a master's cruelty toward a slave who ultimately died was no less than murder. Moore accused Davis and other defenders of Massachusetts's reputation of misrepresenting "how slow and gradual was the amelioration of the conditions of servitude. Impatient at the sluggish movement of humanity, they seem determined to bridge over the long valleys, the deep chasms and perilous gulfs through which their fathers actually struggled to reach the heights of Liberty and Equality." Davis, he said, had an "untimely sensitiveness in regard to the honor of his ancestry or his native State."[40]

Referring to Dunbar as "the 'great gun' of Boston" who sought his "annihilation," Moore dismissed Dunbar's arguments point by point in a lengthy rejoinder. Moore emphasized that he had no quarrel with Massachusetts per se but rather with "her self-righteous historians." Massachusetts was "far more likely to suffer from the cowardice of her friends than the courage of her enemies." Moore claimed that although he never asserted that the 1641 statute "originated" slavery, it was literally the earliest law "establishing slavery in America." Concerning hereditary slavery, Moore found Dunbar's "reasoning . . . utterly futile and worthless," fully in keeping with "the new school of Puritans." The legal status of hereditary slavery in Massachusetts never was formally challenged, Moore explained, mocking "the art with which the champions of Massachusetts have . . . contrived to conceal the truths with which they have always been so familiar."[41]

Modern scholars have sided with Moore in the issues raised by his critics. They credit him with uncovering the legalization of hereditary slavery in Massachusetts in the seventeenth century and the persistence of the institution and the slave trade after 1780. As historian William M. Wiecek has commented, Moore correctly perceived that the *Somerset* case concerned only the removal of slaves from England and, as a result, had no impact on slavery in Massachusetts.[42] Indeed, Moore prefigured by a century Jerome Nadelhaft's revisionist interpretation of the *Somerset* case. According to Robert M. Cover, the ambiguous nature of the records, differing interpretations of "constitutionality" and judicial review, and the absence of judicial opinion have made the history of slavery and abolition in Massachusetts "a historian's perennial football."[43] However, Moore's contemporaries used his book in a dramatically different game.

Published during Reconstruction, Moore's *Notes on the History of Slavery* armed white southerners with ammunition to challenge what they deemed the North's self-righteous position on slavery. New Englanders, "whose pious hands are uplifted in horror over the wrongs of the poor negro," were hypocrites, charged *De Bow's Review.* They retained slavery while it was profitable to do so but freed their slaves when it no longer paid. Northerners, then, had no right to berate southerners who *"happened to remain a few years longer in the practice which they introduced and taught."*[44] To be sure, some white northerners got the message. The old abolitionist Parker Pillsbury, for example, was shocked by Moore's revelations. In 1883 he judged *Notes on the History of Slavery* "one of the most surprising volumes ever issued by the American press." Others, upon discovering that their families once had held slaves, mocked their own false pride and admitted their embarrassment. Writing in the *Nation* in 1886, one New Englander recounted his recent dismay upon learning that ancestors on both sides of his family had been slaveholders. "These evil results of hereditary slaveholding," he wrote, "so apparent (to the New Englander) in the Southern character—was their 'vicious quitch' even in us, also, all 'unbeknownst?' " "May we hope," the writer added jokingly, "that the news of the Emancipation Proclamation" had reached his ancestors in the next world.[45]

There was nothing humorous, however, about race relations in the South in 1866. The controversy over Moore's book raged soon after reports reached the North that the South's Black Codes had reduced the freedmen to a form of quasi-slavery. A few months earlier, the Joint Committee on Reconstruction had paraded the South's unwillingness to free the blacks in deed as well as in word before the American public.[46] Now, Moore charged that even in Massachusetts in 1866, "those disabilities which so strongly mark[ed] the social status of the negro still linger." On the race question, then, Massachusetts continued to preach more than it practiced.[47] This argument, moreover, came from a respected northern intellectual and librarian. From Reconstruction until well into the new century, southerners cited *Notes on the History of Slavery* to document northern hypocrisy regarding racial matters. "Massachusetts," the editor of the *Confederate Veteran* explained in 1897, "had always carried herself with a prudish dignity in the family of States." Moore, however, exposed "the pretty pranks she played when a girl."[48] The message was clear. At the very moment that one southern state after another was passing Jim Crow legislation—riveting blacks into a second-class legal status—northerners should not preach race relations to the South.

After studying the controversy over Moore's book, there is little evidence to support David Van Tassel's assertion that Moore was motivated by jealousy and determined in "justifying and increasing the reputation of New York state." The intensity of Moore's animus against Massachusetts per se was more apparent than real. Rather, *Notes on the History of Slavery* represents the emergence of a school of historical research bent on "exposing unmerited reputations" and revising the filiopietistic national past.[49]

Anticipating the scientific historians and breaking with the romantic historians, Moore viewed history as a factual chronicle. Because he was conscious of what later generations of historians would label "historical relativism," Moore argued:

> It would be to misread history and to forget the change of times, to see in the Fathers of New England mere commonplace slavemongers; to themselves they appeared as the elect to whom God had given the heathen for an inheritance . . . and for their wildest and worst acts they could claim the sanction of religious conviction.

However, just as the scientific historians of slavery later failed in their attempts to excise partisanship and bias from their writings, so, too, did Moore succumb to the frailties of the historian. In spite of his quest for objectivity, *Notes on the History of Slavery* was decidedly Whiggish in orientation, imposing the author's progressive nineteenth-century vision of liberalism and democracy on seventeenth- and eighteenth-century Massachusetts. The book also falls clearly into the ideological camp of neoabolitionist historians such as James Ford Rhodes, who gained prominence three decades later. Although Rhodes, like Moore, emphasized New England's role in the Atlantic slave trade, Rhodes blamed the South for the evils of slavery while Moore censured Massachusetts for clutching onto slavery for so long, as well as for its sanctimoniousness.[50]

Moore's writing echoed the abolitionists, old and new, when he attacked slavery's "brutal customs," its "utter wickedness," and its justifications based on "miserable pretences." Passionate in his language, Moore referred to the captains of slave ships as "pirates" and censured the kidnapping of blacks in Boston in February 1788 as "outrageous" and "atrocious." Moore held Massachusetts slaveholders accountable for what he termed "the looseness" of slave marriages in the colony, lamenting that "marriage was not a matter of choice with them, [no] more than any other action of their life." Again speaking of white interference with slave marriages, Moore wrote that "it was as true then as it is now that the institution of slavery was inconsistent with the just rules of Christian morality."[51]

Moore differed from the later neoabolitionist historians, however, when he did not distance himself from the slaves as persons. Instead, Moore sympathized openly with the "poor Negroes" and "unfortunate creatures." He praised the creativity and contributions of skilled slaves and insisted that in no sense had the blacks been a "deadweight" on Massachusetts society. Moore, in fact, identified black self-assertion as an important force that ultimately worked toward the destruction of slavery. He cited advertisements for runaway slaves that mentioned their "notions of Freedom" and pointed out that as a form of protest free blacks resisted paying taxes. Slave insurrection always loomed as a possibility in Massachusetts, Moore said, but in reality, slaves filed liberty suits and freedom petitions. In 1787, for example, some petitioned the Massachusetts legislature for aid to return to Africa. The next year, black abolitionist Prince Hall wrote a petition on behalf of three kidnapped Boston blacks, protesting their seizure and demanding abolition of the slave trade. At a time, then, when many whites in the Reconstruction North viewed blacks in overtly racist ways, Moore championed "the negro's capacity for intellectual improvement."[52]

On another level, Moore's book illustrates the uses of history in the crucible of legal and social change. Armed with the weapons of the historian, Moore exposed not only slavery's long history in Massachusetts but also the Bay State's lengthy tradition of racial intolerance and proscription. In *Notes on the History of Slavery,* Moore openly attacked the legacy of racism and hypocrisy that lay in slavery's wake. He recognized the ever-present forces of "localism, laissez-faire, and racism" that, according to Eric Foner, "reasserted themselves" at the close of the Civil War.[53] During the war, Moore documented the glacial speed with which the Continental Congress had moved to consider the arming and freeing of black troops during an earlier conflict—the American Revolution. Hinting that the Lincoln administration should move swiftly toward emancipation, Moore declared, "It requires little ingenuity to invent historical parallels—not very profound research to find historical precedent—but it is the highest wisdom to know how to apply the lessons of the Past."[54] There were lessons to be applied. As late as June 1864, the Thirteenth Amendment failed to pass in the U.S. House of Representatives by a vote of 93 to 65, and not until January 1865 could President Abraham Lincoln twist enough congressional arms to enable the amendment to pass the House 119 to 56.[55] At the very moment, then, that the South was expected to seek forgiveness for its sins, the North was demonstrating the longstanding hypocrisy and shoddy treatment of blacks that Moore's book was about to expose.

Moore's *Notes on the History of Slavery* took an important step forward in redefining U.S. nationality. Whereas the old romantic nationalists had glorified the American past, Moore's new critical perspective found plenty of blame on both sides of the Mason-Dixon line. The post–Civil War United States was emerging as a pluralistic society caught up in the throes of an industrial revolution. Simplistic, moralistic notions of good versus bad would no longer suffice. Perhaps with a smirk on his face, Moore concluded his book by making a final slap at Massachusetts. Slavery was not legally abolished there, he reminded his readers, until passage of the Thirteenth Amendment late in 1865, the votes of eight former Confederate states having been crucial in the amendment's ratification.[56] Ironically, slavery's "actual prohibition . . . in Massachusetts" was "accomplished by the votes of South Carolina and Georgia."[57] Moore's history reminded victorious northerners that there were limits to their own virtue, even as they began to tailor the bloody shirt.

2

James Ford Rhodes, Woodrow Wilson, and the Passing of the Amateur Historian of Slavery

In 1892, in his *History of the United States from the Compromise of 1850,* James Ford Rhodes published one of the earliest analyses of slavery as an institution in the Old South.[1] Rhodes, the Cleveland ironmaster turned Boston historian, popularized a nationalistic interpretation of slavery and the coming of the Civil War. By de-emphasizing southern blame, he acquired a reputation for a general "sense of fairness" toward southerners and their region. The generation of Americans around the turn of the century found bitter sectional antagonism unattractive. Rather, it accepted a national consensus based on shared economic and racial attitudes. American imperialism of the 1890s added a major nationalizing force. Though Rhodes condemned slavery as a moral wrong, he viewed it as a national rather than a sectional sin. Slavery, according to Rhodes, was caused as much by the greed of New England shippers who brought the slaves from Africa, as by that of the southern planters who purchased them. Throughout his multi-volume history, Rhodes celebrated "our common human nature North and South." He looked upon sectional harmony with a sense of mission, considering "no work . . . holier than one directed to bringing together the South and the North."[2]

The son of an Ohio Copperhead, Rhodes inherited his father's iron and coal business. He worked until 1884, at which time Rhodes had amassed a fortune substantial enough to finance a historian without portfolio. In many ways, Rhodes represented the literary tradition of the gentleman scholar. Affluence enabled him to study history as well as to hire research assistants and acquire an extensive personal library. An elitist, Rhodes found capitalists "a lot sight better than the proletariat." His 1891 move from Cleveland to Boston was in itself an indication of an attempt to join a people "whose good manners and cultivation give them a distinction rarely seen elsewhere." Unlike the history Ph.D.s who struggled to practice their craft as college professors, Rhodes lived an epicurean life. When not researching or writing, he was vacationing at Bar Harbor, Maine, enjoying novels and the sea, or traveling abroad. Writing in 1900 from Germany, Rhodes found "the cuisine . . . delicate, the attendance excellent, the wines aus-gezeichnet." In 1910 he invited Frederick Jackson Turner to be his guest at Boston's prestigious Wednesday Evening Club. "The men come together at half past nine," explained Rhodes, "supper is served at ten and there is talkee-talkee until midnight."[3]

Untrained in the "scientific" historical methods of his day, prone to view the past and present from the perspective of the northern elite, Rhodes was a most unlikely historian of slavery. Although he considered himself an expert on the South, Rhodes actually was quite unfamiliar with the region. His three trips below the Ohio River, in 1868, 1869, and 1872, were undertaken to investigate iron and coal deposits for his father. Visits to North Carolina, Georgia, Tennessee, and Louisiana brought the Clevelander "in close contact with the ruling 'carpet-bagger' and the 'unreconstructed rebel.'" But these brief excursions hardly made Rhodes an authority on the South in general or slavery in particular. Professor William P. Trent, a native Virginian, encouraged Rhodes to revisit the South to "judge for yourself . . . the Old South and the New. You will find," predicted Trent, "that the survivors of the Old although . . . hardly able to appreciate the spirit and aims of modern historical research, are nevertheless delightful men, well worth cultivating."[4]

Trent, like other southern whites, disagreed with the tone and emphasis of Rhodes's treatment of slavery. Even though Rhodes clearly shared white southerners' belief in the inferiority of the Negro, he wrote undeniably from the perspective of the abolitionist. For example, early in his first volume, Rhodes declared that "The historian whose sympathies are with the anti-slavery cause can most truly write the story" of the slavery issue. Recognizing his limitations, Rhodes admitted that it was "quite easy for one of Northern birth . . . to extenuate nothing; [and therefore] more care must be taken to set naught in malice." These statements notwithstanding, when writing about slavery he focused upon the poor care and treatment of the bondsmen by their masters.[5]

Day-to-day slave life, argued Rhodes, was harsh and often cruel. He cited cases in which slaves were overtasked to the point of injury or death. They were whipped by evil overseers, men who "were generally ignorant, frequently intemperate, always despotic and brutal." When analyzing the food, clothing, and housing available on the plantations, Rhodes concluded that few workers in the world subsisted on as little as did the South's slaves. Their clothes were generally "ragged, unkempt, and dirty," their cabins usually "foul and wretched." Restricted by severe slave codes, the blacks were guarded closely by their masters. White ministers neither were to "preach honesty to men who did not own their own labor, nor chastity to women who did not own their bodies." Much in the tradition of the abolitionists, Rhodes condemned the domestic slave trade, especially slave breeding, which he considered "the most wretched aspect of the institution." All in all, Rhodes endorsed Henry Clay's famous remark that slavery was "a curse to the master and a wrong to the slave."[6]

Rhodes's treatment of slavery generally was well received by the literary world and the historical profession. The *Nation,* for example, praised the Clevelander's careful use of sources, including newspapers, and lauded his honest and judicial results. The reviewer pointed out that Rhodes recognized the broad role of slavery as a southern institution. The *Literary Digest* agreed that Rhodes's discussion of slavery was noteworthy and welcomed its fair treatment of the South. In *Historische Zeitschrift,* the usually critical Hermann E. von Holst praised Rhodes's volumes as "a very sound accomplishment . . . one of the best which the country had produced to date." Taking note of the author's "sympathetic disposition," von Holst complimented his reconciliationist tone and recognized this as a unique quality giving a special stamp to Rhodes's work. Applauding Rhodes's fairness and his use of sources, historian Frederic Bancroft called his analysis of slavery the fullest and most interesting yet written.[7]

But there were criticisms, some of them severe. Von Holst believed that weaknesses in Rhodes's volumes, such as the coarse style and numerous contradictions, resulted from his lack of professional training. He faulted Rhodes's discussion of slavery for failing to emphasize the moral aspects of the institution. "Not that his own ethical position . . . is lukewarm," argued von Holst, "but he [Rhodes] underestimates the weight which the ethical factor has . . . in . . . historical development." Bancroft identified Rhodes's failure to consult southern newspapers and his undue emphasis on the harsh aspects of slavery. Had he discussed border state and urban slavery, noted Bancroft, Rhodes would have provided a more complete portrait of the peculiar institution. Columbia University Professor John W. Burgess was more critical, explaining how in Rhodes's discussion of slavery, "the abolitionist assumes . . . the historian's place." According to Burgess, Rhodes recorded the "sensational and exceptional" and omitted the "regular and ordinary" aspects of slavery. This criticism also was leveled by North Carolinian Patrick Henry Winston, who felt that Rhodes's treatment of slavery was "almost entirely in the abstract." Unlike the bondsmen portrayed by Rhodes, the slaves Winston knew in his youth were "physically comfortable and mentally happy."[8]

The harshest attack on Rhodes's lengthy chapter on slavery was an unsigned review in the *Atlantic Monthly* by Professor Woodrow Wilson of Princeton University. Referring to Rhodes's volumes as "a superior sort of anti-slavery pamphlet," Wilson criticized the author's unwarranted emphasis on and distorted picture of slavery. Wilson condemned Rhodes's analysis of the South and slavery for being perverted by what he deemed ignorance and lack of objectivity. For Rhodes, the South was "a foreign country, whose condition and sentiments he learns piecemeal and at intervals from travelers." Too often, said Wilson, Rhodes relied on rumors from which he made speculative conclusions. Again and again, Rhodes revealed "no authentic knowledge or direct realization" of the South. And Rhodes had no better grasp of the slave system than of the region itself. Instead of a balanced and consistent evaluation of the institution, Rhodes first presented "the evils of slavery in black catalogue," but later, "suddenly . . . and smilingly," noted its more benign features. Wilson explained Rhodes's failure to see slavery as a "whole and in its normal aspects," as being a product of his inability to "digest" his material and his tendency "to give grounds for a conclusion rather than the conclusion itself." Wilson concluded by emphasizing Rhodes's "obtuseness of vision," his crude methodology, and his avoidance of complex problems.[9]

Of all the contemporary criticisms of Rhodes's work on slavery, Wilson's was by far the most significant. Unlike Rhodes, Wilson was a native of the South (Virginia), a trained historian (Ph.D., Johns Hopkins University, 1886), and an academic (professor of political science, Bryn Mawr College, 1885–1888, Wesleyan University, 1888–1890, and Princeton University, 1890–1902). Although schooled in Herbert Baxter Adams's "scientific" historical laboratory at Johns Hopkins, Wilson largely rejected Adams's reverence for facts and archival research. Instead, as he explained in 1884, "My chief interest is in politics, in history as it furnishes object-lessons for the present." The historian, according to Wilson, should neither shy away from making moral judgments nor write in a "dry as dust" style. History, Wilson insisted, was a branch of literature, an art form combining accurate lessons of the past and the writer's imagination. Like Rhodes, then, Wilson also made moral judgments and wrote with an eye to capturing his reader's interest. Both valued popular, not "scientific" history, and tended to synthesize the primary research of others. But the two historians parted ways on the question of slavery. Rhodes, the northern neoabolitionist, lashed out against the horrors of the peculiar institution. Wilson, the southerner, pictured slavery in a far more sympathetic light.[10]

According to one historian, Wilson "was curiously indifferent to the moral iniquity of slavery and accepted uncritically the post-Reconstruction arrangements to keep the Negro in his place." Speaking in 1890 before members of the Johns Hopkins historical seminary, Wilson explained confidently that enslavement "had done more for the negro in two hundred and fifty years than African freedom had done since the building of the pyramids." In *Division and Reunion* (1893), he softened these views but went on nonetheless to reject Rhodes's severe condemnation of slavery. While Wilson held dearly to many of the South's traditions, unlike many southern whites, he stopped short of reviving the old proslavery argument.[11]

A renaissance of proslavery rhetoric emerged among white southerners immediately following the Civil War. They argued that slavery offered numerous positive features for antebellum blacks and whites alike. The slaves, they explained, received benevolent care—abundant food and clothing, adequate housing, and valuable industrial training. Moreover, slave status protected the slaves from competition with whites and offered them the patriarchal guidance of their masters. Proponents of this new proslavery rationale went on to point out that since emancipation the former slaves had regressed physically, morally, and spiritually. Blacks now were feared and distrusted by whites. The races no longer lived in harmony. The Negro would not hold a job, wrote numerous white southerners, and all too frequently unleashed his savage instincts against white women. Images of contented antebellum slaves and beast-like post-war freedmen appeared frequently in late-nineteenth-century literature. Historians and scientists, too, looked back nostalgically to the golden age of race relations "before the war." Even though Wilson viewed slavery more favorably than Rhodes, he embraced only some elements of the new proslavery position.[12]

Writing in *Division and Reunion,* Wilson emphasized the diversity of conditions under which the peculiar institution existed in the Old South. He argued that "scarcely any generalization . . . formed would be true for the" entire region. Too often, said Wilson, antislavery observers judged the institution as it existed in the border states—"upon its edges." Unlike masters in the border states who had to contend with constant runaway attempts, planters in the "heart of the South" knew a "more normal" slavery.[13]

Resembling countless other white southerners of this day, Wilson portrayed the Old South as a land of patriarchal slave masters. The bondsmen resided in comfortable slave quarters and rarely experienced harsh treatment. Inhuman conditions were exceptional, never the rule. Such statements would seem to confirm Wilson's membership in the proslavery school. But unlike the majority of the proslavery writers, Wilson recognized weaknesses in slavery. Slave labor was wasteful and discouraged industrial development, he said. Because the "slothful and negligent slave" was unadaptive to intensive farming methods, lands were only occasionally restored. According to Wilson, life was harsh for slaves on large plantations—especially in coastal rice fields—where supervisors were hired overseers. Wilson's biggest break with historians friendly to slavery, however, was his description of slave marriages as "the most demoralizing feature of the system." This comment prompted an irate reviewer in the *New Orleans Picayune* to refer to Wilson's "ignorance . . . of the real conditions of the slaves." He continued: "Everyone who knows anything about it [slavery] understands that the slaves before '61 were far better off than the inhabitants of the slums and sweatshops of New York are to-day."[14]

While this criticism probably amused, not troubled, Wilson, the sensitive Rhodes chafed at Wilson's earlier harsh criticism. For many years afterward, Rhodes, who never learned the identity of the *Atlantic Monthly* reviewer, brooded over the issue. Rhodes felt that he had been unfairly criticized for overemphasizing slavery. He urged historian Frederic Bancroft to join him in "insist[ing] that without slavery, without Cuffee, there would have been no war. It is not the historians who make slavery too prominent," continued Rhodes, "it is the events themselves and the spirit of the time." When informed of Rhodes's reaction to his review, Wilson referred to him as an "amiable goose" and suggested that men like Rhodes, who lacked proper training as historians, should refrain from writing history.[15]

Wilson's biting review and later criticism of Rhodes underscore more than differences between the neoabolitionist and proslavery interpretations of slavery. When reproving Rhodes, Wilson actually was lashing out against history written by amateurs. Despite the genuine merits of Rhodes's multi-volume history, its scope and method looked backward to the tradition of the early-nineteenth-century literary historians. His research compared unfavorably with that of the new breed of "scientific" historians trained at Johns Hopkins and other pioneer graduate schools. Rhodes's preponderant use of travel accounts as sources in his chapter on slavery, for example, illustrates well that his research techniques lagged behind the times.

Analysis of Rhodes's footnotes in his chapter on slavery reveals that eight of the twenty sources he cited most frequently fall into the category of travel accounts. Harriet Martineau, Frances Anne Kemble, Charles Lyell, James Silk Buckingham, Jean Jacques Ampère, Charles Mackay, Alexis De Tocqueville, and Frederick Law Olmsted dominate the sources Rhodes used. He considered travel narratives valuable primary sources, relying on them in much the same way later students of slavery employed plantation records. In most cases, they reinforced Rhodes's antislavery perspective, although he recognized that some travelers were swayed in their judgments by conversations with house servants or by the hospitality of southern planters. Next to Olmsted, Rhodes relied most heavily on Miss Martineau because she had spoken with hundreds of southerners about slavery. Her discussion of miscegenation in *Society in America* (1837) was indispensable to Rhodes's study of slavery, because, he said, it was "the work of a student of social science who . . . gathered facts with care, and only . . . [drew] legitimate deductions."[16]

Although travelers' narratives remain useful primary sources to the historian of slavery, as a genre they contain serious deficiencies.[17] Too often observers made generalizations based on limited experiences. Without mentioning Rhodes by name, in 1896 Wilson chided his over-reliance on travel accounts. Wilson regretted that when writing about the South, northern historians "almost always" quoted travelers, "just as I would describe Kamchatka, a place which I did not intend to do and did not hope to go." They seemed to prefer, continued Wilson, foreign observers who had only briefly toured a small section of the South. Wilson objected to the technique—"matching this traveler's tale with that traveler's tale"—that Rhodes employed in writing about slavery.[18]

Despite his preference for travel narratives, Rhodes did utilize other types of sources. Most of these, however, were antislavery pamphlets or reminiscences. For the southern side, he relied upon Chancellor Harper's *Pro-Slavery Argument* (1852) and J.D.B. De Bow's many publications. Unfortunately, Rhodes failed to discriminate in his use of these sources. Instead, he freely took material on slavery from the polemical literature, usually without noting its obvious bias.

Also disappointing is Rhodes's failure to use southern newspapers or manuscripts. In his entire chapter on slavery, he cited only a few southern newspapers and most of these were quoted in secondary works. This is surprising, because later in his career Rhodes, like historian John Bach McMaster, acquired the reputation as a leader in using newspapers in historical writing. Although he recognized the value of manuscript evidence, Rhodes's chapter gives no indication that he examined any plantation records or, like Frederic Bancroft, interviewed southerners, black and white. Rhodes did conduct research at the Library of Congress in the early 1890s but it is unclear what materials he studied there. The historian admitted in 1908 that when writing his first volumes, he was handicapped by the scarcity of manuscripts.[19]

His failure to consult the full range of primary sources available to him was a product both of Rhodes's lack of professional training and of his patrician orientation. Unlike the graduate students at Johns Hopkins at work on slavery in the 1880s and 1890s,[20] he missed the importance of searching out diaries, state documents, and other primary sources. Out of touch with the academic world, Rhodes no doubt found it hard to keep abreast of new sources as they became available. While Wilson and the other professionally trained historians hunted documents in libraries and archives, Rhodes generally relied upon those published sources held in his personal library.[21]

On first glance, Wilson's critique of Rhodes appears to have resulted from obvious sectional chauvinism. Here we have the defender of the South's peculiar institution assailing the heir to the abolitionist crusade. But this is, at best, only part of the story. Despite his great popularity among readers at the turn of the century, Rhodes clearly represented the old order among American historians. With only a few exceptions, multi-volume narrative histories soon were replaced by narrow, institutional monographs.[22] Scholarship on slavery illustrates this trend especially well. Not until 1918, when Ulrich Bonnell Phillips published *American Negro Slavery,* would a scholar produce a broadly based volume on slavery. Most historians in these years examined the legal origins and evolution of slavery in particular colonies and states. Minute study after minute study emerged from the graduate seminars. These works served as building blocks for Phillips's important synthesis. By 1920, Rhodes's famous chapter on slavery carried little weight among historians of slavery. As in so many other aspects of early-twentieth-century American life, the professional supplanted the amateur. Wilson's harsh criticisms simply sounded the call. In the opinion of the future president, history should be the province of specialists, not those "whose training and associations have fitted them for something else."[23]

3

W.E.B. Du Bois and Ulrich Bonnell Phillips
Symbolic Antagonists of the Progressive Era

Few scholars were less compatible than William Edward Burghardt Du Bois (1868–1963) and Ulrich Bonnell Phillips (1877–1934). Both men were among the leading students of slavery and race who wrote during the Progressive era. But they approached these subjects with such differing assumptions and reached such antithetical conclusions that it is not surprising that the two men became antagonists. From such fabric, historiographical controversies are fashioned.

Du Bois was undoubtedly one of America's great black intellectuals. The importance of his contributions to American black thought transcends the ninety-five years of his long life. Born in western Massachusetts, Du Bois was proud of his family's free birth. Summarizing his mixed racial background, he claimed to have been born "with a flood of Negro blood, a strain of French, a bit of Dutch, but, thank God! no 'AngloSaxon.'"[1] Du Bois was trained as a historian at Fisk and Harvard Universities and at the University of Berlin. Early in life, he developed the strong belief that a Negro intellectual elite could provide the leadership needed to help destroy social cleavages based on race. And throughout his long career as a historian, sociologist, and polemicist he dedicated his energies toward achieving that goal.[2]

Du Bois was a prolific author.[3] Among his twenty-one books and scores of articles and book reviews were *The Suppression of the African Slave-Trade* (1896), *The Philadelphia Negro* (1899), *Black Reconstruction in America* (1935), and the *Atlanta University Publications* (1898–1913), which he edited. George P. Rawick correctly has credited Du Bois with being a "mighty" exception among black historians because he raised new questions rather than simply responding to the views of white scholars.[4] Du Bois earned a national reputation as a black leader, especially after 1903, when he shifted from supporting Booker

T. Washington's conservative policies to a more radical position favoring higher education and equal rights for Negroes. As the first field researcher in Negro problems, as an author, as second president of the American Negro Academy, as founder, propagandist, and editor of the National Association for the Advancement of Colored People (NAACP), and in countless other ways, Du Bois impressed Americans, black and white, with his brilliance. Ever sensitive and optimistic, yet cool, aloof, and arrogant, Du Bois demanded respect for Negroes and never wavered in his battle against life under the veil of racism.[5]

Among historians living in the first half of the twentieth century, Phillips was far and away the leading authority on American Negro slavery. A native of the South, Phillips looked upon his region with affection and was largely responsible for establishing southern history as a research field. Phillips hailed from west Georgia, not far from the Alabama border, and was descended—on his mother's side—from slave owners. After receiving his A.B. and A.M. degrees from the University of Georgia, Phillips traveled north to Columbia University, where he earned his Ph.D. in history in 1902. He spent the next three and one-half decades explaining the essence of the Old South to students at Wisconsin, Tulane, Michigan, and Yale. By 1934, the year of his untimely death, the Georgian had established himself as the foremost student of southern history of his day. Among Phillips's numerous books are *Georgia and State Rights* (1902), *A History of Transportation in the Eastern Cotton Belt* (1908), *Plantation and Frontier Documents: 1649–1863* (2 vols., 1909), *American Negro Slavery* (1918), and the award-winning *Life and Labor in the Old South* (1929).[6] In these works and many essays and book reviews Phillips revolutionized the study of southern history in general and slavery in particular. He uncovered new sources of evidence and was the first scholar to consider questions of class and race in the South as a whole. A pioneer in analyzing slavery as an economic and social system, Phillips led the way in computing the profitability of slavery on a cost basis and examining relationships between bondsmen and masters that existed under the peculiar institution.[7]

In their writings both Du Bois and Phillips prefigured much later scholarship. In his volumes on the African slave trade, blacks in the Philadelphia ghetto, and Reconstruction, Du Bois anticipated many of the themes espoused by later historians and sociologists. In his brilliant *Souls of Black Folk* (1903), and in essays, Du Bois established himself as an expert on slave culture and folklore. He made important and lasting contributions on slave religion and music, African survivals among the slaves, the economics of slavery, and slave housing and family life. An early devotee of the writings of anthropologist Franz Boas, in *The Negro* (1915), Du Bois foreshadowed the themes and conclusions of a number of African historians including Melville J. Herskovits. Among Du Bois's most significant contributions to black history was his indictment of the one-sided view of the Negro held by white historians. Slaves, for example, were studied only to the degree to which they affected the slaveholder. Du Bois charged that whites grouped the bondsmen "as one inert changeless mass," with "no conception of a social evolution and development among them."[8]

Phillips, too, made salient, contributions to American historiography. The impact of his writings was immense, not only on his contemporaries but on scores of later historians as well. Significantly, in the years after Phillips's death, a "Phillips School" of state studies on slavery appeared. These incorporated the essential organization, sources, and interpretation of Phillips's *American Negro Slavery*. It is a measure of his lasting influence that for four decades following the publication of this work, even his severest critics embraced the source materials, method, and topics that Phillips popularized. Even contemporary historians continue to react on his terms rather than adopt new patterns of inquiry. According to the late Herbert G. Gutman, historians of slavery use his "model of slave socialization." They tend to approach "slave belief and behavior as little more than one or another response to planter-sponsored stimuli." Repeating Phillips's essential premise, they ask, "What did enslavement do to Africans and their Afro-American descendants?"[9]

The contributions of Du Bois and Phillips helped make the Progressive era the formative period in the writing of the history of slavery. Both men were trained in the "scientific" historical methodology of their day, and the two historians shared a dedication to high standards of scholarship. They also had common tendencies toward repetition and ideological inflexibility and rigidity. They formulated their attitudes toward race, for example, early in life and were consistent in promoting their respective views.[10] Both men were propagandists. Du Bois stood for racial equality and black advancement. "I believe," he wrote in 1904, "in the Negro Race; in the beauty of its genius, the sweetness of its soul, and its strength in that meekness which shall yet inherit this turbulent earth." Phillips stood for southern progress built atop the subordination of the black to the white race. For years, he charged, his beloved region had been maligned and abused. Phillips considered the South a section distinct from the rest of the country, the product of "natural organic life," not "forces of perversity."[11]

As historians, Du Bois and Phillips shared a commitment to excellence in their craft. Painstaking researchers, both men sought perfection in their work. They were "scientific" in the sense that the two scholars were indefatigable in seeking obscure sources and, in their historical writings, in their dedication to objectivity. But neither Du Bois nor Phillips wrote in the dry-as-dust style associated with the "scientific" historians of the Progressive era. In fact, they both were masters of exposition. Clearness of expression came more easily to Du Bois than to Phillips. In *The Souls of Black Folk*, Du Bois revealed his brilliant gift of imagery and literary style. Phillips's talents as a writer developed more slowly—not reaching maturity until the publication of *Life and Labor in the Old South*. Few historians were more deliberate in their writing than Phillips. He subjected his sentences and paragraphs to constant revision. His graduate students fondly recalled Phillips's dictum that "the author must take pains to save the reader pains."[12]

Their high standards of scholarship made Du Bois and Phillips quick to point out shortcomings—either in fact or style—in the work of their peers. Du Bois could be a savage critic. He frequently fired salvos at historians, black and white. Outraged by the mulatto William Hannibal Thomas's *The American Negro* (1901), Du Bois faulted the volume's "cynical pessimism, virulent criticisms, vulgar plainness, and repeated and glaring self-contradictions." According to Du Bois, Thomas represented those defeated blacks who looked backward to slavery and not toward the future of their race. In Du Bois's judgment, Thomas exemplified "that contempt for themselves which some Negroes still hold as a heritage of the past." In another review—a scathing critique of *The Negro: The Southerner's Problem* (1904) by Thomas Nelson Page—Du Bois denounced the author's pro-slavery interpretation. Slavery, wrote Du Bois, was so ruinous a force for master and slave that "the only thing that saved Mr. Page's genius to the world was the Emancipation Proclamation,—the very deed that allows the present reviewer the pleasure of criticizing Mr. Page's book instead of hoeing his cotton."[13]

Phillips's critiques were frequently as devastating as those written by Du Bois. For example, when reviewing a monograph on internal improvements in Alabama, Phillips charged, "The author writes apparently from afar off, and gives little indication of ever having seen an old map of Alabama or a newspaper published in the State before the Civil War." Critical of another writer whom he considered unfamiliar with southern blacks, Phillips suggested that he "would probably be materially broadened by a sojourn in the blacker portions of the cotton belt." His twelve-line enumeration of the weaknesses of a folding map of Virginia is an example of how excessive Phillips's criticisms could become.[14]

Despite similarities between them, Du Bois and Phillips were separated by a vast intellectual divide. The New Englander of free black origins viewed slavery and race from the perspective of the neoabolitionist. In contrast, the white southerner once recalled that "A sympathetic understanding of plantation conditions was my inevitable heritage from my family and from neighbors, white and black."[15] Even though the two scholars were trained in similar historical methods, their mentors, Albert Bushnell Hart and William Archibald Dunning, were as far apart in orientation and outlook as Du Bois and Phillips. Hart, who directed Du Bois's doctoral dissertation, took pride in the fact that he was "a son and grandson of abolitionists." Hart interpreted slavery as a force undermining southern prosperity and morality. It was, in his judgment, responsible for the bloody Civil War. These sentiments no doubt helped fuel Du Bois's hostility to the slave system.[16] Dunning, on the other hand, established his reputation by interpreting slavery and the Civil War and Reconstruction from a decidedly pro-southern perspective. Southern graduate students like Phillips found Dunning's seminar congenial to their social philosophies and racial attitudes. Like Dunning, Phillips objected strongly to the neoabolitionism of writers such as Hart and James Ford Rhodes. Writing in 1903, Phillips appealed for new approaches in historical scholarship, he said, because "The history of the United

States has been written by Boston and largely written wrong." Convinced that "New England has already overdone its part," Phillips went on to say that his research in the Old South—"from the inside"—revealed numerous "errors of interpretation by the old school of historians." He insisted that "What must be sought is the absolute truth, whether creditable or not."[17]

Du Bois and Phillips differed also in the sources that they used and in the scope of their scholarship. Following the publication of *The Suppression of the African Slave-Trade,* Du Bois dedicated himself more to sociological than to historical research.[18] Many of these investigations were based on field research—interviews with blacks and first-hand observations among Negroes, including former slaves. And after the first decade of the twentieth century, the black writer's works became increasingly polemical in nature. They were designed to shock readers with the hardships and long-reaching effects of slavery and white racism. In contrast, Phillips centered his research largely on plantation records—account books, ledgers, letters, and diaries. These sources reflected his interest in writing the history of slavery from the perspective of the master class. Although several of his essays were designed to defend southern institutions, the great majority were strictly historical in scope. Overall, Phillips's works lacked the intensity and zeal found in those of Du Bois. He was more detached, less personal, in his writings.

The two historians disagreed most clearly on the questions of slavery and race. Even though Du Bois oscillated between favoring integration and racial solidarity, on numerous occasions he urged blacks to challenge statements branding their race inferior to the whites. Slavery, Du Bois believed, was the genesis of the basic tensions in American culture because it established the tradition of classifying inferiors by race. He condemned slavery, because in his opinion it

> spread more human misery, inculcated more disrespect for and neglect of humanity, a greater callousness to suffering, and more petty, cruel, human hatred than can well be calculated. We may excuse and palliate it, and write history so as to let men forget it; it remains the most inexcusable and despicable blot on modern human history.

Whether analyzing slavery in ancient societies or in the nineteenth-century South, Du Bois's tone was unmistakably antislavery. To him slavery was a system of "crushing repression" that fostered prejudice, misunderstanding, and ridicule. In his opinion, whites were to blame for the peculiar institution, a system characterized by "oppression, cruelty, concubinage, and moral retrogression." "Slavery," wrote Du Bois in 1905, "fostered barbarism, was itself barbaric in thousands of instances and was on the whole . . . blighting to white and black." It left a bitter legacy of hate between the races and forced postwar blacks to resemble "all ground-down peasantries" ripe for "crime and a cheap, dangerous socialism."[19]

Although he professed objectivity, Phillips could escape neither the anti-Negro prejudice of the Jim Crow era nor his inherited perception of blacks as inferiors. "The average negro," wrote the Georgian in 1904, "has many of the characteristics of a child, and must be guided and governed, and often guarded against himself, by a sympathetic hand." Not surprisingly, Phillips found Booker T. Washington acceptable because, in his words, the Tuskegeean represented the "high type of the essentially conservative negro." Phillips, though, considered Washington's 1901 dinner with Theodore Roosevelt "a lapse" in the black leader's sense of judgment. With his vision so encumbered by racial prejudice, Phillips never freed himself from the belief that blacks were humorous, light-hearted, and backward. Basic to his writings was Phillips's assumption of Negro inferiority. According to Phillips:

> The African negro or the Southern negro is essentially inferior to the Anglo Saxon. This is through no fault of the individual negro. It is inevitably so. The negroes in America are only four generations removed from the lowest degree of barbarism and savagery. In friendly contact with the whites (in America) they have taken on a veneer of civilization. The closer the intercourse of the races, the more successful has been the negro's imitation of the customs and the civilization of the whites.[20]

In marked contrast to Du Bois, Phillips interpreted slavery as a benign and benevolent institution. As slaves, blacks were schooled on plantations, which Phillips contrasted favorably with the "social settlement" houses of the Progressive era. Not surprisingly, racial slurs abound in Phillips's writings. His *American Negro Slavery* contained a virtual catalog of what even in Phillips's day must have been considered derogatory remarks concerning blacks. Insensitive to Negroes as humans, he portrayed them as "impulsive and inconstant, sociable and amorous, voluble, dilatory, and negligent, but robust, amiable, obedient and contented." Refusing to recognize the African cultural traits among the slaves that Du Bois and Boas had uncovered, Phillips described the bondsmen as mindless and submissive. Incapable of concerted action, the field hands were acted upon—"a passive element whose fate was affected only so far as the master race determined."[21]

Du Bois and Phillips thus were at odds on several essential points. Their differences on the questions of slavery and race alone set the two scholars on a collision course. Because they were so outspoken in criticizing other scholars, one might suppose that Du Bois and Phillips became bitter adversaries; that a series of heated controversies erupted between them. Curiously, however, those disagreements that did arise were one-sided—initiated entirely by Du Bois. As his stature as an authority on Negro history and culture grew, Du Bois had increasingly less tolerance for racist white scholars like Phillips. Also, it was not in Du Bois's personality to hold back criticisms. Whenever the opportunity arose, he went on the offensive against Phillips. The black historian relished lashing out against him, for in doing so he assaulted the chief exemplar of racist white historiography of his day.

Du Bois fired the first shot in 1913, in an editorial entitled "The Experts." It was published in the *Crisis*—the official organ of the NAACP. Writing in a sarcastic vein, the black historian mocked Phillips's "deep insight and superb brain power," which he had revealed in recent lectures at the University of Virginia. Du Bois specifically attacked Phillips's statement that since the demise of slavery, the productivity of southern black agricultural laborers had declined while that of their white counterparts had increased. Phillips, Du Bois wrote bitterly, "is white and Southern, but . . . has a Northern job and . . . knows all about the Negro." Du Bois chided him for making an unfair comparison; in Phillips's examples much of the land cultivated by blacks was inferior to that worked by whites. Negroes, argued Du Bois, toiled upon the unfertilized and "slavery-cursed Mississippi bottoms where the soil had been raped for a century." Whites, however, worked on better land. Du Bois further criticized Phillips's insensitivity to the unequal conditions under which farmers of the two races lived. The white historian, alleged Du Bois, purposely selected a poverty-struck county—Issaquena County, Mississippi—as representative "of Negro industrial decadence." Phillips failed to explain, however, that the county "spends [only] $1 a year to educate each colored child enrolled in its schools and enrolls about half of its black children in schools of three months' duration or less." Du Bois also added that Phillips omitted consideration of the many southern blacks who were respected farmers and landowners. With typical Du Boisian invective, he asserted that Phillips's logic made him well suited to head the U.S. Department of Agriculture, "Not that it takes brains . . . (perish the assumption!), but it *does* call for adroitness in bolstering up bad cases."[22]

Du Bois struck an even more devastating blow at Phillips in his review of *American Negro Slavery*. This book was Phillips's magnum opus, and it was received enthusiastically by most historians. For example, Philip Alexander Bruce was of the opinion that the book "said the final word" on the institution of slavery. A reviewer for the *Baltimore Sun* found Phillips's volume "a fair and impartial account . . . as interesting as a romance."[23] But Du Bois disagreed.

He faulted Phillips for writing a "curiously incomplete and unfortunately biased" economic history of American slaveholders—without focusing on the slaves or consulting slave sources. The slaves' point of view, charged Du Bois, was completely ignored. And worse, Phillips was so insensitive to blacks as persons that "The Negro as a responsible human being has no place in the book." It was Phillips's racism, remarked the black critic, that blinded him to the many accomplishments of Negroes since emancipation. Phillips, Du Bois said, constructed the characters of the plantation—"subhuman slaves" and "superman" slaveholders—not from fact but from "innuendo and assumption." Neither his benign view of slavery's institutional features nor Phillips's explanation for its economic unprofitability were acceptable to Du Bois. In short, he considered

American Negro Slavery a blatant "defense of American slavery—a defense of an institution which was at best a mistake and at worst a crime—made in a day when we need sharp and implacable judgment against collective wrongdoing by cultured and courteous men." Du Bois emphasized that "the case against American slavery is too strong to be moved by [the] kind of special pleading" Phillips espoused.[24]

On two other occasions, in 1935 and 1940, Du Bois again reproved Phillips. In his classic *Black Reconstruction,* Du Bois placed Phillips's works under the rubric of open and blatant "propaganda"—antiblack, prosouthern, and generally hostile to Reconstruction policy. In 1940, the black historian recalled with seeming delight how thirty years earlier Phillips had become "greatly exercised" upon listening to Du Bois's revisionist paper, "Reconstruction and Its Benefits," read before a meeting of the American Historical Association.[25]

How did Phillips react to Du Bois's criticisms? He all but ignored them. Only in *American Negro Slavery*—and then just on two points—did Phillips choose to take Du Bois to task. On the question of the effect of the 1808 prohibition on African importations, Phillips disagreed sharply with the thesis of Du Bois's *The Suppression of the African Slave-Trade.* He criticized the black scholar's large estimates of the number of Africans smuggled into the South between 1808 and 1860. In Phillips's opinion, the great increase in the antebellum South's black population resulted from natural reproduction, not illicit importations of fresh Africans. Phillips also challenged Du Bois on the question of slave law. According to the Georgian, a high crime rate existed among the bondsmen whether in a rural or urban setting.[26] This interpretation clashed with Du Bois's 1901 statement in the *Annals of the American Academy of Political and Social Science* that "under a strict slave regime there can scarcely be such a thing as crime."[27] Their disagreement on this theme emphasizes how far apart Du Bois and Phillips were in evaluating slavery. Whereas Du Bois viewed the institution as a monolith, a rigid system of repression, Phillips described it as a fluid, adaptive mode of arranging a work force. The slavery Phillips described—"shaped by mutual requirements, concessions and understandings" between master and bondsman—conflicted dramatically with the institution Du Bois condemned so forcefully.[28]

These two strictures notwithstanding, Phillips never really acknowledged Du Bois's criticisms. He responded neither to Du Bois's charges of racism nor to the black historian's denunciations of his scholarship. Why?

It was not because Phillips shied away from controversy. As a young historian at the University of Wisconsin he labored in the cause of Progressive reform—for agricultural reform in Georgia and academic improvements at the state university in Athens. Through numerous letters and newspaper articles, Phillips spearheaded a campaign favoring the reduction of cotton acreage, more crop diversification, and a restoration of large-scale agricultural units.[29] In April 1915, Phillips was an early supporter of historian Frederic Bancroft's ill-fated campaign to reform the American Historical Association.[30] And as a senior faculty member at the University of Michigan, Phillips took a stand that established his credentials as a sincere defender of academic freedom.[31] Yet Phillips chose not to do battle with Du Bois. Rarely, in fact, did he even cite the black historian's writings.

Phillips overlooked the contributions of Du Bois and other black writers because he was unaware of them. Ironically, Phillips mastered the primary sources on slavery left by antebellum white planters yet failed to read the black literature of his own day. Most likely, too, he was suspicious of the work of the black authors because of its polemical nature. And even if he had read their works, Phillips was too much a product of his southern origins and the Jim Crow era to comprehend fully their significance. Resembling most white scholars of the age, Phillips simply did not take blacks—even black intellectuals— seriously. Late in his career, he explained that like other "Southerners in the plantation tradition," he tended to look unfavorably upon blacks "in the mass." He liked them, however, on an individual basis. Phillips also made the distinction between the "better" class of blacks—presumably a definite minority—and the "lowliest" Negroes who formed "the mass" of the race. Of the former group, Phillips wrote:

> Well-informed and thoughtful Negroes of our time have no purpose of wrecking civilization. There are no Gandhis among them preaching noncooperation and reversion to primitive ways. They have no love of tribal superstition or savagery; their ambition for themselves and their people is very much the same as yours and mine. They should be commended, never abused.

Although Phillips found "many of the lowliest" blacks "not without likeable and admirable traits," he had serious reservations about them as a class. He wrote:

> Most of them have yet to show, indeed, yet to begin to suggest, that they can be taken into full fellowship of any sort in a democratic civilized order. Their cousins in Africa demonstrate a wonderful capacity to remain primitive,—to perpetuate the crudest of human beliefs and practices. If most of these cousins in America had an effective suffrage, they could not use it with intelligence or to good effect. Such great disaster might not come as did come in the tragic period of "Reconstruction," but the white community will not assume the risk, and no one of knowledge and calm reason advocates it.[32]

Du Bois, of course, did. And he demanded much more in terms of rights for blacks than simply the vote. But Phillips took little notice of him nor of black historians such as Carter G. Woodson, Archibald H. Grimké, Kelly Miller, and John Wesley Cromwell. These men offered an alternative view of slavery to that which Phillips espoused. For them slavery had a different, more immediate meaning than for whites like Phillips. As the black scholars observed with disgust the inequalities of Jim Crowism and the exclusion of Negroes from Progressive reforms, they held slavery accountable for what they considered the continued backwardness of their race. They argued that an understanding of slavery was necessary if future generations were to be guarded against re-enslavement. Almost uniformly the black authors denounced slavery as the consummate sin in American history.

Phillips included Du Bois among the "better" class of blacks.[33] But his exclusion of the black man from among those writers who influenced and shaped his thought hurt him more than he realized. Du Bois's insights into slave culture and folklore could have benefited Phillips immeasurably in his work. The black scholar's view of slavery—from the vantage point of the bondsman—would have opened new avenues to Phillips's understanding of the plantation South. But no dialogue existed between the two historians. It was an age when even the writing of the past became a casualty of the color line.

Du Bois and Phillips symbolized two conflicting strains among historians of the Progressive era. Whereas the black writer focused upon black accomplishments under extreme adversity, the white scholar explored a lost civilization in hopes of finding meaning in the twentieth-century South. Du Bois looked forward to the unqualified integration of blacks into American history and life. He expressed the spirit of the "New Negro" movement and the Harlem Renaissance of the 1920s. Phillips glanced backward to the "Old Negro"—a character he looked upon with affection, but not with serious regard. In his attacks on Phillips, Du Bois was really assaulting what the Georgian represented—Jim Crowism, racism, and proscription. Unfortunately, Phillips never could comprehend Du Bois's broad social message, one that transcended their differences over slavery. Tragically, the intellectual and racial milieu of the period prevented them from sharing their ideas and their unrivaled knowledge of black history— Du Bois from the black perspective, Phillips from the white. They were symbolic antagonists of the Progressive era.

4

Historical or Personal Criticism?
The Case of Frederic Bancroft versus
Ulrich Bonnell Phillips

In 1931, historian Frederic Bancroft published what has become the standard history of the domestic slave trade. His *Slave Trading in the Old South,*[1] the product of more than three decades of research, was the first scholarly treatment of the subject, totally eclipsing in research, content, and scope Winfield H. Collins's *The Domestic Slave Trade of the Southern States* (1904). For years Bancroft had immersed himself in slave traders' advertisements for bondsmen, city directories, slave ship manifests, letters, wills, and court records. He broke fresh historiographical ground by obtaining oral testimony from ex-slaves, slave traders, and planters. Strongly revisionist in tone, Bancroft's book lashed out against the slave trade, that part of the peculiar institution that he deemed most cruel and despicable.

Bancroft's condemnation of the slave trade clashed with the interpretation of slavery accepted by most scholars during the Progressive era. Historians writing in the early twentieth century revived the essential elements of the old proslavery argument. In their view, slavery was benign and instructive and the slave owners were benevolent and patriarchal. They described slavery as an educational institution offering lifelong courses in civilization, vocational training, and discipline. Upon surrendering his freedom, paying his tuition, the slave pupil could use the plantation as a learning center and the planter as his teacher. The plantation legend espoused by historians, sociologists, and polemicists included a long list of apologies and defenses for slavery. Masters were not guilty of concubinage with their female slaves; bondsmen were neither abused nor overtasked; slave children were not sold apart from their parents; and husbands and wives were not sold separately. Reflecting the racial milieu of the Jim Crow era, these writers suggested that without the guidance of the master race, twentieth-century blacks were regressing to savagery. But Bancroft did not accept such views. In his monograph, he attacked the tenets of the new proslavery argument and especially its chief proponent, historian Ulrich Bonnell Phillips.[2]

Compared with other books of the period on slavery, *Slave Trading in the Old South* resembled an abolitionist tract. Undistinguished in literary style, it had an internal unity spirited by Bancroft's zealous attacks on slavery and its apologists. Slavery, wrote Bancroft, was at heart an economic institution. He estimated that in 1859–1860, at the height of the "negro fever," slave trading was extensive, involving $150 million. "And slave-trading," he continued, "was vastly more important than this suggests: it was absolutely necessary to the continuance of this most highly prized property and to the economic, social and political conditions dependent on it." The slave trade became as vitally important to southerners as the peculiar institution itself because the rearing of slaves brought them a larger percentage of profit than did slave labor in the region's staple crops. Indeed, wrote Bancroft, "Slaves, much more than land . . . came to be popularly considered the standard of value of prosperity, at once the safest investment and the most profitable speculation. . . . Consequently the price of slaves was absurdly inflated and planting rested largely on uneconomic bases."[3] Once Bancroft had established the importance of the slave trade to the southern economy, he went on to destroy what he considered to be myths about the traffic in bondsmen.

First, not all slave traders were despised as the dregs of southern society. Whereas some, the common "nigger-traders," were shunned and treated with disgust, others were among the South's most prominent citizens. Of the former class of riffraff, Bancroft wrote, "Imagine a compound of an unscrupulous horse-trader, a familiar old-time tavern-keeper, a superficially complaisant and artful, hard-drinking gambler and an ignorant, garrulous, low politician, and you will get a conception that resembles the Southern antebellum notion of the 'nigger-trader.'" But in marked contrast were the slave "brokers"—men who made substantial profits from the trade in human flesh and therefore were accorded accompanying respect. "When traders prospered, were honest, thrifty, and bought plantations," explained Bancroft, "they enjoyed the essentials of respectability." Contrary to views of writers like Phillips who argued that slave traders were treated with social opprobrium, Bancroft remarked that "Honest and fairly humane trading . . . especially if on a large scale, seems never to have lowered the standing of a man of good family, and it always improved that of men of humble origin."[4]

Whether conducted by "nigger-traders" or "brokers," Bancroft concluded that the slave trade was an exploitative, dirty business. And he assaulted a number of themes that had been pillars of the plantation legend. Willing to admit that the slave trade "became somewhat less inhuman" as the antebellum decades passed, Bancroft alleged that "it never became humane." It was an immoral fixture of an immoral society, he wrote, where "fancy girls" sold as concubines became a stock of the trade. Slave traders also dealt in "prime" slave women—females purchased specifically for breeding purposes. Their offspring were reared for market sale. Even worse, charged Bancroft, masters openly raised families by their slave women. But his most devastating blow to the plantation legend was Bancroft's evidence that slave traders willfully divided slave families. Throughout the South, he said, forced separation of slaves from their relatives—wives from husbands and young children from parents—became a matter of course.[5]

Reviewers found much to praise in Bancroft's book. Carter G. Woodson, editor of the *Journal of Negro History,* credited Bancroft with overturning the proslavery argument. "He has uprooted so much," explained Woodson, "that it will be necessary to work out another program to cover up the truth in some way during the next fifty years." Bancroft's work served "not only to disabuse our minds of ideas advanced by the propagandists but will drive home forcefully the fact that American historical scholarship has not advanced as far as it should have during recent years."[6] Celebrated black poet Sterling A. Brown praised Bancroft's "cold statistics and keen logic." Although Brown predicted that Bancroft's neoabolitionism would be criticized by white southerners, he wrote: "Let the avalanche come. This book is a solid rock, not to be moved. It is *here* and *will* be here, when time has swept all of the loose dirt away."[7]

A recurring theme noted by reviewers was Bancroft's catalog of criticisms of Ulrich Bonnell Phillips. According to Woodson, Bancroft "exploded so many pet theories of Ulrich B. Phillips that his reputation as an authority on slavery must now find new ground on which to stand."[8] Writing in the *New Republic,* Malcolm Cowley praised Bancroft's book as a necessary "supplement and corrective" to Phillips's *American Negro Slavery* (1918). Cowley agreed with Bancroft: Phillips's treatment of the domestic slave trade was sketchy and open to severe criticisms. Whereas Phillips de-emphasized this side of slavery, Bancroft "dilates, indeed, upon the very features of slavery which Professor Phillips is most inclined to neglect."[9] Another reviewer, Wendell Holmes Stephenson, considered Bancroft's strictures of Phillips excessive. One of Phillips's doctoral students and an early defender of his mentor, Stephenson found Bancroft "overzealous in locating discrepancies in the research of other investigators, sometimes without a clear understanding of the issue involved."[10] Unquestionably, Stephenson referred to Phillips.

Throughout *Slave Trading in the Old South,* Bancroft assailed Phillips and his writings. He charged him with failing to recognize in his own evidence proof of large-scale slave breeding from which the planters earned large profits. He cited Phillips as representative of historians who argued that slave traders were held in contempt by southerners. He corrected inaccuracies in Phillips's publications. He chided Phillips's failure to include the natural increase of plantation slaves as a source of profit. He faulted Phillips for discounting evidence that planters rewarded unusually fecund slave mothers. He mocked Phillips's 1918 statement that young slaves were rarely sold separately from their parents. "Hardly ever sold separately!" wrote Bancroft, "they were hardly less than a staple in the trade. The selling singly of young children privately and publicly was frequent and notorious." And he criticized Phillips for withholding or misinterpreting evidence that might cast unfavorable light on the planter class. Either Phillips was an apologist for slavery, implied Bancroft, or he was terribly naive in underplaying the harshness of slave sales. In any case, Bancroft was outraged by Phillips's benign view of slavery, and in his book, he struck a blow against what he considered Phillips's romanticism and misapplication of facts.[11]

Bancroft's attack on Phillips's work is an example of historical criticism at its best. The strictures Bancroft raised were indeed valid. In fact, they prefigured later critiques of Phillips by historians Richard Hofstadter and Kenneth M. Stampp. Bancroft and Phillips were disagreeing over a complex historical problem: the nature of slavery in general and the slave trade in particular. In 1938 Allan Nevins summarized the differences between the two men essentially in these terms. A close personal friend of Bancroft, Nevins interpreted the rift separating Bancroft and Phillips largely as the result of their inherent biases. Nevins purposely cited the differences between them as a case study in conflicting historical interpretations. In *The Gateway to History,* his primer for beginning students of history, Nevins wrote:

> Ulrich B. Phillips and Frederic Bancroft were in possession of much of the same body of facts regarding slavery; they were both thoroughly honest, and determined to tell the uncolored truth as they saw it; but one arrived at friendly, the other hostile conclusions upon slavery as an institution.[12]

But the Bancroft-Phillips controversy was more complex than Nevins realized. The severity of Bancroft's criticism stemmed from a personal feud that transcended the realm of historical criticism. In *Slave Trading in the Old South,* he pursued Phillips with extreme vengeance. By 1931, Bancroft was absorbed with destroying Phillips's reputation as the premier historian of the South.

The roots of the stormy Bancroft–Phillips relationship actually were laid years before Bancroft chose to do battle with Phillips on the question of the slave trade. Ironically, Bancroft and Phillips were perhaps the two most knowledgeable students of the Old South and were trained in "scientific" historical methods at Columbia University. But despite these similarities, the two men were worlds apart in background, perspective, and personality.

Bancroft was born in Galesburg, Illinois, in 1860. His birthplace was a center of midwestern abolitionism and reportedly a "station" on the underground railroad. During his youth, Bancroft was surrounded by antislavery sentiment; his father was an avowed abolitionist. Included among young Bancroft's earliest heroes were William Lloyd Garrison, Charles Sumner, and John Brown. After graduating from Amherst College in 1882, Bancroft entered Columbia's School of Political Science, which awarded him the Ph.D. three years later.[13] While studying at Columbia, Bancroft joined other young, college-educated professionals who worked in the office of the New York Mugwumps.[14]

An idolater of Carl Schurz, Bancroft favored civil service and tariff reform, sound money, and opposed American imperialism. But the graduate student had little time to devote to politics because his dissertation, *A Sketch of the Negro in Politics, Especially in South Carolina and Mississippi* (1885), demanded extensive field research. It was based largely on personal observations of the South and interviews among southern blacks made on a tour in 1884.[15] In this volume and in a series of articles published in the *New York Evening Post* the following year, Bancroft exhibited racist, antiblack opinions.[16] These clashed with his abolitionist background and his later criticisms of Phillips. In his subsequent publications—*Life of William H. Seward* (1900), *Calhoun and the South Carolina Nullification Movement* (1928), and *Slave Trading in the Old South*—Bancroft was bitterly antislavery and hostile to the state rights interpretation of the Constitution. In these later writings, Bancroft was relentless in censuring the southern "traditions" upon which he blamed the bloody Civil War.

A devoted historian, Bancroft dedicated more than half of his life to the study of southern history. Repeated research trips below the Mason-Dixon line had allowed him to acquire firsthand information on his subject and to amass valuable primary source materials on the South. Especially interested in slavery and the Civil War, Bancroft conducted extensive interviews among ex-slaves and Confederate veterans.[17] As early as 1900, he began preparing a massive, multivolume history of the South. But this work, like many of Bancroft's projected publications, never appeared in print.[18] Bancroft's study of Calhoun and nullification and his book on the slave trade were in fact remnants—mere chapters—of his proposed history of the South. Ironically, Bancroft became one of the most knowledgeable historians of the South, but his list of publications remained remarkably short. What makes Bancroft's career even more curious is that he was a historian without portfolio—a gentleman scholar.

Independently wealthy, Bancroft was freed from classroom responsibilities.[19] This circumstance gave him enormous leisure time to write history. And as a self-proclaimed perfectionist, Bancroft required an overabundance of time revising his manuscripts. Sensitive to his paucity of scholarly productivity, Bancroft argued that his chief interest was historical research and writing, not publishing. He perceived himself as a serious student who would not compromise his standards to rush into print, one who published only mature thoughts, not ill-conceived ideas.[20] But other explanations account for Bancroft's sparse publication record.

First, Bancroft was a raconteur—the writing of history did not consume all his energies as he often boasted. To the contrary, like James Ford Rhodes, he enjoyed the good life whether in New York, Washington, or Paris. Writing in 1900, William A. Dunning described Bancroft "as far as possible from the Dryasdust

[sic] type of scholar," a familiar figure among "the more cultivated circles" of Washington society. Dunning continued, "He is something of a *bon vivant;* can enjoy life and can tell a good story . . . and is popular among the members of some of the foreign embassies."[21] Always active socially, throughout his life Bancroft devoted much time recording his observations and criticisms in lengthy letters and personal diaries.

But other obstacles stymied Bancroft's scholarly productivity as well. Perhaps he possessed too much free time, for he was lazy—what one of his biographers has termed Bancroft's lack of "diligence and industriousness." And because he was combative and vitriolic by nature, Bancroft spent much time and effort feuding with persons who disagreed with him and who were less indolent in the practice of their craft. Exhibiting "an early acquired love of disputation,"[22] Bancroft lacked tact and was intolerant. Whether aiming barbs at his friend Rhodes or revealing his personal dislike for a fellow historian, Bancroft was petulant and carping. As it became obvious to him that he would never publish his history of the South, Bancroft came to direct his criticisms at one historian in particular. His victim, a scholar less prone to lethargy than Bancroft, extolled the new proslavery argument. He had become the reputed authority on slavery and the history of the Old South. That historian was Ulrich Bonnell Phillips.

Phillips was born and bred in LaGrange, Georgia, a small town not far from the Alabama border. He grew to maturity in an environment totally different from that of Galesburg, Illinois. The proslavery attitude that permeates all of Phillips's works had its origins in his background.[23] While his father was of yeoman lower-middle-class stock, his mother, whom Phillips considered his constant "comrade and source of inspiration," had a plantation background.[24] Before the Civil War, her family had owned 1,500 acres of land and twenty-four slaves. Growing up in the 1880s in upland Georgia, a section of the Confederacy hard hit by Union troops, Phillips was surrounded by men whose remembrances of those better days "before the war" were the fabric from which the myth of the "Lost Cause" was fashioned. Phillips lived and labored in the South until the turn of the century when he traveled north to earn his Ph.D. under the tutelage of William A. Dunning at Columbia. After completing his doctorate, Phillips campaigned actively for Progressive-era causes—agricultural and educational reform—in his native state.[25] The Georgian believed that his experiences picking cotton as a youth and living among southerners, black and white, gave him an advantage in writing the history of his region. "The South is a baffling puzzle to virtually all outsiders," explained Phillips in 1923. He was convinced that "it must remain so until insiders give the clues for its solution."[26] And in his college classes at Wisconsin, Tulane, Michigan, and Yale, Phillips shared his knowledge of the South from the perspective of the native.

Unlike Bancroft, Phillips was not a man of independent means. He did, however, marry into wealth and thereby acquired many of the trappings of the patrician. When nominating Phillips for membership in a social club at Yale,

Professor Ralph H. Gabriel described him as "a delightful person and most clubable. One of his regrets at leaving [the University of] Michigan," continued Gabriel, "was that ... [Phillips] could not bring his wine cellar with him"[27] Another friend, Herbert A. Kellar, portrayed Phillips as somewhat the benevolent aristocrat. "*Noblesse oblige* was a very real thing to him," added Kellar, "and he practiced it consistently."[28] But if a patrician, he was not a gentleman scholar in Bancroft's mold. Numerous publications and successful graduate students attest to Phillips's credentials as a tireless historian and teacher.

Phillips left a broad imprint on the historiography of the South.[29] The author of monographs on Georgia politics, transportation in the Eastern Cotton Belt, and a biography of Robert Toombs, his two best-known books were *American Negro Slavery* (1918) and *Life and Labor in the Old South* (1929). These established Phillips's reputation as the premier historian of the South during the first half of the twentieth century. Phillips probed the slave regime in more detail than had any previous scholar, systematically used plantation records as sources, and led the way in examining the interrelationship of race and class in southern society. Specifically, Phillips maintained that slavery was benevolent by nature—a successful mode of social control originally established by the whites to prevent race war and social chaos. Differing from Bancroft, he defended the slave owners and praised them for their many kindnesses toward the bondsmen. Of course, Phillips recognized degrees of brutality in slavery, but he considered these exceptional and de-emphasized the seamier sides of the institution—including the slave trade. For Phillips, slavery was a paternalistic relationship between master and slave, one whereby "The possession was not wholly of the slave by the master, but also of the master by the slave."[30] He considered the plantation system an effective mode of organizing laborers but argued that slave property was an unprofitable investment for the planter.

If Phillips shared only one characteristic with Bancroft—and he shared many—it would have been his aspiration toward perfection. A master stylist, Phillips was a severe critic of his own exposition as well as that of others. "Technique," he once wrote, "is an essence of every craft, but liberation is the mark of every master."[31] As a young historian, Phillips was advised by an editor to "take much more pains with your style."[32] Ironically, his graduate students recall fondly Phillips's dictum that "*the author must take pains to save the reader pains.*"[33] And Phillips followed his own advice: He subjected his writings to the strictest self-criticism. He continually revised paragraphs and rarely was satisfied with his choice of words. At one point, Phillips feared that he, a slow and deliberate writer, would never complete *Life and Labor in the Old South,* the first volume of Phillips's own projected multi-volume history of the South.[34] Yet, he finished that award-winning book and was well on his way to reaching his goal before his death in 1934. That accomplishment underscores a fundamental difference between Phillips and Bancroft. Phillips was an ambitious, opportunistic, and productive scholar. Bancroft, on the other hand, failed to take advantage of his own abilities and wasted his energies in meaningless, petty squabbles with other historians.

The first contacts between Bancroft and Phillips were surprisingly cordial. In 1905, Bancroft remarked that he found Phillips's early studies of plantation economics "very useful," and soon after, he again commended the Georgian. Both Phillips and William E. Dodd, he said, shared a mission as southern historians to serve their region.[35] Although he praised Phillips's biography of Robert Toombs after its publication in 1913, the first sign of a rift between Bancroft and his southern rival surfaced in the following year. On historical matters "Phillips seems to be astride the fence," Bancroft wrote Dodd, "and [he is] rather positive in his views whether on one side or the other." Paradoxically, Bancroft charged Phillips with attempting to lure him into an argument.[36] But the real issue that drew the battle lines between the two men was Bancroft's attempt in 1915 to reform the American Historical Association (AHA).

Supported by Mississippi archivist Dunbar Rowland, John H. Latané of Johns Hopkins University, and a handful of other historians, Bancroft led a crusade to institute minor—albeit necessary—changes in the operation and government of the AHA. Relying upon personal letters, pamphlets, and the columns of the *Nation* as their battlefield, Bancroft and his comrades publicized what in their opinion were corrupt practices by leaders of the historical guild.[37] The control and legal ownership of the *American Historical Review* and the travel expenses of the AHA's Executive Council were among the issues Bancroft investigated. Had he not conducted himself as an aroused muckraker or with the zeal of a committee on un-American activities, Bancroft probably would not have received the scorn of his colleagues. For in the long run, the reformers' efforts brought about overdue administrative changes in the AHA. But in acting with rancor and acrimony, Bancroft and his associates alienated many old friends and made a host of new enemies. In his analysis of this "Tempest in Clio's Teapot," historian Ray Allen Billington correctly interpreted Bancroft as a self-serving, frustrated fanatic whose "suspicion-haunted mind" led him to direct tasteless and unsubstantiated charges of corruption at leading figures in the historical profession.[38]

In 1915 Bancroft and Phillips were both members of the AHA's Executive Council, itself a measure of their high standing among their peers. At first, the Illinois native and the Georgian agreed that reforms were necessary within the association. On April 1, Phillips wrote Bancroft an extremely cordial letter inviting him to join the Phillips family while on its vacation in Long Island. "There are a hundred and one things historical and present-day I would like to discuss with you," said Phillips. Assuring Bancroft that he "warmly" supported his plans to reform the AHA, Phillips requested a list of specific grievances—not generalizations—to be investigated. But five days later, when counseling Bancroft as to tactics, Phillips urged Bancroft to avoid all ill-tempered criticisms and angry statements. Possibly recalling his own earlier interest in Progressive reform,

Phillips endorsed the reformers' plans as long as a sense of moderation and good will was maintained. In a letter published in the *Nation* in September, he cautiously endorsed the insurgents' plans to reform the AHA but urged that historians on both sides shun "recrimination," "exaggeration and harsh words."[39] Even before the publication of this letter, however, Phillips's constant warnings and conciliatory attitude toward the leaders of the association made Bancroft increasingly wary of the historian's reform sentiments.[40]

Unfortunately for Phillips, those historians whom Bancroft branded members of a corrupt "ring"—distinguished scholars such as John Franklin Jameson, George Lincoln Burr, and Worthington C. Ford—took offense at Phillips's apparent sympathies with the insurgents. Jameson, who had warned Phillips in a similar vein earlier in his career, criticized him in October as "young and impulsive, and always somewhat eager to get into print." According to Jameson, editor of the *American Historical Review,* Phillips unwisely succumbed to Bancroft's false accusations.[41] Ford, chief of the Manuscript Division of the Library of Congress from 1902 to 1909, and later editor at the Massachusetts Historical Society, was a stalwart opponent of Bancroft. And as Phillips's uncle (through marriage), Ford considered his nephew's indiscretion a breach of "family discipline." According to "Uncle Worthington," Phillips, as a member of the Association's Council, "made a tactical and personal error" in publicly expressing his opinion on reform. Should Phillips again take such a position, warned Ford, he might lose "the confidence of others in your balance and disinterestedness."[42]

Obviously embarrassed, Phillips admitted to Ford that he had acted impulsively when he published his letter in the *Nation.* But, Phillips insisted, his action was prompted by a sincere "feeling of responsibility" as a member of the council. He planned to write one further letter that, Phillips hoped, would once and for all get him "out of the fracas." Shortly before its publication on October 21, Phillips wrote that he had entered the AHA controversy in an effort "at constructive peacemaking" and regretted that he had "taken a hand in the public discussion at all." In a draft of a letter never mailed to Ford, Phillips admitted "having learned the lesson that a man in a middle position may expect blows from both sides." Ford, after corresponding with his nephew, assured Jameson that Phillips's "apostasy does not seem to be more than skin deep." But regrettably for the Georgian, for years to come Jameson remained doubtful of Phillips's sense of judgment.[43]

Phillips attempted to make amends with Bancroft after the publication of his second letter in the *Nation.*[44] However, Bancroft's abusiveness led him to terminate their correspondence. When Bancroft continued to write insulting letters to him, Phillips replied that thereafter he could only communicate "in words which I prefer not to use."[45]

Unquestionably, Phillips's break with Bancroft over the AHA reform issue sparked Bancroft's one-man crusade to discredit Phillips as a southern historian. It widened the already existing gap between the two men based on cultural and psychological differences. Venting his ill feelings toward Phillips, Bancroft continued to disparage him for the remainder of his career.

For example, in 1918, after the appearance of *American Negro Slavery,* Bancroft asked James Ford Rhodes:

> Have you read U.B. Phillips' *American Negro Slavery?* In it he attempts some surprisingly contemp[t]uous comment on anti-slavery opinions. I have been looking for someone to give him his deserts. What he says in an alleged refutation about slave-breeding would interest you. In my volume . . . I shall cover that question in a manner that will leave no room for doubt. I have a most deadly array of facts.

Bancroft believed that in W.E.B. Du Bois he had found just the right historian to give Phillips "his deserts." Prior to the appearance of Du Bois's review in the *American Political Science Review,* the black scholar received a letter from Bancroft encouraging him to criticize Phillips harshly. After the publication of the review—perhaps the most critical evaluation of *American Negro Slavery*—Bancroft praised it but added, "Naturally I had hoped that you would damage . . . [Phillips] much more, for he is very vulnerable; but all things considered, probably it was best for you to hold the mirror up to him."[46]

Bancroft's assault on Phillips continued into the next decade. He repeatedly criticized Phillips whenever the opportunity arose. In 1924, for example, Bancroft attacked his writing style: "Phillips is fond of literary stilts and seems to be very proud of some of his performances on them." Five years later, when the historical profession heralded Phillips's *Life and Labor in the Old South* as among the best books of the decade, Bancroft chose to reprove him for a statement he had made soon after leaving graduate school, more than twenty years before. Ignoring Phillips's significant contributions to the history of the South, Bancroft insisted that "The key to Phillips" was found in his 1905 remark that only "men who have inherited Southern traditions" should write southern history. Bancroft was outraged with the attitude of Phillips and other southern-born scholars that they could preempt the field of southern history. He was confident that he brought a more-detached, less biased perspective to the task. Phillips's assertion so infuriated Bancroft that in 1932 he judged it the thought of one "as callow as an ass's colt."[47]

Bancroft's obsession with criticizing Phillips reached its peak in 1931 with the publication of *Slave Trading in the Old South.* Cocky and vitriolic, Bancroft relished the fact that no reviewer had even attempted "to answer my criticisms and ridicule of Phillips." "From the numerous approving comments . . . on my pin-pricks of Phillips," he wrote historian Harrison A. Trexler, "it is obvious that I am not alone in thinking that he has displayed undue complacency as Sir Oracle of Southern history." At last, Bancroft had triumphed.[48] Not only had his book helped demolish the proslavery argument, but in doing so he had won a victory over his bitter personal and professional rival.

For his part, Phillips probably tried to wipe the infuriating Bancroft from his consciousness. But he failed. In 1924, Phillips, aware of Bancroft's forthcoming book on the slave trade, requested that the editor of the *American Historical Review* allow him to review *Slave Trading in the Old South*—"in which . . . [Bancroft] makes occasion to dispraise my writings." Seven years later, when the book finally appeared, Phillips was too busy to review it: He was courageously fighting throat cancer and laboring on his history of the South. Also, Phillips wrote, in the intervening years, "I've lost much of my taste for battle." Although unable to "slash" Bancroft in print, Phillips ripped into him at least symbolically in a letter to the editor of the *Review*. Challenging the importance of Bancroft's work, Phillips inquired why the editor was "magnifying" the significance of *Slave Trading in the Old South* "by your copious assignment of space?" for the review.[49]

Thus ended the conflict between Frederic Bancroft and Ulrich Bonnell Phillips. Unquestionably, it resulted in large measure from fundamental differences—in background, perspective, and personality. These factors were themselves enough to lead the two historians down different paths in their interpretations of slavery. But personal factors go even further to explain Bancroft's antagonism toward Phillips.

First, Bancroft believed that Phillips had betrayed him during the AHA controversy. In Bancroft's opinion, Phillips's commitment to reform the AHA was shallow at best. When the luminaries of the historical profession began to look upon the reformers with disfavor, Phillips unveiled his true colors. Quickly, he deserted the reformers in favor of the corrupt "ring" Bancroft charged with mismanaging the association. Second, Bancroft exhibited a deep distrust of academicians. Never affiliated with a college or university, he came to resent the leadership of the historical guild by "Professors of history [who] of course, always know everything."[50] And to Bancroft, Phillips probably symbolized the consummate professor of history: the aggressive, productive university teacher. But Bancroft identified Phillips with an even more sinister personage—the "professional Southerner," a historian who marshaled his evidence to uphold southern myths and "traditions" in spite of evidence to the contrary.[51] Finally, Bancroft resented Phillips's stature as the leading southern historian of their day.

What, then, does the case study of Bancroft and Phillips teach us? When analyzing historiographical questions, students must first determine the validity of the historical criticism presented. In the case of Bancroft and Phillips, Bancroft's analysis of Phillips's writings on slavery was carefully reasoned. He raised important questions and underscored Phillips's racial bias. But neither man could free himself from his ingrained preconceptions and prejudiced outlook. This situation explains the surface differences separating the two scholars. Human factors, however, reveal a new personal dimension. Feelings of betrayal, distrust, and jealousy amplified basic disagreements between Bancroft and Phillips. Their conflict was more than a case of historical criticism. It involved human, intensely personal criticism as well.

5

The Historiographic Rise, Fall, and Resurrection of Ulrich Bonnell Phillips

"The ghost of U.B. Phillips haunts all of us," wrote John W. Blassingame in 1978.[1] Ulrich Bonnell Phillips—the very sound of his name conjures up historical bogies for many scholars. By the 1960s, Phillips had come to symbolize the reactionary and racist strains in southern historiography in general and of the historiography of slavery in particular. Phillips was condemned for ignoring the agony of the slaves. He was the classic apologist for an inhumane, brutal, and exploitative system. Professors rarely assigned Phillips's books to their students. When they did, they offered them as case studies in flawed historical scholarship. Phillips not only asked the "wrong" questions, his critics charged, but his conclusions were made ludicrous by overt elitism, extreme antipathy toward blacks, and methodological imbalance and imprecision.[2] To this generation of scholars, Phillips exemplified the many evils of racist white historiography of an earlier day.

Phillips died in 1934. Had he lived, the criticism of the 1960s and 1970s would have dumbfounded him. During the first three decades of this century, Phillips had reigned as the master of slave historiography. His nine books and more than fifty-five articles had established him as the most thorough, systematic, and resourceful student of plantation slavery.[3] Phillips's work dominated the literature on slavery until the 1950s. During the last three decades, however, the pioneer historian has been dethroned and, according to some critics, all but repudiated. The rise and fall of Phillips as a historian of slavery provide an essential backdrop for a third phase of the historiographic cycle: the resurgence of interest in his work in recent years. Several scholars have looked at Phillips anew and—while strongly critical of his racial and class bias—paint a more positive image of the man and his contributions.

When analyzing writings of Phillips on slavery, students usually focus on his two landmark books, *American Negro Slavery* (1918) and *Life and Labor in the Old South* (1929). Attention, however, also should be given to a number of pathbreaking essays that he published in the fifteen years after completing his doctorate in 1902. In these early articles, Phillips introduced many of the themes and utilized most of the manuscript and plantation sources that he developed and used in his two famous books.[4]

Phillips described slavery as a necessary and successful mode of racial control. He equated the plantation with both the modern factory and the social settlement houses of the Progressive era. In his view, the plantation served a vital social function: it created a controlled environment in which the master and slave lived in peace and harmony.[5] Slavery, then, was a benign, paternalistic institution. The blacks received adequate housing, food, and clothing. Slave laws were enforced only casually, and "except in emergencies," masters rarely sold slaves. The planters' "dominating consideration was not that of great profit," wrote Phillips, "but that of comfortable living in pleasant surroundings, with a consciousness of important duties well-performed." Considerable give and take, argued Phillips, characterized labor relations on the plantation. Masters, out of self-interest and genuine kindness, were benevolent patriarchs. "The slaves," Phillips explained, "had many leverages, and oftentimes . . . ruled their masters more than the masters ruled them." And life under this "paternalistic despotism" also included an educational component. The plantation, in his opinion, was a school that trained "ignorant," "unenterprising," "barbaric," "childlike and credulous" Africans in the ways of civilization. Phillips concluded that slavery offered "the most efficient method ever devised for the use of stupid labor in agriculture on a large scale."[6]

Despite its importance in ordering southern society, Phillips judged slavery an utter economic failure. He even predicted that, had the Civil War not intervened, financial considerations would have led to its disestablishment in some peaceable way. Phillips criticized slavery for what he termed "capitalizing the prospective value of the labor of each workman for the whole of his life."[7] Although varied and flexible as a social system, slavery was too inelastic and rigid to be profitable as a labor system. It locked up and exported too much scarce capital, thereby retarding industrialization and making the section susceptible to financial crises. Slavery further discouraged the immigration of wage-earning whites into the South, limited crop diversification, and wasted the fertility of the soil. "It was only in special industries," wrote Phillips in 1905, "and only in times of special prosperity, that negro slave labor was of such decided profit as to escape condemnation for its inherent disadvantages."[8]

Phillips refined and elaborated these themes in *American Negro Slavery,* his magnum opus, and the first systematic analysis of slavery in the entire South.[9] This volume thrust Phillips into the role of the unexcelled authority on the peculiar institution. It eclipsed in scope and detail prior books on North American slavery and has influenced virtually all subsequent works on the subject. His chapters on West African culture, the slave trade, Caribbean slavery, and anti-slavery in the North actually added little to previous scholarship, but his use of the comparative method to examine slavery in the West Indies offered a fresh perspective to American historians. He also made penetrating observations regarding the mechanics of plantation agriculture, the plain folk of the South, and overseers.[10] Even so, Phillips focused predominantly on the masters and their slaves.

He identified a sense of fellowship between the two, a relation characterized by "propriety, proportion and cooperation." Through years of living together, Phillips maintained, blacks and whites developed a rapport not between equals, but of dependent unequals. Under slavery, the two racial groups became interdependent—the blacks "always within the social mind and conscience of the whites, as the whites in turn were within the mind and conscience of the blacks." Though masters controlled the privileges that the slaves enjoyed, Phillips considered blacks "by no means devoid of, influence." Foreshadowing historian Eugene D. Genovese's work by a half-century, Phillips interpreted slavery as a labor system "shaped by mutual requirements, concessions and understandings, producing reciprocal codes of conventional morality" and responsibility.[11]

In *Life and Labor in the Old South,* Phillips's award-winning social history, he did not revise his interpretation of slavery to any significant degree.[12] In fact, the basic arguments—the duality of slavery as an economic cancer but a vital mode of racial control—can be traced back to his earliest writings. He modified neither his view that blacks were inherently inferior nor his belief that they retained few of their African cultural traits after enslavement. "The bulk of the black personnel," explained Phillips, "was notoriously primitive, uncouth, improvident and inconstant, merely because they were Negroes of the time."[13] Less detailed and presented in a more attractive literary style than *American Negro Slavery,* his *Life and Labor* was a general synthesis rather than a monograph. His racism consequently appears less pronounced in *Life and Labor* because of its broad scope. Fewer racial slurs appeared in 1929 than in 1918, but Phillips's overt prejudice remained.[14]

Most white historians greeted Phillips's two books with praise. They complimented the breadth, lack of partisanship, fairness, and factual accuracy of *American Negro Slavery.* Several noted Phillips's use of new sources—plantation records, letters, and diaries. According to southerner Philip Alexander Bruce: "The work is a monument of research, and equally so of fair and discriminating presentation. I venture to assert that you have said the final word."[15] *Life and Labor* enjoyed an even more enthusiastic reception. Historian J.G. de Roulhac Hamilton described the publication of the book as "a real event in American historiography." Because of its broad portrait of southern culture, another reviewer considered *Life and Labor* a prime example of James Harvey Robinson's "New History."[16] Others argued that Phillips's analysis of slavery in *Life and Labor* surpassed that of his earlier work. Henry Steele Commager spoke for many of his fellow historians when he judged the later Phillips book as "perhaps the most significant contribution to the history of the Old South in this generation."[17]

The writings of Phillips on slavery impressed not only his white contemporaries but scores of later historians as well. In the years after his death, a "Phillips school" of state studies on slavery appeared. These incorporated the essential organization, sources, and interpretation of *American Negro Slavery*.[18] Even his severest critics have often embraced the source materials, method, and topics that Phillips popularized. According to Herbert G. Gutman, many historians of slavery still use Phillips's "model of slave socialization." They tend to approach "slave belief and behavior as little more than one or another response to planter-sponsored stimuli." Repeating Phillips's essential premise, they ask, "What did enslavement do to Africans and their Afro-American descendants?"[19]

Despite the generally favorable responses to Phillips's writings, black historians leveled serious criticisms at them as early as 1913. In that year, W.E.B. Du Bois attacked Phillips's proslavery attitude, specifically his argument that since emancipation the productivity of southern black laborers had declined, while that of their white counterparts had increased. Phillips, Du Bois wrote bitterly, "is white, and Southern, but . . . has a Northern job and . . . knows all about the Negro." Du Bois struck a more devastating blow at Phillips five years later, in his review of *American Negro Slavery*. He faulted Phillips for writing a "curiously incomplete and unfortunately biased" economic history of American slaveholders—without focusing on the slaves or consulting slave sources. Phillips was so insensitive to blacks as persons, that "The Negro as a responsible human being has no place in the book." Du Bois considered *American Negro Slavery* a blatant "defense of American slavery—a defense of an institution which was at best a mistake and at worst a crime—made in a day when we need sharp and implacable judgment against collective wrongdoing by cultured and courteous men."[20]

Others mirrored the criticisms of Du Bois. The black historian Carter G. Woodson faulted Phillips for ignoring evidence of slave rebelliousness and for not comprehending "what the Negroes have thought and felt and done." Objecting to Phillips's denial of slave breeding, white historian Frederic Bancroft admittedly was "looking for someone to give him his deserts."[21] Other white reviewers chided Phillips for approving, seemingly endorsing, slavery as the best mode of race relations. A Michigan journalist quipped that Phillips seemed "rather to ignore the fact" that "freedom, in itself, counts for something." The reformer Mary White Ovington disagreed with Phillips's tolerant spirit toward slavery. In contrast to Bruce's statement, she feared that "unless the descendant of the slave writes an exhaustive book from his standpoint this might be the last word on the subject."[22]

Life and Labor also received considerable criticism. Again, blacks led the way in reproving Phillips. Historian William M. Brewer attacked him for ignoring slave artisans. Phillips, charged Brewer, erroneously grouped all slaves together as a monolith. This, he explained, "is still the policy of white Americans in thinking of Negroes and prescribing a place for them." Brewer cogently described Phillips as "a disciple of the color line and a staunch defender of the faith of the South." Frederic Bancroft dubbed Phillips "Sir Oracle of Southern History" and accused him of failing to recognize in his own evidence proof of large-scale slave breeding from which the planters earned immense profits. Either Phillips was an apologist for slavery, said Bancroft, or he was terribly naive in underplaying the extent and harshness of the slave trade.[23]

These criticisms by pioneer black historians and a few white scholars indicated just how vulnerable Phillips was to the forces of revisionism. During the 1930s and 1940s historians continued to chip away at Phillips's major themes. Lewis C. Gray disagreed with the economic indictment of slavery by Phillips. Gray found slavery a highly profitable business enterprise but conceded that the institution had pernicious effects on the economy of the region. In Gray's opinion, Phillips misread the fluctuations in slave prices. Over-capitalization was "at most only a temporary phenomenon," and for the entire antebellum period "there was a considerable reduction in cost of producing cotton."[24] Other economic historians added to Gray's critique. Robert R. Russel absolved slavery from several charges made by Phillips. He blamed the attractiveness of staple agriculture for the backwardness of the antebellum economy of the South. Thomas P. Govan and Robert W. Smith questioned Phillips's bookkeeping methods. The pioneer historian calculated as plantation expenses items that were, in reality, profits. And he erroneously used appreciated values of bondsmen as capital investment in figuring profit.[25] Through the years, Phillips's work on plantation economics has fared poorly. Today, few subscribe to his belief in the unprofitability of slavery.[26]

Nor have historians withheld criticisms of Phillips's method. As early as 1944, Richard Hofstadter impugned his use of inadequate and misleading data— the records of large plantations. Influenced strongly by Frank L. Owsley's researches on the plain folk of the Old South, Hofstadter faulted Phillips for slighting small slave units, where the vast majority of the bondsmen lived. Further, Hofstadter accused Phillips of holding "certain preconceptions which disposed him to throw out materials that showed the institution in a less favorable light."[27] Another critic identified examples of "unbalanced selection, misquoting and inaccurate paraphrasing" which, he said, "raise a strong doubt in regard to the objectivity of Phillips's works."[28] Recently, students have uncovered inaccuracies in Phillips's slave price data for New Orleans and occupational records from the 1848 Charleston Census. For years, unsuspecting historians have relied upon these sources.[29]

Phillips's racism, however, always has been his most vulnerable weakness. Innumerable historians have objected to his racial slurs. In 1943, for example, Herbert Aptheker pointed out that Phillips's racism prevented him from identifying large-scale resistance on the part of the bondsmen.[30] But among mainstream, "establishment," white historians, Phillips's reputation remained intact until the

1950s.[31] White Americans in general, and white historians in particular, simply were unaware of how much anti-Negro prejudice had clouded their attempts to document the past. It was not until the post–World War II years, in the midst of third-world revolutions abroad and a black revolution at home, that white American intellectuals became ripe for a complete repudiation of Phillips. Racism, while still very much a part of American life, then came under fire.

Historian Kenneth M. Stampp led the assault on Phillips. While mindful of his predecessor's significant accomplishments, Stampp reproved Phillips for ignoring slave life on small plantations and farms, for "loose and glib generalizing" about slavery, and for failing to view the institution "through the eyes of the Negro." In treating slavery, explained Stampp, Phillips overemphasized the "mild and humorous side and minimized its grosser aspects." Because Phillips was incapable of taking blacks seriously, Stampp concluded that he had lost his relevance for Americans of the 1950s. Summarizing the best anthropological thought of his day, Stampp wrote, "No historian ... can be taken seriously any longer unless he begins with the knowledge that there is no valid evidence that the Negro race is innately inferior to the white, and that there is growing evidence that both races have approximately the same potentialities."[32] To underscore his commitment to racial equality, Stampp assured his readers that he had "assumed that the slaves were merely ordinary human beings, that innately Negroes *are,* after all, only white men with black skins, nothing more, nothing less."[33]

That statement, of course, came back to haunt Stampp. Much like Phillips's books, Stampp's excellent work, *The Peculiar Institution: Slavery in the Ante-Bellum South* (1956), underwent revisionism of its own.[34] In retrospect, though, Stampp was remarkably restrained in his criticism of Phillips. But historians of the 1960s used Stampp as a symbol. His work represented a victory over those evils in American life—racism, elitism, proscription—so conveniently identified with Phillips. Unconsciously, many historians may have "scapegoated" Phillips. By focusing upon his racism—projecting onto him their own racial ambivalence—they could keep their feelings safely outside of themselves, all the while justifying their self-images as liberals.[35] By the mid-1960s, it was easy—even stylish—to abhor Phillips.

Then came Eugene D. Genovese. More than any other historian, Genovese is responsible for the resurgence of interest in Phillips. According to historian Charles B. Dew, in these years Genovese was "engaged in a one-man crusade to focus scholarly attention on Phillips's work instead of his anti-Negro bias."[36] In 1966, he read a revisionist paper on Phillips before the American Historical Association and wrote an interpretive foreword to the paperback edition of *American Negro Slavery.* Two years later, he edited a collection of Phillips's articles. "Phillips," wrote Genovese, "came close to greatness as a historian, perhaps as close as any historian this country has yet produced." Admitting that Phillips's racism "prevented him from knowing many things which he in fact knew very well," Genovese praised Phillips because he "asked more and better questions than many of us still are willing to admit, and he carried on his investigations with consistent freshness and critical intelligence."[37]

Genovese's rise as a Phillips booster paralleled his climb as an authority, first on the planter class, then on the slaves. The radical historian seemed to delight in shocking liberal historians with his overly zealous defense of the arch-racist Phillips. Genovese chided Stampp, for example, for failing in *The Peculiar Institution* to attain the objectivity that Stampp had found so wanting in Phillips. Yet Genovese also was annoyed at Phillips because he "failed to draw the necessary conclusions from his extraordinary lifetime efforts."[38] Put another way, Phillips fell short of his admirer's own perception of the Old South as a quasi-feudal, pre-bourgeois, pre-industrial society under the thumb of the master class. Yet Genovese undervalued his own intellectual debt to Phillips. Even though he credited blacks with transforming plantation paternalism "into a weapon of resistance," the Marxist's use of the paternalism construct was strikingly similar to that first espoused by Phillips.[39]

Genovese's influence permeates what might best be described as a Phillips revival. Since 1969, Phillips has been the subject of one dissertation and twelve articles.[40] Far from uncritical, each acknowledges the historian's racism, but places it into the context of the Progressive era. These authors are generally sympathetic to Phillips, despite having been students during the 1960s when Phillips and his works were anathema. Their studies tell us much about Phillips—as historian, intellectual, progressive, liberal, archivist, and proslavery ideologue.

Does Phillips deserve all this attention? Unquestionably, yes. Ironically today's historians of slavery owe a tremendous debt to this racist, white southern historian. Although we may not wish to admit it, Gutman is correct: Phillips continues to dictate the manner in which many historians approach the study of slavery. His works remain standards against which we judge the new scholarship on slavery. Writing in the era of Jim Crow, not civil rights, Phillips focused squarely on the complex interrelationship of class and race in southern history. He was the first historian systematically to evaluate slavery as a social system and to measure the effect of its social role. For him, the peculiar institution was as much a mode of interracial adjustment and control as a system of organizing labor. Phillips also possessed an uncommonly broad conception of slavery as an economic institution. He pioneered the examination of slavery on a cost basis. Anticipating much recent work, Phillips recognized the importance of comparative slave studies. He identified the value of comparing Caribbean and North American slavery. Through Phillips's innovative use of various plantation sources, he further revolutionized the study of slavery. And his analysis of the workaday world of master, slave, and overseer was on a scale unprecedented by the historian's peers. Recently, no less a critic than Kenneth M. Stampp has admitted that "In their day the writings of Ulrich B. Phillips on slavery were both highly original and decidedly revisionist."[41]

But Phillips was far from flawless. As an economic historian alone, his work is subject to severe criticisms. He underestimated the long-range value of slave offspring. Though Phillips spoke a great deal of the draining of money out of the South, he failed to show where the money went. He paid too little attention to the workings of the credit system that enabled white southerners to purchase their bondsmen. Phillips failed to show how the planters could lose money while the South prospered as it did throughout the decade of the 1850s. He erroneously criticized planters for reinvesting their profits in additional slaves. By Phillips's own analogy, slaves were fixed capital to planters much as machines were to factory owners. And throughout his writings, Phillips was unclear on the relative efficiency of slavery to individual masters and its effect on the southern economy at large.

Undoubtedly, Phillips's racism weakened every word he wrote on slavery. The historian became trapped by his favorite sources—plantation records. To these materials he applied his own elitist, pro-southern, and antiblack beliefs. Not surprisingly, many of Phillips's interpretations differed little from those of the planters whose accounts he accepted. Failing to employ slave sources to any significant degree, he also ignored the work of contemporary black scholars.[42] Phillips never considered that what he interpreted as examples of the "crudity" of black labor might have been expressions of slave resistance. Even though he recognized the fear of slave revolts among whites, Phillips perceived slave resistance in a vacuum—a product not of self-assertion by blacks, but of a reversion to savagery.

We cannot honestly fault Phillips, however, for viewing slavery from the veranda and not from the slave cabin. There is much truth in historian Clement Eaton's observation that "young liberal historians tend to charge . . . [Phillips] out of the context of his sources."[43] Phillips was limited in the types of sources that were then available. And he was not entirely unaware of the limitations of plantation records. Phillips admitted, for example, that planters' rules for overseers presented "too idyllic a view of the system," that they were "rather the aspirations of the high class planters than the actuality on the average plantation."[44] In 1929, he complained that despite his efforts to locate them, few slave materials of any value were available from Delaware, Maryland, Kentucky, Missouri, or Arkansas. In Phillips's judgment adequate records to describe slave life on small plantations and farms simply did not exist.[45] Long before Owsley and his students, however, Phillips had employed census statistics as sources. But the large scope of his subject—slavery in the entire South—prevented him from delving fully into the county and court records. And finally, Phillips did cite "Oral testimony gathered . . . from old residents in various quarters of the South," as well as letters from slaves and narratives of ex-slaves.[46] Although he cautioned against the uncritical use of the latter source, in both *American Negro Slavery* and *Life and Labor* Phillips cited accounts—if only a few—written by former bondsmen.

From the vantage point of the three historiographic cycles presented here, Phillips's contributions to the study of slavery clearly outweigh his deficiencies. Neither saint nor sinner, he was subject to the same forces—bias, selectivity of evidence, inaccuracy—that plague us all. Descended from slave owners and reared in the rural South, he dominated slave historiography in an era when Progressivism was literally for whites only. Of all scholars, historians can ill afford to be anachronistic. Phillips was no more a believer in white supremacy than other leading contemporary white scholars.[47] That his antiblack bias did not prevent him from becoming the foremost student of slavery is less an indictment of American historical scholarship than an indicator of how completely he represented white American racial attitudes of his day.

Yes, Phillips grossly undervalued the oppression of slavery. His treatment of the African Americans was patronizing at best. His insensitivity to the suffering brought about by the slave trade is difficult for us to comprehend. And how could a careful historian fail to treat miscegenation? In short, to our eyes much of what Phillips wrote is insulting and offensive. But his inability to satisfy us reflects radically changed social values and racial mores. It is unrealistic to expect Phillips's pioneering work to keep pace with a half-century of revisionist writings, not only on slavery, but in genetics and cultural anthropology as well. Let us treat Phillips as we would any other historian—critically, but with balanced judgments. We must read Phillips carefully and cautiously, but read him nevertheless. Tackle his ideas squarely and fairly. We cannot approach him as a symbol who must be rejected *a priori*. For in spite of his shortcomings as a historian, that haunting figure—Ulrich Bonnell Phillips—still has much to tell us about slavery.

II

Trends

6

Alfred Holt Stone

Mississippi Planter and Archivist/Historian of Slavery

Mississippi planter and tax administrator Alfred Holt Stone (1870–1955) published widely on the subjects of race relations and southern history.[1] Early in this century, he was regarded as one of the nation's foremost white experts on the "Negro problem."[2] Stone's essays spanned a broad range of topics—from critiques of the "race problem" literature of his day, to the significance of the boll weevil; from experiments in plantation labor management, to competition between European white immigrants and the South's black work force.[3] As a measure of his status, in 1901 Stone was invited to address the American Economic Association.[4] Six years later, he delivered a paper before the American Historical Association.[5] He also was appointed a research associate in economic history at the Carnegie Institution of Washington. In these years, Stone befriended Ulrich Bonnell Phillips, destined to become the outstanding historian of slavery of the first half of the twentieth century. Stone provided Phillips invaluable support—both as guarantor of a book contract and as a source of plantation records.[6] Through vacations at Stone's Greenville home "Dunleith," Phillips gained important glimpses into the workaday world of the modern cotton plantation.

Despite the contemporary importance of his research and writing, Stone's work generally has been ignored by historians. In 1933, for example, in his *Slavery in Mississippi,* Charles Sackett Sydnor cited none of Stone's writings.[7] To be sure, some scholars have relied upon Stone. In *The Negro in Mississippi, 1865–1890* (1947), Vernon L. Wharton drew upon several of Stone's works as well as his huge collection of writings on blacks deposited at the Mississippi Department of Archives and History.[8] Nevertheless, Stone plays at best an uncertain role in southern historiography. In 1951, historian Albert D. Kirwan attacked conclusions Stone had made in a 1944 article as "conventional but not to be trusted."[9] And recently Eugene D. Genovese criticized Stone in passing in his *Roll, Jordan, Roll* (1974). According to Genovese, Stone joined Phillips and other "openly racist writers" in explaining the slaves' work ethic as a product of "Negro traits."[10] Racist and outmoded in methodology, Stone's pioneer work holds little appeal to modern historians. Written from the perspective of the slaveholder, not that of the slave, it flies in the face of today's scholarship. Yet Stone made two important, although little known, contributions to the historiography of slavery.

First, early in the century, Stone scoured the South for documentary records of slavery. Researching the peculiar institution before the establishment of the great archival repositories at Chapel Hill, Durham, and Baton Rouge, pioneer historians had to locate manuscript materials on slavery for themselves.[11] They operated largely through personal contacts. In 1907, for example, Stone wrote to historian William E. Dodd seeking "documentary manuscript and other materials bearing particularly on the ante bellum and earlier post bellum aspects of" southern blacks. At that time Stone was collecting information for a projected book, *The Negro in Slavery and Freedom.* He believed that a great deal of manuscript material on slavery was available, but too widely scattered for use by historians. And obtaining these records was all the more difficult because they were deposited mainly in the hands of private families or individuals. Requesting names of families with manuscripts dealing with slavery, Stone informed Dodd:

> I am in search of all forms of sugar, rice, tobacco, indigo and cotton plantation records,—such as journals, diaries, account books, account sales, cotton picking records, instructions to overseers. . . . In fact, I want anything which will throw the least light upon the economic side of the institution of slavery, as it existed at various . . . places in the Southern and border states. This would of course include all other forms of economic activity in which the negro was employed before the war as well as that of the plantation.[12]

Early in the century, Stone also published a pamphlet/questionnaire outlining the precise types of records on slavery of most interest to him.[13] *Material Wanted for an Economic History of the Negro* is a remarkable document not only for the student of archival history, but for students of slave historiography as well. In it, Stone explained that he was in quest of "original material" for use in his research on blacks under slavery and since emancipation. "The South is full of valuable documentary material," he explained, "but it is widely scattered, difficult to locate, and its importance not always appreciated. Such material can be supplemented and rendered more valuable by the personal information of older men who are rapidly passing away." Again, Stone hoped to employ personal contacts as sources of manuscript records. He realized all too well that no union list of manuscript collections existed for the nation at large, or the South in particular. What's more, southern libraries were especially lax in collecting records of their region's past.[14]

To remedy this archival problem, Stone planned to contact individuals with manuscripts in their possession. "Such material is largely in private hands," noted Stone, "and it is on the kindness of private individuals that I shall have to rely both for information as to its location and for its use after I have found it." The Mississippian realized that because slavery differed from locale to locale, it was imperative that he obtain manuscripts from throughout the South. "The economic life of the South and of the negro varied so widely," Stone added, "that it is necessary to localize this study in order to avoid misleading generalizations." He set for himself a most ambitious goal: "to locate material in each county in which the negro was economically important before the war."

Just what types of sources did Stone expect to find tucked away in old attics and corn cribs? For information on slave prices, and for descriptions of slaves, he sought bills of sale, advertisements, and administrators' accountings. To document plantation buildings—slave quarters, plantation homes, overseers' houses, gins, smokehouses, barns, dairies—Stone solicited diagrams, photographs, and descriptions. Contracts or accounts with plantation physicians and instructions to overseers would serve to illumine the medical care of the bondsmen. To uncover the police control of slaves, Stone sought written instructions of owners to overseers or slave drivers. His greatest concern, however, was to uncover "reliable descriptions of the practical, everyday routine of plantation life and work—for both white and black." The workaday world of masters and slaves, Stone explained, could best be recreated by salvaging a broad range of paper records. These included not only staple crop account sales, but also

> "plantation books," diaries, letters, overseers' reports, ledgers, journals, time books, weight sheets, or records, gin books, or any other books, papers or memoranda, showing methods of cultivating, yield per acre or per hand, method of marketing, profits or loss, or throwing light on any phase of slavery economics or slave life whether on plantations, or farms, or in mines or in towns, or under contractors on public or private work.

"Everything of the kind," Stone cautioned, "no matter how apparently worthless is of some value."

Stone possessed an uncanny ability to uncover archival gems that might be overlooked by other investigators. An early student of the role of cotton factors in the Old South,[15] he searched for names and addresses of antebellum factorage houses and commission merchants. Stone also sought accounts of transportation facilities—roads, canals, rivers, and railroads—used to carry the South's crops to market. And although generally insensitive to blacks, as individuals or as a group, Stone recognized the importance of documenting the slaves' African origins. "I would like to secure," he wrote, "even meager information touching various tribal groups of negroes which remained intact for a number of years, as, for example, the 'Moors,' in Delaware, and the 'Malagasy,' or 'Mollygasters,' in Virginia."

Stone's quest for the documentary records of slavery and the plantation system was only part of his overall contribution to slave historiography. While searching for these materials, he also raised significant questions pertaining to the slave experience. These revealed a probing mind, one that viewed slavery not as a monolith, but rather as a fluid system of racial and economic control. Although rigidly conservative on the race question of his day, Stone saw considerable flexibility in the slavery system of the Old South. The queries included in his pamphlet, quite surprisingly, prefigured much later scholarship. Stone in fact posed many of the questions that still elude modern historians of slavery. That he asked them at all is a measure of Stone's importance.

Like Phillips, Stone too led the way in probing the economic history of slavery. Whereas previous scholars ignored slave economics, especially quantifiable data, Stone and Phillips eagerly sought it out. Stone, for example, wished to compile slave price data with an eye to assessing slavery's overall profitability. Among the questions he posed were: "What were the economic advantages and what [were] the economic evils of slavery? . . . How did the two offset each other? When and why was it a profitable system and when and why unprofitable? What was the general effect of the system on the economic life of the South, as compared with the development of other sections of the country?" Stone, ever sensitive to the varieties and subtleties within the peculiar institution, hoped to analyze the effect of unit size on the day-to-day routine of farms and plantations. "Was there any difference," queried the Mississippian, "between slavery on a large plantation and in towns or small farms? If so, what? Was there much absentee landlordism? What caused it, and what was the effect on the treatment of slaves and on plantation management?"

Stone wanted to unearth the most minute aspects of plantation agriculture. Which methods did planters employ to prepare ground, to plant, to cultivate, to gather crops? What types of tools—plows, planters, hoes, frames—did slaves use? He also desired to profile the slave work force. What, he asked, was the division of labor, the nature of skilled versus unskilled workers? How proficient were plantation craftsmen—blacksmiths, carpenters, painters, masons, brickburners, millers, and wheelwrights? What hours did bondsmen work? At what age did slave children begin to labor? How did the task system compare with the gang system? And to what degree did antebellum planters experiment with "scientific" agriculture? An innovator himself in turn-of-the-century cotton production, Stone hoped to learn to what extent his predecessors worked to fertilize the soil, select planting seed, and avoid soil depletion.

Anticipating questions posed a half-century later by historian Robert S. Starobin,[16] Stone also expressed interest in industrial slavery. To what extent, he asked, were slaves leased to contractors? What was their role in railway, canal, and building construction? Were they employed in shipyards? He was eager, too, to identify the role of the bondsmen in manufacturing, both in factories and in "hand" work on the South's farms and plantations. Central to Stone's investigations was the adaptability of blacks in general, and slaves in particular, to industrial life. "Why," asked Stone, "was slave labor more profitable in agriculture than in other industries?" How commonly were slaves used in mining operations? And to what degree, Stone wondered, were plantations self-sufficient? Not only did he seek to document the slaves' production of cloth, thread, shoes, clothes, and saddles, but such staple items as soap, candles, lard, and foodstuffs as well. The inquisitive Stone even wanted to obtain "descriptions of methods and means of curing meat."

The conditions of slave life—food, housing, medical care, recreation—held special significance to Stone. Not until historians had an accurate record of conditions under slavery could they place into proper perspective the conditions of life of free blacks in the New South. Surprisingly, Stone seemed little interested in the diet of the bondsmen. Instead, he inquired into the logistics of supplying rations to a work force by way of a common kitchen. And he also wished to learn how much free time bondsmen received in order to tend garden truck patches. As to housing, Stone desired in-depth data on the slave quarters—dimensions, material, the details of construction, heating, and ventilation. He went so far as to request descriptions of the water supply available to the slaves, whether streams, springs, or cisterns.

Stone's interests included the medical care of the bondsmen, especially the aged, infirm, pregnant women, and children. He was on alert for descriptions of plantation hospitals and nurseries. The Mississippian also questioned the nature of the slaves' leisure activities. He realized that even within the controls of bondage, the slaves enjoyed certain amusements and recreations. What restrictions, asked Stone, were placed upon their use of firearms? Stone queried, "To what extent was crap-shooting or other gambling, permitted?" While the slave codes prohibited even the most elementary education for blacks, Stone suspected that some masters violated the full letter of the law. "Why," he asked, "were slaves educated at all? Did they thereby become more efficient or more valuable? How far were the general laws regulating slavery disregarded or observed in the domestic control of slaves?" On the topic of police control, he sought information pertaining to plantation discipline, punishment of bondsmen, slave patrols, and fears of slave revolts.

As the above questions suggest, Stone focused clearly on topics that remain critical to the ongoing slavery debate. He raised other points—on black slaveholders, slave breeding, the domestic slave trade, and the hiring out and self-purchase processes—that still demand attention from historians. Overseer-slave relations, as well as overseer-planter contacts, were yet other topics that captured his attention. Stone's fascination with the most minute aspects of slavery surpassed that of any researcher of his day, including Phillips. For example, the

Mississippian wanted to learn just "How common was the keeping and use of dogs for trailing runaway slaves?" And Stone wished to uncover precisely which terms were most commonly used to designate the bonded laborers—"slaves, negroes, niggers, blacks, hands, people, or servants."

Alfred Holt Stone neither located the volume of archival material he desired nor answered the questions he so carefully posed. In fact, Stone contributed surprisingly little on the subject of African American slavery.[17] The bulk of his writings instead assessed the contemporary "race problem." Although Stone added little to the scholarship on slavery, this should not diminish the importance of his inquisitive spirit. Then, as today, it was far easier to ask than to answer difficult queries. An untrained, amateur historian, Stone tended to view the past through the prism of the present. His real interest in slavery was as a comparative model for race and labor relations in the era of Jim Crow. To his generation, Stone possessed the necessary credentials for this work. He was a planter, with extensive firsthand knowledge of plantation blacks. Readers, North and South, considered him an authority on the racial dilemmas of their day. So too did the prestigious Carnegie Institution of Washington, which awarded Stone financial support to conduct his research. A solid son of the New South, Stone took a pessimistic view of the future of black agricultural labor in the South. He regarded blacks as inferiors, destined to fall further and further behind whites. By inference, Stone's writings served to buttress the South's decision to separate the races by law and by custom.

Stone reigned as the consummate southern white "race thinker" of his day. His significance as a historian of slavery lies in the fact that he recognized how little his generation really knew about the peculiar institution. In spite of Stone's class and racial bias against blacks, he realized the importance of integrating the history of slavery into the economic history of America's labor force. Stone exhibited considerable prescience—he anticipated by more than a half-century many of the topics of interest to today's historians of slavery. What's more, he was keenly aware of the importance of identifying and conserving the South's archival records. Much in the tradition of his friend Phillips, Stone performed invaluable self-archival work. In the absence of archival repositories below the Mason-Dixon line, the two men raised the consciousness of southerners on maintaining the vital documents of their past. Beyond that, they actively went out into the field and collected manuscripts and other records to prevent their destruction and to assure their availability for later scholars. Stone's efforts, then, comprise an obscure but nevertheless important chapter both in archival history and the historiography of slavery.

7

Neglected but Not Forgotten

Howell M. Henry and the "Police Control" of Slaves in South Carolina

Over the past twenty years, American historians have witnessed a virtual explosion of interest in African American slavery.[1] The black revolution of the 1960s inspired numerous scholars to probe the origins of white racism and its accompanying institution, chattel slavery. But the fascination of slavery for historians is no new phenomenon. Back at the turn of the century, and throughout the Progressive era, slavery held the focus of many students.[2] During these years dissertation after dissertation on slavery emerged from the Johns Hopkins University and other pioneer graduate schools. Slavery held a curious attraction for historians in this period. Many found it analogous to the conditions of labor in both the industrial North and the agricultural South.[3] Others investigated slavery because it fitted well into the legal-institutional focus of the new "scientific" history.[4]

These writers, claiming objectivity, impartiality, and a devotion to factual data, worshipped Darwinian science. In their seminars, they emphasized the evolution of non-political institutions such as slavery. As early as 1880, a reviewer in the *Nation* argued, "Slavery takes its turn with other fossil remains in adorning our cabinets of curiosity and of science, and in being studied under the microscope."[5] The investigation of slavery further afforded a perspective on contemporary race relations. These historians wrote in an age of racial tension—of Jim Crow laws, poll taxes, literacy and property tests, and white primaries. From their research on race relations in the Old South, white southerners fashioned a new proslavery argument.[6] It served as an ideological basis for much of the regulation, proscription, and extra-legal harassment of blacks in the first years of the twentieth century.

One early historian, South Carolinian Howell M. Henry (1879–1956), clearly viewed slavery through the prism of social, or what he termed "police control." Henry grew up in Newberry, which during Reconstruction established itself as a rural cotton center.[7] Although he was descended from yeoman farmers, not planters, during the antebellum period Henry's family owned at least one slave. After the war, the Henrys tilled a family farm of less than fifty acres.[8] They were prosperous enough, however, to send their son to Newberry College, where the curriculum stressed theology and the classics. He graduated in 1898.[9]

After teaching public school for six years, Henry entered Vanderbilt University to pursue graduate work in history. He earned his master's degree in 1908 and five years later received the second Ph.D. in history awarded by the Nashville school.[10] Henry's graduate work focused upon South Carolina. As early as 1909, when beginning work on his doctorate, Henry informed Alexander S. Salley, secretary of the South Carolina Historical Commission, of his serious interest in the history of his native state.[11] Henry's completed dissertation, "The Police Control of the Slave in South Carolina," was in its day an excellent analysis of slave control. Published almost seventy years ago, Henry's study has played a seminal role in the historiography of slavery in the Palmetto State. Yet Henry remains obscure, and his book has generally been omitted from the ongoing slavery debate.[12] It is time to rescue Howell M. Henry from oblivion.

Upon completing his doctorate, Henry joined the faculty at Emory and Henry College in Virginia. He spent his entire career there, as professor of history and economics (1913–1918, 1940–1953) and as dean (1918–1940). With the exception of an article on Tennessee's slave laws, his dissertation remained Henry's sole contribution to the slavery field. Instead of publishing, he devoted his energies to guarding Emory and Henry against the encroachments of intercollegiate athletics.[13] "Henry," wrote historian George J. Stevenson, "was committed to stringent academic standards and upholding . . . the reputation of a small, respectable college in the face of an overweening lust for gridiron glory."[14] Henry's inability to compromise, and what some considered "his unsympathetic and untactful relationship with the students," made him an unpopular campus figure.[15]

Although Henry disagreed with many of his peers over the merits of college football, he shared the prevailing antiblack bias of his day. Henry was, according to a former colleague, "one of his generation who 'loved a Negro and had absolutely no use for the Negro'" "an unreconstructed Southerner," "a 'gentleman of the old school—South' (in the best and worst sense of the phrase)."[16] Strongly opposed to integration, he feared that racially mixed schools would result in inferior education for blacks and whites alike.[17] A friend recalled one Methodist Race Relations Sunday in the 1950s, when Henry "caused some stir by getting up and walking out of the . . . chapel service." The minister had addressed too "clearly and unconventionally" the civil rights question.[18]

Threads of Henry's later antipathy toward blacks appeared throughout his 1914 monograph on slave control in South Carolina. Like most white historians who studied slavery in these years, Henry viewed blacks through racist eyes. South Carolina's 1712 slave code was designed, he said, to control "African negroes with barbaric traits." Much of the slave legislation concerned thievery by slaves, which Henry considered still "the colored person's inherent weakness." Slave patrols resulted from the early need to "hold in check this irresponsible and often dangerous part of Southern society." And Henry agreed with antebellum southern whites who asserted that the slaves' "primitive condition" and "lack of moral responsibility" made them unfit to testify in court cases against whites. In his judgment, overseers were necessary to manage labor in antebellum South Carolina. It was incomprehensible, he said, that "the best results could be had from a large plantation entrusted entirely to negroes."[19]

In spite of his racism, Henry's research was exhaustive. He examined what in his day was an overwhelming volume of printed and manuscript sources in addition to "testimony of ante-bellum people still living." His use of pamphlets, government documents, and newspapers—materials that he called "purely original sources"—set a standard for later historians. Especially noteworthy were his findings in town and city ordinances, district records, and newspapers. For example, in order to determine how the slave laws were enforced, Henry examined the manuscript records of every geographic section of South Carolina. He also gleaned valuable information on slave trial procedure from criminal court records contained in the various Sessions Journals. But Henry's most significant methodological contribution was his examination of the files of thirty-seven newspapers located in the Charleston and University of South Carolina libraries, and in private collections.[20]

Henry was one of few early historians of slavery to examine in any detail *why* the various slave laws were passed. He argued that most slave laws were shaped by expediency rather than from a fixed theory of slave treatment or management. Whites drafted statutes for emergencies such as insurrections and rarely consulted these regulations for the daily plantation routine. Laws against slaves trading with white merchants, for example, generally were established "as occasion demanded." Sectional differences within South Carolina, explained Henry, also influenced slave legislation. In the upland regions, with a low concentration of slaves, farmers made few demands for rigid slave laws. Their lowcountry neighbors, however, the affluent Carolina planter elite, lobbied for strict slave regulations because of the large slave population in their districts.[21]

Throughout his monograph, Henry stressed the great power of this planter class in shaping slave legislation. Planters favored slave laws designed to keep the bondsmen laboring at their highest efficiency. But they also shaped laws to fit their specific needs. An example is the public reimbursement paid a master if his slave was convicted of a capital crime. Henry also reached the highly significant conclusion that slave laws indirectly benefited non-slaveholders, who feared the results of an uncontrolled population of blacks in their midst. In his opinion, "Slavery was not only an economic and industrial system . . . but more than that, it was a gigantic police system, which the poor man in the up-country as well as the wealthy planter in the lowlands did not know how to replace."[22]

Henry concluded that most slave legislation resulted from an unwarranted fear of slave revolts. The 1739 Stono revolt and several other conspiracies notwithstanding, he argued that the widespread paranoia among white South Carolinians over slave rebelliousness was largely unwarranted. Regardless, each alleged uprising prompted increasingly severe slave laws. In the wake of the Stono insurrection, whites passed a strict slave code to supplement the 1712 code. Similarly, in 1822, after the Denmark Vesey plot, they enacted new measures designed to tighten controls on all blacks. Legislative action was begun to oust free Negroes from the state, new manumissions were prohibited, and the Seamen Acts were passed restricting blacks aboard ships docked in South Carolina ports.[23]

For the day-to-day regulation of their bondsmen, South Carolinians established slave patrol ordinances and slave patrols. According to Henry, enforcing these laws proved more difficult than passing them, however. On the one hand, masters frequently were lax in their handling of slaves, allowing them to visit friends or relatives on neighboring plantations. On the other hand, masters feared the mishandling of their chattels by non-slaveholding patrollers who "looked upon the patrol as the guarantee of . . . [their] safety from evils often perpetrated by the black race." Henry considered the abuse of slaves by patrollers "the greatest evil of the system." In his opinion, it gave police power over the bondsmen to "unscrupulous persons" rather than to "the better class" of whites.[24]

One of the more important features of Henry's work was his analysis of the enforcement of slave laws. He concluded that some slave laws rarely were enforced. These included prohibitions against importing slaves, hiring bondsmen out, and allowing them to trade with whites. Slave patrols commonly ignored all but the most suspicious slave conduct and generally allowed blacks from adjacent plantations to congregate. Whites also tolerated separate church services for bondsmen with black preachers, which were in direct violation of state law. And Henry doubted whether slaves were punished for such petty "crimes" as swearing, smoking, and loitering—although all of these activities were prohibited by various slave ordinances. More serious, laws for the punishment of whites guilty of killing or excessively punishing slaves were enforced only sporadically—when evidence proved a blatant violation.[25]

Certain laws, however—the Seamen Acts and ordinances against slave stealing—never were evaded. Slave stealing was a capital offense and was enforced vigorously by whites. In Henry's judgment, the fact that slave stealing was considered a more heinous crime than murdering a bondsman underscored the power and influence of the master class in antebellum South Carolina. Killing a slave while correcting him was justifiable, he added, under the ownership rights of chattels personal. But, he explained, slave stealing threatened the "entire stability of the whole system and was subversive of the interests of society." To the South Carolina planter, the slave stealer became "the anarchist of Southern serfdom."[26]

Regardless of which South Carolina slave ordinances were enforced, Henry rated Charleston the most difficult location to police slaves. Anticipating historian Richard C. Wade's later work, Henry recognized that the city contained several impediments to effective slave control. First, the urban environment offered slaves more opportunities to abuse laws than were available in rural areas. This situation required flexible laws and police enforcement, he said. Second, many of Charleston's bondsmen were skilled and therefore were permitted to hire themselves out. Regulated only minimally by their masters, these slaves were granted considerable personal "freedom." The presence of large numbers of free blacks in the city was yet another force that worked against the strict enforcement of slave ordinances. Despite these factors, Henry concluded that the amount of slave crime in Charleston was relatively small. Serious crimes were punished in the city's workhouse, which he considered "an intelligent method of dealing with the troublesome problem of police control." Still, the Charleston Neck remained an impregnable haven for runaway slaves.[27]

Few of the problems of urban slave control appeared on the large plantations where overseers disciplined the bondsmen. Henry's chapter on the overseer was one of the earliest and most perceptive scholarly analyses of the role of that figure in the slave system. He argued that the overseer, not the slave driver, was the most powerful force on the plantation next to the master. By virtue of the 1712 law requiring all absentee masters to have a white man present on their plantations, the overseer became a permanent fixture on the plantation. As a "plantation quasi-police officer," he generally dictated plantation discipline and became "an economic necessity" for plantation management. Although overseers as a class lacked definite legal status, they held all of the responsibilities accompanying slave ownership. And frequently the overseer took "the place of the master in his paternal relation of duty and responsibility to the slave."[28]

The best overseers, Henry argued, served both the master and slave well. They contracted with the slave owner to provide slaves with adequate food, clothing, and humane treatment. But the average overseer was "a misfit, a makeshift," who neither fully accepted his "middle position in society" nor completely satisfied his employer. Low wages and the nature of the job—"Stern necessity . . . forbade even a tendency toward kindliness"—often made the overseer cruel, "coarse and brutal." Further, the overseer usually came from the non-slaveholding and non-propertied class of southern whites, according to Henry, rendering him "the least fitted morally and temperamentally for the position." He often was distrustful and jealous of the slaveholders, because, for him, "Overseeing was a step to nothing." "In a sense," concluded Henry, the overseer, "like the slave he controlled, found no hope or ambition in the system."[29]

Contemporary reviewers found considerable merit in Henry's monograph. In the *Mississippi Valley Historical Review,* Wallace Carson praised it as exhaustive both in research and coverage. He considered the scope of the book broader than its title suggested.[30] The reviewer in the *Journal of Negro History* complimented Henry's documentation and made no reference to his racism.[31] Ulrich Bonnell Phillips, the leading student of slavery of his day, agreed with Henry's argument that men more than laws controlled slaves. His own research confirmed the thesis that slave laws were employed predominantly in emergencies. Phillips, himself a pioneer in the use of plantation records, found Henry's citations to court records "especially welcome." He lauded the author's statements that responsible South Carolinians sought to reform abuses in the state's slave code, especially in slave trial procedures.[32] But both Carson and Phillips noted weaknesses in the book. It contributed "nothing strikingly new ... either in theory or in fact," charged Carson. Phillips faulted Henry's style, "that which is unhappily common in doctoral dissertations."[33]

Despite Phillips's disclaimer, he was impressed enough with Henry's book to cite it several times in his own writings. In *American Negro Slavery* (1918) and *Life and Labor in the Old South* (1929), Phillips drew upon Henry's dissertation to document references to such topics as slave revolts, patrols, trial procedures, and free blacks. And from among the mass of state studies on slavery, he chose *The Police Control of the Slave in South Carolina,* along with one other book, as "monographs of note."[34] Other historians, too, have incurred a heavy debt to Henry. Examination of books, articles, and graduate theses pertaining to slavery in South Carolina reveals the high degree of dependence of Henry's successors upon his pioneer work. References to the monograph fall into thirty-five subject categories. Students most often have cited Henry as a referral on slavery and slave law in South Carolina. Other subjects, in order of decreasing frequency, include slave patrols, slave religion, the Vesey plot, the enforcement of slave laws, free blacks, and slave homicides. The remaining references span a wide spectrum from slave hiring to the Laurens County plot of 1831.[35]

Although students of slavery in South Carolina certainly are aware of Henry's book, they have all but failed to assess its worth. In 1934, David Duncan Wallace remarked blandly that *The Police Control of the Slave in South Carolina* was "valuable for the entire history of South Carolina slavery."[36] This statement represents well the rather thin level of analysis that the book has generated. Peter H. Wood's comment—"This work is now rather dated, and it devoted little attention to the formative colonial years"—typifies the attitude of most recent scholars toward Henry's book.[37] Regrettably, such observations add little to our understanding of the historiography of slavery.

Several students, however, have questioned specific aspects of Henry's work. Writing in 1943, Herbert Aptheker challenged his statement that forty-four blacks and whites died during the Stono uprising. Aptheker's research led him to conclude that "probably about twenty-five whites and twice that number of slaves were killed."[38] More recently, Michael S. Hindus also faulted Henry's statistics. Whereas Henry argued that "the usual number" of slaves executed annually for criminal offenses "was two or three," Hindus found that, "The total number of executions averaged six per year or about twice as many as previous estimates."[39] And three other historians, Alan F. January, A. Leon Higginbotham, Jr., and David W. Cole, have uncovered flaws in Henry's book as well. January discovered a "grossly inaccurate" account of enforcement of the Seamen Acts. Higginbotham and Cole identified unsupported assertions.[40]

In the light of modern scholarship on slavery, Henry's work is subject to more severe criticism. Its racist and elitist bias—written from the perspective of the veranda, not from the slave quarters—clearly dates the volume. Unlike recent authors, he ignored both the psychological damage that the slaves may have endured and the blacks' unquenchable thirst for freedom. Henry's method of treating South Carolina slave laws implied—without sufficient evidence—that conditions for bondsmen in that state were unique. As Robert William Fogel and Stanley L. Engerman have noted, he made no attempt to relate slave control to the economic aspects of the institution.[41] Further, by emphasizing that many slave laws were not enforced, Henry argued implicitly that slavery was mild in the Palmetto State.

Even so, it is surprising that historians have missed the many strengths in Henry's monograph. In several important ways it is unique among the mass of books and articles on slavery written during the Progressive era. Many of these studies focused narrowly on slave law and resembled verbatim listings of statutes and court decisions.[42] But Henry's book was more broadly based and interpretive, underscoring the importance of slave law as a system of social and racial control. When *The Police Control of the Slave in South Carolina* is evaluated solely as an investigation of slave law as a system, its special merits become even clearer. Henry was the first historian to follow William T. Laprade's 1911 mandate that students should evaluate, not describe, the enforcement of slave laws.[43] Because of this analysis and his thorough research, Henry's study far surpassed in quality the only other book-length study of slave law, Gerald Montgomery West's 1890 Columbia University dissertation.[44]

Henry also examined several aspects of slavery—overseers, slave drivers, hired slaves, special slave courts—in greater detail than had any previous investigator. His analysis of the Vesey plot was, for its day, quite acceptable. It must be recalled that the traditional interpretation of this abortive revolt remained virtually unchallenged until historian Richard C. Wade sounded his alarm in 1964.[45] Years before the appearance of Wade's work, however, Henry appreciated fully the difficulties involved with maintaining discipline over urban bondsmen. Observing that white mechanics in Charleston protested the competition of skilled slaves, Henry, like Julia A. Flisch before him, also prefigured the focus of Robert S. Starobin's later work on industrial slavery.[46]

Where, then, does the largely ignored Howell M. Henry rank in the historiography of slavery in South Carolina? Surprisingly high. Through the years Henry's book has remained a virtual fixture in the literature of South

Carolina slavery. While few have read it cover to cover, fewer still have pondered its place in the scholarly literature on African American slavery. But many have found it a useful reference for specific slavery-related topics, despite their general disdain for old-fashioned, racist, legalistic books. Unfortunately, today's scholars must still depend on Henry for information pertaining to many aspects of slavery in South Carolina. This state of affairs will continue until a monograph is completed on slavery in the antebellum period comparable to Peter H. Wood's excellent study of slavery in colonial South Carolina. Until this void is filled, Henry's book should be used carefully and selectively, but used nevertheless. In its day *The Police Control of the Slave in South Carolina* was a pioneer, pathbreaking study. Henry took slave law out of the statute books and placed it in the workaday world of master, overseer, and slave. Although he may well remain neglected, his book should not be forgotten.

8

A Different View of Slavery

Black Historians Attack the New Proslavery Argument, 1890–1920

The importance of slavery in the racial thought of the late nineteenth and early twentieth centuries has been vastly understated by scholars.[1] Yet slavery held an unusual attraction for historians, popular writers, editors, and polemicists in these years.[2] Not since the late antebellum period had so much attention been devoted to the peculiar institution. Many scholars investigated slavery because it fit well into the legal-institutional focus of the new "scientific" history. Writing in 1892, Anna Julia Haywood Cooper commented that "after so long a time," authors "have begun at last to draw subjects and models" from the slaves.[3] Other writers identified slavery with such vital issues of their own day as peonage[4] and wage slavery,[5] thus giving an enlarged significance to the study of it. Baffled by what they perceived as an insurmountable "Negro problem," most southern whites looked back to slavery to gain some perspective on contemporary racial tensions. They were even more convinced of the "scientific" or biological inferiority of the Negro than their Old South forebears. These writers revived the fundamentals of the old proslavery argument—interpreting slavery as a benign school in which blacks fared better than freedmen.[6] By justifying the second-class citizenship accorded blacks in these years, southern writers offered an old creed for the New South.[7]

Although the paternalistic interpretation dominated views of slavery during the Progressive era, it did not go unchallenged. Black historians formed a vanguard for members of their race in assaulting slavery.[8] But because there was only a handful of professionally trained black historians in these years, a broad range of other writers—clergymen, social scientists, editors—joined them in interpreting slavery.[9] African American intellectuals thus assumed the role of historian.

As on other questions, black thought regarding slavery was not a monolith, but rather a maze of inconsistencies and contradictions. For example, many blacks stressed the importance of slavery to understanding the contemporary Negro problem. But others urged members of their race to de-emphasize slavery—to look forward to a bright future, not backward to a sordid past.[10] They disagreed on other slavery-related questions as well. Were blacks inherently inferior? How sophisticated was ancient African civilization? Was slave treatment cruel? How did the slaves react to captivity? Such influential writers as Booker T. Washington, Kelly Miller, and William H. Councill had mixed reactions to slavery, concurrently denouncing it as an evil[11] and finding benefits[12] in it for the bondsmen. Regardless of conflicting views, a common theme pervaded black thought on slavery. It was considered the severest form of bondage in world history, the consummate sin in the American past. Professor John W. Work of Fisk University could not comprehend "all this latter day talk about the happiness and contentment of the slave." It was "either inexcusable ignorance, or a culpable effort at gross deception; for slavery, was horrible in every aspect."[13] With the zeal of the abolitionists, blacks attacked the new proslavery argument and the racism upon which it was based.

African Americans dwelt upon slavery because it constituted the best-known and most controversial aspect of their history. Unless the story of slavery was told by blacks, they said, generations born since emancipation would not learn fully of its horrors.[14] And for blacks, too, slavery was laden with parallels to Negro life in early twentieth-century America—Jim Crow and peonage laws,[15] the crop lien and convict lease systems,[16] industrialism and industrial education,[17] American imperialism,[18] and the anti-Negro policies of the Wilson administration.[19] "Slavery is no more," wrote the editor of the *Indianapolis Freeman,* "but in its stead stalks race, caste, business and commercial ostracism, civil oppression and debarment, political persecution and all the brood of evils that survived the demise of the parent evil."[20]

The slavery that these pioneer black historians described clashed dramatically with the romanticized plantation school of the white proslavery apologists. Blacks objected forcefully to the tendency among whites to write the history of slavery solely from the perspective of the master class. In 1898, W.E.B. Du Bois charged that although whites devoted sufficient attention to the legal side of slavery,

> of the slave himself, of his group life and social institutions, of remaining traces of his African tribal life, of his amusements, his conversion to Christianity, his acquiring of the English tongue ... of his whole reaction against his environment, of all this we hear little or nothing, and would apparently be expected to believe that the Negro arose from the dead in 1863.[21]

Blacks also criticized specific white scholars. For example, Thomas N. Baker, a black clergyman, condemned the treatment of slave women in the writings of

James Ford Rhodes and Joseph A. Tillinghast. These historians, accused Baker, were "so prone to 'Jim Crow' the Negro, that they feel they must use a 'Jim Crow' logic in discussing him."[22] Carter G. Woodson was one of several African Americans who lashed out against Edward B. Reuter's *The Mulatto in the United States* (1918). This openly racist study blamed slave females for inviting miscegenation. According to Woodson, Reuter's book signaled "the return of the antebellum proslavery philosopher disguised as a scientific investigator."[23] And blacks did not fail to attack Ulrich Bonnell Phillips, the foremost student of slavery of his day. In 1913, Du Bois laced into what he termed Phillips's arrogant, proslavery statements. Five years later, he branded Phillips's "curiously incomplete and unfortunately biased" book, *American Negro Slavery*, a blatant "defense of an institution which was at best a mistake and at worst a crime." Reviewing the same volume, Woodson accused Phillips of being unable "to fathom the negro mind"—not comprehending "what the Negroes have thought and felt and done."[24]

Slavery obviously had a different, more immediate meaning for these black writers than for whites. Indeed, a few black historians knew slavery from first-hand experience while all had felt the stares born of prejudice and discrimination. Observing with disgust the proscription and inequalities of Jim Crowism, and the exclusion of blacks from Progressive era reforms, many blacks looked backward to slavery to explain Negro degradation in America. They considered an understanding of the peculiar institution necessary to guard future generations from re-enslavement.[25] Blacks used slavery—their special history—as a tool to lash out against Progressive racism. In the process, they prefigured the focus and conclusions of much recent scholarship.

Blacks tackled the proslavery argument head on when they challenged the assertion that they were members of an inferior race and hailed from a backward continent. Drawing on the writings of anthropologist Franz Boas, they advanced the idea of fundamental racial equality.[26] African Americans welcomed Boas's argument that the differences between whites and blacks were "exceedingly small as compared with the range of variability found in either race."[27] What had previously been assumed to be racial characteristics, he said, were actually the result of many interrelated factors—environmental as well as hereditary. Boas's influence is found in the writings of black men from all walks of life, including historians, sociologists, editors, clergymen, and physicians.[28] "The unity of the human race is no longer a disputed question," concluded journalist T. Thomas Fortune in 1896.[29] To a reviewer in the *A.M.E. Church Review*, Boas's work demonstrated that "the Negro is endowed with capabilities, that color is no badge of mental ability among human beings."[30]

Blacks also adopted Boas's findings that in antiquity their African forebears had a highly developed civilization.[31] Edward A. Johnson, a lawyer and amateur historian, commented that "all the science and learning of ancient Greece and Rome was, probably, once in the hands of the foreparents of the American slaves."[32] African Americans with as contrasting perspectives as Washington and Du Bois were among the earliest writers who used Boas's anthropological findings to challenge myths of African backwardness and to popularize the beauty and significance of slave culture.[33] In numerous articles, Monroe N. Work argued that Africans were among the world's first people to smelt iron and to develop agricultural implements. They established military organizations, trade centers, courts, and archives, and produced skilled artwork.[34] By arguing that slavery and contact with Caucasians was a backward step for the Africans, black historians turned the tables on the apologists for slavery. Du Bois, for example, charged the planters—not the Africans—with "inhumanity, barbarism and the methods of the jungle."[35]

Although some black historians did refer to slavery as a school, most found the analogy repulsive. That blacks were content as slaves, they said, was a white man's myth—the propaganda of those who could not free themselves from treating the African American as a child. Richard T. Greener, the first black graduate of Harvard, condemned the slavery/school analogy, mocking the lessons the slaves allegedly received from bondage:

> The Negro has no tears to shed over that "wonderful school of slavery, under Providence" so often quoted. He is no such hypocrite as to go through the pretence of believing that slavery is ever a good, a necessary, or beneficial school. Much less does he grant that any phase of that school, at any stage, affected him morally, socially, or physically except adversely, while he does know from bitter experience, how utterly phar[i]saical, how absurdly hypocritical, and how thoroughly unchristian the entire system was in practice, example and influence.[36]

A year later, John W.E. Bowen seconded Greener's critique of the school of slavery. Bowen, the son of a slave, received a Ph.D. from Boston University and taught historical theology at Gammon Theological Seminary in Atlanta. In his judgment, slavery was a "pit of seething, reeking and nauseating corruption"—"a dehumanized and bestialized thing"—where blacks were "worked like dumb, driven cattle ... crushed with the iron hoof of oppression and repression; [and] whipped, torn, bleeding, in body, mind and soul." Blacks, charged Bowen, must challenge the whites' version of slavery as the halcyon days of purity and moral power for the Negro. What sort of school, asked Bowen, was taught by the slave driver's whip and bloodhounds?[37] Bowen, Greener, and other blacks agreed that the intellectual and religious qualities African Americans possessed emerged in spite of, not because of, slavery.

Black historians found the slavery/school analogy vulnerable to two specific criticisms. First, conditions under the peculiar institution were deplorable. Slave life was degrading—designed to diminish self-respect and growth in the bondsmen.[38] Almost uniformly, these writers complained that the slaves were systematically overtasked—they were underfed, forced to live in hovels, dress in rags, and submit to dehumanizing tortures.[39] Ex-slave Frederick Douglass disagreed with the proslavery theory that considerable give-and-take characterized the master/slave relationship. "The master is always the master," quipped Douglass, "and the slave is always the slave."[40] Blacks agreed that the modicum of care that the slaves received resulted from the masters' financial, not humanitarian, interests. Even Booker T. Washington, who pointed repeatedly to the educational benefits of slavery, admitted that the bondsmen toiled under poor conditions. Drawing upon his own recollections as a slave, the Tuskegean recalled vividly his "miserable, desolate, and discouraging surroundings," his insufficient food and clothing, his "bed of rags," his coarse flax "tow" shirt. Another ex-slave, Dr. William A. Sinclair, recalled that life in thralldom was "gruesome and unholy," barbaric, "brutalizing," and "debasing." Like Sinclair, Carter Woodson described the punishments meted out to slaves as "crude and abusive."[41]

But blacks considered miscegenation the most heinous subject offered in the slavery/school curriculum. Slave owners not only raped black women at random, but destroyed the racial integrity of the black race.[42] Woodson blamed the extensive miscegenation in the Old South on the lust of the master class. He charged white historians, "ashamed of the planters who abused helpless black women," with "trying to minimize the prevalence of this custom."[43]

Black historians assailed a second bulwark of the proslavery school: that without the guidance of slavery, postwar African Americans were reverting to barbarism. Negro authors admitted that slavery did teach the bondsmen some lessons—lessons in blind obedience, servility, hatred, and humiliation. But these were lessons to be unlearned. Hightower T. Kealing, editor of the *A.M.E. Church Review*, blamed slavery for a long list of deficiencies in blacks—shiftlessness, incontinence, intolerance, extravagance, and improvidence. He maintained that slavery taught blacks to be sloppy, unreliable workers and to be dishonest in their dealings with blacks as well as whites.[44] Other black writers complained that slavery instructed the Negroes to despise and disrespect one another; to fear spies in their midst, who, like in the days of bondage, would betray their secrets to the whites.[45] In the opinion of Benjamin G. Brawley, dean of Morehouse College, slavery left a legacy of contempt for labor. Washington often referred to this theme, urging his students at Tuskegee, and blacks in general, to distinguish the "vast difference between working and being worked."[46]

W.E.B. Du Bois held slavery accountable for the lax morals and poor habits characteristic of Philadelphia ghetto blacks who had served as bondsmen in Virginia and Maryland. In his study of Negroes in the Georgia black belt, Du Bois concluded that they farmed on exhausted soil, lived in squalor, and frequently suffered separation from their spouses. These conditions, he said, were products of "long custom, born in the time of slavery." "A slave ancestry and a system of unrequited toil," argued Du Bois, made these blacks resemble "all ground-down peasantries"—ripe for "crime and a cheap, dangerous socialism."[47]

Of all slavery's many crimes, blacks considered its effect on the African American family to be most grievous.[48] In Du Bois's judgment, the planters' major crime was that they "debauched, destroyed, and took from" the African the organized home. Neither the sale of relatives nor the forced concubinage of female slaves was conducive to a stable family life. In 1899 Du Bois argued that "with all its shortcomings," the powerful, polygamous, "strictly guarded savage home life of Africa" offered more protection for women than "the promiscuous herding" of the slave plantation. Even though traces of African family institutions persisted, the slaves "were raped of their own sex customs and provided with no binding new ones." "Slavery," Du Bois continued, "gave the monogamic family ideal to slaves, but it compelled . . . only the most imperfect practice of its most ordinary morals." Paradoxically, "the greatest social effect" of slavery was the substitution of the polygamous Negro home with one "less guarded, less effective, and less civilized."[49]

Du Bois concluded that the living arrangements under slavery contributed to the unstable black family in the postwar South. Slave cabins were "dirty one-room lodges where, crowded like cattle, men slept in dreamless stupor after endless hours of forced and driven toil." The slave quarters evolved, he said, into "filthy hovels" with "no family life, no meals, no marriages, no decency." And the slave home lacked strong paternal leadership. Fathers were denied authority to govern the family. Their wives and daughters were liable to sexual abuse by the whites and any member of the family could be sold at the master's whim. Tragically, lamented Du Bois, the emasculated slave husband was a "male guest in the house, without respect or responsibility." Lacking unity or a sense of permanence, the slave family was reduced to a temporary, disjointed "agglomeration of atoms" devoid of force or pride. According to Du Bois, such living conditions typified the dehumanizing and destructive effect of slavery on the Africans.[50]

Many black historians went beyond simply answering the new proslavery argument. They broke fresh ground by focusing on the slaves' responses to captivity. These early black writers celebrated the strength of the Negroes who, unlike the Indians, withstood slavery's cold brutality.[51] They identified a black subculture—the slave community—in which members shared a group life. There were gifted slave artisans, talented slave poets, and mysterious slave preachers.[52] Black writers found "The Negro Genius" present under slavery despite conditions that would have destroyed the creative instinct in a lesser race. According to Benjamin Brawley, Negroes had an "instinct for beauty" that was strengthened, not diminished by slavery. Woodson's pathbreaking research into the strivings of slaves for education further shattered the stereotype of the bondsmen as mindless, satisfied beings.[53]

Some African American historians expressed pride that their slave ancestors laid the foundation for black protest and self-help in America. Bondsmen broke their chains—at least symbolically—by seeking refuge in their music, leisure activities, and religious folklore. Slave songs, according to Kelly Miller, were "the first expression of the imprisoned soul of an imprisoned race"—"the smothered voice of a race crying in the wilderness." "They breathed the prayer and complaint of souls overflowing with the bitterest anguish," explained Frederick

Douglass. One student of slave culture interpreted the slaves' "ring plays" as a "safety valve, a sweet solace, a blessed forgetfulness" when the hardships of enslavement became too oppressive.[54] While some writers described the slaves' faith as a religion of resignation, others portrayed it as a form of dissent—a mode of implicit resistance. Sinclair, for example, maintained that the slaves "hoodwinked" their masters by singing religious songs "while the words echoed and re-echoed deep down in their hearts" the thirst for liberty. Writing in 1900, Du Bois argued that the bondsmen drew upon their religion—Obi worship, exorcism, spells, and blood sacrifices—to resist slavery. Religion was the slave's weapon against captivity—"the dark triumph of Evil over him." Through song and prayer the bondsmen vocalized their agony and their innermost appeals for freedom.[55]

These early black historians of slavery credited the bondsmen with employing all manners of artful intrigue to protest the indignities of the slave regime. Day-to-day resistance to slavery took various forms—disobeying orders, running away, attacking overseers, organizing secret societies, aiding Union troops— each revealing the constant desire by African Americans for freedom. Just as they detailed with pride the Africans' skills as warriors and craftsmen of weapons, these authors identified a militant spirit in the blacks throughout slavery.[56] In 1883 historian George Washington Williams asserted that masters remained in constant fear of slave revolts—the only "safety-valves" available to the slaves. Williams argued that the small number of slave insurrections resulted not from any fear on the part of the blacks, but because of a lack of leadership among them. Although "under-fed and over-worked; poorly clad and miserably housed," slaves rarely became the "too goodish, too lamb-like, too obsequious" Uncle Tom figure. "The lion slumbers in the Negro," concluded Williams, and this spirit was strengthened, not destroyed, by enslavement.[57]

To a few blacks living in the age of Jim Crow, rebellious slaves such as Denmark Vesey and Nat Turner became folk heroes. Historian John Wesley Cromwell, referring to slave revolts as "a constant menace to the safety and security of slavery," maintained that before the American Revolution alone, approximately twenty-five insurrections had occurred. Lawyer and civil rights activist Archibald H. Grimké regretted that despite Vesey's brilliant planning and "underground agitation," his revolt failed when he was betrayed by a co-conspirator. According to Grimké, Vesey was a "grand master in the art of intrigue" among the slaves—one who helped train the bondsmen "in habits of deceit, of deep dissimulation . . . that *ars artium* of slaves in their attempts to break their chains." Similarly, Cromwell glorified Turner's revolt as an example of the assertive, active Negro. He struck "to help himself rather than depend on other human agencies for the protection which could come through his own strong arm."[58]

Such emphasis upon slave resistance can be misleading. Grimké, for example, applauded slave insurgence when writing about Vesey, but, in another instance, asserted that the bondsmen were passive, lacking feelings of resentment and revenge.[59] Similar complexities and subtleties appear throughout the early black scholarship on slavery.[60] On the one hand, these authors celebrated advancements under slavery as proof of the essential strength and equality of their race. Only an exceptional people, they said, could have withstood the horrors of American slavery. Yet at the same time, black historians admitted the degradation of the Negro. They criticized the behavior—subservience, negligence, extravagance—that blacks learned as slaves and retained as freedmen.[61] The paucity of professionally trained black historians goes a long way toward explaining the contradictory nature of their writings on slavery. Few studied slavery in a systematic manner, and—understandably sensitive on the subject —African Americans countered white racism with their own filiopietistic interpretation of the black past. Propagandists for black advancement in the early twentieth century, they were prone to exaggerate the achievements of their race under the peculiar institution.

Even so, the early black historians of slavery prefigured recent scholarship. They examined questions and adopted themes that did not become popular among historians until the 1960s and 1970s.[62] Emphasizing racial pride and unity, African creativity and nationalism, these blacks anticipated the racial mood of the Negro Revolution of the 1960s. Years before the appearance of Melville J. Herskovits's writings, and a half-century before John W. Blassingame published *The Slave Community: Plantation Life in the Antebellum South* (1972), they observed the survivals of African culture and identified a subculture among American slaves. Their research in black folk life—songs, dances, jokes, and religious practices—foreshadowed the recent work of Sterling Stuckey, Lawrence W. Levine, and Shane and Graham White. By arguing that the bondsmen actively resisted enslavement and struggled to acquire the rudiments of formal education, these pioneer historians further outlined themes popularized by succeeding generations of scholars. Finally, they shared with later historians a sensitivity to the long-range effects of slavery and racism upon American life.

Despite the important contributions of the early black critics of slavery, white historians in the early twentieth century generally ignored their arguments. In 1905 one such historian, Walter Lynwood Fleming, remarked disapprovingly that whenever African Americans discussed slavery "we hear the clank of chains and the cutting swish of the lash; the slaves, we infer, hate the whites with a consuming hatred, and the cruel masters endeavor to crush out the human feelings of the black."[63] Modern scholars, too, have missed the significance of slavery in black thought during the Progressive era. The early black historians used their study of slavery to attack white racism, to explain Negro degradation in America, and to bolster race pride and Negro solidarity. Unlike their white contemporaries, they portrayed the slaves as real persons with mature, not childlike, emotions and with human sensitivities. These blacks were writing the history of slavery from the perspective of the bondsman seventy-five years ago. Theirs was a decidedly different view of slavery, one that years later is not so different after all.

9

The Unveiling of Slave Folk Culture, 1865–1920

In recent years historians of African American slavery have made great strides in probing the inner lives of the bondsmen. Few scholars today undervalue the horrid conditions of slave life and fewer still approach the blacks as passive actors in the plantation tragedy. Works on slavery now emphasize blacks as activists and slavery as a malleable institution. Not satisfied with viewing slavery as a static system of control, historians analyze the institution from numerous perspectives to discern how and why it became responsive to the changing needs of master and slave. They stress the human relationships that grew under slavery. They emphasize the diverse ways that blacks resisted their captivity. Current studies approach the slaves as persons with human needs, strengths, and deficiencies. Significantly, much of the best scholarship on slavery has focused upon the cultural adaptation of African Americans in slavery.[1] This trend has been so pervasive that historian August Meier recently referred to "the new paradigm of slave historiography, which makes the slave community and its culture central to the discussion."[2] The folk culture[3] of the slaves—folk songs, tales, religious practices, family and housing customs—today ranks among the most popular and innovative subjects of inquiry for students of black history.[4]

But we must acknowledge our debt to scholarship on slavery of an earlier age—that of the period 1865 to 1920. In the immediate post–Civil War years, slavery remained a major topic of discussion for a broad range of American writers, North and South, black and white.[5] Pioneers in analyzing folk elements in slavery, historians, social scientists, clergymen, and others anticipated many of the topics and themes examined by modern historians. These early students introduced the basic sources and methodology employed by subsequent investigators. And the questions they raised are strikingly similar to those addressed by present-day writers.

Music provides the best example of the long-range importance of the early scholarship on slavery. During the Civil War a number of well-educated northern teachers, missionaries, army officers, and newspaper correspondents collected slave songs while living in the South. The earliest was Thomas Wentworth Higginson, Massachusetts Unitarian clergyman and colonel of the first black regiment inducted into the Union Army. Higginson recorded the texts for slave songs he heard in South Carolina. These formed the basis for his article, "Negro Spirituals," the first postbellum publication to appear on the subject.[6] To the slaves, Higginson said, their music offered "a stimulus to courage," a "tie to heaven" that allowed them to withstand the cruelties of the peculiar institution. Through Biblical allegories the bondsmen "could sing themselves . . . out of the contemplations of their own low estate, [and] into the sublime scenery of the Apocalypse."[7]

Following Higginson's lead were the editors of the first comprehensive collection of slave songs, William F. Allen, Charles P. Ware, and Lucy McKim Garrison. Each served during the war in relief organizations on the Sea Islands off the South Carolina coast.[8] Their seminal book, *Slave Songs of the United States* (1867), set high standards for later students of black music. Not only did they appreciate the exotic, African qualities of slave music, but the three northerners genuinely respected the musical style and technique employed by the bondsmen. They were fully aware of the historic importance of notating black folksongs and disseminating them to a broad audience. By uncovering the elements of black folk music—syncopation, call-and-response form, strong rhythm, and short melodic phrases—the editors contributed greatly to the public awareness of a distinctive African American musical genre.[9]

Slave Songs of the United States included 136 texts with both words and music. Allen, Ware, and Garrison, according to musicologist Dena J. Epstein, overcame major obstacles in collecting and publishing the songs. First, working without tape recorders, the collectors struggled to reduce the sounds they heard to musical notation. Even transcribing the words posed difficulties, especially the Gullah dialect and its "unconcern with syntax." Variants of songs further dumbfounded the students as they sought a "correct," authoritative version. And even Garrison, who possessed musical training, was uncertain just how to use conventional symbols to notate this strange music that seemed to violate all standard musical rules. Notwithstanding these difficulties, the book was an extraordinary accomplishment for its day. True, the editors failed to comprehend fully the African qualities of slave music, but they stressed its distinctiveness and identified a syncretism of Africanisms and the unique experiences of slaves in the New World. And not only did the editors recognize important qualities in slave music, they noted its value in "illustrating the feelings, opinions and habits of the slaves" as well. Of special importance were the editors' observations concerning language. Rarely, they explained, did the bondsmen make distinctions of gender, case, number, tense, or voice. As Epstein correctly concludes, "The editors, despite the limitations of the period in which they worked, did an exemplary job, well deserving our admiration."[10]

Equally valuable to the historiography of slave music were the writings of black historian/sociologist W.E.B. Du Bois and Edward Krehbiel, white music critic of the *New York Tribune*. In his famous essay, "Of the Sorrow Songs," Du Bois argued that the essential meaning of slave melodies was "that sometime, somewhere, men will judge men by their souls and not by their skins." Beautiful but sad, articulate but veiled, in Du Bois's judgment the spirituals reflected the day-to-day features of slave life. They emphasized the out of doors in which the bondsmen worked and the monotony of field labor. Few of the songs dealt with happiness and love. When they mentioned family members, the songs rarely included the father—in Du Bois's opinion the emasculated and tragic figure of the slave community. The themes were necessarily narrow, Du Bois observed, because of "the limitations of allowable thought" imposed by the whites. Still, the slaves sung of hope in ultimate justice.[11]

Du Bois praised Krehbiel's 1914 work, *Afro-American Folksongs,* as "the most important contribution to the literature of Negro art that has been made for several years." Krehbiel addressed squarely the question that puzzled folklorists and musicologists throughout the period: whether slave songs originated in Europe or in Africa. He disagreed with authors who claimed that their basis was in European folk songs or in the music of the white masters. Instead, argued Krehbiel, the "essential elements" were derived from Africa, and the individual songs were "the product of American institutions; of the social, political and geographical environment within which their creators were placed in America." Slave songs contained many "African idioms"—variations of both major and minor scales joined with rhythmic and structural characteristics. According to Krehbiel, this was "the crude material which the slaves brought with them from their African homes." He also challenged the assumption that slave songs were sad. To the contrary, Krehbiel explained, most of the music was optimistic in tone because the slaves, like the ancient Israelites, were hopeful that they too would soon be delivered from bondage and given freedom in the hereafter. Krehbiel believed that much of the confusion resulted from the false assumption that the songs were predominantly in the minor key. His own examination of over 500 slave songs revealed that more than half were in the major, not the minor key.[12]

Krehbiel's emphasis on the African origins of slave music underscores a major theme in the early literature on slave folk culture. These writers anticipated by several decades the later emphasis on the African American heritage of blacks in the United States.[13] For example, in the 1870s and 1880s Thaddeus Norris and George Washington Cable wrote articles on slave folk culture in Louisiana stressing the impact of African customs on American blacks. According to Norris, the African hoodoo ritual kept New Orleans blacks in a constant state of fear. Although he considered them a nonsensical folk belief, Norris acknowledged that the frog-bones and conjuring gourd that held such power over the city's blacks were "handed down from their African ancestors."[14] Cable's more detailed articles, "Creole Slave Dances" and "Creole Slave Songs," described the rich African folk culture he had observed when living in antebellum New Orleans.[15]

On Sunday afternoons, for example, field hands were called by African drums and horns to assemble at "Place Congo" where, to the "wild" sounds of African musical instruments, the Creole slaves performed the *bamboula,* the *cata,* and other tribal dances. In Cable's judgment, the shrieks, chants, and leapings of the dancers indicated "a frightful triumph of body over mind." These dances closely resembled the leapings and writhings of the Louisiana slaves' forest voodoo ritual. He recognized that Louisiana bondsmen appeared primitive to the whites who observed their behavior with suspicion. But actually these blacks had descended from one of the most advanced tribes, the Mandingoes, who were leading warriors, metal workers, and merchants of Africa.[16] Summarizing the impact of the Africanisms on slave folk culture, Jeanette Robinson Murphy wrote, "The greater part of their music, their methods, their scale, their type of thought, their dancing, their patting of feet, their clapping of hands, their grimaces and pantomime, and their gross superstitions come straight from Africa."[17]

Just as these writers identified African qualities in the music and dance, others found them in black folktales. In 1877 William Owens observed that the Negroes' fables were most influenced by the Dark Continent and were "as purely African as are their faces or their own plaintive melodies."[18] Numerous folklorists writing in the period—from T.F. Crane in 1881 to Elsie Clews Parsons in 1919—agreed with Owens. They recognized that the true origin of the stories was found in the folktales of the slaves' African forebears. Many went on to say that the slaves' African-based folktales also had prototypes in European as well as South American folklore.[19]

When authors in these years mentioned Negro folktales, invariably they referred to Joel Chandler Harris's Uncle Remus stories, first published in the late 1870s in the *Atlanta Constitution.*[20] Harris's animal folktales were immensely popular in their day. After all, on the surface they adhered to the racist view of blacks then held by most white Americans. Blacks were portrayed as undignified, immature, and incapable of independent judgment. Harris's reputation, not surprisingly, has fared poorly among recent critics who tend to equate Uncle Remus with Uncle Tom and brand Harris a proslavery ideologue.[21] Such a view is only half correct and is unfair both to Harris and to the slaves whose folktales he popularized.

Harris neither invented nor altered the animal fables he heard as a youth in Middle Georgia.[22] He considered his role in the stories simply as "compiler" and informed Samuel L. Clemens that his relation to the tales resembled that "between an almanac-maker and the calendar."[23] Deeply respectful of the stories as literary genre, Harris was the first folklorist to transpose and record them accurately with correct dialect and inflections.[24] He thereby took a major step forward in preserving the folk heritage of black Americans.

Harris's avowed goal was to render an authentic portrait of the slave. He was seriously handicapped, though, by his fundamental ambivalence toward blacks. Harris was a segregationist, a white supremacist, a solid son of the New South. He created the Uncle Remus figure not only to serve as narrator, but to symbolize the happy slave of the Old South. According to the poet and critic Sterling Brown, Uncle Remus represented the "venerable, pampered, Negro . . . having (or allowed to have) only pleasant memories." He served as Harris's "mouthpiece for defending orthodox southern attitudes."[25] In the cycle of animal tales, Uncle Remus defends the social mores of the Old South, admires the white folks, criticizes uppity blacks, and admonishes blacks not to migrate to the North. On more than one occasion, Uncle Remus warns his audience that over-aggressiveness by Brer Rabbit led to trouble even for the wily hare. Blacks were to watch their step and know their place. So much for Harris's creation.

But a radically different view of slavery emerges in the slaves' actual folktales. Harris realized that the bondsmen used storytelling as a safe vehicle for explaining their life in thralldom. He failed, however, to grasp just how critical the tales actually were. The animals interact in an atmosphere of constant hostility and danger. The slaves, in the role of the weak animals, score paradoxical victories over their masters, the strong animals Brer Wolf, Fox, and B'ar. In Harris's first book, *Uncle Remus: His Songs and His Sayings* (1880), Brer Rabbit defeats Brer Fox in nineteen of twenty encounters between the two characters. The world of Brer Rabbit, Possum, and Tarrypin was actually the cruel, violent, sadistic world of the black slave. Like these folk tricksters, the slaves too had to manipulate their oppressors in order to survive. By lying, cheating, stealing, and simply enduring, the slaves resisted their captivity. Harris, then, misread the folktales he so scrupulously collected. Brer Rabbit was motivated not by "mischievousness" as he believed, but rather by "malice." The slaves told their folktales to attack slavery as well as the hegemony of whites. Without fully recognizing it, Harris uncovered an invaluable corpus of folk evidence that slaves did whatever they had to do to resist their bondage.[26]

Harris's stories had a profound influence on black novelist and lawyer Charles W. Chesnutt. His collection, *The Conjure Woman,* appeared in 1899.[27] Chesnutt became fascinated with the folklore of the ex-slaves while teaching as a young man in Freedmen's Bureau schools in North Carolina. But it was Harris's Uncle Remus tales that demonstrated to Chesnutt the potential of the folktale as literary form. The two men differed in method and argument. Whereas Harris based his stories exclusively on genuine tradition, Chesnutt's dervied almost totally from his imagination.[28] Chesnutt improvised freely with his folk sources, while Harris worked to maintain the integrity of the old tales. And Chesnutt excluded any positive image of slavery from his pages. Instead, his tales of slave magic and conjuration exposed slavery's cruelties and injustices, its vile economic underpinnings, and its potentially destructive effect on the black family.[29]

On the surface, Chesnutt's book appears to be an entertaining collection of tales set in slavery times. They offered parables for blacks and whites without seeming to upset the postwar southern racial caste system. But on another level, Chesnutt employed the double narrative structure to expose white racism before and after slavery, especially the insensitivity of whites to the social and economic plight of blacks.

In *The Conjure Woman* Chesnutt actually worked a conjure on his audience.[30] He intentionally manipulated the language of his main character, Uncle Julius, the venerable ex-slave.[31] When Uncle Julius spoke of the supernatural—men changed into trees or animals, whites transformed into blacks—he was uncovering the essential inhumanity of the slave system, its barbarity, and the strength of the slave family to endure. In "Mars Jeems's Nightmare," the brutal slaveowner is "goofered" into a black slave and discovers the harshness of slavery when forced to work under his own overseer. Whereas Chesnutt credited the blacks with the power to use nature to fight enslavement, he portrayed whites as constantly at odds with nature, exploitative, and greedy.

Not only did Chesnutt's folk stories attack slavery, they provided folk evidence that blacks responded to slavery in ways other than obsequiousness. Chesnutt's slaves retaliated against their masters overtly and covertly, maintained group solidarity, and sought to retain their humanity in spite of gross inhumanity on the part of the whites. Drawing upon African influences,[32] Chesnutt argued that slaves used their folk culture to interpret their world and to shape a slave community totally alien from that of their masters. In this manner the slaves actively controlled their lives, no matter how oppressive slavery became.

Like Chesnutt, Du Bois also credited the slaves with employing folk sources to fashion vital survival mechanisms—what another author referred to as "folk-repression."[33] Du Bois recognized that the bondsmen retained African folk elements in their religious and domestic lives. Although the blacks experienced a harsh "social revolution" in their removal from Africa, he argued that their nature worship and medicine man were recreated in the South in the form of the voodoo ritual and slave preacher. The preacher was the central figure in the slave's religion.

> He early appeared on the plantation and found his function as the healer of the sick, the interpreter of the Unknown, the comforter of the sorrowing, the supernatural avenger of wrong and the one who rudely but picturesquely expressed the longing, disappointment and resentment of a stolen and oppressed people. Thus, as bard, physician, judge and priest, within the narrow limits allowed by the slave system, rose the Negro preacher, and under him the first Afro-American institution, the Negro church.[34]

Not until the publication of Eugene D. Genovese's *Roll, Jordan, Roll: The World the Slaves Made* in 1974 would a historian probe as deeply into slave religion as Du Bois. He maintained that despite the veneer of Christianity given slave religion by masters and missionaries, for more than a century it retained the imagery and superstitions of the African forest. The slave, asserted Du Bois, drew upon "the resources of heathenism"—exorcism, witchcraft, Obi worship, spells, and blood sacrifices—to resist slavery. His religion was the slave's weapon against a bondage that the Negro envisioned as "the dark triumph of Evil over him." By 1750, Du Bois explained, planters succeeded in indoctrinating their slaves to Christianity. Passive submission replaced the bondsmen's active resistance. With the removal of their tribal rites, the blacks slipped into a "deep religious fatalism." According to Du Bois, the slaves' new Christian "religion of resignation" resulted in better, more docile laborers who were prone to indulgence and crime.[35]

Du Bois not only recognized African folk tradition in slave religion, but in family life as well. Writing on the slave family, he argued that "with all its shortcomings," the powerful, polygamous, "strictly guarded savage home life of Africa" offered more protection for women than "the promiscuous herding" of the North American slave plantation. In 1908 Du Bois again charged slavery with "crushing out . . . the African clan and family life" of American blacks. "No more complete method of reducing a barbarous people to subjection," he argued, could be devised than to destroy the ancient African conception of family. Even though traces of African family institutions persisted, the slaves "were raped of their own sex customs and provided with no binding new ones. Slavery," Du Bois continued, "gave the monogamic family ideal to slaves but it compelled . . . only the most imperfect practice of its most ordinary morals." Du Bois charged that paradoxically, "the greatest social effect" of slavery was the substitution of the polygamous Negro home with one "less guarded, less effective, less civilized."[36]

Du Bois identified still more Africanisms in the slaves' folk housing. Focusing on three distinct types of slave quarters, he examined a subject that remains almost totally neglected by historians. The first African American slaves built their homes on the African model: windowless huts with woven walls and thatched roofs constructed around four posts. These, argued Du Bois, could be kept clean and shady. But as "the cold brutality of slavery" increased, slave cabins began to reflect the harshness of the institution. "The homes of the slaves became dirty one-room lodges where, crowded like cattle, men slept in dreamless stupor after endless hours of forced and driven toil."[37]

One housing group noted by Du Bois was arranged on the feudal model—one-room log cabins positioned close to the Big House. These slave quarters usually contained a stone chimney and board floor. House servants frequently enjoyed larger, superior housing, sometimes with two rooms. Despite the close master-slave contact under these living conditions, slavery destroyed the ancient customs of the African home. And as some masters acquired several plantations, or became absentee landlords, they often placed their bondsmen beyond sight of their residences and under the control of overseers. According to Du Bois, this second housing arrangement widened the distance between slave and master. Subsequently, he explained, the blacks were denied the whites as models upon which to shape their habits and behavior. The slave quarters became "filthy hovels" with "no family life, no meals, no marriages, no decency."[38]

More favorable was the housing arrangement that existed in antebellum southern cities. Urban slaves, said Du Bois, enjoyed considerable freedom and lived in small but adequate one or two room homes behind their masters' houses. In Du Bois's opinion, the major drawback of housing conditions under slavery in the cities was the "sexual looseness" learned by the blacks through close association with the whites. Although he admitted exceptions, Du Bois concluded that the housing conditions under slavery contributed to an unstable black family in the post–Civil War South. Slave homes lacked strong paternal leadership because fathers lacked authority to govern the family. Their wives and daughters were liable to sexual abuse by the whites and any member of the family could be sold at the master's whim. Tragically, lamented Du Bois, the slave husband was a "male guest in the house, without respect or responsibility." Lacking unity or a sense of permanence, the family was reduced to a disjointed "agglomeration of atoms," devoid of force or pride. According to Du Bois, such living conditions typified the dehumanizing and destructive effects of slavery on African Americans.[39]

While many of Du Bois's comments on the slave family have been revised by recent scholars, his work on slave music, religion, and housing remains indispensable to historians of slavery.[40] The same may be said for the contributions of Higginson, Krehbiel, Harris, Chesnutt, and many other pioneer writers. To be sure, their writings were more narrative than analytical in emphasis, more irregular than systematic in methodology. And many of the early folklorists were little more than "collectors"—antiquarians in search of curious remnants of slavery.[41] But by focusing on slavery-related cultural themes, investigators between 1865 and 1920 laid the foundation for the modern study of African American slave folk culture. They recognized clearly the significance of the cultural lives of the slaves. They understood that much could be learned about slave life by examining the manner in which the slaves expressed themselves. How, they asked, did the bondsmen reconcile the constant tension between self-expression and the restraints imposed by the master class?[42] Recognizing too that the slaves' behavior reflected African characteristics, these writers probed folk materials to discern how effective enslavement was in modifying or destroying inherited cultural traits.

The first students of slave folk culture accomplished much despite laboring under two broad handicaps: the racial bias of the period and the difficulty of acquiring authentic, unedited folk sources. Antiblack racial stereotypes appear in nearly all of the discussions of slave folk culture contributed by whites. No doubt many of these writers maintained a belief in black inferiority. Their investigations into the cultural lives of the slaves may have reinforced this prejudice. In his early works, even Du Bois wavered on the question of the equality of the races. In some instances he described blacks as backward, childlike, underdeveloped, and in need of white role models.[43]

The early analyses of slave music, for example, contain many of the most racist characterizations of blacks found in the entire literature of slavery in this period. Howard W. Odum's 1909 dissertation, "Religious Folk-Songs of the Southern Negroes," exhibited the scientific racism so prevalent among white scholars of his day. Odum believed that slave spirituals revealed the simplicity of the Negro as a race. To him, they clearly presented the blacks' primitive "love of rhythm and melody"—their "faith in dreams and visions quickly exaggerated into fabrications." Emotional and repetitious, slave songs satisfied the black's "social wants" and relieved to a degree his alleged "child-like psycho-physical cravings." For Odum and the majority of white students of slave music, the spirituals contained those qualities—"the narrative style, the inconsequential, disjointed statements, the simple thought and the fastidious rhymes"—that they considered typical of the black mind.[44]

Despite their racist underpinnings, the bulk of books and articles on slave folk culture actually served to combat racism. By taking the slaves' cultural lives seriously the authors recognized—if only implicitly—the humanity and creativity of blacks as people. They helped establish the fact that blacks, too, had made important contributions to American civilization. This was no small feat given the racial assumptions of the era of Jim Crow. Black writers like Du Bois and Chesnutt emphasized the slaves' cultural accomplishments under extreme adversity. Only a strong race, they argued, could have withstood such oppression and made lasting cultural achievements. Race pride and identification were key goals of the Negro History Movement and were served well by these writings.

The pioneer students of slave folk culture partially overcame the shortage of sources by interviewing ex-bondsmen. By doing so they unearthed valuable songs and tales. In 1919, for example, Elsie Clews Parsons recorded material from former slaves in South Carolina that provides important insights into slave punishments, work loads, recreational activities, and funeral customs.[45] And some of the black writers drew upon their personal recollections as slaves. Regrettably, the early folklorists ignored an invaluable primary source: the large corpus of ante- and postbellum slave autobiographies. Not until recent years have students recognized the value of these vital sources of information about slavery. Had researchers tapped the slave narratives, they would have uncovered abundant folk evidence from the perspective of the blacks themselves.

Even so, the folklorists and musicologists discussed here led the way in presenting the black man's view of slavery. In the process, they foreshadowed many of the topics examined and sources employed by later scholars such as Melville J. Herskovits, John W. Blassingame, and Lawrence W. Levine. The contributions to slave historiography by the early writers prove that post–Civil War investigators did not ignore black social history. In fact, their research into the cultural history of slavery helped challenge the revived proslavery interpretation of Thomas Nelson Page, Ulrich Bonnell Phillips, Joseph A. Tillinghast, and other historians and "race thinkers." While they certainly did not contribute the last word on the subject of slave folk culture, the first generation of scholars still deserves recognition. They created an awareness of slave culture as a serious research field. Their work provided important folk evidence that the slaves drew upon their rich cultural heritage to withstand the horrors of enslavement. These writers took the vital first step in our understanding of the inner lives of the bondsmen.

10

E. Merton Coulter, the "Dunning School," and *The Civil War and Readjustment in Kentucky*

Historians recall E. Merton Coulter (1890–1981) as one of the deans of southern historiography. He wrote or edited thirty-seven books and more than 100 articles, coedited the multi-volume series *A History of the South,* published by Louisiana State University Press, and edited the *Georgia Historical Quarterly* for forty-nine years.[1] Yet Coulter's modern reputation rests primarily as a conservative, racist, unreconstructed white southerner. Over the last four decades, historians have branded his work on Reconstruction, especially *The South During Reconstruction, 1965–1877* (1947), an anachronism. Out of touch with post–World War II historiography, the book reportedly harkened back to the method, interpretation, and biases of historian William A. Dunning and his graduate students at Columbia University. As early as 1948, historian John Hope Franklin identified major weaknesses in Coulter's study of Reconstruction. According to Franklin, Coulter misrepresented and distorted his sources. He allegedly rejected documentation that undercut his arguments, confusing "his own attitudes with those of contemporaries under the claim of writing in the spirit and atmosphere of the period." In Franklin's opinion, Coulter exhibited flagrant antiblack bias.[2] In 1959, Bernard A. Weisberger agreed, judging Coulter's assumptions "excessively conservative" and his book "something of a setback."[3] The late Joe Gray Taylor recently wrote that "the real significance of Coulter's volume is not so much what he said but that it was the last major work on Reconstruction to set forth that particular point of view." Historian La Wanda Cox has characterized Coulter's 1947 study as "the last major work on Reconstruction to be totally unreconstructed."[4]

Born in 1890, Coulter inherited a sympathetic view of the Confederacy and scorn for Reconstruction as he grew up in a middle-class southern family at the turn of the century.[5] "No, I am not a 'Yankee' by 'a durn site,'" he informed an inquiring Kentuckian in 1946. "I was born in North Carolina where my ancestors lived from Colonial times. I had two grandfathers who were Confederate soldiers, one was killed in the war and the other was captured at Gettysburg and was held prisoner at Point Lookout until the end of the war."[6] After his release, Coulter's grandfather joined the Ku Klux Klan and later was arrested, indicted, tried, and acquitted for violation of the Enforcement Acts of 1870–1871. Ellis Merton Coulter took history classes as an undergraduate with J.G. de Roulhac Hamilton at the University of North Carolina (A.B., 1913), served briefly as principal of a high school, and in 1914 entered graduate school at the University of Wisconsin.[7] Studying under Carl Russell Fish, Coulter completed his doctoral dissertation, "Commercial Relations of Kentucky, 1860–1870," in 1917.[8] A year earlier, he had published the first of two pathbreaking articles on the impact of the Civil War on trade in the Mississippi Valley. These appeared in the prestigious *Mississippi Valley Historical Review*.[9] After two years of teaching at Ohio's Marietta College, Coulter joined the faculty at the University of Georgia, where he taught from 1919 until his retirement in 1958.

Early in his career, Coulter focused on the field of Kentucky history because the state's past had been inadequately treated by previous scholars and because its complexity tested the "scientific" methodology of his day.[10] He judged the available secondary literature weak and unanalytical, describing Lewis and Richard H. Collins's *History of Kentucky* (1882) as "a mine of undigested and unrelated information."[11] As a graduate student, Coulter uncovered vast source material on Kentucky in Madison, especially at the State Historical Society of Wisconsin. In 1922, after extensive manuscript and newspaper research in Chicago, Frankfort, Louisville, Lexington, and Washington, DC,[12] he published a monograph on the Cincinnati Southern Railroad and southern commerce during Reconstruction. This was reprinted from the five-volume *History of Kentucky*, edited by Charles Kerr, and coauthored by Coulter and William E. Connelley in the same year. According to Coulter, Connelley "wrote only the pioneer period of the Kentucky book." Actually, Coulter wrote sixty-five of the chapters while Connelley contributed fifteen.[13] Ongoing post-doctoral research enabled Coulter to expand his dissertation on Kentucky commerce and the Civil War into a monograph that included Reconstruction, an era he dubbed "Readjustment," because "Kentucky really never seceded in 1861 and so it could not be *Reconstructed*."[14] In 1925, after ten years of effort, the historian completed his book. "I believe that I have investigated about all the material there is on the subject—written and manuscript," Coulter told Louis R. Wilson, then director of the University of North Carolina Press, which published Coulter's *The Civil War and Readjustment in Kentucky* a year later.[15]

This important book examined the forces in Kentucky that led the Commonwealth down the unprecedented constitutional path of neutrality, not secession, and ultimately to its stormy relationship with the United States government as a loyal border state. Excluding military campaigns from his focus, Coulter devoted almost a quarter of his book to analyzing why white Kentuckians took refuge in neutrality. At the start of the war, explained Coulter, Kentuckians had divided loyalties. Allied historically and emotionally with the South, they were connected through their pocketbooks with the Old Northwest and the North. Three groups dominated Kentucky politics. At one extreme stood the anti-South, anti-slavery, unconditional Unionists, and on the other the radical secessionists, or Conservatives. The majority of white Kentuckians, however, championed the South on social, political, and racial lines, but favored the North for economic reasons. When they were forced to take a stand, this large middle group led the state down the road to compromise in the form of neutrality. Only when this strategy proved ineffectual did Kentucky favor the Union over the Confederacy. Significantly, Coulter criticized the Confederacy for both its economic policies and for invading the Commonwealth in September 1861. "The South," he wrote, "too impatient to be tolerant and too impetuous to be tactful, lost the greatest prize of the West—Kentucky." All the while, charged Coulter, Abraham Lincoln had been careful "to commit himself to nothing" and, by allowing the state to trade with both sides, "lulled Kentucky into a sense of security behind her neutrality." In point of fact, the United States government had been violating Kentucky neutrality for months by recruiting and arming troops in the state.[16]

In spite of its decision to side with the Union, explained Coulter, Kentucky's commitment to the Union war effort always was thin. After 1862, this ambivalence translated quickly into disbelief, pain, and anger when the state was treated as a "conquered province" by federal military and civil personnel. According to Coulter, by 1863 most white Kentuckians had concluded that some independent status, not necessarily secession, would have been preferable to the state's treatment by its Union brethren. In his opinion, Kentuckians interpreted federal occupation to mean "widespread and menacing persecution." "No person could be too important to escape the suspicion or ill will of a general, or too lowly to escape the grudge of a provost marshal." They voiced their dissatisfaction by voting against Lincoln and Unionists in state and national elections as well as by refusing to serve in the Union army. By war's end, Kentuckians assembled a long list of grievances against the Lincoln administration: wartime emancipation, recruitment of black troops, the draft, confiscation and impressment of property, arbitrary arrests, banishments, martial law, suspension of the writ of habeas corpus, interference with the judiciary and elections, suppression of the press, and manipulation of trade. These actions by the federal government uniformly led Kentucky whites to reassess their allegiance. They felt deceived, hoodwinked by Lincoln and the state's military occupation forces. Many concluded that the Commonwealth's first impulse—neutrality—had been right after all. As a result, wrote Coulter, after Appomattox, Kentucky "showed herself more Southern in habits of thought and sympathies, than, perhaps, any part of the former Confederacy itself."[17]

The reality of federal military occupation shattered the hopes of Kentucky

Unionists and fueled the fires of discontent among southern sympathizers, ex-Confederates, and Democrats. The peace that followed Appomattox, according to Coulter, "was the peace of the erstwhile vanquished over the victor. It was the peace that existed between the frog and the snake which had swallowed it." The period of "Readjustment"—or to use Coulter's metaphorical phrase, "the war after the war"—resulted in the renaissance of prosouthern sentiment in the Commonwealth, the supremacy of former Confederates, the removal of Unionists from power, and the emergence of a coalition of Conservatives renamed the Democratic party. Because Kentucky never was "reconstructed," Democrats easily blocked the growth of a Republican party in the state and generally proscribed blacks. "Perhaps," concluded Coulter, "it was not so surprising after all . . . that Kentucky waited until after the war was over to secede from the Union."[18]

The Civil War and Readjustment in Kentucky received warm praise from contemporary reviewers. Kentucky's press and the state's two historical journals applauded the monograph. "This is a book," proclaimed the *Louisville Times,* "that every Kentuckian should have in his library." "Mr. Coulter writes with almost incredible impartiality," asserted the *Lexington Herald.* Its reviewer suggested that "Thoughtful negroes should be interested in reading how the federal government and the Republican party played cat-and-mouse with their emancipation as a political device and by no means as a human right." Inspired by less chauvinism, the *Filson Club History Quarterly* praised Coulter's monograph as one "that no Kentucky historian . . . can afford to neglect." Similarly, the *Register of the Kentucky State Historical Society* assessed it as "the most thorough and accurate diagnosis of Kentucky's attitude of mind during the period we have ever read."[19]

Among academic historians, R.S. Cotterill, a contemporary of Coulter's at Wisconsin and an expert on Kentucky history, judged the book "the most important contribution to Kentucky history since the days of Mann Butler and one of the most significant of recent books in American history. It is scholarly, heavily documented, [and] rests on scrupulous research. . . . It fills a yawning gap in our history." Frank Lawrence Owsley of Vanderbilt University agreed. He complimented Coulter for exhibiting

> considerable courage in sifting the mass of compelling and conflicting evidence. . . . He has done a brilliant piece of work. . . . Every statement is documented with source material, garnered as with a fine-tooth comb from the correspondence of the Breckinridges, Holt, Watterson, Crittenden, Harrison, Stevenson, Durrett, and from the newspapers . . . and the government documents. . . . It is, in many ways, the best book on this period.

Another reviewer, William Kenneth Boyd, lauded Coulter for writing in the spirit of James Harvey Robinson's "New History"—recognizing that political action reflects social and economic motivation. Still other reviewers found *The

Civil War and Readjustment in Kentucky comparable to the state studies on Reconstruction prepared at Columbia University under Professor Dunning.[20]

Even those who welcomed the book, however, recorded some critical observations. J.G. de Roulhac Hamilton, Coulter's former professor at Chapel Hill and the author of a study on Reconstruction in Dunning's series, wished that Coulter had included more information pertaining to economic conditions in Kentucky during the war.[21] Cotterill had four specific objections. He faulted Coulter for stating—but not solving—the problem of Kentucky's neutrality, "receiving at face value every word of the Kentucky politicians." He regretted Coulter's failure to treat the military campaigns, writing "of war without writing of warfare." In Cotterill's view, "sentimentalists" had dominated Civil War historiography "long enough; surely the professional historian might profitably employ himself in taking it over. Professor Coulter . . . has . . . neglected his duty and deliberately failed to keep his appointment with opportunity." Cotterill went on to identify a prosouthern bias in Coulter's treatment of the postwar rise of the Democratic party in the Commonwealth. And the reviewer was amused at Coulter's failure to discuss Kentucky's postwar congressional delegation. "At times," he quipped, "it seems that Professor Coulter's avoidance of James Guthrie amounts to a religious ritual."[22]

In spite of these strictures, modern scholars have found surprisingly little to criticize in Coulter's pathbreaking work. While taking Coulter's *The South During Reconstruction* to task in 1948, Professor Franklin noted that *The Civil War and Readjustment in Kentucky* was "regarded as the definitive work on that subject." Thirteen years later, in his own *Reconstruction After the Civil War* (1968), Franklin noted that Coulter's approach resembled that of the earlier Dunning studies on Reconstruction, which had concluded that "little good came out of the reconstruction experience."[23] In 1966, Thomas L. Connelly first challenged Coulter's interpretation of post–Civil War Kentucky politics. According to Connelly, "Instead of party and intra-party struggles, perhaps Kentucky's politics in this period might better be interpreted as a power vacuum which power groups sought to control, rather than a resurgence of Confederate sympathy." In contrast to Coulter's explanation, Connelly suggested that "The real struggle may have been not along party lines, but between rival trade, commercial, social, agricultural and even personal groups which found support in both the supposed Democratic and Republican party groups." Three years later, historian Ross A. Webb raised similar questions about Coulter's argument. While respectful of Coulter's "monumental," "well-researched and scholarly" work, Webb nonetheless charged that *The Civil War and Readjustment in Kentucky* perpetuated the "myth" of Kentucky as a pro-Confederate state. "Coulter," wrote Webb, "treated his subject with the devotion of a Southern scholar, sometimes losing sight of the true nature of Kentucky's postwar attitudes and sentiments." According to Webb's research, the majority of Kentuckians never favored the rebel cause, and the Reconstruction era reaped marked benefits for Kentuckians, black and white. During these years of Republican control in Washington, Webb explained, the most common sentiments in the Commonwealth were "anti-administration and anti-congressional," not pro-Confederate. A decade later, Webb labeled Coulter's book "decidedly pro-Confederate in its interpretation," yet "invaluable as a reference work."[24] Others have apparently agreed with the latter assessment. In 1977, *The Civil War and Readjustment in Kentucky* finished second in a poll to determine the most significant books published in Kentucky history before 1960. James C. Klotter, in his important 1982 overview of Kentucky historiography, judged Coulter's book "the basic starting place" for studies on the "Readjustment" period in the Commonwealth. According to Klotter, "if the obvious faults" in *The Civil War and Readjustment in Kentucky* "are recognized, the book has held up remarkably well."[25]

Coulter's work, nevertheless, is vulnerable to serious criticism. In both a 1979 article and in an unpublished biography of Coulter, Michael Vaughan Woodward touched on the historian's lifelong paternalistic view of blacks. He charged that in *The Civil War and Readjustment in Kentucky,* Coulter depicted blacks "as a confused mass of humanity. Whatever eagerness they possessed for volunteering [for service in the Union army] is attributable [by Coulter] to their child-like natures." According to Woodward, Coulter regretted the destruction of slavery, especially the master-slave relationship. He considered emancipation too sudden and blamed it for unleashing crime, disorder, and political corruption in the Commonwealth. Charging that Coulter's book "fit the prevailing historiographical climate," Woodward noted that the historian judged the slaves unfit for freedom, praised the Black Codes as necessary to Kentucky's well-being, and damned the Freedmen's Bureau as the source of much of Kentucky's postwar violence and lawlessness. In Coulter's view, Democratic victory in 1870 "saved [Kentucky] . . . from the saturnalia of extravagance and fraud that made government a mockery in the former Confederate states."[26] If anything, Woodward understates his case.

Coulter, like many whites living in the age of Jim Crow, held an intensely racist view of blacks. He perceived blacks as a "problem"—not as equals endowed with the same strengths and weaknesses as whites. No sooner had the war begun, wrote Coulter, than the slaves became "boisterous and unruly . . . a menace to the peace of the community." He recognized in their behavior not even a hint of resistance. Instead, Coulter depicted the slaves as a "simple" people, unable to protect themselves from Yankee recruiters and incapable of coping with being torn from their familiar surroundings. He treated them as an amorphous group in a perpetual state of locomotion—"drifting," "straggling," "milling," "wandering." "They were a constant menace to peace and good order and in some places they added to their petty thievery, the pillaging and plundering of" public buildings. What especially irked Coulter was that the federal government treated blacks "as a class apart from other people." He failed to realize that the South's slave codes in general, and Kentucky's slave laws in particular, had done the same thing since the eighteenth century. And Coulter identified a further deterioration of black behavior during the "Readjustment" period, when the former slaves succumbed to the alleged "meddling" of the Freedmen's Bureau. In his opinion, emancipation generally rendered the blacks "worthless" laborers "who after receiving the suffrage became even more ungovernable."[27]

While Coulter's racism tends to leap out at the modern reader, many of his statements, especially in the postwar portions of the book, are blurred by a more subtle problem of tone or voice. The reader is left unclear as to whether Coulter's statements reflect his views or those of his sources. Commenting, for example, on white Kentuckians' reaction to the Thirteenth Amendment, Coulter remarked that "the legislature would not put off the day so long for the contemptuous burial of the outrageous amendment." Analyzing the Conservatives' dissatisfactions with federal regulation of the state election of August 1865, Coulter wrote that "the military authorities had acted outrageously." Summarizing the Radicals' assessment of their electoral defeat, Coulter stated that "[General J.M.] Palmer had run rough shod over Kentucky as if it had fewer rights than the conquered South." Explaining the Democrats' attitudes toward black suffrage, Coulter said that the legislators devised "means to delay the evil as long as possible."[28] Many other examples could be cited. Significantly, Professor Franklin identified a similar problem in his 1948 critique of Coulter's *The South During Reconstruction*. More than two decades after Coulter published his Kentucky study, he was still "injecting his point of view . . . misconstructing . . . when he is not satisfied with permitting the characters to speak for themselves and [Coulter] feels called upon to explain and, perhaps, to extend their feelings."[29]

Contemporary reviewers of Coulter's *The Civil War and Readjustment in Kentucky* failed to identify these problems in his book. Indeed, they praised its impartiality, contrasting the work favorably with the products of Dunning's famous seminar.[30] Those dissertations, according to historian David Donald, were heavily researched, written "with an air of objectivity," and "were acclaimed as triumphs of the application of the scientific method to historiography." Weisberger describes these authors within the context of their day as "fair-minded," "thorough," and "scrupulous," and credits them with unearthing valuable source materials of lasting importance.[31] In the 1920s, Coulter no doubt welcomed identification with Dunning's students, whose works were recognized as model studies. Yet long before Franklin leveled his 1948 attack on Coulter, the "Dunning school" was under fire for its racism, its opposition to black participation in Reconstruction, and its hostility toward the Republican governments in the South. For example, in 1935 W.E.B. Du Bois listed Coulter's *The Civil War and Readjustment in Kentucky* along with the Dunning dissertations under the heading "Standard—Anti-Negro." "These authors," he explained, "believe the Negro to be subhuman and congenitally unfitted for citizenship and the suffrage."[32] According to a modern student, theirs was "a tale of carpetbagger and scalawag venality, black incompetence, and Democratic virtue and rightful triumph."[33] The forces of revisionism have not looked with favor upon the "Dunning school."

Coulter's treatment of "readjustment" in Kentucky falls unmistakably in the Dunning camp. In his last chapters, the historian abandoned the scrupulous objectivity he had employed early in the work, especially in his lengthy discussions of Kentucky's neutrality and the state's economic concerns. The final chapters, however, fall into the "chamber of horrors" interpretation of Reconstruction—anti–U.S. Army, anti-northern, anti-Republican, and antiblack. Conservatives, Democrats, and "the Confederate tradition" are idealized at the expense of the allegedly hapless and corrupt Radicals and blacks. Again and again, Coulter blasted the federal government for what he termed "war rubbish, burdensome and galling." This included the Thirteenth and Fourteenth Amendments and the Freedmen's Bureau. Like Dunning's disciples, Coulter bemoaned "the tightening rigors of reconstruction [that] throttled the South." "The sudden freedom of the negro and his ambitions, aspirations, and hopes perverted by designing and crafty white leaders . . . developed into a dangerous and ominous" scenario for the Commonwealth. He attacked the Freedmen's Bureau in Kentucky for "manipulating the negroes for political purposes" and "for alleging brutal treatment of the freedmen by their former masters." Coulter considered the Bureau "one of the greatest causes of violence and disorder" in the state. "It left suspicion and hatred between the two races, where understanding and friendship should have prevailed."[34]

But despite his Dunning-like tone, Coulter recognized the importance of fair and balanced analysis. He admitted that when assessing accountability for the problems of the "readjustment" period, "the blame was not all on one side." Coulter quoted a Shelby County farmer in 1870 who believed that white Kentuckians exhibited a "stubborn indisposition to accept their present situation," an unwillingness to shed the "prejudice of previous habits." And for all of his blistering attacks against the Freedmen's Bureau, Coulter admitted that "it produced certain tangible results." The Bureau encouraged blacks to save money and fed, clothed, and educated thousands of black Kentuckians. By 1869, the Bureau had aided in establishing 391 schools in the Commonwealth with over 1,000 teachers instructing almost 19,000 pupils. Even Coulter had to recognize this important achievement. He considered the "miserable school system" of the Conservatives among the greatest embarrassments of Kentucky's postwar Democratic regimes.[35]

All in all, despite its shortcomings, Coulter's book was a tremendous achievement, one that still deserves high praise and ranks among the most important works in the field of Kentucky history. It surpassed the Dunning state studies in virtually every category—breadth of research, sophistication of method, impartiality, interpretation, and readability. It contained noticeably fewer overt racist slurs than other contemporary works. Coulter was far more thorough in his research than Dunning's students, setting a lofty standard in the use of manuscript collections, local newspapers, oral testimony, and an array of government documents. These qualities become evident when one compares *The Civil War and Readjustment in Kentucky* with the only other contemporary book-length study of Kentucky in the Civil War period: Mary Scrugham's slender study, *The*

Peaceable Americans of 1860–1861 (1921), a Dunning dissertation that dealt with Kentucky's decision to remain neutral and ultimately to cast its lot with the Union. While employing manuscript collections as sources, her dissertation lacked depth and adhered to the racist tone of the other Dunning studies. For example, in Scrugham's opinion, "The greatest calamity" of Reconstruction "was the debasement of political morality . . . brought about by the injection of a mass of totally ignorant negroes into the electorate." Contrasting Coulter's book with Scrugham's work clearly underscores Coulter's achievement.[36]

Throughout his volume Coulter broke fresh factual and interpretive ground. Better than any previous investigator, he sketched Kentucky's complex and constantly changing political alignments before, during, and after the war. Coulter interpreted Kentucky's neutral stance not as irrational behavior, but rather as the result of white Kentuckians' overriding individuality—their love for the Union, their self-concept as mediators, and especially their determination to trade with all sections of the country without interference. Resembling other Progressive historians, especially those schooled at Wisconsin in the era of Frederick Jackson Turner, Coulter emphasized geographic, geologic, and economic causation.[37] He argued that Kentuckians feared that if they entered the war their state would become a battlefield—a frontier invaded from all sides. Agriculture and commerce would suffer immeasurably. Espousing an economic interpretation, Coulter downplayed ideology, race, and political factionalism as causes of Kentucky's alignment with the Union. State rights, economics, and racial control provided the ordering principles for his interpretation of Kentucky's ultimate disaffection from the Lincoln administration and the state's move into the solidly Democratic ranks.

Coulter's interpretation of Kentucky's economic interests squared nicely with the facts. As the state's relations with the federal government steadily deteriorated during the war, and as the North garnered control over Kentucky, the Commonwealth was beset by independent, marauding guerrilla bands. "Their hatreds and revenges seemed insatiable," explained Coulter. "They stole, plundered, and burned as they hurried along their career of destruction." Yet in spite of the guerrillas, wartime dislocation, and what Coulter termed "the blighting and pestilential presence of the Federals," Kentucky's economy somehow prospered during those chaotic times. The state's banks and government finances remained stable throughout the war.[38]

Such insights have rendered *The Civil War and Readjustment in Kentucky* one of the most durable works in the field. This is not meant to suggest a blind endorsement of Coulter's arguments. On many levels his book is seriously flawed and obviously dated. But it would be unfair to fault him too strongly for adhering to, and even surpassing, the accepted historiographic canons of his day. The fact remains that in over sixty years no scholar has even approached writing a comprehensive, revisionist history of the Civil War and Readjustment period in Kentucky. Coulter's book still has much to teach us.

11

Ulrich Bonnell Phillips's World Tour and the Study of Comparative Plantation Societies

> So long have plantations been a concern of mine that they have become perhaps an obsession. On a journey around the world last year I visited shrines, temples, towns and ruins more or less under a mild compulsion; but cultivated fields or groves and the people drawing substance from them caught my strongest attention, particularly where there were signs of tangible system.[1]

University of Michigan historian Ulrich Bonnell Phillips (1877–1934) stood atop his profession in 1929. That year, his book *Life and Labor in the Old South* received rave reviews. It already had won Little, Brown and Company's $2,500 cash prize for the best unpublished manuscript in American history. This accolade, in addition to his ranking as the foremost historian of slavery and the Old South, led to what Phillips termed "a very flossy job at Yale" University. This appointment, a chair in American history, meant more money, more prestige, and a very light teaching load. Phillips looked eagerly ahead to possessing "much more time than heretofore for authorship." Even before the details of the Yale job offer were announced, however, Phillips was awarded an Albert Kahn Foundation Fellowship. This prestigious $5,000 grant allowed Phillips to make a year-long world tour before joining the Yale faculty. As Kahn Fellow, Phillips sought to study plantations worldwide, especially in Africa. The tour, he explained, "indulged a wish of many years to broaden my grasp of Negro traits, to see the quality of primitive life where least disturbed, and to test a few theories." In fact, Phillips's trip to Asia and Africa provides an invaluable litmus test to measure his racism. To what extent did Phillips's world tour reinforce his previous racial views? Or did his trip force Phillips to redefine his notions of race? Unaware of this dimension of his forthcoming trip, and exuberant over his good fortune, Phillips wrote, "1929 is a year of grace indeed."[2]

In mid-August, Phillips embarked westward by train from Ann Arbor, stopped at Berkeley, California, sailed to Oahu, Hawaii, and then on to Japan. En route Phillips remarked that though he would investigate plantations in Asia, he was determined "to see how the Negroes handle the cotton crop in the forks of the Nile." Phillips's plan was to make his way to the Sudan, then send his wife and children to France where the latter would attend school. Along the way, Phillips visited Kyoto, Japan, where his inane remarks about the inability of the Japanese to speak English suggested his utter unwillingness to grapple with racial and cultural differences. Phillips's comment, that he was "getting in a degree Oriental and most pleasurably," expressed clearly his white, Eurocentric way of interpreting the world. A month later, Phillips visited Shanghai, Hong Kong, Manila, Singapore, and Penang—"diverse orderly confusions of tongues and races," he observed. After traveling more than halfway around the globe, Phillips still had made no significant statements about comparative plantation life or culture.[3]

In November, Phillips finally examined plantations—tea and rubber estates in Ceylon, the British colony off the coast of India. These observations fit nicely, Phillips explained, into his "general study of plantations." Phillips inspected the Hantane tea plantation in the mountainous region near Kandy. The tea shrubs grew on steep slopes and were shaped broadly at waist level so that workers engaged in the semi-weekly plucking could easily toss the shoots into baskets secured on their backs. Like African American slave women, Ceylon women frequently worked in the fields with babies on their hips and plucked the tea bushes with one hand. Baskets laden with shoots were dried and then processed, as Phillips explained, "rolled, fermented, rolled again, dried, sifted, picked over, graded and packed." He found the process "suggestive of old-time sugar planta-tion doings in Louisiana." According to Phillips, quality tea production depended on carefully drying, rolling, and fermenting the leaves after the first rolling had bruised them. As he descended the mountain plateau southwestward to Colombo, Phillips passed cocoa plantations and, he remarked, rice fields and coconut groves run by natives without white management.[4]

From Colombo, Phillips again ventured inland, this time to observe the Hangwella rubber plantation. Phillips was impressed by the fact that the planta-tion owners supplied their Tamil coolie laborers, imported from southern India by contract, with a hospital, school, Hindu temple, concrete swimming pool, and day nursery. He commented that the coolies were "near enough black to make one look for kinks in their hair." The coolies systematically tapped and collected latex from the orderly rows of rubber trees. Phillips noted the precision with which each tapper "conserved with a miserly care" the precious bark of the rubber trees. At the mill, workers strained, measured, and tested the milky sap and then diluted it with acid. This rubber was destined for European or American tire plants.[5]

Phillips was especially interested in labor relations on the Hantane tea and

Hangwella rubber plantations. The owners employed *kanganes*—Tamils who served as recruiting agents among their people in southern India—to import workers and then to manage their labor. The kangane in charge received the equivalent of two cents per day for each Tamil laborer he supervised; sub-kanganes or gang bosses received three cents for each laborer in his unit. Compensation for the coolies included roundtrip transportation from India, housing, hospitalization, a midday meal, and schooling for the children. Most Tamils were paid on a piece-work arrangement, receiving less than the equivalent of twenty cents per day. Phillips commented that the Tamils fared well physically and, from his observation, had a positive working relationship with the white managers who ran the plantations for the absentee owners back in England. Much like his impression of master-slave relations under American slavery, Phillips described management-labor contacts in Ceylon as illustrative "of not merely good temper but of cordiality and affection." "Of course," Phillips added, "a few heart-to-heart talks with coolies might change this estimate." But Phillips remained convinced that managers and workers on Ceylon's tea and rubber plantations shared a reciprocal relationship resembling the plantation paternalism that he had described in the Old South. Slavery at its best, Phillips wrote in 1918, was an institution characterized "by mutual concessions and pledges." Impressed with the British resident managers, Phillips was confident that "these lonely white men are evoking from crude labor good service in loyal temper, which means they are giving a valued *quid pro quo*."[6]

In early December, Phillips next sailed from Colombo to Suez and then made his way to Cairo to prepare for his trek up the Nile. There he bade his family farewell as they departed for Europe, determined "to contemplate cotton and primitive Negroes," he said, "if the crocs or the coons don't get me." Phillips first stopped at Fashn, about 100 miles south of Cairo, to observe Ragheb Bey's 2,500-acre Gafadoun Ezbeh plantation on the fringe of the Sahara. The cash crop was the long and silky Sakellarides variety of cotton that, at Gafadoun Ezbeh, yielded on average an unusually high 700 or 800 pounds per acre. This high productivity resulted from the effective use of fertilizer and seed selection.[7]

Plantation management at Gafadoun Ezbeh, according to Phillips, exhibited "a striking mixture of the very old and the very new." In one field, he observed twelve traditional plows constructed from logs, poles, and iron sheathings, drawn by twin bullocks. In another field, modern steam-powered machinery dragged a massive gang plow. Phillips described labor relations at Gafadoun Ezbeh as "patriarchal." The overall agricultural operations were directed by a steward, but workers on the plantation were supervised by a *nazir* (overseer), a *bash kholly* (field boss), and several *khollys* (foremen). Watchmen guarded the cotton when the crop stood ripe in the fields. Phillips was especially amused by an unusual member of the proprietor's staff, an Albanian bodyguard armed with an umbrella (to shield his master from excessive sun) and a shotgun (to protect him from possible assassins). With one exception—on a Mississippi plantation years before—Phillips had never observed an armed member of a plantation supervisory force. He considered it "curious" that Ragheb Bey, "a native among natives," would require protection from his fellow Egyptians. Perhaps not everyone at Gafadoun Ezbeh considered Ragheb Bey so "patriarchal" a master after all.[8]

Phillips next ventured south by train to Kom Ombo near Assouan. There he observed gigantic steam-driven centrifugal pumps delivering Nile water through canals to convert the porous, sandy loam into fertile sugar fields. After three days of travel south by ship and west across the desert by rail, Phillips arrived in Khartoum, the capital of the Sudan. Phillips's destination was the extensive operations of the Sudan Plantations Syndicate in the Gezira, a fertile district between the White Nile and Blue Nile. Phillips settled in for a two-day visit at the syndicate's headquarters at Barakat, observing all that he could of its 300,000-acre cotton plantation operations. He joked that "even at meals and at a polo game I was crammed with all the data that I could ask for."[9]

Phillips took careful note of the modern canals, the experimental farm where seeds were bred to supply the entire plantation, and the cotton gin that employed buffalo hide cylinders to separate the sleek Sakellarides fiber from the seed without damage. Tenants cultivated thirty acres each and were required annually to rotate the crops. It was a labor system that no doubt reminded Phillips of sharecropping in the post–Civil War American South. Leaseholders provided the labor, drawing upon almost 100,000 Arabs and Negroes, including workers from the White Nile region as well as pilgrims en route to or from Mecca. In return for furnishing the labor, tenants received all the millet and lubia and 40 percent of the cotton crop they produced. The syndicate supplied seasonal advances for tenants, water for irrigation, steam- or diesel-powered plows, and seed. It also ginned the cotton and marketed the crop. Phillips judged the fiber to be finer than Egyptian cotton and marveled because the fields averaged 400 pounds of cotton per acre. This, Phillips wrote, "invites envy from the rest of the cotton-growing world."[10]

Phillips next traveled to central Africa "where," he explained, "the naked, pagan, tribal Negroes are as yet untouched by projects of organized industry." Phillips's visit to Africa held special meaning to him, having devoted almost three decades to analyzing the life and labor of African American slaves and American race relations. Phillips was convinced that his knowledge of African Americans would help him overcome his inability to communicate with the Africans. "Luckily," Phillips wrote, unaware of his thoroughly engrained racism, "being Georgia-bred, all Negroes have never looked alike to me." He gawked at the first black Africans he encountered, judging their backwardness "simply incredible . . . with little promise of essential change in another century or millennium." To Phillips, Africa represented "a museum of the primitive."[11]

Phillips began his African trip in early December, venturing south in the Anglo-Egyptian Sudan from Khartoum up the White Nile to the area between latitudes ten and thirteen. Phillips next traveled on the Bahr-el-Jebel, its western tributary the Bahr-el-Ghazal, and then "as far south as the steamers ply," to

Terrakekka (latitude six) south of the Sudd. On board the *Fateh,* a paddlewheel steamboat, Phillips met Major J.R.N. Warburton and Captain H.F. Kidd, Sudan officials returning to their frontier posts after home-leave in England. According to Phillips, the two administrators "sized me up over the bridge table" and invited him to accompany them to central Africa. "Part of their prompting," explained Phillips, "was the fact no American had previously gone into their zone."[12]

Phillips and his new friends ventured westward from Terrakekka with a lorry, touring car and trailer, supplies, and five servants. Phillips joked that "Fords, Flit [an insecticide] and fly-swatters" were "America's contribution to Sudan progress." They spent three days driving west to Amadi, then in a southwestern direction to Maridi and Yambio, where they crossed the fifth parallel, and northwest to Source Yubu where Phillips spent Christmas. He noted the causal relationship between topography, agriculture, rainfall, latitude, disease environment, and race. Phillips argued, for example, that in the latitudes near the equator annual rainfall was sufficient to grow virtually any crop, including cotton. Such observations, however, suggest little real insight into African agricultural life and labor.[13]

Phillips was especially interested in viewing cotton cultivation forty miles on either side of Maridi and near latitude nine along the banks of the Bahr-el-Gazal. This crop flourished despite relatively little moisture and no irrigation. The soil retained water and drained slowly, allowing the plants to thrive even in drought. African cotton—the product of short staple cottonseed imported from the United States—grew as tall as any cultivated in the Mississippi Delta, Phillips said. But African cotton succumbed to more diseases and insects than its American counterpart and suffered from poor scientific management. High transportation and seed costs, Phillips concluded, prevented African cotton from ever competing seriously on the international market.[14]

At Maridi, Phillips became enamored of the Azande, a homogeneous tribal group. He marveled at the subtlety of the song and dance at a Zande celebration at Source Yubu. The music, Phillips said, "began softly, swelled to a shout and sank again, while feet shuffled, arms jerked and fingers jiggled." Perplexed by the apparent lack of syncopation, Phillips admitted that his "familiarity with Negro music in America was of no help at all." He was confident, however, that few traces of Azande music or dance survived among African Americans. The blacks "discarded them long ago," insisted Phillips, "to take the melodies of their white masters and modify these into new forms." Though mindful of the limitations on a casual observer to comprehend "the collective savage mind," Phillips could not free himself from his long-standing negative view of blacks and exhibited little recognition of cultural relativism. He judged the Azande "good farmers in a casual savage way." In his opinion, the Africans were undeniably "primitive." Phillips was entertained, for instance, by the sight of "the veriest pickaninnies" performing a tribal custom adopted from the British military. He also made condescending remarks about the traditional grass clothing worn by Azande women. "To a visitor the effect is not unlike that of the bare-breasted show-girls of the Folies-Bergere, but to the natives this nakedness is merely a matter of course. Old women, with wrinkled skin and shriveled breasts, have the same lack of covering as their buxom daughters."[15]

From Source Yubu, Phillips ventured northward with Captain Kidd over treacherous, "jolting" terrain (sometimes forcing them to stop to cut a path for the lorry), across the Bo and Busserie Rivers, and finally to the provincial capital of Wau. There, Phillips explained, he was in "touch again with comfort and good fare, and even with tennis and auction bridge." Taking leave of Captain Kidd, Phillips took a rickety old Ford to Meshra, where he boarded the steamboat *Kaibar* for the voyage through the Sudd, on the Bahr-el-Ghazal to Lake No, and on the White Nile to Malakal. Phillips's journey covered 800 miles spanning the Nile-Congo divide, "where," he wrote proudly, "no American has gone before." Along the way, he contracted malignant tertian malaria and, in mid-January 1930, steamed to Khartoum for hospitalization. His bout with malaria left Phillips wary of traveling again where anopheles mosquitoes preyed so easily on white men. "Central Africa," he wrote, "will not see me more, though I shall see it again and again with dimming memory's eye, striving to discern the significance of its phenomena." Phillips next trekked to Cairo, from which point he sailed to Italy and then on to France to be reunited with his family.[16]

Phillips came away from his African trip with a cache of specimens—African weapons, tools, ornaments, and musical instruments—that confirmed his belief in the natives' "primitiveness and . . . savage contentment." African backwardness, Phillips insisted, resulted from its low literacy rate and widespread belief in magic, which, in turn, were influenced by the continent's diversity of languages and cultures. "Literacy," he explained, "has compacted tribes into nations" and "has at the same time in large degree promoted particular loyalties as against the sense of continental or world-wide identity." As a result, Phillips said, "Africa . . . is in the world but, except for her northern and southern extremes, not of it." Unwilling to judge African contributions in their own light and within the context of time and place, Phillips went on to conclude that the continent largely lacked any "civilization which the outer world will dignify by that name." Though Phillips judged black Africa to be so fragmented "that we may as well say that no Negro world exists," he nonetheless observed essential uniformities in Negro architecture, implements, weapons, and crafts. Phillips explained the apparent contradiction between heterogeneity of African languages and homogeneity of artistry as the result of the Africans' "struggle for existence." They imitated, modified, and adopted cultural forms over time.[17]

Yet Phillips remained perplexed as to why African blacks had not adapted to Western ways after centuries of contact with Europeans. "The Negroes," he asserted in terms reminiscent of nineteenth-century proslavery rhetoric, "have contributed no inventions to the world's advantage." After all, Phillips reasoned, West African Negroes easily could have demanded tools, carts, and weapons from European traders in exchange for African slaves. But no, "the Negroes continue to live in a manner which seems to us impossibly bare." Unwilling to accept African customs nonjudgmentally, Phillips argued that the Negroes exhibited little inclination to adapt to "civilized" ways. He doubted that the Africans retained traditional practices consciously but argued that blacks were not as imitative as white southerners generally supposed. "The [African] Negroes differ from the rest of us," Phillips wrote, "mainly . . . in their greater esteem of leisure, for which their climate is in large part responsible, and their prolonged contentment with primitive conditions." American blacks, concluded Phillips, retained little of the culture of their African forebears. Rather, they exhibited "a special capacity for survival by an adaptation which at every stage has been schooled directly or indirectly by the whites."[18]

In general, Phillips went abroad to study plantations. He ventured to Africa presumably to observe blacks at the same stage of development as their American slave forebears. Examined critically, however, one cannot but question Phillips's rationale for the African phase of his trip and the observations he made. Historian Eugene D. Genovese correctly has wondered why Phillips chose "to study the African not in West Africa, which supplied most of our slaves, but in primitive east-central areas, which supplied few or none." Phillips's argument that he sought to observe blacks "where least disturbed," in their natural state, perhaps made sense anthropologically, but not historically, at least not in the American context. "It never occurred to him," Genovese explains, "that those particular Africans had never approached the level of pre-European West Africa." And Phillips's method—examining a people and a culture in the 1920s, ostensibly to understand it centuries earlier—is open to serious question.[19]

Unfortunately, Phillips never explained fully his motives or his intentions for his trip in the first place. There is no evidence from his earlier writings that he ever sought to explore "primitive" life, that this had been a long-term goal. He neither recorded what he thought he would find in Africa nor how he planned to use his observations. "What he found," historian Merton Dillon explains, "neither surprised nor disappointed him, for at every point his impressions were conditioned by opinions he long ago had formed about the cultural tendencies of Negroes and the function of the plantation." In fact, his study of comparative plantation cultures and working-class peoples worldwide taught Phillips remarkably little. He died in 1934 and with the exception of narratives of his trip, Phillips never published any of his insights into comparative plantations. His few references to agricultural operations consisted of pedestrian observations at best. Most white Americans of Phillips's day surely would not have found his comments regarding African "backwardness" surprising or especially perceptive. They wholeheartedly agreed with him.[20]

Phillips's observations of central Africa reinforced and intensified his longstanding view of blacks as persons inherently inferior to whites. Within a year of his return to America, Phillips wrote that the tribal black, "so primitive as to be styled a savage, merely dwells in a world of his own, with crafts and conceptions outgrown by most other men." These Africans, Phillips added, "demonstrate a wonderful capacity to remain primitive,—to perpetuate the crudest of human beliefs and practices." Phillips, like the South's "Bourbon" politicians, neither forgot the past nor learned from the present. He adopted the same "Orientalist" perspective on Africa and Africans—"a kind of Western projection onto and will to govern over the Orient"—as the British colonial administrators whom he so admired. Like them, Phillips viewed the Africans as "pagans" whose refusal to adopt "civilized" ways left them totally apart from modern man.[21]

His world tour also confirmed Phillips's belief that the plantation system and slavery played constructive roles in the acculturation of Africans in North America. Rejecting the writings of W.E.B. Du Bois, Franz Boas, and Melville J. Herskovits, Phillips asserted that African Americans retained "no memory of African scenes or tribal ways or Negro languages." He saw this as a positive. Instead, they "cheerfully made American plantation life their own, for the most part accepting slavery . . . and adopting their masters much as a child appropriates his parents or a pupil his teacher."[22]

Ironically, Phillips's negative impressions of African blacks contributed to a slightly more favorable opinion on his part of American blacks. He came away from viewing blacks in Africa with a newly refined racism, one with more nuances, yet still an ideology grounded firmly on the idea of inherent black inferiority. After returning from his world tour, Phillips differentiated more clearly than ever before between black Africans and black Americans. Black Africans, Phillips concluded, were incapable of progress. Black Americans, however, under certain conditions, could inch along toward what Phillips defined as civilization. This minute shift in Phillips's racial thought is significant because in the decade between the publication of his two most influential works—*American Negro Slavery* (1918) and *Life and Labor in the Old South* (1929)—he had articulated no such change. In the unpublished draft of Phillips's account of his African trip, for example, he wrote that American blacks "made their masters' culture their own in large degree, and attained considerable excellence in civilized husbandry and handicrafts. Of course the generality remained uncouth," he added, "but even this crudity came to be more American than African."[23]

To be sure, in 1931 Phillips subscribed as much as ever before to the tenets of white supremacy in the American South. He feared, for example, the "mass" of American Negroes who "have yet to show, indeed yet to begin to suggest, that they can be taken into full fellowship of any sort in a democratic civilized order." Phillips predicted that even if blacks received the vote, "they could not use it with intelligence or to good effect."[24]

Phillips's world tour convinced him that whites had to play even more significant roles in uplifting and controlling blacks in Jim Crow America. "The most effective promoters of their improvement," he informed the General Education Board in 1931, "must be selected whites." Gone were the old plantation masters and mistresses who had provided guidance and regulation. It thus was in "the best interests of their own social order" for whites to educate blacks. No doubt shocking his white audience in July of that year in Blacksburg, Virginia, Phillips announced that he welcomed having blacks in his university classes in the North. It was important, he said, to encourage those "informed and thoughtful" blacks not intent on "wrecking civilization. There are no Gandhis among them preaching non-cooperation and reversion to primitive ways. They have no love of tribal superstition or savagery."[25]

Phillips, then, journeyed many miles in what he termed his 1929–1930 "circuit of this curious globe." His trip, however, unearthed few new insights into comparative plantations. It cemented Phillips's view of Africans as hopelessly backward and only subtly altered his opinion of African Americans. Phillips remained so blinded by his preconceptions and prejudices that in reality he had not traveled very far at all.[26]

12

A Southern Historian on Tour
Clement Eaton's Travels Through the New South

Writing in 1966, North Carolina-born Clement Eaton heaped praise upon the first book of a younger historian.

> The author represents the new breed of southern historians, who have emancipated themselves from old assumptions and stereotypes, who dig deeply in the sources, maintain a very liberal outlook, and write with sophistication and charm.[1]

For years historians have described Eaton in similar terms. Until his death in 1980, Professor Eaton long remained the "dean" among social and intellectual historians of the Old South.[2] Throughout more than a half-century of studying the South, Eaton championed the cause of liberalism in his native region. Eaton's liberalism did not always come easily or mature rapidly. His admiration of the architectural treasures left by planter aristocrats, his respect for historical tradition, and his own temperament kept him from embracing wholly recent historical criticisms of southern institutions and values. Eaton's was a liberalism of the old school—inclusive, firm but polite, and altogether lacking the tribalism, smugness, and hellfire of the Vietnam generation. Whatever its deficiencies and seemingly outmoded civilities, Eaton's liberal outlook became his principal legacy for students of the southern past.

Eaton was born in Winston, in the tobacco growing Carolina Piedmont, in 1898. By no means wealthy, Eaton's family was solidly middle class and secure financially.[3] "They were both democratic and aristocratic in feelings, manners, culture, and self-esteem," explained Professor Eaton in 1979.[4] In the tradition of several early southern historians, Eaton's forebears had strong ties to the Old South. The Cliftons in South Carolina were planters, while the Clements and

Eatons in North Carolina were small slaveholders. Eaton's grandfather and great-grandfather served as officers in the Confederate Army.[5] Two forces—Eaton's family and his educational experiences at the University of North Carolina and at Harvard—were most instrumental in shaping the historian's liberal views.

Forced to earn his own way through the university at Chapel Hill, Eaton's father instilled in his son an admiration for hard work and a strong competitive spirit.[6] Looking back over his life, Eaton credited his father with inspiring in him "the desire for distinction, for winning honor rather than devoting . . . [his] life to the acquisition of money or to the pursuit of pleasure."[7] The senior Eaton spent several years teaching, then moved to Winston-Salem where he became an accountant to a tobacco manufacturing firm, then mayor of the community and a real estate broker.[8] Eaton recalls fondly when, in the racially tense era of Jim Crow, Mayor Eaton greeted Booker T. Washington at the Winston-Salem train station.

> I remember vividly hearing my father introduce Booker T. Washington to the audience in a large theatre in Winston-Salem. I was then, I think, twelve years old. The great Negro educator spoke to a segregated audience, the blacks sitting in the gallery. He did not seem to mind speaking to a segregated audience. My father . . . was popular with black audiences to whom he was invited frequently to speak in churches and colleges. They called him "the mare," and were profuse in compliments.[9]

From his father, young Eaton gained a strong sense of sympathy for the underdog.[10] There was a vast difference between a patriarchal regard for the Negro and accepting him as a social and political equal. Years later, writing of his early racial views, Eaton recalled with his characteristic candor, "I accepted the ideas of my parents and friends about the Negro but I was wrong and it is the path of a good historian to search the truth and change his ideas with new evidence."[11]

From his parents Eaton also inherited a love for literature and the arts. According to Eaton's brother, their father "could quote more poetry from the entire English tradition than anyone I have ever met." Young Clement's intellectual and artistic interests derived, too, from his mother, an accomplished painter. Together, Eaton's parents tutored their son in what historian Albert D. Kirwan has referred to as "a curious mixture of stern Calvinism in religion and liberal principles in politics."[12] Slowly Eaton's liberalism took form. Reflecting in 1979 on the gradual growth of his mind, the historian defined his liberal creed as including sympathy for the downtrodden, "the preservation of civil liberties, especially freedom of expression," and "a catholic point of view as regards social questions and . . . fundamentalism in religion." These elements in Eaton's thought were shaped and sharpened in the stimulating academic centers at Chapel Hill and Cambridge.[13]

Eaton entered the University of North Carolina in 1915 and Harvard five years later. These schools left so profound an impact on the young scholar that in 1964 he dedicated the revised edition of his first book to his two alma maters.[14]

At Chapel Hill, Eaton reveled in the intellectual ferment then emerging at the university. The atmosphere there demanded academic honesty,[15] stimulated inquiry, and encouraged dissent. As a sophomore at North Carolina, explains Eaton, "I . . . [was] liberated from orthodox religion . . . but I was careful not to broadcast my heterodox opinions."[16] As an undergraduate, he "belonged to a group of young liberals who felt that they had emancipated themselves from the shackles of old authority. We were innocents . . . living in a changing world that we did not understand."[17]

First among those teachers who nurtured Eaton's skepticism was Professor Horace Williams. The iconoclastic Williams, dubbed "the gadfly of Chapel Hill,"[18] taught Eaton philosophy and logic. From English professor Edwin Greenlaw, the young Carolinian gained an appreciation for fine exposition. Eaton esteemed Greenlaw's "vast scorn for superficial thinking and sloppy work." Under the tutelage of Norman Foerster, a student of American literature, Eaton came to admire the writings of Henry David Thoreau and Ralph Waldo Emerson. After reading and rereading the New England Transcendentalists he became imbued with the spirit of the individualist.[19] This remained Eaton's foremost trait.

Like many historians before and after him, as an undergraduate Eaton majored in English. During his senior year at Chapel Hill, he roomed in the ramshackle "Old Inn," next to a student destined to become one of America's foremost novelists, Thomas Wolfe. Although he never knew Wolfe intimately, Eaton recalled vividly his behavior at the dining table in Swain Hall: "We were constantly passing food to him, for his appetite was huge and his manners Rabelaisian."[20] In the fall of 1920, Eaton, having received the A.B. and A.M. in English at North Carolina, joined Wolfe in the graduate school at Harvard. Unlike Wolfe, Eaton elected to pursue a doctorate in history, not English. Like Wolfe, Eaton entered the national culture. He would always retain his love and concern for the South, but his Harvard experience and subsequent teaching in the North would free him from the provincialism and defensiveness characteristic of so many other southern scholars of his generation.

Harvard opened new horizons for Eaton. By the 1920s, the university's history program—featuring such scholars as Frederick Jackson Turner, Edward Channing, Samuel Eliot Morison, Roger Merriman, and Arthur M. Schlesinger—ranked among the nation's best. Not only had Harvard's history department surpassed Johns Hopkins's as the premier training ground for historians, but also the entire graduate school was unsurpassed in what was then coming to be called the "social sciences."[21] At Harvard, Eaton learned quickly the difference "between the easy standards of a southern university and the sophistication and intellectual competition among students in a great graduate school."[22] He gained a newfound appreciation for factual detail and a corresponding wariness of facile generalizations. Eaton's Harvard education also extended beyond the classroom. Whether at the Fogg Museum, Boston's Repertory Theatre, or "Old Howard" burlesque theatre, Eaton was broadened considerably by his years in Cambridge.[23]

During his Harvard years, Eaton's liberalism was aroused by one of the key culture conflicts of the 1920s: the Scopes trial of 1925. Already skeptical of religious orthodoxy, Eaton pitied William Jennings Bryan, the symbol of funda-mentalism in the evolution controversy. In May 1925, the graduate student re-corded his views of Bryan after having heard the great silver-tongued orator speak on evolution. Eaton particularly objected to Bryan's imprecise logic and faulty judgments. Writing to his mother back in North Carolina, Eaton complained:

> I am sorry to say that . . . [Bryan] did not adopt the right attitude toward his subject, "Evolution." Instead of treating it in a serious fair-minded way, he ridiculed the supporters of it and told one joke right after the other without giving any clear logical argument against it. I heard Bryan once when his eyes flashed and his voice was resonant and magnificent, but this time he had a hunted look and his voice was strained and high-pitched. I had hoped that he would rise to the occasion in battling with the best minds of this generation and give us some thoughtful and keen criticisms of the scientific theory. My impression of Bryan was that he was intensely sincere, but that his mind was rambling and mediocre. His heart has always been on the right side in the great questions that have confronted the nation, but he has usually erred in his solution. I have the feeling that he does not study and carefully meditate on the problems which face him. Consequently his oratory lacks the solid sub-soil of effort and ref[l]ection.[24]

As a graduate student, Eaton determined to build his own work on the bed-rock of effort and reflection. At Harvard, he developed an almost implacable, critical spirit. Doctoral training sharpened his analytical powers, no doubt, but without dulling his enthusiasm or ambition. Under the tutelage of Frederick Merk, then in the seedtime of his own successful historical career, Eaton chose to write a dissertation on intellectual freedom in the Old South. It was a difficult and unwieldy topic. However diffuse, the subject appealed to Eaton's growing concern over the fate of liberalism in America.

For Eaton, studying the freedom-of-thought struggle in the antebellum South enabled him to probe the growth and wane of liberalism in his native region. Eaton looked back with affection to what he deemed the golden age of southern history—the late eighteenth and early nineteenth centuries. In these years, he argued, southerners welcomed discussion and tolerated dissent. In contrast were the decades that culminated in the South's secession. This was a period when the southern mind became clouded, then closed, by proslavery politicians and ideo-logues. "I was strongly attracted to the Jeffersonian ideas in the liberal period of Southern history," explained Eaton, "and repelled by the illiberal period preced-ing the Civil War."[25] Merk shared his student's enthusiasm, but urged Eaton to interpret his subject broadly. The dissertation, advised Merk, should go beyond the slavery question alone to treat freedom of religious, political, and social discussion as well.[26]

Aside from assisting Eaton in shaping his thesis, Professor Merk also helped him refine his literary style. According to Albert D. Kirwan, "It was under Merk's guidance that Eaton perfected his clear, lucid style, with its cogent simplicity, its well-balanced sentences, its spontaneous power."[27] Writing to his pupil, Merk urged Eaton to strive for simplicity in literary form. "The great masterpieces of art in whatever field," explained Merk, "are magnificent in their simplicity and in the completeness of their fusion of use and ornament. Your ornament lies a little on the surface—it is too clearly ornament in many cases, and particularly you use too many adjectives."[28] By late 1928, when Eaton had completed his dissertation, Merk expressed pride in his student's achievement. It was, wrote Merk, "much the best thesis that has been prepared under my care at Harvard."[29] So impressed was Merk with Eaton's manuscript that in 1934 he chided his former student for having not yet published it. "In these days of suppression of free speech and free opinion everywhere in the regimented states of Europe," stated Merk, "a study of a similar condition in our own South would be particularly well timed."[30] Six years later—having broadened both his focus and research—Eaton published his award-winning *Freedom of Thought in the Old South*.[31]

Unlike his early years, the remainder of Eaton's teaching and publishing career is much better known. Eaton's northern sojourn continued for many years after his graduation from Harvard. After brief teaching appointments at Whitman College and Clark University, in 1930 Eaton joined the faculty at Lafayette College in Easton, Pennsylvania, where he rose in rank to professor of history. In 1946, he finally came home to the South. Two persuasive Kentuckians, Professor Thomas D. Clark and J. Winston Coleman, lured Eaton to the University of Kentucky.[32] He stayed at Kentucky for twenty-two years, until his retirement as Professor Emeritus in 1968.[33] While teaching at Kentucky, Eaton, along with Professors Kirwan and Clark, established one of the region's better doctoral programs in southern history and helped to make Lexington a congenial haven for moderate and liberal southern scholars.

Eaton's own reputation also soared during his tenure at Kentucky. His textbook on the Old South, first published in 1949, has gone through three editions and ranks as the seminal work on the subject.[34] His *History of the Southern Confederacy* (1954) is considered by many Civil War specialists to be the best and most balanced military account of the South in the war.[35] In 1957, Eaton published a highly readable and remarkably concise biography of Kentucky nationalist Henry Clay.[36] According to one reviewer, "Objective balance and judicious evaluation are maintained throughout this book, and it is clear that Mr. Eaton admires the great Westerner, though one suspects that he would not have joined the Clay camp."[37] Four years later, in *The Growth of Southern Civilization*,[38] Eaton synthesized the fruits of his many years of research in the social and economic history of his native region. In many ways, this book placed Eaton on a par with Ulrich Bonnell Phillips, considered by many to have been the foremost historian of the antebellum South. Reviewing another of Eaton's books, *The Mind of the Old South*,[39] historian Carl N. Degler argued that "No historian of the South since U.B. Phillips has been as productive and has commanded as unrivaled a knowledge of the sources of antebellum southern history as Clement Eaton."[40] Yet as much as Eaton's work demands comparison with Phillips's, the former historian surpassed the latter by focusing upon such seriously neglected subjects as southern urban and cultural life, and the Old South's forgotten people—the middle and lower classes, women, and the handicapped.[41]

In addition to publishing three other books, including a biography of Jefferson Davis,[42] Eaton contributed more than a score of articles to scholarly journals.[43] His outstanding publishing record brought Eaton many rewards, including visiting teaching appointments at Wisconsin, Princeton, and Columbia, as well as Fulbright and Guggenheim Fellowships. In 1968–1969, he served as Pitt Professor of American History at Cambridge University.[44] Among Eaton's highest tributes was his election in 1961 as president of the Southern Historical Association. Breaking with tradition, the historian used his presidential address—ostensibly on Professor James Woodrow and academic freedom in the 1880s—as a platform from which to challenge his peers to assume "a bold and courageous stand on the integration of the races in our educational system. I refer," Eaton continued, "particularly to immediate integration in our colleges and universities and to gradual integration in our schools."[45] He implored historians no longer to ignore racial discrimination, "for it now has reached the point of interfering with the free trade of ideas in our profession."[46] Clearly viewing the historian not as a passive narrator of previous events, Eaton interpreted his role broadly, as an agent of social change. On the race question, at least, historians were to do more than simply "teach and write history but also to influence even in a small degree, the course of future history."[47]

Eaton's liberal views most likely shocked those conservative white southern historians who came to Chattanooga to hear a historical address, not a polemic on the civil rights question. At least the southern press expressed outrage. According to the *Chattanooga News-Free Press,* in his speech Eaton "slipped disturbingly away from education and into the realm of opinion with an outcry promoting racial integration."[48] In an editorial entitled "Quackery, Not History," Charleston's *News and Courier* condemned Eaton for "making sociological quackery with the posture and attitude of scholarship."[49] First, the editor was astounded with Eaton's ahistorical perspective. "Only by ignoring constitutional history," he wrote, "could this historian-by-vocation pass indifferently by the infamy that was the 1954 [*Brown v. the Board of Education of Topeka, Kansas*] integration opinion."[50] Professor Eaton also was charged with being "oblivious to crime statistics, to the deplorable conditions of integrated schools" in the North, and having succumbed to "the myth of racial equality." In conclusion, the editor cautioned his readers to beware of scholars like Eaton—"who so misuse the dignity and integrity of their calling."[51] It was, of course, that very dignity and integrity of his profession that Eaton sought to enlist in the cause of southern liberalism.

By today's standards, Eaton was anything but a radical; indeed, his liberalism was already dated and even "quaint" in the 1970s. Eaton's courtly manners, stately bearing, and respect for tradition gave him the appearance of a southern Bourbon, but his writing proved otherwise. Throughout a long teaching and writing career, he exhibited a constant forward-looking, liberal view. As a young man, he accepted uncritically his society's prejudice concerning black inferiority and the "proper" social order. As a mature scholar, Eaton came to condemn racial injustice. Increasingly during the 1960s, Eaton assailed segregation and came to appreciate southern history from the perspective of the blacks. In his revisions of earlier works—especially *The Freedom-of-Thought Struggle in the Old South* (1964) and *The Mind of the Old South* (rev. ed., 1967)—Eaton accorded attention to black thought and attacked slavery and prejudice more forthrightly than ever before.

Fortunately for students of southern historiography, Eaton left manuscript diaries of three research trips in the lower South in 1935, 1946, and 1953.[52] Not written for publication, these diaries reveal Eaton's private thoughts and reflections. The diaries provide valuable insights into the author's persistent fascination with all facets of southern history and culture and, as the products of one so long out of his native South, they reveal Eaton's reacquaintance with the charms and riches of southern life. They also illustrate the slower pace of academic life and the personal contacts that once undergirded the southern historical establishment. Southern food, agriculture, dialect, architecture, design, intrasectional and state differences—these and numerous other features of the South captured Eaton's perceptive eye. Comparison of the diaries with Eaton's writing career points up his growing sensitivity toward black culture and his impatience with southern demagoguery. Still, the "Big House" always struck him more profoundly than the black shanty, and he never entirely sloughed off a liberal paternalism toward poor folks in general and blacks in particular. Even in his last work, the biography of Jefferson Davis (1977), Eaton displayed a sympathy for the "great men" of the Old South and an awe for the society they built.

Like many diarists, Eaton recorded his random, but often detailed, impressions in a newsy, gossipy style. In other instances, his pen portraits are crisp, precise, and polished. Throughout the diaries Professor Eaton noted both the humorous and the tragic, the unusual and the commonplace. Certain passages, too, illuminate the background behind Eaton's writing projects, such as his research on Professor James Woodrow. What makes his diaries of special importance is the manner in which Eaton weaves the history of his native region into a personal odyssey through the New South.

The three diaries are reproduced here in their entirety. Eaton's original spelling, capitalization, and punctuation are retained with all their irregularities. For the sake of clarity, endmarks are supplied where they were lacking in Eaton's texts. Any other editorial additions or emendations are set in brackets. The diaries are published here with the kind permission of Mrs. Allis Eaton Bennett, Professor Eaton's literary executrix, and the Department of Special Collections, University of Kentucky, where the diaries are deposited.

Travels in the Deep South in 1935

In the late summer of 1935 I left Atlanta by a slow train for Montgomery Alabama. We travelled over a rough hill country in Georgia made of red soil. Several small towns and villages lay on our route, such as Lagrange, Lanette, and West Point. Some large cotton mills vitalized the existence of these interior villages of the South. In the purely agricultural villages, the chief thrill of the day was watching the train pull into the station and let off a few passengers and drop the evening newspapers. I have never seen the train pass by negroes working in the fields without their stopping their work to gaze at the train.

After we crossed the Chattahoochee River, we had arrived at the Promised Land of Alabama. We passed through Opelika and other towns bearing strangely-sounding Indian names. After we left Auburn, Alabama, we saw negroes picking cotton in the fields. They did not seem to be in a hurry. They were wearing nondescript clothes mostly blue over-alls, but I saw one picturesque darky with a brilliant red shirt. I saw wicker baskets of cotton in the fields and cotton piled on the porch floors of negro shanties. The cotton pickers were of all ages, sizes, and of both sexes.

In the Montgomery newspapers I read that the Communists are seeking to organize a strike among the cotton pickers of Alabama.[53] The negroes are now getting 40¢ a hundred pounds, but the Communists wish them to demand $1, a hundred pounds, or strike. As a result of the disturbance over organizing the Negroes one negro has been killed and two wounded. The whites are very much incensed at such foreign interference in the labor question.

I was told by a gentleman connected with the *Montgomery Advertizer* that the Communist drive was really a racket by which to exploit the negro. He was threatened with violence if he did not join the organization and pay the dues, which are pocketed by the agitators. I talked to Miss Frances Hails,[54] the archivist at the Capitol, about the situation. She declared that Lowndes County where the disturbance has broken out contains a population of about 80% negroes. The whites there will not put up with any foolishness and some of the agitators will be killed if they continue their work of meddling with the negroes. Such language and such an attitude is an echo from the days when the Abolitionists tried to interfere with the southern race problem. I heard native Alabamians speaking of "the ruling white race."

As we approached Montgomery, I noticed the unmistakable sign of the deep South—the appearance of Spanish moss drooping from the trees. The land became more level and the soil changed its red color. The rural districts seemed to be inhabited almost entirely by negroes.

Montgomery is a delightful old southern town—apparently not too intent upon making money. It is dominated by one of the loveliest public buildings in the South, the Capitol. This fine old building stands on a hill at the end of the principal street, a wide spacious street of paved bricks. It has recently been painted white by the federal funds of Roosevelt's administration. (Atlanta has also benefited by federal aid in having the Capitol of Georgia scraped and cleaned.) The Montgomery Capitol gleams softly between its grove of elms and its shrubbery. It is old in appearance and yet it is youthful. The large white columns are perfect in proportions and the corinthian and Ionic capitals are beautiful. Montgomery has palmettoes, oleanders, and flourishing magnolia trees that betoken a southern climate. I stood on the porch of the Capitol on the exact spot where Jefferson Davis delivered his inaugural address as president of the Confederate States. The Capitol grounds are defaced by only two monuments, one colossal monument to the Confederate soldiers, and another queer monument to a Confederate surgeon, John Wyeth.[55] The Capitol grounds at Atlanta, however, have two exceedingly undignified statues, one of Tom Watson[56] with his coattails flying as he delivers a passionate gesture and the other of Gov. Joe Brown[57] and his wife. Joe Brown and Tom Watson both were leaders and idols of the common man—Brown before the Civil War and Watson during the Populist movement of the 1880s and 1890s.

I talked a great deal with the archivist at the state capitol about Alabama and Alabamians. She told me when the stars fell on Alabama—Dec. 13, 1833. She told me how chagrinned Alabama was that Duke University invaded the country[58] and bought the priceless manuscripts of Clement C. Clay.[59] Finally, she described how quickly Carl Carmer,[60] the author of *Stars Fell on Alabama,* had to flee the country, without staying for his hat or telling his wife good-bye, owing to his personal conduct—immorality with a co-ed. She admitted that Carmer was right on one thing. He had told the truth about the "Cajuns." This strange people (a mixture of Creole and negro stock) represented a deplorable problem of Alabama. One Cajun family might have one child as white as the purest Caucasian while another would be as black as a negro. They were a proud, sensitive people, who withdrew from contact with strangers. Miss Hails declared that before she would marry into one of the families around Mobile she would scrutinize closely the family tree. Only recently the leading honor student in one of Mobile's high schools, a girl, was proven to be a "Cajun" and forced to abandon the school without receiving the merited honor.

I take my meals at the dilapidated home of an old, gray-haired lady, Miss Mary Moore. She has not the slightest desire to make money apparently. She loads her table with a profusion of food and charges the ridiculous sums of 20¢ for a liberal breakfast, 30¢ for dinner, and 25¢ for supper. People in the South, especially if they are of the old school, have dinner at noon instead of in the evening.

Montgomery has some attractive old houses—rather neglected and decaying. The Pollard house is now used as a transient home. It has immense white columns supporting the roof of the porch; the capitals are painted brown. Several old homes are on Adams Street, where I am living. Most of these antebellum homes have magnificent magnolia trees in the yard and crepe myrtles that have grown to be large trees.

The federal government has undertaken a very fine task of photographing most of the old homes in Alabama. I studied most of these pictures & chose the Gorgas home at Tuscaloosa, as the model for my future home. It is brick and has a double porch, the upper story of which is approached by graceful winding stairs. Most of the imposing homes built before the war in Alabama were constructed after the planters had attained wealth, especially in the decade of 1850. Alabama was not a state until 1819, and then it was largely wilderness.

The style of architecture here differs from the Georgian homes of the Valley of the James in Virginia. It is largely Greek revival—some homes are adaptations of the Parthenon. This style is very imposing, but not particularly homelike. The houses were built of wood, and consequently many of them look very dilapidated & in need of fresh paint. In fact, the whole South suffers from a scarcity of paint—except on the cheeks of the women.

Inside these houses of the Greek revival, there is a good deal of ornamentation of stucco. Some of them have black marble mantels imported from Italy, while others have beautiful classic mantels made of wood. I prefer the latter.

Montgomery has a very modern side as well as retaining the relics of old days. Her residential sections contain beautiful and luxurious homes. (Cloverdale & Country Club sections) In the center of town is an attractive fountain, which is peculiarly refreshing to look upon in this warm climate. As a sign of the utilitarian ideal conquering the love of the old—the town councilmen have ordered some of the trees shading the principal street, Dexter Street, leading to the Capitol, to be cut down. Fearing a wave of protest, they stationed a negro with an axe at each tree early one morning and started them simultaneously to destroying the old trees.

I made a special trip to Demopolis, a hundred miles away. Demopolis (City of the People) was founded by a band of French people (1500 in number), Napoleon's old soldiers & officers, who came to Alabama in 1817. They were given a tract of public land on the condition of introducing the cultivation of the olive & the grape vine. I was shown at "Gaineswood" one of these old olive trees that still survives. The experiment was not a success & most of the French soldiers drifted away.

However, one of the beautiful homes of the old South was erected at Demopolis by Col. Nathan Bryan Whitfield.[61] Whitfield was a very wealthy planter who came from North Carolina. He devised the plan of a beautiful home "Gaineswood" according to his own ideas. Inside, some of the rooms remind one of the remains of Pompeii—classic columns and stucco relief on the ceilings—

colored in some cases—beautiful mirrors set in the walls. "Gaineswood" was built in the 1850s.

It is now owned by a Mr. Kirven,[62] formerly a poor boy of Demopolis, who aspired someday to be the lord of "Gaineswood." He made his money in lumber, purchased the old mansion for $30,000.00 and spent $35,000.00 restoring it. One of the huge mirrors, for example, cost $1500.00. The exterior of "Gaineswood" is imposing with its columns, its circular balustrade on top of the roof, and its formal French garden.

In Demopolis is another fine old home, "Bluff Hall," on the banks of the Tombigbee. It is much severer in architectural style than "Gaineswood," with square pillars instead of the usual round fluted columns. I was told that the inheritor of "Bluff Hall" married a divorcee—one night he and she returned from a wild party, and later he found her untrue to him & shot her, her two children & himself. In this beautiful home an unlovely home life must have existed.

I looked at the waters of the Tombigbee River with great interest. Enormous cotton warehouses stand on its banks at Demopolis and here the cotton freighters come from Mobile. The banks are very steep. A short distance above Demopolis the Black Warrior River joins the Tombigbee.

Demopolis is in the heart of the so-called Canebreake or Black Belt—once, this region was covered with dense fields of cane & groves of trees. Now it is great cotton country. The soil is a rich black loam, very fertile. Here the large planters lived and today the population is composed of about one white man to ten negroes. Riding along the road to Demopolis, I saw many gangs of negroes picking cotton. They get 40¢ a hundred pounds (an average picker, 200 lbs. of cotton a day), hence, the exploitation of the negro.

I talked to a negro man picking in the fields who showed me how he did it. He said he could pick 200 lbs a day. Much of the black belt land is now devoted to cattle raising.

Demopolis & Selma are typical country towns of the deep South. These villages consist mostly of small stores that have iron or wooden awnings shading the street held up by iron poles, and the court house. The people move slowly, and call on the negroes at the slightest provocation to run errands, hand them things, etc.

We passed through Uniontown, a tiny village. Here Yancey delivered his greatest speech (in his own judgement) in 1856.[63] Now it is an insignificant place. I did not get to Greensboro, where stands the home of Richmond Pearson Hobson.[64]

In Demopolis I met accidentally on the street the Baptist minister, an alert young man, about my age, I should say. He invited me to lunch and I had a very enjoyable time talking to him. He introduced me to an old negro, "Uncle" Richard Smith, who was a quaint old religious negro. "Uncle Richard" could not read, but he could remember scripture in a garbled fashion. His expressions were "killing" so ludicrous were they. The preacher took a great delight in the idiosyncrasies and humor of this old darky.

On my return I stopped at Lowndesboro, which is an anachronism in these modern days. It has a number of fine old Greek Revival style houses. Here I went through the house of Dixon Hall Lewis,[65] Senator from Alabama in 1848. He weighed 430 lbs & had to have a special chair made for him in the Senate. The house is now occupied by Judge Thomas of the Supreme Court of Alabama & his wife, a descendant of the elephantine Senator.[66] The house was built in 1827 and is very quaint. It has a fine hallway through which the cool breezes can blow. The judge was very cordial & invited me to spend the night with him. Then I visited the Haygood home, which is in a bad state of repair. The family had rather spend money giving the children a college education than fixing up the old house. Finally, I visited the Dixon home—an imposing classical building on the outside but very disappointing within. The master was a hale, weather-beaten man, bald-headed, very jovial. He told me of his forty fox hounds, of the Walker breed, and he blew on his horn made from an antler— which set his dogs to baying & yelping. He said that he owned 6,000 acres of land. He was proud of his little son, seven or eight yrs old, a suntanned little fellow, who had just killed his first bird in flight. He also had a daughter, who was entering Goucher College this fall. Yet there was an unpleasant side to "Bob" Dixon—he had killed, I was told, several Negroes, and he acted as though slavery had never been abolished.

Journal of Travels of a Guggenheim Fellow in the Lower South in 1946

Columbia S.C. Feb. 6, 1946
On my route from Raleigh to Columbia I crossed two of South Carolina's most famous rivers, the Peedee near Cheraw and the Wateree near Camden. At Cheraw I saw many cotton bales piled up in the freight station, and I knew I was in Dixie. Also the station waiting rooms, clearly marked "White" and "Colored," were another indication. I saw very few cattle or horses or pigs on the route between Raleigh & Columbia—a considerable number of peach orchards, how- ever, also pecan trees. Last year's corn and cotton fields were the chief evidence of southern agriculture—a traditional pattern. Frame houses in the country were frequently unpainted. From the car window I could see little of the towns of Cheraw or Camden, but judged them to be rather small; Cheraw has 5,000 people, I was told.

In Columbia I was much impressed with the public market—a low shed extended at great length in the middle of a very wide street (in fact Columbia has very wide streets and a spacious air). Maybe Sherman has conferred this benefit on posterity.[67] I strolled through the market, which appeared to me like an agricultural bazaar of Bagdad—Here were found colorful fruit, temple oranges, cumquats, tangerines, lemons, large apples, bunches of small yellow bananas, pineapples, coconuts, black walnuts, pecans, immense turnips, cauliflowers, string beans, salad greens, carrots, chickens, eggs, and quantities of pine hearts for kindling wood fires.

I secured a room near the University at Senate & Marion Streets, $1.50 a night.

On the train I had heard conversation on inflation and on soldiers who had fondly thought of their families & children, only to learn that their wives wanted a divorce—the result, a victim for the psychopathic hospital.

In Columbia I met my Uncle Jim Hough for the second time in my life. He has been Asst. Attorney General of S.C. for eleven years. He is now 73 years old, deliberate in manner, seldom looks you in the eyes and appears rather lacking in emotion, but possessing a keen sense of dry humor. He looks like my grandmother Hough, who refused to grow old.

He told me about my S.C. relatives and ancestors. My great grandfather, Jesse Chalmers Clifton, lived at Fort Long, (18 miles from Rock Hill) and was a large slaveholder—had 300 slaves. Sent two of his sons, my grandmother's brothers, to the University of Va., & one to Univ. of N.C. The Cliftons were tall people and Uncle Jim says they were Welsh in origin but I question this. He said we are related to the Gastons & that Mama was named after Mary Gaston, a Revolutionary heroine. Other relatives were the Walkers and the Chalmers. My Grandfather Hough, Minor Jackson Hough, was tall, had brown eyes and black hair—was a student of the law—solicitor of a District of four counties, also a county judge after the Civil War—a major in the Confederate army at the close of the Civil War.

Uncle Will, a Phi Kappa Psi at the University of S.C., was described as a handsome man and the most likeable fellow in the world.

Columbia, now a city of over 100,000 people, is near an army camp & the streets at night are flooded with soldiers[68]—the streets are brilliantly lighted—theaters and eating places doing a thriving business.

Rested in the lobby of the modern Wade Hampton Hotel.

Columbia, February 10, 1946

The glimmerings of Spring are apparent—the flowering of the yellow jasmine—of a small white flower on a bush which has a nostalgic fragrance—also a stray dandelion & hyacinth—hundreds of black-birds roosting in the trees in the evening.

I walked down Senate Street this morning and noted a tremendous magnolia tree in an old yard—I have never seen furniture made from magnolia wood—I should like to design a desk made of this peculiarly southern wood.

On Senate Street also is an obelisk erected to the memory of N.G. Gonzales,[69] 1858–1903, the founder and editor of *The State,* founded in 1891, South Carolina's largest newspaper to-day. It was placed there by subscriptions of the citizens. Gonzales, I understand, was a fighting liberal, whose newspaper crusaded for public education and social reform—he was anti-imperialist and bitterly opposed to the Tillman crowd—The inscription on the monument praises him for his great courage. He was killed by a Tillman follower.[70]

Throughout the city are iron placards commemorating historic events & persons—near my rooming house is one in honor of General Maxcy Gregg,[71] a leader in the Southern Rights movement—one in front of the University tells how the name South Carolina College was changed to University of S.C. when the institution was reopened after the war in 1865, then changed back to S.C. College, then changed again to the University of S.C.[72]

South Carolinians apparently believed in doing things unanimously—unanimous in adopting secession ordinance—unanimously the student body of S.C. College volunteered in 1861; when Preston Brooks[73] beat Charles Sumner[74] & a resolution to expel him was defeated in Congress he resigned & was *unanimously* reelected to his seat.

In the South Caroliniana Library, (an attractive old building with columns, 1840) there is a marble placard, a tribute to Brooks who died in 1857, the year after he beat Sumner—Brooks was young at the time, born in 1819—he had remorse for this stupid deed.

The University of S.C. has a quadrangle of plain brick buildings painted gray—dominated by the new library at one end of the quadrangle—the buildings are named after the great men connected with the institution—Maxcy College, Rutledge College, the Chapel 1805, planned by Robert Mills,[75] Petigru College (law), Pinckney College, etc.

There is a huge girls' dormitory recently constructed and some new naval buildings; the old gymnasium at the end of Sumter St has a facade like a Roman temple; the stadium is a modest field with wooden benches.

I talked at length with Prof. Davis, head of the English Dept., who lives in one of the gray brick houses facing the campus.[76] He is a grandson of Prof Joseph Le Conte,[77] and he is a very genial and modest old gentleman who has taught here for 45 years. He taught one year in the University of Washington but he wanted to devote his services to his own people & state, and thus return[ed] to become a living part of the old university.

I have been working on the papers of Prof. James Woodrow[78] who was dismissed from his position as Professor of Natural Science in connexion with Revelation in Columbia Theological Seminary in 1884, because he taught the doctrine of evolution. I have been in his home, a large brick structure on Sumter St, now used as the home of the Richland County Library. He became President of S.C. College 1891–97.

I understand that [in South Carolina] there are state-supported traveling libraries for the counties—an excellent idea—also no sales tax in S.C. such as there is in N.C.

I heard the artist Rockwell Kent[79] speak here—although he is 64 yrs old he is very vital—his youth renewed by fighting for the cause of labor—he spoke in behalf of art for every one—told a delightful story from Hans Christian Anderson "The Emperors Clothes"—to illustrate the necessity of the people stating frankly their likes & dislikes of pictures—his view of art is that a man in love with life wants to talk about it through the medium of art—an enthusiast who says "Look!" Art is different from a photograph as the editorial page is from the news page.

Columbia Feb 11, 1946
Still working hard on the papers & publications of "James Woodrow, Champion of Evolution in the South."

Saw the First Baptist Church where the secession convention first met. It is an impressive building of the Greek Revival style—in form of a Greek Temple with massive columns & no steeple. Fitting that the secession convention should meet in such a building.

At Caldwell's Friendly Cafeteria (supposed to be one of the best eating places in the city) I met a Mr Callison[80] the other Asst. Attorney General—he had recently killed a hog on his place about 12 miles from here. He stoutly defended the poll tax qualification for voting—said it did not prevent people from voting—it is law for every one to pay the poll tax regardless of whether they vote—resented pressure groups in North to repeal—the measure to repeal passed the state senate but [was] defeated in the house—present requirements for voting in addition to poll tax—read the state const. or give a reasonable interpretation of it, *or* own $300 worth of property. Callison said present Atty General[81] has been in office 20 yrs—although one party system obtains, there is division within the party. [He] said that in some S.C. counties the property tax was almost nominal—a sales tax only on luxuries like cigarettes 3¢ a pack & cosmetics—South Carolina has a rural philosophy.

Talked with Uncle Jim—he believes in [the] Baptist Church because it is a true democracy—apparently believes in Hell. Says Houghs were very sensitive and high-strung people. I think he is very saving of his nickels and conservative. Lives very plainly and cheaply.

Placard in front of the University of South Carolina: "Chartered 1801, as the S.C. College; Opened Jan 10, 1805; Entire Student body volunteered for Confederate Service, 1861; Soldiers Hospital, 1862–65; Reorganized as University of S.C., 1865; Radical Control, 1873–77; Closed, 1877–80; College of Agriculture and Mechanic Arts, 1880–82; S.C. College, 1882–87; University of S.C. 1887–90; S.C. College, 1890–1905; U. of S.C. 1906. Faithful index to the ambitions and Fortunes of the State" written by Mrs Meriwether,[82] wife of Head of History Dept.

Talked to Attorney General of S.C.—called "General"—a very fat man with a mane of white hair—twirled his glasses as he talked—had enormous pair of "britches" on—a mediocre man who for 20 yrs has been reelected to his post. Shares prejudices of his state—South Carolinians are obsessed with the idea of repelling outside interference with their conduct of affairs—"the General" seemed convinced of the need of keeping the negroes in their place—I heard him refer to Tillman—I wonder if the shadow of the dead Tillman still troubles the state.

I went out to see "Millbank," the home of Wade Hampton II[83] & III,[84] built before 1820. Only six tall white columns in a semi-ruined condition are standing after Sherman burned the place. They (made of brick, with white stucco over them, fluted) stand at the foot of an avenue, behind which a modern white house has been erected. On the way out I talked with the widow Rucker,[85] widow of an old prof in the University. She said her husband was doubtful whether N.C. was a southern state, & in North Alabama Florence, her home, they hated the people of East Tennessee who had invaded the area and committed outrages.

I also strolled through the graveyard of Old Trinity Episcopal Church, where the generations of the Hamptons are buried, also Dr Thomas Cooper,[86] Henry Timrod,[87] W.C. Prestons,[88] & the Mannings[89]—a repository of the bones of governors, senators, and generals of the state.

On the capitol grounds opposite is the statue of General Wade Hampton on a stallion—the general appears very dignified—the stallion's provocative append-age painted red, probably by some irreverent student—a country wit who was looking at this defacement said to me—the Confederate general's horse "had been shot in the balls."

Also on the capitol grounds is a young cork tree recently planted to encourage the domestication of the cork tree in S.C.

The wide streets of Columbia I am told are not the result of Sherman's destruc-tion,[90] but the planning of the city by the state when it was laid off in 1786.

There is a very interesting bust of Dr Thomas Cooper in the South Car-olinia[na] Library—looks like a man of great will and decisiveness—his dome peculiarly square & bald—made of cement.

More conversations with Uncle Will. He spoke of the inherited bashfulness of the Houghs—my grandfather was not a mixer and rather diffident except when he spoke before a jury and then he was a power.

I talked with Mr Salley[91] who is in charge of the state archives—a very old gentleman who is supposed to be very learned in S.C. history. He maintains the battle of King's Mountain was fought in S.C. although [the] town of King's Mountain is in N.C.[92]—stoutly maintains Jackson [was] born in S.C. & it is doubtful whether President Polk was born in N.C. or S.C.

Augusta, Ga., Feb 13, 1946
In coming from Columbia to Augusta I noted peach and pecan orchards, cotton and corn fields—houses covered as a rule with tin—no basements—Passed through Graniteville, near Aiken & Augusta—a fine school built by the cotton mill company. Graniteville in the Old South set the pattern of the paternalism of the southern cotton Mill[93]—Vaucluse, near Graniteville, is another cotton mill town and textile factories, I am told, form a large part of the industrial activity of Augusta. As we neared the Savannah River saw large numbers of cypress trees standing in swamps covered with Spanish moss—the Savannah, a muddy river no larger than the Delaware at Easton.[94]

At the Columbia station I talked to a soldier who had just come from

Burma—he had taken so much atabrine to ward off malaria that he became yellow in color. He was impressed with the miserable living conditions of the people in that country—saw people lying dead on the streets from starvation. Said much of the land was undeveloped—needed irrigation, but the British do not want to invest large sums, for fear that they will lose India & Burma.

Augusta has unusually spacious streets shaded by trees and a nice business district. I rode out to the resort hotels and walked to the famous golf course. On the way I passed many beautiful large homes with columns—and beautiful lawns. In the middle of Feb. the lawns were green, robins were flying about, daffodils, hyacinths, japonica, and especially red camelias—looking much like roses.

Talked with a man on the bus who says Gene Tallmadge[95] the demagogue, did many good things—reduced car licenses or tags from $12.50 to $3.00, made taxes very low on small homesteads and farms. Predictions are he will win the next election.

Athens Ga Feb 14, 1946
I regretted leaving Augusta, which seemed to me a nice town. I wonder if the beautiful residences were built by Yankees who made their money from soap, iron, bath fixtures, coal, cement, etc. Probably so—but the homes were attractive nevertheless.

In Augusta I talked to an old fellow who sat at the same table with me in the S & W Cafeteria. He was opposed to our government loaning the British government a dime—opposed to feeding Europe, which made a business of war. Was also strongly anti-Roosevelt—said "Gene" Tallmadge, the old demagogue, was the leader of the anti-Roosevelt forces. Tallmadge's strength is in the rural districts—he gets the vote of the "wool hat boys" by chewing tobacco and wearing red galluses.

Georgia has just broken a tradition by electing a woman to Congress—it is charged that she won her election by the C.I.O. [Congress of Industrial Organizations] and *Negro vote.*[96]

I rode by bus to Athens—passed through the village of Thomson where Tom Watson, the Populist leader, lived and through the village of Washington, the home of Robert Toombs.[97] The latter had a rather garish court-house and the town was not romantic-looking—at least from the bus windows.

Athens is built on red hills. The University is in the heart of the town—a nucleus of old buildings—some of them brick, painted gray as at S.C., and others red; [I saw] two nice old buildings which housed the literary societies. These institutions played a great role in the college life of the Old South.[98] In addition to the old campus there are many new buildings—especially an enormous Navy Pre-Flight School, a big gymnasium, and a big stadium. Apparently the University is providing culture for the masses.

I talked to a nice young man, a returned veteran, a graduate of the College of Charleston, who told me that his college was superior to the University of S.C. in giving a liberal arts education. Tuition is free to residents of Charleston and Charleston County.

Athens, February 15, 1946

Had a nice talk and lunch with Mr Coulter, head of the History Dept.[99] He spoke in bitter terms of Tallmadge—described the ousting of Chester Destler from his job in a small college near Savannah, for using books on the Negro which were liberal.[100] Said that Tallmadge in lowering the price of license tags conferred a great boon on trucking corporations.

Saw the Georgia football players initiate some players into the monogram club—a thoroughly rah rah spectacle in the middle of the street, strapping them with belts on their bended rears—dropping eggs from a balcony on their heads—this university must be crazy about foot-ball. Some of the players looked as though they read only the comics.

Athens has white columns everywhere—on the porches of the large houses on Milledge Ave, on the churches & business buildings and on the college buildings the Greek temple form is seen frequently.

Met an attractive young man in [the] History Dept named Walter Martin,[101] a PhD from University of N.C. who wrote a history of the territory of Florida & now is working on a biography of Flagler.[102]

Milledgeville Ga, February 16, 1946

Left Athens at 1 o-clock. Yesterday evening I rode on the bus down Milledge Ave in Athens, the home of the aristocrats—white columns! white columns! On the way to Milledgeville passed through Eatonton, the home of Joel Chandler Harris.[103] Talked with one of the residents, who told me that none of the Eatons were living there now. The town has several small industries, an aluminum plant, a brick plant, etc.—illustrating the decentralization of industry possible as a result of extension of electricity into the country. Also saw a fence for cattle consisting of a single wire charged with electricity.

Arrived at Milledgeville and secured a room in the principal hotel—a miserable and filthy place, similar to the antebellum taverns described by Olmsted.[104]

Nevertheless, the town is a charming old town of Middle Georgia, the capital of the state from its founding in 1804 until the end of the Civil War—The Capitol building was not destroyed by Sherman's troops. It is a unique state house in the South, since it is Gothic in architecture with a crenellated wall. It is now occupied by the Georgia Military Academy, a prep school. The price of tuition and board, between $700 and $800, makes it one of the cheapest military schools in the country. Milledgeville is also the location of the Georgia State College for Women—having an enrollment of 1200 girls—very cheap—$4½ per month for room. J.C. Bonner, one of the younger writers on southern history, teaches there—a splendid person.[105]

He drove me to "Mount Nebo" the plantation of Governor David Brodie

Mitchell, a former Indian agent & after his governorship implicated in illicit slave smuggling.[106] The plantation has some very interesting gates or portals of round brick columns, covered with stucco. The avenue to the mansion is lined with cedars an[d] yuccas—Bonner said the avenues of cedars were an outgrowth of southern nationalism. The house was recently burned—Bonner said that the cause for the burning of so many of the fine old antebellum homes was the defective chimneys, which were built in the house and the failure to use enough brick. In Va, however, the chimneys were usually built outside of the houses.

We drove back along the Sparta road and saw the old Crowley Place, an unpainted house with an unpretending porch and detached kitchen connected by a covered porch.

Much of Georgia's red Piedmont land is eroded and abandoned. Bonner drove me a few miles out of Milledgeville and showed me the famous gulley described by Sir Charles Lyell in his *Second Visit to the United States*.[107] It has grown wider with the passing of time.

We also saw the original building and site of Oglethorpe University, where Sidney Lanier[108] studied and Prof James Woodrow taught—a plain brick structure which is now used for a private hospital for mental cases. Oglethorpe University passed out of existence during the Civil War. Years later it was revived in name and transferred to Atlanta.

Bonner also showed me the fine home of Herschel V. Johnson,[109] the opponent of secession, a large Greek revival home which during the Depression was purchased for $2,750.

Milledgeville is the site of the state insane asylum, with a population of 9,000 people as compared to 26,000 for the town, of whom 1200 are the college girls. Also the town has a model boys reformatory.

From Milledgeville I rode by bus to Macon. Macon is a city built on hills. It has wide streets, a modern-looking business district, and a remarkable classic auditorium. My principal excursion was to Mercer University, a collection of Victorian buildings with several modern structures. Talked to John Carter Mathews,[110] the American historian there, who is full of ideas. He described Macon as a decadent matriarchy where a man under 50 was regarded as a young man. Mercer has about 500 students and did not impress me favorably.

The Dean of the Law School, a man named Feild,[111] a Carolina man, said there is no liberalism in the New South.

From Macon I rode by train to Atlanta along the Ocmulgee River. An old fellow on the train told me how the boll weevil has caused his father to change from cotton to peaches, but he was unlucky in this adventure on account of diseases and low prices. Also pecans have bad & good years.

In Atlanta I went to ten hotels before I could get a room for the night. Atlanta is a hustling large city, not very different from a Northern city. I went out to Decatur several times to work in the Columbia Theological Seminary on the faculty records in the Woodrow controversy over evolution. I had to put in a telephone call to Davidson College to the president of the Seminary to get permission to use the Seminary archives.

From Atlanta to Montgomery I rode in an old-fashioned coach. Saw eroded red fields—time changed one hour back after leaving Atlanta. At Opelika (could see Alabama Polytechnic at Auburn) as we approached Montgomery, noticed many deserted Negro shacks—was told that the Negroes had left the black belt permanently. The movement began during and after World War No 1—first to Memphis and Maryville, and from there to Detroit, Chicago, & points north.

Feb 24, 1946

Montgomery has become the capital of a cattle country. All around the level or slightly rolling dark earth is no longer in cotton but furnishes nourishment for thousands of black and red and white herds of cattle. Also a considerable number of pigs can be seen "rooting."

Alabama, I understand, is one of the most progressive states in the Union in developing public health service.

The town is somewhat affected now by the proximity of Maxwell Field, the great army aviation camp.

I rode through the residential district, "Cloverdale," [and] saw the governor's mansion, an unattractive stone Victorian mansion, and some beautiful new homes with azaleas and other attractive shrubs and flowers in the lawns.

I rode with some friends to Troy, fifty miles from Montgomery, and to Brundige—typical little Alabama towns.

The capitol grounds now have some beautiful dignified new state buildings since I was last here—a Public Highway Building and a building for the Department of Archives and History.

In this building I did some work in the Charles and James A. Tait Papers.[112]

Rode by bus to Tuskeegee, an hour away. The country contained some black soil as well as red soil—pecan orchards, cattle, and cotton fields. The juxtaposition of red land and gray soil was curious.

Tuskeegee has a number of old homes of the Greek Revival type, some sadly in need of paint, others well cared for.

I met a lawyer in Tuskeegee, a graduate of Emory University, who was the attorney for Tuskeegee Institute. He told me that race relations were excellent—but they were determined to uphold white supremacy—since the Negro population was 7 to one over the white population.

Walked out to Tuskeegee Inst—one mile out—The University is run by mulattoes—very light in color.

Talked with a sociol[o]gist, Coe,[113] a crippled mulatto with a high excited voice and highly active mind—a Communist. Also Robert Reid,[114] professor of history, a very light mulatto with a facile personality. Talked with him about his thesis, "Slavery in Alabama."

Talked to President Patterson[115] at great length—he says Tuskeegee will continue the Booker T. Washington idea of education.[116]

He is a conservative in regard to seeking to force the issue of race equality—says extremists like Richard Wright, author of *Black Boy,* would cause destruction of the race.[117]

Stayed in Mobile, Alabama, the first night of Mardi Gras season there—in an old hotel on the main square, the "Bienneville." The city is old but has been considerably modernized—not as quaint as New Orleans—[the] French quarter smell[s] of incense in the air.

Rode out to the Bellingrath Gardens—really delightful experience—Bellingrath[,] a southern man made his money on Coca-Cola, & devoted it to creating the garden, a thing of beauty.[118]

Rode by bus along the shore road to New Orleans—passed through Pascagoula, Miss, Ocean Springs (Old Biloxi), Biloxi, Pass Christian—Beautiful homes lined the shore at Biloxi and Pass Christian.

Journal of a Historian's Southern Journey in the South in the Summer of 1953

August 18, 1953. Left Raleigh by bus for Fayetteville at 8:45 A.M., cloudy and relatively cool—passed through a little cotton mill town Erwin, which had a Church of God prominently located in the village—the forests in N.C. seemed to be completely uncared for—mostly pine trees of no great height—tobacco—one field with paper bags tied over the top leaves—peas—corn, much dried by the drought, and cotton are the main crops—the land rather flat, sandy, and the reddish slightly rolling land hard-baked by the sun. The houses visible from the railroad cars are frail frame structures—painted white—often with tin roofs [and] no cellars—frequently in need of paint.

Arrived at Fayetteville at 10:24. The chief attraction of Fayetteville is its curious brick structure, thro[ugh] the center of town, called the Old Slave Market. It is a small brick structure with a cupola and clock on its roof. The remarkable feature of it is that it rests on stilts of stone buttresses—beneath the building on the street level slaves were sold in the antebellum period—its architecture is Georgian, in style, with white classic pilasters. As I looked at it I thought of the human suffering it witnessed. Now it is occupied by the Chamber of Commerce—whose motto, I guess, is material progress. Although there are some old houses remaining—most of the old structures have been replaced by colorless, utilitarian buildings—Fayetteville has broad modern streets—a town of 50,000 population "as of now" said the young girl at the desk of the Travellers Aid Society. Its main industry is cotton mills—but it must have been affected greatly by the location of Camp Bragg—the largest military camp in the United States.

Left Fayetteville at 11:17 A.M. Aug 19 on the Atlantic Coast Line—am in an air-conditioned car with 23 colored people, mostly women, and nine white peo-

ple, mostly men. Stopped at Dillon another cotton mill town and shortly after-
wards crossed the Pee Dee River—a moderate-sized muddy river—my Uncle
Joe used to say that the stream of the family farm near Mocksville, N.C., ran into
the Great Pee Dee River.

Near Dillon [I] see some cotton fields with cotton on the plants—in the area
around Raleigh the cotton is only in bloom. The train stops at Florence, where
passengers change trains for Sumter and Columbia—does not appear to be much
of a town—a railroad center—few people get on the train except Negroes.

Pass some cypress swamps—the trees having a bulbous base—this train is called
the Havana Special connecting with an over-night steamer at Miami for Havana.

August 18, 1953.
Arrived in Charleston in the rain—rode in a bus from the station to the Francis
Marion Hotel on the square, where the Old Citadel is located. On this square is a
huge towering statue of Calhoun with the inscription that he was an upholder of
the Constitution. In the Charleston *News and Courier* is an editorial opposing
mixed schools and suggesting that abolishing segregation is against the Constitution and that the only way to abolish segregation in schools is to adopt a constitutional amendment. The *News and Courier* claims to be the oldest newspaper in the
South, founded in 1803. Both it and the *Charleston Evening Post* are very conservative papers (owned, I understand by the same company). They are opposed to
increasing the power of the central government and to increase taxes. The Francis
Marion has air-conditioning in its rooms and a television set, which gave a program showing a Charleston Negro playing Beethoven's Moonlight Sonata, Arthur
Godfrey's folksy program, and a guessing game for a prize of money.

As I was walking down Meeting Street, a Charlestonian Ashmead Pringle of
the old colonial family invited me to ride with him and he pointed out some of
the old houses and told me about their owners.[119] He is a business man engaged
in the processing of phosphate rock for fertilizer. As I rode in to the city from the
station I saw some of the phosphate and fertilizer plants which have kept
Charleston alive—the advent of which is described in Owen Wister's novel,
Lady Baltimore.[120] Pringle says the Florida rock is much better than the Carolina
phosphate and is now used exclusively—brought by freight cars cheaply because
of the competition with ocean vessels. We drove to the docks and saw two pretty
good-sized vessels from Rotterdam and Norway. On account of the bar, the
largest ships that enter the harbor are not more than 12,000 tons. Pringle is a
graduate of the College of Charleston and of the business school at Harvard. He
was at Harvard when I was a graduate student there. During a trip to Europe in
1937 he met a Danish girl whom he married and now he has five children.

Charleston is a city of about 150,000 people, and being a seaport and naval
base, it has some of the characteristics of a seaport. For example, at night, I
wandered along Market and King Streets and noticed many sailors in the bars
and on the streets. Two establishments were engaged in tattooing sailors' arms.

In the afternoon I went to the Post Office at the corner of Broad and Meeting Streets and sat on a step, smoking a cigarette and contemplating St Michael's Church on the opposite corner. It is a beautiful church and its interior is in restrained good taste. Inside, I noticed how high were the pews—so that a child could easily play or go to sleep on a bench without being observed—even a small man could take a comfortable siesta.

August 19—Today I went to the Charleston Library Society to do research. It is a private organization—has about four to five hundred members, who pay a fee of $5—researchers from out of town pay 50¢ for 2 weeks privileges. I got some excellent material in the J.B. Grimball diary,[121] original at Chapel Hill—diary of a Charleston aristocrat and rice planter—a mirror of the life of the rice aristocracy and of the conservative South Carolina mind. In the afternoon when my eyes became tired I wandered through the grounds of the Unitarian Church just opposite—founded in 1819, the oldest Unitarian Church in the South. Dr Samuel Gilman,[122] who wrote "Fair Harvard" in 1836, was pastor of this church for nearly 40 years—now, I understand, the congregation is only 70 or 80 persons and that it has to be supported in part by the national church organization.

I again met Mr Pringle & he told me about the St Cecilia Society, of which he is a member—about 400 members—the great event of the society is the ball, for which the tickets are $15, but they have a supper and champagne—the dance is entirely by formal program—and the men run it. There is a very exclusive society here called the Carolina Plantation Society—which has not yet admitted Mr Pringle.

Went down Tradd Street—and saw the Sword Gate of an old house on Legare Street. Charleston needs thousands of buckets of white paint.

August 21—Yesterday after working in the Charleston Library Society on King Street I took a long walk down to the Battery and along East Bay Street—I could see Fort Sumter in the distance—The houses of Charleston have a wealth of porches—two or three stories high—the end of the house is adjacent to the street and the porches look out on gardens—the trees most often seen are crepe myrtle, which become more attractive particularly the satiny trunks as they grow older, a profusion of magnolias, which attain a considerable height, oleanders and of course palmettoes. I walked along Tradd and Church Streets where you see old stucco houses, painted in pastel colors and some of them with iron balconies. It is surprising how many people speak to a stranger in this city.

Today, I worked in the South Carolina Historical Society, which is housed in the Fireproof Building on Meeting Street, built in 1826 by Robert Mills, the South Carolina architect who designed the Washington Monument and the Treasury Building in Washington. I took a walk in the park adjacent to the Fireproof Building where there is a very attractive bronze bust of Henry Timrod and a statue of William Pitt belonging to the year 1766. Saw the building on East Bay

St. where pirate Stede Bonnet[123] and his crew were confined in 1718 and where the provincial legislature of the Revolutionary period met—also walked in the arcade of the Slave Market—here Negro peddlers sell fruit and vegetables.

Savannah—Aug 23–24—staying at DeSoto Hotel, which boasts a sprinkler system. Savannah has some nice old squares with semitropical flowers and trees. Worked at the Georgia Historical Society building which is near Armstrong Junior College. Great industry of the city is [the] manufacture of paper bags.

Aug 25—Took the bus for Brunswick, Ga—country level and uninteresting—the highway passed by numerous herds of cattle—Florida and Louisiana have the open range, so that if you hit a valuable steer with your car you are liable for damages. Passed through Darien—a very small village devoted to shrimp fishing. The South is definitely changing. One of the Savannah newspapers points out that the Yankees are coming South, the Negroes going North, cotton going West, and cattle coming east. The manufacture of paper is a great industry of the lower South. Good school buildings are now very prevalent.

Brunswick, August 25, 1953—Rode by bus from Savannah—2 hrs—through flat, very uninteresting country—passed through two villages[:] Riceborough and Darien—the latter a shrimp fishing village—near Butlers Island, where Fanny Kemble languished.[124] Also in the distance was Sapelo Island—Arrived in a downpour of rain which flooded the streets to the curb—am staying at an old Victorian Hotel—the *Oglethorpe,* where the Rotary Club, in shirt-sleeves, was assembled—Here at Brunswick is located a large rosin and turpentine mill—town reported to have a population of 25,000. Brunswick is a modern village, a conventional southern town. Near Brunswick the Hercules Powder Co has a huge turpentine factory.

Aug 26—went out to Sea Island, Ga. and St Simon's Island by bus over the Causeway. The hotel "The Cloisters" is a luxury hotel, $20 per person per day in the season Feb 1–May 1—$16 out of season.

St Simons is a flat island, formerly a sea island cotton area—with Frederica at one end, now abandoned. On this island Oglethorpe built his cottage,[125] the Wesleys preached,[126] the battle with the Spaniards of Bloody Marsh, 1742 was fought,[127] and Fanny Kemble visited and wrote her *Journal of a Georgian Plantation 1838–9* [*Journal of a Residence on a Georgian Plantation in 1838–1839*]—not published until 1863, and then as an anti-southern work.

Baton Rouge Sept 6, 1953—Rode across the Mississippi River twice on the ferry to the little village of Port Allen—a crude conventional southern village. As I rode on the steamboat, I thought of "Huckleberry Finn" and the romantic days of the Mississippi steamboats. I also wondered why the Confederacy couldn't transport troops and supplies across the river after the fall of Vicksburg and Port Hudson. The Mississippi makes so many bends that it seems to me it would have been not too difficult to elude patrollers. The levees are very high at Baton Rouge.

The city has doubled its population in the last ten years—now has 134,000 people—it has huge industries in the northern part of the town on the river—oil refineries, aluminum plant, etc.

III

Method

13

"Keep 'Em in a Fire-Proof Vault"

Pioneer Southern Historians Discover Plantation Records

Writing in 1910, and again a year later, William Thomas Laprade addressed the problems that confronted students of African American slavery.[1] The young assistant professor of history at Trinity College in North Carolina urged historians to be innovative in the sources that they employed when examining the South's peculiar institution. For too long, Laprade argued, writers had depended exclusively on biased travel narratives and accounts to document the history of slavery and the plantation regime. In addition to advocating the use of fresh sources, Laprade suggested that investigators free themselves from the legalistic framework that dominated the historiography of slavery. Critical of the majority of the volumes, Laprade wrote:

> Of making many books on American slavery there does not seem to be any prospect of an end in the immediate future. And if much of the study which has been expended on it has not resulted in a weariness of flesh, this must be due to the perennial interest which seems to attach to the subject rather than to any useful conclusions which have resulted from such study. For in spite of all this work some of the most fundamental questions with regard to slavery in America still await authoritative answers.[2]

Laprade's comments on the literature of slavery written during these years were in the main correct. "Fundamental questions" did remain to be answered; yet "useful conclusions" had been reached by historians of slavery who wrote during the Progressive era.[3] Heretofore an emotionally charged issue for Americans North and South, during the Progressive era slavery came to be examined calmly, "scientifically." Whether studied systematically as an institution or mentioned in the context of contemporary racial problems, slavery emerged in the period 1890–1920 as a major topic of discussion. Not since the late antebellum years had so much attention been devoted to it. Professor Laprade's concern with the sources for the history of slavery was mirrored in the writings, both published and unpublished, of a generation of southern historians and archivists. They recognized the value of a previously unexploited source material—plantation records and manuscripts. And for a number of southerners locating these documents became a major preoccupation.

Both an appreciation of the importance of manuscripts and access to them were necessary before historians could study slavery in what was then considered a "scientific" manner. Southern historians were at a marked disadvantage in this field because of the region's negligence in establishing collections of source materials. True, the southern state historical societies, organized in the nineteenth century, published some official documents and encouraged the study of history. For example, as early as 1818, South Carolina took steps to appropriate money for preserving state records. By 1856 the state historical society held the papers of Henry Laurens, documents that were particularly valuable for research on the history of the slave trade. On the whole, however, according to historian J.G. de Roulhac Hamilton, the South's historical societies neglected their "fundamental function," which, he believed, was collecting source materials and making them available to scholars.[4]

Nor did the creation of the Southern Historical Society in 1869 and the Southern History Association in 1896 remedy this defect of inadequate sources on the history of slavery. The Society was almost wholly dedicated to Confederate history. The Association had broader interests, and its *Publications,* described as the region's "first modern historical magazine," contained essays on slavery. But the organization did little toward collecting or publishing manuscript sources on the peculiar institution. Unfortunately, too, the meetings of these organizations, which might have stimulated the study of slavery and southern history in general, were attended mainly by affluent nonprofessionals. Few professors attended; most were unable to come because of distance and lack of funds.[5]

Scholars were, however, beginning to emphasize the importance of historical manuscripts. In 1887 Justin Winsor of Harvard urged the American Historical Association (AHA) to seek a national repository for manuscripts "before it is too late." By the turn of the century, according to Wendell Holmes Stephenson, southern historians had begun recognizing the historical significance of plantation records, including diaries, journals, and account books. As early as 1892, William P. Trent made extensive use of over 1,000 manuscript letters in his biography of William Gilmore Simms. Three years later, Trent, who like Laprade was trained at Johns Hopkins University, emphasized the historians' need for the collection of sources such as old letters, plantation account ledgers, and files of newspapers. Unfortunately, the South's first great collector of primary materials,

North Carolina's Stephen B. Weeks, became discouraged with the regional apathy held toward his work. "If I had studied Egyptian history in Idaho as thoroughly as I have N.C. history," he wrote with sarcasm in 1899, "I should have been much more appreciated in my native State!" Weeks's decision to sell his valuable collection of North Caroliniana in fragments instead of contributing it en masse to a library seriously retarded its use by early researchers.[6]

The increasing emphasis on primary sources in the study of slavery was especially apparent in the works of two early twentieth-century figures. In 1907 Alfred Holt Stone, a planter from Dunleith, Mississippi, wrote to historian William E. Dodd seeking information on "documentary manuscript and other materials bearing particularly on the ante bellum and earlier post bellum aspects of" southern blacks. Stone was collecting information for a projected book, "The Negro in Slavery and Freedom." He believed that a great deal of manuscript material on slavery was available but too widely scattered for use by historians. It rested mainly in the hands of private families or individuals. Requesting names of families with manuscripts dealing with slavery, Stone informed Dodd:

> I am in search of all forms of sugar, rice, tobacco, indigo and cotton plantation records,—such as journals, diaries, account books, account sales, cotton picking records, instructions to overseers. . . . In fact, I want anything which will throw the least light upon the economic side of the institution of slavery, as it existed at various . . . places in the Southern and border states. This would of course include all other forms of economic activity in which the negro was employed before the war as well as that of the plantation.

Two years later the reform journalist, Ray Stannard Baker, made a similar request. Planning several articles "on slavery as it existed," Baker had already accumulated much primary source material "both in the way of personal experiences and documents." He still desired Dodd to offer hints on additional sources of materials, unpublished documents, pictures, and pamphlets.[7]

Most students of the history of slavery at this time, however, lacked any real way of gaining access to the records of the South's past. For years, southern scholars had recognized the seriousness of the region's archival problems. A reviewer in the *Sewanee Review* in 1892 summarized the urgency by declaring that "a true history" of the southern people ought to be written before the materials for that history had vanished.

The following year a correspondent advised Professor Herbert Baxter Adams, in whose famous Johns Hopkins seminar many of the pioneer students of slavery were trained, to begin a study of southern blacks. "I earnestly hope that you will," wrote Lynn R. Meekins, then literary editor of the *Baltimore American,* because "this is an important dividing line between generations and valuable material will soon be slipping away."[8]

Too often manuscripts pertaining to the South were either lost or hoarded in attics and, according to Stephenson, early in the century were "fast disappearing because of a lack of knowledge of their value as historical evidence." To help correct this, John Franklin Jameson, the first editor of the *American Historical Review,* planned an extensive manuscript search throughout the South in 1905. Albert Bushnell Hart, professor of history at Harvard, advised him that the region's famous families held the key to uncovering the South's manuscripts. Hamilton, who by the 1930s had assembled the South's greatest archival collection at the University of North Carolina at Chapel Hill, accurately recalled how in 1906 the South lacked any "great collections of historical manuscripts." Philip M. Hamer, when chief of accessions at the National Archives, said that the preservation of sources such as plantation records, which could have been valuable to researchers on slavery, was generally "the result of chance and less the result of foresight." Had southern families preserved rather than destroyed their papers, large caches of slave owners' records might have been available to early researchers. Those saved usually were located in such informal repositories as corncribs and outbuildings.[9]

Historians widely lamented this lack of sources. Dodd asserted in 1904 that students of southern history were limited because "only one first rate library of reference" (probably referring to the Library of Congress) existed in the entire South. A year earlier, Professor Jameson had warned southern historians that "a hundred years from now inquiring minds will be eagerly seeking for knowledge of American slavery as an actual institution and for an understanding of the social system which was bound up with it, but now is the golden time to collect the data, before it is too late." Worthington C. Ford, a pioneer archivist at the Boston Public Library and the Library of Congress, regretted that, although the South had possessed abundant historical sources early in its history, they had been wasted. "Now that the trained historian is ready," he added, "the material is wanting." Professor Eugene C. Barker of the University of Texas believed that the absence of sources in the South had allowed New Englanders to dominate the writing of southern history. Walter Lynwood Fleming, then professor of history at Louisiana State University, complained that his university library lacked the materials necessary "to form a basis for an adequate course in Southern history." Fleming even doubted whether an acceptable course on any phase of southern history could be offered below the Mason-Dixon line. As late as 1923, William H. Kilpatrick, a Georgian transplanted to Columbia University, spoke of the dreadful condition of the South's primary sources.[10]

Despite these complaints, the South was in fact a pioneer in the establishment of state archival programs. Led by Thomas M. Owen, in 1901 Alabama founded its Department of Archives and History. A contemporary hailed the state's decision to collect systematically its documents of the past as "the most far reaching step yet taken in the South looking to the support of historical work and research." Owen, described by historian Ulrich Bonnell Phillips as "an extremely valuable and attractive man," was a national leader in state archival management and emerged as the dominant figure in a region lacking "an overplus of active men in the historical field." In 1903, according to Phillips, the Alabama Department of Archives and History joined only two other libraries in the United States—the Library of Congress and the Wisconsin State Historical Society—as depositories of primary materials for the writing of southern history. Owen took pride that Alabama was the first state to recognize the importance of caring for and preserving its archives by establishing a separate state agency. Nonetheless, in a report on manuscripts in 1900, he noted the conspicuous absence of plantation materials and other records of slavery. Six years later, Owen also acknowledged that he could not locate "any manuscript material . . . on slave insurrections" when asked for citations.[11]

Following Owen's lead, Dunbar Rowland and Franklin L. Riley worked for the establishment of Mississippi's Department of Archives and History, which came to pass in 1902. A decade later, Frederic Bancroft, an expert on the domestic slave trade, praised the department as "perhaps the most civilizing influence in Mississippi." By 1911, its collections contained records that were highly useful to students of slavery, including slave auction lists and emancipation petitions. Similarly, in 1903 North Carolina chartered its Historical Commission. Directed by R.D.W. Connor, it quickly acquired valuable manuscript collections with valuable information on slavery. The Jonathan Worth Papers, for example, contained material on slave treatment, slave sales, and slave law. Contemporary researchers on slavery also had access to the Manuscript Division of the Library of Congress, established in 1897. Within eight years, the division held over 120,000 manuscripts pertaining to many aspects of southern history. As early as 1815, the library had acquired the Thomas Jefferson manuscripts containing primary materials on slavery. During its first years, the library also acquired a collection of "Slave Papers," including slave appraisals, mortgages, and birth certificates of bondsmen. In 1899, Richard West added to this collection an important group of "Plantation Reports." But despite these holdings, as late as 1914, Frederic Bancroft complained of the weak collection of plantation records at the Library of Congress—it contained only "a few plantation books," he said. Not until well into the twentieth century did the Library of Congress hold collections of records adequate for the writing of a satisfactory history of slavery.[12]

One scholar, however, Ulrich Bonnell Phillips (1877–1934), overcame this paucity of sources. A native Georgian, Phillips studied with both Frederick Jackson Turner and William A. Dunning before embarking on a teaching career on the faculties of Wisconsin, Tulane, Michigan, and Yale. Phillips was a prolific author. In addition to more than a score of articles, his two best-known books— *American Negro Slavery: A Survey of the Supply, Employment and Control of Negro Labor as Determined by the Plantation Régime* (1918) and *Life and Labor in the Old South* (1929)—earned him a reputation as the foremost historian of slavery of his day. Not until the publication of Kenneth M. Stampp's *The Peculiar Institution: Slavery in the Ante-Bellum South* (1956) was Phillips dislodged as the master of slave historiography.[13]

Although historians' evaluations of Phillips's writings on slavery have undergone cyclical revision, they agree that he merits praise as the dominant figure in the collection and use of plantation materials. These became fundamental sources in Phillips's paternalistic interpretations of American slavery. Despite his racism and his overdependence on the records of large planters, Phillips revolutionized the study of slavery. He uncovered new sources of evidence, analyzed the profitability of slavery on a cost basis, and examined relationships between bondsman and master that existed under the slave regime.[14]

Phillips's role as a pioneer in the use of plantation records and a variety of other sources is an important factor in his reputation as a "scientific" historian and as one of the South's foremost scholars. The Georgian was the only student of slavery in the early twentieth century to exploit planters' letters, diaries, ledgers, and pamphlets on a large scale, and to employ census statistics in conjunction with such records. Phillips also paved the way in the extensive use of southern newspapers and of correspondence between masters and overseers. Moreover he gleaned much statistical information for numerous charts and graphs from city directories, bills of sale, slave price quotations, slave ship manifests, and cotton factors' account statements. By popularizing the use of such sources, Phillips anticipated the major sources employed by many of his successors. He made an additional contribution by identifying the location of plantation documents and encouraging their preservation. Phillips undoubtedly possessed a broader understanding of the value of plantation materials than did any of his peers. He considered it to be the historian's obligation to utilize any and all sources that served to reconstruct "the old system [of slavery] as an organic whole."[15]

Phillips believed strongly in plantation records because he looked upon them as unconscious sources for the study of slavery. To evaluate objectively the peculiar institution, always a topic charged with emotion, required, in Phillips's opinion, special sources. "The most reliable source of knowledge," he said, "and the source least used thus far," were plantation records—"documents written with no thought of reaching the public eye, writings whose purpose is to give the plain facts and nothing else." Phillips was convinced that the hostile attitude of northern writers toward slavery and the South resulted largely from their unfamiliarity with the region's primary sources. Writing in 1909, Phillips explained, "Original material for Southern history has been so scarce at the centres where American historiographers have worked, that the general writers have had to substitute conjecture for understanding in many cases when attempting to interpret Southern developments."[16]

From the time of his experiences as assistant librarian in graduate school at the University of Georgia, Phillips appreciated the value of books and documents. Even after his appointment in 1902 as instructor of history at the University of Wisconsin, he proposed an arrangement whereby he would spend half of each year teaching at Madison and half as librarian for the Georgia Historical

Society. In Phillips's opinion, "the two kinds of work" were "really supplementary in character." With much the same kind of fervor as that of such pioneer southern archivists as Alabama's Owen or Mississippi's Rowland, Phillips argued that if southern history was to become a serious research field, the region's manuscripts and other primary sources had to be preserved. In 1903, for example, he lamented that so little had been accomplished in Georgia for the maintenance of the state's records, that important documents in the State House were being devoured by rats. Similarly, he found the town records of his hometown, Milledgeville, Georgia—poorly arranged and cared for—"some . . . damaged by mice, and all . . . exceedingly dusty and disagreeable to use." Three years later, Phillips admonished his friend Yates Snowden of the University of South Carolina to guard the plantation records that he was collecting. "For God's sake," implored Phillips, "Keep 'Em in a Fire-Proof Vault."[17]

As a young historian, Phillips scoured the South for all types of plantation records and located important materials in city, state, and local archives. Many of his most noteworthy discoveries, however, came from private collections, access to which he gained through such personal contacts as Georgia planter John C. Reed. It was through Reed that Phillips obtained the papers of Robert Toombs. Phillips relied heavily on these manuscripts for his biography of the Georgia fire-eater.[18] Summer appointments at several universities granted him the opportunity to investigate southern records much more thoroughly. At the Virginia State Library, for example, he uncovered 1,300 vouchers of bondsmen convicted of capital crimes. These served as the basis of Phillips's "Slave Crime in Virginia," published in 1915 in the *American Historical Review*.[19]

Besides supplying him with valuable primary sources for his books, Phillips's position as the authority on southern manuscript collections brought him other rewards. Several of the more valuable sources that he uncovered were published in their raw form as edited documents. In such works as *The Correspondence of Robert Toombs, Alexander H. Stephens, and Howell Cobb* (1913) and *Plantation and Frontier Documents: 1649–1863* (2 vols., 1909), Phillips made important manuscript materials available for the use of other scholars. He also gained appointments to the AHA's Public Archives and Historical Manuscripts Commissions. Throughout his career, Phillips continued to extol manuscripts as the most important sources in the study of southern history.[20]

Between 1903 and 1906, Phillips contributed articles to the AHA's *Annual Reports* that offer a glimpse into his conception of the limitless value of manuscripts to the student of slavery. In two of these essays, analyses of Georgia's public and local archives, Phillips emphasized the importance of property inventories and manuscript census returns. He considered them important instruments in compiling numbers and values of slaves on farms and plantations over specific periods of time. From such information, Phillips said, plantation tendencies—such as average slave and land holdings—could be determined.[21]

Phillips considered information in town and county records of special value in the study of the economics of slavery. Local archives, he argued, contained vast amounts of significant material in contrast to the printed sources on the subject, that were "scanty and fugitive, and often unreliable." Phillips added: "The county records of appraisements and sales of estates at auction comprise the chief source from which knowledge may be had of the rise and fall of slave prices. A comparative study of data of this sort . . . will be essential as a basis for any definitive economic history of slavery in America." Such raw materials as wills, oaths, court minutes, and local slave ordinances joined plantation records as important sources used in Phillips's writings. He predicted that as these sources became increasingly available to researchers, they would replace the generally "fallacious" antebellum travelers' accounts.[22]

Phillips's correspondence reveals his great dependence on personal and professional contacts in locating and gaining access to the various plantation records that he used in his writings. Through adventuresome manuscript hunts in the South with agricultural historian Herbert Anthony Kellar (1887–1955) and others, Phillips acquired a rich collection of pamphlets, journals, and manuscripts. The buying, selling, and trading of these sources became for him a hobby closely related to his historical work. And Phillips was generous with his rare books and manuscripts. Many of his former colleagues and graduate students recall how he shared with them his prize archival finds. When visiting the Phillips home at Ann Arbor, historian Avery O. Craven admired one of his host's rare volumes. Upon returning to his own residence, Craven discovered that Phillips had slipped the volume secretly into his suitcase as a gift.[23] According to Fred Landon, Phillips possessed "the same zest for manuscripts that a fisherman might have for a trout stream." Not surprisingly, Phillips warmly recommended in 1928 that funds be allocated to help establish the Southern Historical Collection at the University of North Carolina. J.G. de Roulhac Hamilton—founder of the collection and longtime friend of Phillips—guaranteed the Georgian first crack at a "most wonderful body of plantation material." Hamilton explained that this was "a reward of virtue," but no doubt it was influenced by Phillips's endorsement of the funding of the collection.[24] Such personal connections and his affluence enabled Phillips to become the leading figure in the use of plantation materials. These sources were not easily obtained and Phillips's rise within the historical profession was attributable partly to his unusual access to them.

Among the papers of Kellar is a valuable and entertaining document that illustrates the lengths to which Phillips and other early southern historians had to go to procure plantation manuscripts. A native Nebraskan and educated at Chicago, Stanford, and Wisconsin, for almost four decades Kellar served as director of the McCormick Historical Association in Chicago. He was a resourceful and energetic collector of manuscripts and at the McCormick Library developed one of the best collections of colonial and nineteenth-century agricultural materials in the United States. Like Phillips, Kellar enjoyed uncovering manuscripts—especially those pertaining to the farm and plantation. During the 1920s, the two historians exchanged letters in which they discussed the location and value of sundry manuscript collections. At different times, Phillips and Kellar exchanged or sold historical materials to each another.[25]

Kellar's unpublished "Notes on Trips to Virginia with Ulrich B. Phillips in Search of Manuscripts" is a charming reminiscence of a manuscript expedition in Virginia's Shenandoah Valley in the spring of 1926. Collecting materials for his projected *Life and Labor in the Old South,* Phillips joined Kellar in Lexington, Virginia, on April 17 after a number of stops at archival repositories in the lower South. Joining the two historians was James Rion McKissick (1884–1944), a South Carolina journalist who later served as president of the University of South Carolina. McKissick shared his colleagues' interest in manuscripts and was an avid collector of historical materials relating to the Palmetto State.[26]

The trio embarked on their manuscript-hunting trip through rural Virginia armed with a thirst for uncovering virgin manuscripts and fortified by two quarts of bootleg whiskey that the resourceful McKissick had acquired. On the first day, they traveled by bus from Lexington to Greenville, located in Augusta County, about twenty-four miles away. They next rented an automobile and drove to the home of Kellar's acquaintance George W. Armentrout, a farmer and antiquarian who several times previously had invited Kellar to examine his collection of old documents. Upon reaching Armentrout's farm, the three researchers were stunned when the Virginian's elderly sister informed them that her brother had been dead for three years. Not to be denied their opportunity to look through the Armentrout collection, Phillips, McKissick, and Kellar persuaded their hostess to take them to one of her late brother's farms, then inhabited by a tenant. As Kellar later wrote in his recollection of the trip, "because the roads were rough, and our own car none too reliable, we accepted an invitation to ride in her Ford." Kellar described the remainder of this journey as only a participant could:[27]

> After Ulrich, McKissick, George's sister, and myself had gotten into the car, together with a boy to drive, we had a rather full load, but we did not care for adventure lay ahead. The ride was not at all [what] it might have been for the wind was cold and raw and we were half frozen before we reached our destination. Ulrich with his long arms vainly attempted to hold down the curtains of the car to keep out the cold wind. Eventually descending into a deep valley, we stopped at the edge of a bawling creek, where the Ford disgorged its passengers, and we made preparations to cross a rickety foot bridge of the suspension type—the house was set back a few yards from the bank on the other side. The bridge did not look particularly trustworthy, but McKissick bravely volunteered to try it first. Our apprehensions proved correct for McKissick almost fell into the water, but finally to the accompaniment of free advice, he crossed safely and profiting by his example we quickly followed.
>
> At the house George's sister knocked on the door and the wife of the tenant appeared. In answer to a request for George's papers, the woman nodded an assent and presently reappeared dragging a large and disreputable looking gunny sack. Like feasters at a banquet we eagerly gathered around the sack

and opened it. At once we perceived that it was full of old letters and papers. Digging down into the mass, I pulled out a letter and looking at it found that it was dated 1732. I asked the woman if there were any more bags, and eventually she brought out four other sacks similar to the first. By this time Phillips and McKissick, not to mention myself, were becoming quite excited. Tying the sacks on the fenders and on the top of the car, and presenting a most bizarre appearance to anyone who might happen to meet us on the road, we started back to the . . . Armentrout house. On the way Phillips whispered to me: "I think we ought to get this material if we can." I replied in the affirmative, and suggested we make an offer. Phillips then wanted to know what I thought would be proper, and I said, "Well, suppose we offer $5.00 a sack, sight unseen." To our surprise and gratification, George's sister accepted the proposition and we promptly paid over the twenty-five dollars.

At the Armentrout house we transferred the treasure to our own car and as quickly as we decently could, made our departure, fearing all the while that the sister might change her mind about letting us have the material. As it turned out our fears were quite unfounded, because she was delighted to be able to obtain the amount stipulated in order to clear up some matters in connection with her brother's estate, of which she was the administratrix.

Reaching Greenville we found that the train, which ran to Lexington once a day, was due shortly, and accordingly decided to travel by that means since it would make it easier to carry our newly acquired possessions. At the station we bought tickets and turned over the sacks to the agent, asking him to express them with us to Lexington. A few moments later the agent came up to me with a puzzled expression on his face and regretfully imparted the information that he could not accept the bags for shipment. Upon asking the reason, he said that he had looked all through his express schedules and could find no designation which covered the content, which he had been told were old papers. I then told him that if he could not accept our papers, we would take them with us in the coach. The agent kindly, but firmly, said that this could not be done. In this impasse the agent suddenly had a brilliant idea, and asked if we objected to his shipping them as "corn shucks." So corn shucks they were and Phillips gravely paid out thirty cents to ship five sacks of corn shucks from Greenville to Lexington.

Upon arrival at our destination we hired a taxi and proceeded to the Dutch Inn. The guests in that somewhat sedate establishment were greatly astonished to see two colored boys, bending and staggering under the weight of five huge gunny sacks, proceeding through the front door, solemnly followed by three scholars, disheveled in appearance, but with the light of victory glowing in their eyes. An ominous pause ensued, but Mrs. Louise Owen, the proprietress, who is used to my vagaries, gallantly rose to the occasion and rented us a room for the gunny sacks.

Thereupon for two days and two nights with the aid of the major portion of the two quarts of whiskey and the enthusiasm of the quest for the unknown, Phillips, McKissick and myself proceeded to examine the twenty-five thousand or more documents contained in the gunny sacks. Befitting our enterprise and belief in cooperation, the arrangement that we made was practical and efficient. Taking one bag at a time, each of us selected a goodly portion for inspection. After due industry each had two piles, one of large proportion which was chaff, and one of smaller size which was wheat. In the course of our endeavor Phillips found about two thousand slavery items; I found several thousand iron furnace papers and McKissick, curiously enough, a few South Carolina items. When Phillips and McKissick finished, I still had three documents to go through. One turned out to be worthless. The second proved to be an iron furnace item. The third, the last document of the twenty-five thousand to be examined, nearly gave me apoplexy. I read it through once and then passed it to Ulrich with the remark "Do my eyes deceive me?" Ulrich took one look at what I handed him and let out a whoop of joy in which he was soon joined by McKissick. The document was a contract in the handwriting of Daniel Boone and signed by him, in which he accepted some several hundred pounds from a Mr. Johnson of Augusta County in return for which Boone proposed to locate a large tract of land for Johnson on his next trip to Kentucky. We voted that the occasion was dramatic and called for the finishing of the second bottle, which we did.[28]

The cache of documents uncovered by Phillips, Kellar, and McKissick is impressive even when contrasted with the large volume of plantation and slavery-related materials now readily available to researchers. But the 1920s was a different era both in the development of southern archives and in the serious study of southern history. It was the start of what one scholar has recently termed the "take-off point" of southern historiography.[29] Modern archivists, conditioned to think in terms of records managers, data banks, and endowment grants, frequently fail to appreciate the problems under which their forebears labored. Men such as J.G. de Roulhac Hamilton of the University of North Carolina and William K. Boyd of Duke University were successful collectors because they possessed uncanny abilities for ferreting out manuscripts from a variety of obscure places. Historians accustomed to the rich collections of plantation manuscript materials at Chapel Hill, Durham, and other southern repositories also should recall the barriers that their predecessors faced in locating sources. Even when Phillips and his contemporaries had the luxury of examining archival materials in the confines of a library, rarely were the documents carefully arranged and cataloged.

Owen, Rowland, Hamilton, Phillips, Kellar, and Boyd—to mention only a few of the better-known pioneer historians and archivists—performed several vital functions for southern archival development. They educated southerners in the importance of preserving past records and helped establish the nuclei of important manuscript libraries that today rank among the nation's best. Through their writings, they further helped advance the "scientific" and objective study of the southern past. Following Laprade's suggestions, early students of slavery helped solve the South's archival problems. Their efforts form a key chapter both in archival history and the historiography of slavery.

14

The Historian as Archival Advocate
Ulrich Bonnell Phillips and the Records of Georgia and the South

Students of American archival history recognize that in the early twentieth century the South led the way in the establishment of state-sponsored archival institutions.[1] Writing in 1905, Mississippi archivist Dunbar Rowland remarked that "the work of the archivist, in preserving the sources of truth, is fast becoming one of the most important activities in which historical agencies can engage." "Progressive States," Rowland explained, especially in the South, had already established "special departments for the care, classification, and publication of official archives" to provide historians with primary source materials.[2] Led by Thomas M. Owen, in 1901 Alabama founded its Department of Archives and History. Following Owen's lead, Rowland campaigned for the establishment of the Mississippi Department of Archives and History, which was established in 1902. A year later, North Carolina chartered its Historical Commission directed by Robert D.W. Connor. Despite the South's national leadership in documentary preservation, pioneer southern historians nevertheless labored under serious problems as they sought evidence to document the history of their region.[3]

Among historians of these years, Georgia native Ulrich Bonnell Phillips (1877–1934) proved most successful in locating, utilizing, and promoting the importance of antebellum southern historical records. Phillips identified—and urged the preservation of—manuscripts, especially those pertaining to slavery and the plantation system. Phillips employed these sources in writing or editing eight books, most notably *American Negro Slavery: A Survey of the Supply, Employment and Control of Negro Labor as Determined by the Plantation Régime* (1918) and *Life and Labor in the Old South* (1929). These works, though by today's standards methodologically backward, racist, paternalistic, and pro-

slavery, thrust Phillips into the first rank of American historians of his generation. He dominated the historiography of slavery in the first half of the twentieth
century. His use of plantation manuscripts, then relatively obscure and arcane
sources, enabled Phillips to delineate slavery's institutional features, to analyze
its profitability on a cost basis, and to probe the dynamics of the master-slave
relationship.[4] Though Phillips's Jim Crow–era interpretations lost favor with
historians in the 1950s, his contributions as a pioneer historian and advocate of
systematic archival practice deserve careful analysis.

Significantly, Phillips uncovered vast riches of southern manuscripts—plantation
records as well as those pertaining to other aspects of southern history. Well
ahead of his time, he underscored the precarious, neglected condition of the
South's widely dispersed private papers and official documents. Phillips emphasized the importance of arranging and preserving these records. In 1903, for
instance, he complained that northerners had dominated the writing of American
history. "It must be written anew before it reaches its final form of truth, and for
that work the South must do its part in preparation." Regrettably, Phillips added,
southern history lagged behind other research topics principally because "most
of the [region's documentary] material is inaccessible." Three years later, Phillips admonished historian Yates Snowden of the University of South Carolina to
take pains to conserve the plantation records in his care. Indeed, Phillips took
advantage of every opportunity to encourage the establishment of repositories of
historical manuscripts in his native region.[5]

Trained in the "scientific" historical methodology of his day at the University
of Georgia and Columbia University, Phillips was determined to attain "objectivity" by allowing the primary sources to speak for themselves. Phillips believed
strongly in plantation records because he looked upon them as unconscious
sources for the economic and social history of the South. He regretted that
because "original material" on the history of the South had been so scarce,
previous writers substituted guess work "for understanding in many cases when
attempting to interpret Southern developments." "The most reliable source of
knowledge" for the history of slavery, Phillips explained, "and the source least
used thus far," were plantation records—"documents written with no thought of
reaching the public eye, writings whose purpose is to give the plain facts and
nothing else." He predicted that once plantation records were made available to
researchers, "travelers' accounts, fallacious as they usually are, will be duly
relegated to a place of very minor importance."[6]

Phillips was the only southern historian early in the twentieth century systematically to exploit planters' letters, diaries, and ledgers on a large scale. In 1903,
in one of his first publications, he implored researchers to integrate a broad range
of primary sources into their writings on the South. "For a complete view of the
life of the community," Phillips explained, "the town records must be supplemented with the county archives, the state documents, the newspaper files,
travelers' accounts, and private correspondence."[7] He also employed census data

in conjunction with these records. Phillips similarly paved the way in the extensive use of southern newspapers and of correspondence between masters and overseers. He gleaned much statistical information for charts and graphs from city directories, bills of sale, slave price quotations, slave ship manifests, and cotton factors' account statements. Phillips not only utilized numerous plantation manuscripts in his writings, but published as edited documents some of the more valuable papers that he unearthed, including *Plantation and Frontier Documents: 1649–1863* (2 vols., 1909) and *The Correspondence of Robert Toombs, Alexander H. Stephens, and Howell Cobb* (1913). He also innovatively mined such hitherto unknown sources as 1,300 vouchers of slaves convicted of capital crimes. Phillips uncovered these records at the Virginia State Library.

As much as any archivist, Phillips understood the value to the historian of rare books and documents. While in graduate school at Georgia, he served as assistant university librarian. In 1901, the university's chancellor, citing Phillips's willingness to undertake "special training" in library science, heartily recommended his appointment as librarian, a proposal that never came to pass. After joining the history faculty at the University of Wisconsin in 1902, Phillips proposed an arrangement whereby he would devote one-third of each year teaching at Madison, and the remainder as librarian at the Georgia Historical Society in Savannah.[8] With much the same commitment to the preservation of manuscripts as archivists Owen, Rowland, and Connor, Phillips linked the future of southern history as a research field to the availability of the region's primary sources. Accordingly, in 1903, Phillips accepted a proposal from Herman V. Ames, chair of the American Historical Association's (AHA) Public Archives Commission, to prepare an extensive inventory of Georgia's official records. Phillips was especially well suited to the task, having examined many of Georgia's records while researching his award-winning doctoral dissertation, *Georgia and State Rights* (1902). Even before starting his project for the AHA, Phillips remarked that problems awaited anyone who sought to identify and urge the preservation of Georgia's archival records. "There are stacks of valuable documents now being eaten by rats in the state capitol," he complained, "and lots of others in private hands in every part of the state."[9]

Phillips linked the deplorable condition of Georgia's documents to what he considered to be the overall backwardness of the state's historical activities. Influenced strongly by the ethos of professionalism and efficiency espoused by Progressives in Wisconsin and elsewhere, he advised Georgians to establish a modern historical society, one staffed by "scientific" historians. "In general," argued Phillips, "the most important policy is . . . to keep the old fossils out of office, and prevent the society from becoming antiquarian rather than historical. . . . Of course, the genealogists and the collectors of arrow-heads, who think they are historical students must be coddled sometimes." But, he insisted, "for practical work men of true historical interest and training must be had." Phillips argued that only a trained professional should tackle the overwhelming task of organizing the Georgia state papers in their confused condition. "Even a synopsis of them," he wrote, "cannot be made without heavy work. It should not be attempted by anyone who does not know the relative value of historical documents, or who has not had a technical training in historical work." Phillips proposed that the first step in the process would be the kind of preliminary report of the state's records that he was preparing for the AHA.[10]

Phillips began his canvass of Georgia's archives by conferring with Governor Joseph M. Terrell and former Governor Allen D. Candler, the latter serving as Georgia state historian and compiler of records. After his thorough examination of the documents, Phillips concluded that Georgia's state and local records constituted "one of the most valuable collections of unexploited official documents now to be found in America." But as elsewhere in the South, Phillips lamented, Georgia's state and local records suffered from problems of arrangement, description, and conservation. These problems were exacerbated, he said, by the fact that Candler, though well intentioned, was "sure to do no work of value in his present office." According to Phillips, Candler not only lacked historical training, but spent most of his time merely "drawing his salary." In Phillips's judgment, Georgia's archives would suffer as long as they were entrusted to an untrained "political employee." The state drastically required "expert and enthusiastic service" in its archival and documentary publication programs.[11]

Phillips deplored the fact that many of Georgia's early records had gone astray. He judged possibly "the most serious loss" to have been the letters to the governors prior to around 1840, that never were transcribed. Other records, that had no direct connection to Georgia history, had erroneously been placed with the state's documents. Many early documents that belonged in county and municipal offices lay instead in the state archives in Atlanta. To illustrate another problem, Phillips described a volume of bills of sale and deeds of gift, located among the executive department's archives, that should logically have been deposited in the state department. Other historical records had simply vanished, grumbled Phillips. He was disappointed, for instance, to discover that manuscript state census returns "for but few of the counties are to be found in any degree of completeness," and those for 1824 and 1831 were "fragmentary." Virtually no records existed before 1858 for the city of Athens. Though its modern records were well housed in fireproof vaults, Phillips surmised that the university town's early documents were destroyed by Union troops, "or that the documents were hidden by the townspeople during Sherman's invasion and have never been restored to the archives room." In any case, he regretted that the surviving documents reflected "many signs of neglect" and supposed "that at some period the custodian destroyed part of the archives as rubbish."[12]

Phillips also criticized the arrangement of Georgia's records—even those in the capitol building—describing them as "to a large degree haphazard." Except for the land records in the department of state, Phillips discovered little systematic arrangement anywhere. Even these important records were "preserved in a thousand or more pigeon-hole boxes." Phillips found the records of the colonial period "numbered in some obscure system with letters of the alphabet." He described a collection of "miscellaneous original documents"—reports and letters—tied in packages with labels and stacked upon four shelves in the main archives room of the state department. These documented Georgia's relations with the French and Spanish at Natchez and St. Augustine "concerning desperadoes on the Florida boundary." Records pertaining to postbellum expenditures, explained Phillips, were located "around the walls of the main document room of the executive department" in "tall cases of dust-proof pigeonholes."[13]

More troublesome, in Phillips's opinion, was the arrangement and description of Georgia's antebellum records and those for the Civil War and Reconstruction periods. Phillips described these as "among the most important in the capitol." Located in the "overflow document room"—an obscure, isolated room on the third floor of the capitol—these documents were stored in packages, some labeled, some not. "From careless handling many of the documents have become displaced from the packages in which they belong," Phillips explained. He wrote with disgust that these packages were stacked carelessly "along the walls in open shelves or bins, with just the faintest hint of classification. For practical research, the documents might almost as well be in a promiscuous heap upon the floor. The room has no attendant, and apparently is not visited as often as once a year. There are 160 of these bins full of papers, each bin about 3 feet long and a foot high." These manuscripts included the "Rough Minutes" of the Governor's Council for the colonial period, "discovered" in the basement of the capitol only a few years prior to Phillips's survey. According to Phillips, they contained valuable information regarding appointments and passports granted for travel into the Creek nation.[14]

Phillips regretted that other noteworthy documents had suffered from the vicissitudes of Georgia's history and from poor handling. In Milledgeville, which preceded Atlanta as Georgia's capital, the frequent removal of records, and what Phillips termed "the destructive work of Sherman's troops" in 1864, wreaked "sad havoc . . . among the loose documents" and damaged bound material as well. A volume of eighteenth-century wills, for example, had been "mutilated by the cutting out of pages, possibly blank, at the back." He fumed that the gaps in the early nineteenth-century county records housed in the Milledgeville courthouse resulted not only from a courthouse fire in 1861, but from "the inattention of the officers in charge and the lack of any secure vault or case for the volumes and papers." Records found in the Milledgeville town clerk's office, Phillips said, lacked any semblance of arrangement or care. "Some of them have been damaged by mice, and all of them . . . are exceedingly dusty and disagreeable to use."[15]

Phillips was glad to report that the offices of the county clerk and ordinary in Lexington, Oglethorpe County, were equipped with a fireproof vault for their local archives. Though some of the county's records were disorganized, he wrote happily that the original records in the ordinary's office were "well classified, tied in packets, clearly labeled, and stacked upon open shelves in very good arrangement." Similarly, the archives of Habersham County in Clarkesville were protected in a fireproof vault. Phillips found the bound volumes "in fairly good order, but the original documents not in books are in extreme disorder, with very many of them probably lost." He noted that the court records for Habersham County included valuable deeds, bills of sale, wills, and inventories, as well as a group of private records—merchants' account books, cash books, day books, journals, and ledgers. Unfortunately, the historian said, the court documents were "scattered in utter disarrangement in open pigeonholes and packing cases." Although the clerk's office had "a good set of dust-proof filing cases in the vault," Phillips complained that "very few documents have been arranged therein." The bound volumes were unlabeled and, Phillips griped, were largely maintained in a "slovenly fashion."[16]

Similarly, the archives of Clarke County, located in Athens, were protected in a fireproof vault. Phillips found the original writs, fifas, and orders "in good preservation, and mostly well arranged in metal dust-proof filing cases." Though many of the bound volumes in the clerk's office had their bindings scorched in a courthouse fire, fortunately, Phillips declared, "no important documents appear to have been destroyed." He complimented the arrangement of these records that "show evidences of much care in their keeping." Included in the clerk's office were bound volumes of rare nineteenth-century Georgia newspapers and "an old trunk" containing miscellaneous private manuscripts. In the ordinary's office, Phillips encountered many documents filed in no special arrangement in a set of wooden pigeonholes. The vault contained "several trunks and cases of private papers" as well as a packing case full of loose newspapers, pamphlets, and manuscripts. Among these documents was an 1823 committee report on Clarke County's regimental fund, enumerating persons liable to drill, with fines collected and uncollected.[17]

Phillips gained many insights into the nature of slavery on the local level from his survey of Georgia's records. Using Taliaferro County as an example, he compared data drawn from the 1827 state census and the 1860 federal census. This county, typical of the upland Georgia cotton belt, showed a decrease in white population (2,038 to 1,693) in these years but increases in its free black (32 to 41) and slave (2,394 to 2,849) populations. In terms of slaveholdings, Phillips identified 178 slaveholders who owned fewer than ten slaves each in 1860 as compared with 198 in the same category in 1831. In contrast, 93 slaveholders held ten or more slaves in 1860 as compared with 81 in that category in 1831. From this rough data, Phillips concluded that the small holdings of slaves in this portion of Georgia "were gradually decreasing in number and also in size, while the large holdings were gradually increasing in number and in size as well." Phillips interpreted "this tendency as a general law of the plantation system—that, within the limit at which plantations grew too large to be manageable, the tendency in the staple-producing region was for the size of plantations under good management to increase until the maximum efficiency was reached, while the size of those under weak management tended to decrease until they lost their complex organization and became simple farms."[18]

By comparing the 1824 manuscript census for Crawford County with the 1860 federal enumeration, Phillips gleaned valuable demographic information regarding slavery's place in the settling of west Georgia's cotton belt. In 1824, the county was dominated by small farmers. Sixty-five percent of all white families in the county held no slaves, and 50 percent of those remaining held fewer than four slaves each. Only eleven families of the 330 in the county held as many as eleven bondsmen each. By 1860, however, planters increased their holdings both of land and slaves. Plantations gradually encroached upon the land hitherto controlled by small farmers. As a result, many small farmers moved in search of fresh lands, "where they might live more cheaply as self-sufficient producers, having little to do with staples, money, or markets." By 1860, the number of slaveholding families had increased to 369, holding a total of 4,270 bondsmen. Phillips concluded that "The pioneer work throughout the South seems to have been done by the yeoman class and the younger sons of the well to do, while the wave of planters followed later and was confined to the staple-producing areas and to the districts lying in reach of markets."[19]

From his examination of Baldwin County records of sale and estate inventories, Phillips concluded that the records of appraisements and sales of estates "comprise the chief source from which may be had of the rise and fall of slave prices." Because the available published data on slave prices and the economics of slavery was so "scanty and fugitive, and often unreliable," Phillips predicted that a comparative study, juxtaposing data from throughout the slaveholding regions of the North and South, will be essential as a basis for any definitive economic history of slavery in America."[20]

His study of tax digests for Oglethorpe County enabled Phillips to draw conclusions concerning not only slaveholding, but also postwar labor and race relations in the Georgia Piedmont. From an average slaveholding of five in 1794 (395 slaveholders owned 1,980 slaves), to an average slave holding of twelve in 1860 (549 slaveholders owned 6,589 slaves), this county exhibited "a fairly continuous increase in the proportion of Negroes to whites in the population." Phillips pointed to an 1899 indenture agreement—one among many on file in Oglethorpe County—between a planter, James M. Smith, and a black, Anderson Benson, as illustrative of "the degree to which the plantation system has been maintained in spite of the overthrow of the institution of slavery." In the agreement, Benson bound himself to labor for Smith for a term of five years. Resembling the labor contracts that blacks signed during Reconstruction, Benson agreed "to work faithfully" under Smith's "direction, respect and obey all orders and commands" and "at all times demean himself orderly and soberly." In addition to furnishing his apprentice with board, lodging, clothing, and fifty dollars a year as compensation, Smith agreed to teach Benson "the trade of husbandry in all its details."[21]

Phillips's insights into the condition of Georgia's archival materials enabled him in 1905 to broaden his analysis to include the records of the entire South. He concluded that archival conditions in the region still left room for vast improvement. While Phillips regretted that many of the South's most valuable documents had found "refuge" in Washington and in the North, he was forced to admit that in these repositories southern manuscripts "received more care and attention than if they had remained in their original localities." Though his earlier study of Georgia's records had underscored its rich holdings of public records, Phillips now complained that the state had not yet begun to systematize the manuscripts held in the capitol building. And researchers would find few valuable manuscripts at the Georgia Historical Society in Savannah. Indeed, Phillips said, "the most important documentary collections" were held privately. While Phillips generally considered Virginia's archives to be more accessible than others in the region, he nonetheless urged that state to provide some sort of finding aid—"a calendar or even a finding list for the whole body of archives." He criticized Virginia's documentary publication program, the Virginia State Papers series, as "an unsystematized mass of heterogeneous and often worthless items." And Phillips found fault with Tennessee's archives. Aside from some newspaper collections at the Tennessee State Library and the Tennessee Historical Society, he identified "no other public collection of material in the State worth the mention, nor any noteworthy publication of documents."[22]

Phillips noted similar problems in South Carolina. The state had undertaken no major documentary publication program and the strength of its archival holdings lay mostly in newspaper collections. In Charleston, Phillips located newspaper files "of quite phenomenal extent," dating from the earliest newspaper published in the colony in 1732. South Carolina's state records, however, located in Charleston and Columbia, stood "in great confusion." The old volumes of colonial records at Charleston, deplored Phillips, "have had their brittle and broken pages mended in an atrocious way by the pasting of a heavy white cloth over one side of each sheet. The cloth is absolutely opaque. Every alternate page is thus blotted out of the record, and such volumes thereby [are] rendered almost useless." And despite his repeated efforts to examine the manuscripts at the South Carolina Historical Society in Charleston, Phillips found access to these records most difficult. As in Georgia and throughout the South, most of the valuable collections of South Carolina family and plantation records lay in private possession.[23]

Phillips concluded that while the South had indeed made progress in organizing and preserving its historical materials, archival management in the region remained largely in its infancy. Although the South held vast quantities of manuscripts, few historians could gain access to them and they remained unused. Most of these documents rested in private hands and stood "unclassified, undigested, unknown." Phillips complained that even the pioneer efforts of southern archivists had been "partly wasted," because their "need of training, enthusiasm, and personal force" had partially been ignored. As a result "the documents and their use have suffered accordingly." He judged the region to be disadvantaged because no southern university had yet begun to collect historical manuscripts. Phillips hoped that southerners would come to grasp the broad benefits of studying history, not for "utilitarian purpose," but "for history's sake." He feared, however, that "from their lack of social self-consciousness," southerners "are not likely to develop a genuine passion for preserving and publishing their records."[24]

Phillips's doubts ultimately proved to be well founded. Notwithstanding his pathbreaking efforts to identify, preserve, publicize, and utilize the South's historical manuscripts, southern historians continued to encounter major difficulties in locating sources until the 1930s. The establishment of the Southern Historical Collection at the University of North Carolina in 1930, and Duke University's Manuscript Department in 1931, ushered in an era of systematic archival collection and management in the South. Significantly, in 1928, Phillips had recommended that funds be allocated to help establish the collection at Chapel Hill.[25] But this and other infant collections of southern Americana would take decades to mature into major repositories.

In the years before his death in 1934, Phillips continued to comb the South's countryside in search of the plantation documents that he cited in his books and articles. He received valuable assistance in collecting manuscripts from Herbert A. Kellar, curator of the McCormick Historical Association. By the late 1920s, according to historian Merton L. Dillon, Phillips "had become a dealer in manuscripts and Americana as well as a scholar and collector."[26] Since the turn of the century, Phillips had actively promoted archival practices and the use of primary sources for the study of southern history. Many of the manuscripts that he unearthed in the early 1900s were employed again and again in his later writings. These records provided a foundation for his lifelong research into the history of slavery and the South. They reinforced Phillips's conservative social ethos and paternalistic view of blacks.

In part, Phillips's motives as a historian who favored the establishment of archives were self-serving. An aggressive, competitive scholar, he sought not only to establish southern history as a research field, but to dominate it. In order to do so, Phillips required primary sources. But as a southern Progressive and spokesman of the New South, he linked his region's future to an understanding of its past.[27] Phillips believed that his lobbying for modern archival practices in the South would reap both personal benefits as well as those for the intellectual life of his region. Significantly, Phillips helped lead the South away from antiquarianism to modern historical methodology. As a propagandist for the systematic care of Georgia's public records, Phillips helped pave the way for Georgia archivists Allen D. Candler, William J. Northen, and Lucian Lamar Knight. In 1918, Georgia established its Department of Archives and History.[28]

Though a collector, Phillips encouraged southern archives and libraries to acquire manuscripts for the use of the broad scholarly community. He implored southern state legislatures to build manuscript collections, to conserve them, and to staff their repositories with trained professionals. Although Phillips once aspired to a joint professor-librarian position, he never performed archival functions to more than a limited degree. His substantial contribution to archival development in the South was an insistence on adequate resources for the systematic care of historical records by trained professionals. Phillips was an effective advocate because of his professional standing, his deep commitment to the use of primary materials, and his keen familiarity with archival conditions in the South. Though a historian, Phillips provided leadership at a time when the archival profession was just beginning to emerge. As historian and archival advocate, then, Phillips provided an important impetus to the development of archives in the South. He serves as a valuable example of the role that a scholar—a historian sensitive to the importance of archival materials—can make to the preservation of historical records.

15

Ulrich Bonnell Phillips's *Plantation and Frontier Documents: 1649–1863*

The Historian as Documentary Editor

After a half-century of debate over his significance to the historiography of the South, Georgian Ulrich Bonnell Phillips (1877–1934) remains a controversial and enigmatic figure.[1] A Georgia native, Phillips viewed the South with affection and sought to defend it from attacks by neoabolitionists. He did so in part by establishing southern history as a research field. Trained in the "scientific" historical methodology of his day, Phillips ultimately surpassed all others of his generation in the appreciation and use of plantation records and other southern manuscript materials. Similarly, as a conservative on the race question and a member of the white southern intellectual elite, Phillips had few rivals. Although he repeatedly professed objectivity, Phillips escaped neither the antiblack prejudice of Jim Crow America, nor his inherited perception of blacks and other working-class peoples as inferiors. Following in the footsteps of his friend Frederick Jackson Turner, early in his career Phillips applied Turner's geographic and economic determinism to the study of slavery and the South. Phillips later expanded his outlook and interpreted slavery, and much of southern history, as falling within the broad realm of social history. Phillips's *American Negro Slavery: A Survey of the Supply, Employment and Control of Negro Labor as Determined by the Plantation Régime* (1918) and *Life and Labor in the Old South* (1929) attest to the thoroughness of his research, the broad influence of his sometimes controversial interpretations, and the high literary quality of his exposition.[2]

Despite all that has been written on Phillips and his valuable scholarship, his work as a documentary editor has remained largely unexamined, possibly because many historians themselves have a bias against editing as second-class work.[3] Much, however, is to be learned about Phillips's view of history and his methodological approach to it by examining his contributions as an editor. His best-known edited works include *Plantation and Frontier Documents: 1649–1863* (2 vols., 1909), *The Correspondence of Robert Toombs, Alexander H. Stephens, and Howell Cobb* (1913), and *Florida Plantation Records from the Papers of George Noble Jones* (co-edited with James David Glunt, 1927).[4] This essay focuses largely on *Plantation and Frontier Documents.*

Several factors inclined Phillips toward editorial work. First, he ranked as one of the South's most persistent advocates of modern archival practice in the early twentieth century. Phillips underscored the difficulties historians of the South experienced accessing the region's historical records. In 1903, the American Historical Association (AHA) appointed Phillips to its Public Archives Commission, and he served on the AHA's Historical Manuscripts Commission from 1909 to 1913.[5] He perceived documentary publication as a natural corollary to the preservation of records.[6] Phillips felt compelled to make available to a broad audience the rich manuscript sources that he personally had uncovered. Second, Phillips valued scholarly accuracy with a passion and relished the give-and-take of historical criticism. Finally, he was ambitious and almost obsessed with publishing. In 1907, he described himself as "a man in a hurry."[7] Recognizing this trait, John Franklin Jameson, editor of the *American Historical Review,* once advised Phillips "that you have a good deal of time before you and need be in no haste to publish." Jameson added: "Secure reputations, valuable when a man is fifty or sixty, are not to be had but by taking a good deal of pains and time for the execution of everything that a man prints over his name when he is young." A decade later, Jameson described Phillips as "young and impulsive, and always somewhat eager to get into print."[8]

And publish Phillips did, authoring five books, editing three documentary collections, and writing scores of articles and reviews.[9] In 1902, when Phillips earned his Ph.D., the field of historical editing was poised for change. The movement toward the collection, preservation, and publication of historical records began in France in the 1830s. But in nineteenth-century America, literary, filiopietistic editors doctored, altered, omitted, and mutilated texts bordering on deliberate falsification.[10] In 1895, the AHA established a Historical Manuscripts Commission that adopted modern principles of editing patterned on the third Versammlung deutscher Historiker that also met in 1895. By 1909, when Phillips's first significant documentary appeared, the AHA had already published four major editing projects: the letters of John C. Calhoun, Salmon P. Chase, the French ministers to the United States, 1791–1797, and the diplomatic archives of the Republic of Texas.[11]

As the new century unfolded, the editing field thus lay wide open for a professional scholar like Phillips. He stood armed with scholarly standards and determined to establish himself quickly as a leader in the new field of southern history.[12] Phillips appreciated the labor involved in editing and recognized the value of documentaries as primary sources. His edited work, in fact, played an important role in Phillips's reputation as the leading scholar of his day on the Old South. He employed many of the plantation materials that he located and edited in the early twentieth century again and again in his later writings.

In a review essay written in 1903, Phillips first exhibited the sharp critical sense that later characterized his editions. He considered the volume under review, a monograph on internal improvements in Alabama, "superficial, undigested, and in scope too limited to fit the title. The author ... gives little indication of ever having seen an old map of Alabama or a newspaper published in the State before the Civil War." In 1905, Phillips fired a broadside at Virginia's documentary publication program, the Virginia State Papers series. According to the historian, the *Calendar of Virginia State Papers and Other Manuscripts, 1652–1781* (1875–1893) constituted "an unsystematized mass of heterogeneous and often worthless items." Years later, Phillips excoriated an author because his book was "regrettably hard to use," lacked a table of contents, chapter titles, coherent footnote citations, an index, and, Phillips added, any "readily apparent sequence of themes." It was not beyond Phillips, even as a mature scholar, to comment on the poor quality of indexes and shoddy proofreading. More happily, in 1927, Phillips praised Helen T. Catterall's *Judicial Cases Concerning American Slavery*, judging "the editing beyond reproach." Such enthusiasm, however, resulted not from a lack of troubleshooting on Phillips's part. He confessed that for a brief moment, at least, he thought that he had spotted a typographical error or a misspelled word. But no, Phillips admitted, "the dictionary trapped the trapper." And in 1931, Phillips even detected a "superfluous and erroneous" footnote in his own edition of *Florida Plantation Records*. Phillips judged this "a fearful example of what ought not to be" and wisely observed that "the fewer the notes one inserts, the smaller the prospect of error." Phillips assumed full responsibility for the erroneous footnote which, he admitted, "is all my own."[13]

Phillips's earliest edited work appeared in a series of undistinguished articles in the obscure *Gulf States Historical Magazine* in 1903–1904. Teaching at the University of Wisconsin, Phillips had easy access to the Draper Manuscript Collection at the State Historical Society of Wisconsin. His articles basically provided "copies" of documents from that collection, including an 1800 bill for newspaper advertising in Kentucky, manuscripts pertaining to Indian wars along the frontier, and territorial land grants. One article was an admittedly "rambling" piece based on selected nineteenth-century town records of Milledgeville, Georgia. During these years Phillips also conducted extensive surveys of Georgia's records for the AHA.[14] In his edited articles, Phillips provided brief introductory remarks and sparse annotations. They exhibited little of the editorial rigor found in his three more mature documentaries. For example, Phillips offered the reader scant information concerning his editorial style, especially the method of transcription he selected.

Although these early articles reveal little concern on Phillips's part for any logical or consistent editorial procedures, he nonetheless recognized the documents' value as primary sources. From the land records he concluded, like Frederick Jackson Turner before him, that "the keynote of the land policy in the [Old] South was the demand for liberality." Phillips believed that the central theme of western expansion "was the belief in the rights of the people," especially their "impatience with any policy which hindered their enjoyment of the bounties of nature." Phillips interpreted land acquisition as a "process" and emphasized the fundamental importance of inexpensive and plentiful lands "for the profitable use of slave labor and the plantation system." Commenting on the uncalendared hundreds of volumes of Draper manuscripts, Phillips wrote enthusiastically that they "include a very great amount of all sorts of historical data" for social and economic analysis. "The only trouble," he added, "is to find it." From the Milledgeville documents, Phillips deduced that "materials exist for a complete . . . history of any given community and of the South as a whole." He cautioned, however, that access would be achieved "only by diligent search, and it can be wrought into history only by intelligent and persevering interpretive study." He promised that "the rewards awaiting the patriotic historian who sets forth the clear and convincing truth about the South will be great enough to blot out the memory of his tedious labor."[15]

By 1908, having already published two monographs and numerous articles on slavery and the plantation system, Phillips was a rising star in the field of southern history. He moved south for the first time when Tulane University hired him away from Wisconsin to come to New Orleans. A year later, in 1909, Phillips published *Plantation and Frontier Documents*, his most important documentary edition. These hefty tomes, totaling over 750 letterpress pages, comprised volumes one and two of the ten-volume *Documentary History of American Industrial Society* (1910–1911), published by the American Bureau of Industrial Research (ABIR). In 1904, reform economists Richard T. Ely and John R. Commons established the ABIR at Wisconsin and planned their monumental documentary spanning three centuries of American labor history. Commons had primary responsibility to see the series through to publication in 1910 and 1911. After heated discussions, Ely, Commons, and the publisher, Arthur H. Clark, agreed to issue Phillips's volumes separately, in 1909.[16] The cumbersome project was delayed by financial problems in 1907 and was racked by bitter personal feuds between Ely and Commons over royalties and over control of the ABIR, and between the editors and the directors over whose names would appear on the title pages and spines of the volumes. Phillips entered the latter fray head-on. He informed Ely "that my name shall appear upon the back of the volumes which embody my work, I must make a positive condition."[17] Though he described the brouhaha as "one over mere details" and stated that "the tempest has a teapot scope," Phillips participated fully in the fight and ultimately prevailed.[18]

The ABIR represented one of America's earliest collaborative scholarly editing projects. Significantly, Ely and Phillips termed the scope of Phillips's volumes southern "industrial society," knowing full well that most citizens of the Old South earned their livings from the soil, not from manufacturing. A Wisconsin Progressive, Ely considered their project not "a mere antiquarian pursuit," but "a prerequisite for interpreting the truly urgent and menacing problems of today." Ely and Commons were among the first to conceptualize labor conditions in America as a whole, including slave laborers. As Ely said, the ABIR was concerned with "the labor problem in all its ramifications, whether as a race problem in the South, a trade union problem in the North, or a political problem in both."[19] Commons emphasized the need for a documentary on the economy of the Old South and referred to Phillips's volumes as "the most interesting, original and unique of the whole collection."[20]

Phillips, who confessed to having a "sympathetic understanding of plantation conditions," intended his volumes to correct "the conjectures of hit-or-miss writers," who had generalized unfairly about his beloved South. His concern was with "men and manners," which he defined as "a phase of social history." As early as 1904, Phillips had interpreted economic history "chiefly as a means of interpreting political history." Ely observed that while previous historians focused on wars and politics, the new generation of scholars was examining "movements of the masses." He added:

> To the historian of today it is the very peace and obscurity of these industrious millions that furnish the object of diligent search. The vulgar but precious documents they unearth and edit are the tax receipts, the bills of exchange, the leases, wills, and other every-day records of the life and living of the people, written perhaps on papyri and preserved by their fortunate use as covers for their mummies. Eventually, out of this patient search, with a new wealth of economic material, a new Gibbon may picture to us the work and industry that sustained the masses while they suffered beneath the wars and politics so graphically portrayed by the elder Gibbon.

In their own way and in their own day, Ely, Commons, and Phillips were mapping out the contours of sources and research methods that later historians would describe as the "new" social history.[21]

With his research subsidized by the ABIR and by grants from the Carnegie Institution of Washington, Phillips worked independently of the other editors searching far and wide for documents for inclusion in his documentary. In *Plantation and Frontier Documents,* he also included "a large number" of documents that he had collected previous to joining the ABIR. For several years, Phillips had labored along with historian Charles McCarthy, director of the University of Wisconsin's Legislative Reference Library, gathering sources for an economic history of the Old South.[22] "The only way of obtaining approximately complete information," Phillips explained, "is to seek documents in every promising nook and cranny in the land, and to glance through every document in search of data—for in study from sources one often finds what one little expects." He visited libraries in Richmond, Charleston, Columbia, Atlanta, Savannah, Lexington, Louisville, Nashville, Washington, and New Orleans. He unearthed private collections in such out-of-the-way spots as Pinopolis, South Carolina, and Stovall, Mississippi. Along the way, Phillips employed copyists to transcribe the documents. His industriousness bore rich fruit, leading Phillips to conclude that "finding rare and hidden materials [was] largely a consequence of the unworked nature of the field."[23]

In selecting items for inclusion, Phillips kept three qualities in mind: "rareness, unconsciousness, and faithful illustration." He sought accounts by "actual participators who wrote with no expectation that what they wrote would be published." Phillips admitted a certain unevenness in the items that he selected for inclusion. Some topics—like free blacks who voluntarily enslaved themselves—were chosen because of their uniqueness. "On the subject of small farms," however, Phillips said that "the reader must keep in mind that there is a hiatus in the documents," and explained that he employed "distinct caution" in selecting documents that exhibited "prevalent philosophy and public opinion." He acknowledged that "the method of the whole work has its obvious limitations or unevenness and incompleteness." While Phillips considered "the result . . . fragmentary at best," he nonetheless hoped that "the result can not fail to be suggestive, at least, and furnish a basis for true knowledge."[24]

Unlike his earlier edited articles, in *Plantation and Frontier Documents,* Phillips followed the professional editorial practices that were just then taking shape. He obviously had grown as an editor, this time taking "great care" in reproducing the 386 documents accurately and providing "reasonable assurance . . . that no serious errors have crept in." He identified each document by source and location and employed ellipses or a full line of dots to indicate where material within a document had been omitted. Occasional misspellings, explanations, and clarifications were identified in brackets. His publisher employed special typography to reproduce the archaic tailed "s." Phillips said that, with only two exceptions (where he was forced to rely upon abstracts, not "verbatim copies"), "no conscious departure from the text of the original has been made." For the two volumes Phillips provided only twenty-two conventional annotations and no introductions to the volumes' twenty-three sections. While these might have assisted readers in moving from one document to another, Phillips rationalized his editorial decision on the grounds that most of the documents "are well able to tell their own story."[25] Because documents generally included information on more than one topic, Phillips cautioned readers to beware of the categories that he had assigned to them. His scheme of organization was "loose as well as broad," Phillips explained, and "it is safer to use the collection as a whole, or any single document from it, rather than to take the material under any single heading as being at all fully descriptive."[26]

Plantation and Frontier Documents is an accumulation of primary materials from throughout the South that illustrate the diversity of the region's economic and labor history. Phillips included planters' diaries, instructions, contracts, and letters; newspaper advertisements; certificates of freedom; manuscript petitions; municipal records and ordinances; travelers' journals; and merchants' account books. He uncovered these in libraries as well as in such informal repositories as corn cribs and outbuildings. *Plantation and Frontier Documents* was the first documentary record of cotton, rice, indigo, sugar, and tobacco cultivation, as well as what Phillips referred to as plantation "by-industries"—cultivating cereals, keeping bees, weaving, spinning, and fishing. Volume 1 dealt almost exclusively with plantations—management, routine, crops, supplies and factorage, health care, and the maintenance of the work force, black as well as white. In it, Phillips rescued from obscurity plantation regulations that he admitted gave "too idyllic a view of the [slavery] system." Such records illustrated "the aspirations of the high class planters," he said, not "the actuality on the average plantation." Phillips devoted Volume 2 largely to slavery and frontier life, with sections treating poor whites, immigrants, migration, manufacturing, and artisan and town labor. Phillips observed that the documents on "Fugitive and Stolen Slaves" underscored "the weakest spots in the whole slaveholding system, the precariousness of slave labor as a form of wealth, the injustice and hardships of slavery when imposed upon the exceptional 'person of color,' and the failure of the rigid legal system to allow for evolution and readjustment." He noted that the records on slave crime illustrated "the necessity, the degree of success and failure, and the results of subjecting the imported Africans to a tyranny of Anglo-American law and industry." Phillips also remarked that because poor whites "left no records of their own . . . satisfactory evidence regarding them is hard to find."[27]

Phillips included documents on southern miners, textile workers, craftsmen and women, and mechanics—groups still largely omitted from consideration by southern historians. He supplied annotations that explained, for example, the matlaying of sugar, the task system in rice cultivation, and the "country marks" among African tribesmen. Phillips pointed out that the documents regarding public regulation of industry resulted from "the spirit of conservatism, even of medievalism, and not of progress." Commenting on the documents of mechanics' associations, he said that "in most cases" such groups were "not of the nature of trades unions." He pointed out that trades unions were but sporadic in the South and not characteristic."[28] Taken as a whole, *Plantation and Frontier Documents* reflected the central themes of Phillips's many writings: the diversity of conditions in the South, and slavery as a social necessity for whites, a cultural and educational boon for blacks, and an economic albatross for the region.[29]

Plantation and Frontier Documents included a lengthy introduction that still provides one of the best explanations of the growth of the plantation system. Many of Phillips's generalizations have become accepted in the historical literature on the South. He defined the plantation as "a unit in agricultural industry in which the laboring force was of considerable size," where "the work was divided among groups of laborers who worked in routine under supervision." He insisted, however, that the unique quality of the Old South's plantation system lay in its use of unfree labor. Drawing upon the Darwinian model, Phillips argued that in the Old South, frontier units, farms, and plantations competed in local areas for supremacy. In the end, "the most efficient for the main purpose at hand would conquer." Phillips, like Turner before him, concluded that much of the economic history of the plantation South experienced a similar process of evolution. The plantation supplied a successful system of agriculture, one predicated on a "constant and even" work force. Implicit in Phillips's introductory essay was the differentiation that he had made in his early articles between the *plantation* on the one hand, and *slavery* on the other.[30]

Scholars generally greeted *Plantation and Frontier Documents* with enthusiasm. In the *Political Science Quarterly,* William R. Shepherd praised Phillips for producing "a great pioneer work" and complimented him "for the scholarly care with which he has selected and arranged the collection." Reviewers in the *Atlantic Monthly* and the *Dial* lauded Phillips for fashioning a documentary free of partisan bias by seeking out "unconscious" sources never intended for publication. Mississippi planter, economist, and Phillips's friend, Alfred Holt Stone, extolled *Plantation and Frontier Documents* as "an event of first importance to students of American history and economics." He praised the collection for illustrating "the economic inertia of the plantation system," in both the Old and the New South, and for providing a "corrective" to false representations of the Old South by chauvinists on both sides of the Mason-Dixon line. As late as 1961, historian Fletcher M. Green esteemed Phillips's documentary as "the most important single collection of published source documents on the plantation regime of the pre-Civil War South."[31]

Some reviewers, however, were less gushing. Max Farrand, who found many of the documents "really illuminating," nonetheless criticized Phillips for failing to be "exhaustive" in his collecting. Phillips erred, in Farrand's opinion, both in arranging and in organizing the documents "with reference to the material selected," ignoring "a logical analysis of the subject in hand." And Farrand feared that the absence of explanatory text rendered many of the documents "misleading and sometimes . . . unintelligible" to non-specialists. Farrand, who awarded the third and fourth volumes of *A Documentary History of American Industrial Society* "unqualified praise," complained that Phillips's volumes would serve best as collateral material to an economic and industrial history of the South. But until then, he said, "the collection as a whole will hardly serve the purpose for which it was intended." An unidentified reviewer in the *Nation* agreed. While judging the volumes "indispensable," he found their "annotation . . . parsimonious," and the level of "editorial analysis and comment" insufficient. The reviewer further questioned Phillips's rigid topical arrangement and his inclusion of texts that were "a bit wearisome and not over instructive."[32]

Plantation and Frontier Documents certainly contains flaws. Modern scholars will cringe at the generally passive role Phillips assigned to African Americans. Phillips interpreted the plantation as a school that provided "efficient control and direction" of unfree workers and "incidentally trained a savage race to a certain degree of fitness for life in the Anglo-Saxon community." For example, his documenting the voluntary enslavement of free blacks was in line with Phillips's benign view of slavery. He included in his edition an article from the *Milledgeville Federal Union* that noted the unusual nature of one of the voluntary enslavement cases, describing it as "a nut for Yankee philosophers to crack." While Phillips certainly allowed the documents to speak for themselves, he selected documents that reinforced his own vision of slavery as a positive good for blacks. *Plantation and Frontier Documents* decidedly has the flavor of the "big house," not the slave quarters.[33]

In terms of mechanics, Phillips's introductory essay provides insufficient context for interpretation of the documents. Though in some cases he supplied supplementary titles and brief introductory remarks, the dearth of conventional annotations places *Plantation and Frontier Documents* in a narrative and analytical void. The documents stand like relics frozen in time and space. Introductory essays for each section—as in Walter Lynwood Fleming's *Documentary History of Reconstruction* (2 vols., 1906–1907)—would have provided readers with a better sense of the ways in which the Old South's economy was integrated. The absence of an index poses another serious access problem—one not even partially solved by the detailed table of contents. This omission is all the more inexplicable because Arthur H. Clark, the publisher, specifically requested that Phillips and the other editors prepare indexes. Phillips disagreed, however, arguing unpersuasively that "the presence of analytical tables of contents . . . obviates the need of . . . indexes."[34]

And for all of Phillips's pioneering labors in unearthing manuscripts, only 27 percent (104 of 386) of the items published in *Plantation and Frontier Documents* were from holographs (see table on page 163). The largest single number of manuscripts came from Mrs. Alexander S. Erwin of Athens, Georgia, a daughter of Georgia politician Howell Cobb. In 1905, Mrs. Erwin expressed her willingness to have Phillips publish her father's letters. Phillips culled the manuscripts from ten private collections and nine libraries or archives. The number of manuscripts from private collections and from libraries or archives were roughly equal: fifty-five from private collections and forty-nine from libraries or archives. The remaining 73 percent of the documents were drawn from printed sources, some of which (like the works of Frederick Law Olmsted, W.H. Russell, and Charles Lyell) were readily available.[35]

Nevertheless, within the context of its day, *Plantation and Frontier Documents* was a tremendous editorial achievement. Without diminishing the significance of Phillips's antiblack bias, it must be recalled that the master class kept the records and documented the history of slavery and the plantation from their perspective, not from that of the slaves. It would be unfair to Phillips, writing and

Sources for *Plantation and Frontier Documents*

Source	Number of Documents
Mrs. Alexander S. Erwin, Athens, Georgia	21
Georgia Historical Society	15
Draper Collection, State Historical Society of Wisconsin	13
Mrs. C.G. Brandon, Natchez, Mississippi	12
Mrs. Hawkins Jenkins, Pinopolis, South Carolina	11
Virginia Historical Society	8
Library of Congress	5
Alexander S. Salley, Jr., Columbia, South Carolina	4
Charleston, South Carolina, Library	3
Georgia State Archives	2
Ravenel Family, Pinopolis, South Carolina	2
John W. Stovall, Stovall, Mississippi	1
William M. Bridges, Richmond, Virginia	1
Mississippi State Department of Archives and History	1
Milledgeville, Georgia, Town Records	1
Ulrich B. Phillips Personal Collection	1
Virginia State Archives	1
E.S. Hammond, Blackville, South Carolina	1
Gaspard Cusachs, New Orleans, Louisiana	1
Total	104

editing during the age of segregation, to expect him to have viewed slavery from the vantage point of the slaves. In the Progressive era, only a handful of professionally trained black scholars and white neoabolitionists challenged the tenets of the old proslavery argument.[36] Phillips, in fact, was sensitive to this point. In reviewing a documentary in 1931 on the slave trade, he remarked: "The volume gives little of the slaves' point of view. . . . that is the lament, certainly not the fault, of the editor."[37] To his credit, years earlier Phillips included documents in *Plantation and Frontier Documents* that mentioned the harsh conditions of slavery for mulattoes and for slaves at the hands of slave stealers and overseers. He also published documents that showed blacks in assertive roles—as skilled laborers, as runaways, and as opponents of the slavery system. Phillips included, for example, the testimony of Billy Proctor, a Georgia slave who sought to purchase himself. The editor described Proctor's handwriting as "clear" and "strong."[38]

Phillips's unwillingness to interpret the documents was in line not only with contemporary editorial practice, but with the canons of "scientific" history as well. He refused to generalize because most of the documents, he said, "furnish their own warranty." Phillips explained that the documents in his collection were written "concretely, unconsciously, and in evident faithfulness with a special matter with which the writer was concerned in a matter-of-fact way."[39] In 1918, Phillips remarked eloquently that "for twenty years I have panned the sands of the stream of Southern life and garnered their golden treasure. Many of the nuggets rewarding the search have already been displayed in their natural form." He referred to *Plantation and Frontier Documents*.[40] His reliance on printed primary sources also must be placed into perspective. Phillips worked generations before the availability of union catalogs, automated finding aids, and computerized bibliographical systems. His compilation of numerous published items—advertisements, broadsides, editorials, and accounts from hard-to-find newspapers—represented a major scholarly accomplishment. It remains so today.

As the table on page 163 suggests, Phillips gained access to private manuscript collections by aggressively cultivating personal connections among the South's gentry, whom he referred to as the region's "grandees." In 1907, for example, Dunbar Rowland, of the Mississippi Department of Archives and History, arranged for Phillips to borrow records from fellow Mississippian John W. Stovall. "So thanks to your good graces," Phillips wrote Rowland, "I shall doubtless have another good haul for my volume of plantation and frontier documents."[41] In doing so Phillips emerged as a major transitionary figure whose self-archival work prefigured the systematic acquisition of manuscripts by the South's archives and libraries.

By the 1920s, according to his biographer Merton L. Dillon, Phillips had become "a dealer in manuscripts and Americana as well as a scholar and collector." Dillon attributes Phillips's "large reputation as a discoverer and user of such manuscripts . . . in great measure" to manuscripts that Herbert A. Kellar helped him procure. Dillon argues that Phillips relied upon travel accounts and newspapers for much of his documentation in *American Negro Slavery*. The manuscript materials that he and Kellar later acquired, however, "presented a wider range of topics and portrayed a more diverse South" in *Life and Labor in the Old South*.[42]

Plantation and Frontier Documents played a role in Phillips's maturation as a scholar and provided valuable documentation for his analyses in *American Negro Slavery* and *Life and Labor in the Old South*. Dillon has suggested that the documents Phillips edited for the ABIR enabled him to move from "theoretical and general" studies of plantation economics, to more specific topics. For years historians have relied upon Phillips's edition to document the workaday world of planter, preacher, lawyer, merchant, servant, free black, slave, and yeoman. As historian John Herbert Roper has argued, the coverage of *Plantation and Frontier Documents* was so broad, so rich "that it successfully gives the lie to the common complaint that Phillips ignored nonelite whites." The volumes reflected Phillips's Progressive, conflict orientation, especially his interpretive focus on class and race along the South's evolving frontier.[43]

Phillips's ambition, industry, and connections with the South's gentry overcame the handicaps that contemporary scholars faced accessing the records of the South's past. *Plantation and Frontier Documents* was the first and remains one of the most comprehensive collections of documents on the Old South. Though flawed, the documentary established Phillips as an editor and propelled him forward as the foremost historian of slavery in the age of Jim Crow.

Notes

Notes to Preface

1. See John David Smith, *An Old Creed for the New South: Proslavery Ideology and Historiography, 1865–1918* (1985; reprint, Athens: University of Georgia Press, 1991).

2. Ulrich Bonnell Phillips, *American Negro Slavery: A Survey of the Supply, Employment and Control of the Negro Labor as Determined by the Plantation Régime* (New York: D. Appleton, 1918), 401.

Notes to Chapter 1

1. David D. Van Tassel, *Recording America's Past: An Interpretation of the Development of Historical Studies in America, 1607–1884* (Chicago: University of Chicago Press, 1960), 111, 121.

2. Moore to Charles Deane, February 28, 1868, Charles Deane Papers, Massachusetts Historical Society.

3. The elder Moore "combined journalism, publishing, mill operations, and landowning." He "left New Hampshire in 1839," reportedly, "a bankrupt man." David J. Russo, *Keepers of Our Past: Local Historical Writing in the United States, 1820s–1930s* (Westport, CT: Greenwood Press, 1988), 36–37.

4. See, for example, Moore to Parkman, February 27, 1846, March 2, 3, 1857, January 8, 1874, Francis Parkman Papers, Massachusetts Historical Society; Moore to O'Callaghan, September 13, 1860, Edmund Bailey O'Callaghan Papers, Manuscript Division, Library of Congress; Moore to Winsor, April 15, 1880, in Lenox Library Memorial to James Lenox, Houghton Library Reading Room, Harvard University.

5. Lee to Moore, November 25, 1839, James Freeman Clarke Papers, Houghton Library, Harvard University.

6. Robert W.G. Vail, *Knickerbocker Birthday: A Sesqui-Centennial History of the New-York Historical Society, 1804–1954* (New York: New-York Historical Society, 1954), 97–98; Pamela Spence Richards, *Scholars and Gentlemen: The Library of the New-York Historical Society, 1804–1982* (Hamden, CT: Archon Books, 1984), 34–42, 44; Rush C. Hawkins to the editor, *New York Times,* May 19, 1892. Moore's best-known work was *"Mr. Lee's Plan—March 29, 1777": The Treason of Charles Lee* (New York: C. Scribner, 1860).

7. Moore to Charles Deane, January 24, 1887, Deane Papers; George H. Moore, *Notes on the History of Slavery in Massachusetts* [hereafter cited as *Notes*] (New York: D. Appleton, 1866), 14, 23. I have edited Moore's spelling and capitalization to conform with modern usage.

8. Moore to Charles Deane, January 24, 29, 1887, Deane Papers.

9. Moore to Bancroft, July 15, 1875, George Bancroft Papers, Massachusetts Historical Society.

10. Moore to Abbot, June 28, 1852, George Jacob Abbot Papers, Yale University.

11. Moore to Henry H. Edes, July 6, 1889, Henry H. Edes Papers, Massachusetts Historical Society.

12. Moore to Bancroft, August 17, 1877, June 19, 1882, Bancroft Papers.

13. Moore to Deane, January 27, 1868, Deane Papers; Moore to George Bancroft, August 5, 1875, June 19, 1882, Bancroft Papers; George Washington Williams, *History of the Negro Race in America*, 2 vols. (New York: G.P. Putnam's Sons, 1882), 1:173n. Moore assisted Williams with his research, according to John Hope Franklin, *George Washington Williams: A Biography* (Chicago: University of Chicago Press, 1985), 106.

14. "Personal," *New York Times*, March 27, 1869.

15. Sections of Moore's book appeared during the Civil War years under his pseudonym "E.Y.E." See "Historical Notes on Slavery in the Northern Colonies and States— Parts 1–4," *Historical Magazine* 7 (November 1863): 342–345, and (December 1863): 363–367; *Historical Magazine* 8 (January 1864): 21–30, and (June 1864): 193–200; and "Additional Note on the History of Slavery in Massachusetts," *Historical Magazine 9* (February 1865): 57.

16. George H. Moore, *Historical Notes on the Employment of Negroes in the American Army of the Revolution* (New York: C.T. Evans, 1862), 4–5.

17. Moore, *Notes*, 1, 224. In his book, Moore did not differentiate between the Plymouth Colony and Massachusetts Bay. He held them equally culpable for the origins of slavery. "In this connection," Moore wrote, "they may justly be regarded as one" (32).

18. Moore, *Notes*, 110, 98, 124, 68–69, 1–2, emphasis added.

19. Moore, *Notes*, 1, 5–6, 9, 29, 65–66, 7–8, 30, 10.

20. Moore, *Notes*, 11, 12, 16, 21, 11, 18–19. The wording, but not the content, of Sumner's quote appears in a slightly different form in *The Works of Charles Sumner*, 15 vols. (Boston: Lee and Shepard, 1871), 3:384. George Washington Williams remarked that in *Notes on the History of Slavery in Massachusetts*, Moore "summoned nearly all the orators and historians of Massachusetts to the bar of history. He leaves them open to one of three charges . . . evading the truth, ignorance of it, or falsifying the record." Williams, *History of the Negro Race in America*, 1:173n.

21. Moore, *Notes*, 49, 52, 52–53, 54–55, 53.

22. Moore, *Notes*, 111–124, 132, 115–116. Moore added that "the absurdity of the claim set up for Massachusetts is not diminished by the fact that no case in the history of English Law has been more misunderstood and misrepresented than the Somerset case itself." See 115n.

23. Moore, *Notes*, 71.

24. Moore, *Notes*, 59, 111, 142, 144.

25. Moore, *Notes*, 153, 162–163, 176–200, 180, 191, 200.

26. Moore, *Notes*, 203, 203–204 (emphasis added), 209, 224, 221–222.

27. Moore, *Notes*, 224, 227, 230, 237, 229, 230, 240.

28. Moore, *Notes*, 241, 224, 242.

29. Van Tassel, *Recording America's Past*, 161; Peter Novick, *That Noble Dream: The "Objectivity Question" and the American Historical Profession* (Cambridge: Cambridge University Press, 1988), 59.

30. Van Tassel, *Recording America's Past,* 161; [Dawson], review of Moore, *Notes on the History of Slavery in Massachusetts,* in *Historical Magazine* 10 (December 1866 [Supplement 2]): 48, 57. For another favorable review, see *Spectator* (London) 39 (September 22, 1866): 1063.

31. "Notices of New Publications," *New York Herald,* June 3, 1866; "New England Negroism and Hypocrisy," ibid.

32. "Slavery in Massachusetts," *Springfield Weekly Republican,* June 16, 1866; Moore to Bancroft, June 29, 1866, Bancroft Papers.

33. "A Touchstone for Massachusetts," *Nation* 2 (May 22, 1866): 645.

34. "Was Massachusetts the Mother of Slaves?" *Independent* 18 (June 7, 1866): 4.

35. See *Correspondence Concerning Moore's Notes on the History of Slavery in Massachusetts: Two Letters from the Historical Magazine* (New York: n.p., 1866), 2. This letter and Moore's response appeared originally in the *Historical Magazine* 10 (September 1866 [Supplement 2]): 81–82, and (October 1866 [Supplement 3]): 105–108.

36. Moore to Bancroft, September 24, 1866, Bancroft Papers.

37. "Slavery in Massachusetts," *Boston Daily Advertiser,* September 18, 1866. Dunbar's criticism also appeared as "Slavery in Massachusetts: The Boston Critics on Mr. Moore's Notes," *Historical Magazine* 10 (December 1866 [Supplement 2]): 138–143, and in *Slavery in Massachusetts: The Boston Critics and Mr. Moore* (n.p., n.d.), 1–17.

38. Doe to Bancroft, July 13, 1875, Bancroft Papers; Moore to Bancroft, November 22, 1875, Bancroft Papers.

39. "Mr. Moore's Reply to His Boston Critics," in *Slavery in Massachusetts: The Boston Critics and Mr. Moore,* 22; Moore to Deane, January 27, 1868, Deane Papers. Moore's response also appeared in *Historical Magazine* 10 (December 1866 [Supplement 6]), 186–198.

40. Moore, "Letter from George H. Moore to the Editor," in *Correspondence Concerning Moore's Notes on the History of Slavery in Massachusetts,* 10, 6–7, 12.

41. Moore to George Bancroft, September 24, 1866, Bancroft Papers; "Mr. Moore's Reply to His Boston Critics," 19, 25, 33, 21, 29–31, 55.

42. Lorenzo Johnston Greene, *The Negro in Colonial New England* (New York: Columbia University Press, 1942), 16–17, 64–68, 382; Lawrence William Towner, "A Good Master Well Served: A Social History of Servitude in Massachusetts, 1620–1750" (Ph.D. diss., Northwestern University, 1955), 134, 247; William M. Wiecek, *The Sources of Antislavery Constitutionalism in America, 1760–1848* (Ithaca: Cornell University Press, 1977), 44n; Wiecek, "Somerset: Lord Mansfield and the Legitimacy of Slavery in the Anglo-American World," *University of Chicago Law Review* 42 (Fall 1974): 115.

43. Jerome Nadelhaft, "The Somerset Case and Slavery: Myth, Reality, and Repercussions," *Journal of Negro History* 51 (July 1966): 193–208; Robert M. Cover, *Justice Accused: Antislavery and the Judicial Process* (New Haven: Yale University Press, 1975), 44–45.

44. "The Massachusetts Slave Trade," *De Bow's Review,* After War Series, 2 (August 1866): 296.

45. Parker Pillsbury, *Acts of the Anti-Slavery Apostles* (1883; reprint, Freeport, NY: Books for Libraries, 1970), 72; E.R.S. to the editor, *Nation* 43 (October 21, 1886): 329–330; H.W.S. to the editor, *Nation* 43 (November 4, 1886): 371–372.

46. See *Report of the Joint Committee on Reconstruction at the First Session Thirty-Ninth Congress* (Washington, DC: Government Printing Office, 1866).

47. Moore, *Notes,* 111.

48. Sister Sallie, *The Color Line Devoted to the Restoration of Good Government Putting an End to Negro Authority and Misrule, and Establishing a White Man's Government in the White Man's Country, by Organizing the White People of the South* (n.p.,

[1868?]), 65; Thomas Nelson Page, *The Old South: Essays Social and Political* (1892; reprint Chautauqua, NY: The Chautauqua Press, 1919), 292–296; Robert F. Campbell, *Some Aspects of the Race Problem in the South* (Asheville, NC: The Citizen Company, 1899), 1; Mrs. Andrew M. Sea [Sophie Irvine Fox], *"Slavery in Massachusetts": A Brief Synoptical Review of Slavery in the United States* (Louisville: Albert Sydney Johnston Chapter U.D.C., 1916), 3–12; "Slavery in Massachusetts," *Confederate Veteran* 5 (January 1897): 21. The editor of the *Confederate Veteran* quoted a review of Moore's book published in the *New York Commercial-Advertiser*, n.d.

49. "Mr. Moore's Reply to His Boston Critics," 34; Van Tassel, *Recording America's Past*, 122.

50. Moore, *Notes*, 204, 71. On the Whig interpretation of history, see Herbert Butterfield, *The Whig Interpretation of History* (1931; reprint, New York: Norton, 1965), 24, 62, 94–95. On Rhodes, the neoabolitionist school of historians, and the inadequacies of "scientific" historical methodology as applied to the study of slavery, see John David Smith, *An Old Creed for the New South: Proslavery Ideology and Historiography, 1865–1918* (1985; reprint, Athens: University of Georgia Press, 1991), 117–130, 155–157, 190–191.

51. Moore, *Notes*, 9, 72, 87, 226, 227, 225, 227, 27–28, 56, 55.

52. Moore, *Notes*, 109, 63, 230, 198, 208, 129, 111, 135, 225, 226, 63n. On anti-black sentiment in the North during Reconstruction, see Forrest G. Wood, *Black Scare: The Racist Response to Emancipation & Reconstruction* (Berkeley: University of California Press, 1968).

53. Eric Foner, *Reconstruction: America's Unfinished Revolution, 1863–1877* (New York: Harper & Row, 1988), 34.

54. Moore, *Historical Notes on the Employment of Negroes in the American Army of the Revolution*, 24.

55. Mark E. Neely, Jr., "Thirteenth Amendment," *The Abraham Lincoln Encyclopedia* (New York: McGraw Hill, 1982), 308.

56. Moore, *Notes*, 242; J.G. Randall and David Donald, *The Civil War and Reconstruction* (Boston: Heath, 1961), 396–397. Randall and Donald considered it "one of the many anomalies of reconstruction," that Arkansas, Tennessee, North Carolina, Virginia, Louisiana, Alabama, Georgia, and South Carolina were "considered competent to ratify the antislavery amendment, such ratification being essential to its enactment, and yet be rejected by Congress and not considered states in the Union."

57. Moore, *Notes*, 242.

Notes to Chapter 2

1. The Macmillan Company published Rhodes's work in nine volumes between 1892 and 1922. His famous chapter on slavery appeared in Volume 1, pages 303–383. References to the first volume will hereafter be cited as *History* with the appropriate page number.

2. James Schouler to James Ford Rhodes, November 28, 1909, James Schouler Papers, Massachusetts Historical Society; Rhodes to William P. Trent, April 10, 1902, William P. Trent Papers, Columbia University; Rhodes to Hilary A. Herbert, November 12, 1904, Hilary A. Herbert Papers, Southern Historical Collection, University of North Carolina at Chapel Hill.

3. Rhodes to John T. Morse, Jr., August 11, 1923, in M.A. DeWolfe Howe, *James Ford Rhodes: American Historian* (New York: D. Appleton, 1929), 345; Rhodes to Robert Grant, March 3, 1912, Robert Grant Papers, Houghton Library, Harvard University; Rhodes to Andrew D. White, June 23, 1900, Andrew D. White Papers, Cornell Univer-

sity; Rhodes to Frederick Jackson Turner, November 8, 1910, Frederick Jackson Turner Papers, Henry E. Huntington Library. The standard biography of Rhodes is Robert Cruden, *James Ford Rhodes: The Man, The Historian, and His Work* (Cleveland: Western Reserve University Press, 1961).

4. Frederic Bancroft, "James Ford Rhodes," *Harper's Monthly* 36 (December 17, 1892): 1219; Trent to Rhodes, March 21, 1893, James Ford Rhodes Papers, Massachusetts Historical Society.

5. Rhodes, *History,* 152, 303.

6. Ibid., 307–308, 307, 332–333, 315.

7. "Rhodes's History of the United States," *Nation* 55 (December 29, 1892): 499–500; "Books," *Literary Digest* 6 (December 31, 1892): 242; Holst in *Historische Zeitschrift* 77 (1896): 337, 338, 342; Bancroft, "A New History of the United States," *Critic* 19 (February 18, 1893): 93.

8. Holst in *Historische Zeitschrift,* 337, 338, 340; Bancroft, "A New History of the United States," 93; Burgess in *Political Science Quarterly* 8 (June 1893): 342–343; Winston to Rhodes, October 22, November 15, 1901, Rhodes Papers.

9. Wilson, "Anti-Slavery History and Biography," *Atlantic Monthly* 72 (August 1893): 272–274.

10. Wilson to Ellen L. Axson, November 13, 1884, in Arthur S. Link, ed., *The Papers of Woodrow Wilson,* 69 vols. (Princeton: Princeton University Press, 1966–1994), 3:430. The standard treatment of Wilson's early years is Link, *Wilson: The Road to the White House* (Princeton: Princeton University Press, 1947). On Wilson as historian, see John M. Mulder, *Woodrow Wilson: The Years of Preparation* (Princeton: Princeton University Press, 1978), 139–143.

11. Henry Wilkinson Bragdon, *Woodrow Wilson: The Academic Years* (Cambridge: Harvard University Press, 1967), 11, 237.

12. See John David Smith, "An Old Creed For the New South: Southern Historians and the Revival of the Proslavery Argument, 1890–1920," *Southern Studies: An Interdisciplinary Journal of the South* 18 (Spring 1979): 75–88.

13. Wilson, *Division and Reunion, 1829–1909* (New York: Longmans, Green, 1893), 125.

14. Ibid., 126–128, 105; review in *New Orleans Picayune,* May 28, 1893, in Link, ed., *The Papers of Woodrow Wilson,* 8:218–219.

15. Rhodes to Mrs. Roger Merriman, September 6, 1918, Merriman Family Papers, Massachusetts Historical Society; Rhodes to Frederic Bancroft, August 5, 12, 1893, Frederic Bancroft Papers, Columbia University; Wilson to Horace E. Scudder, August 14, 1893, in Link, ed., *The Papers of Woodrow Wilson,* 8:310.

16. Rhodes, *History,* 342.

17. Many foreign travelers held negative preconceptions of blacks. See William L. Van Deburg, *The Slave Drivers* (Westport, CT: Greenwood Press, 1979), 117–124.

18. Wilson, "Remarks by Prof. Woodrow Wilson," *Annual Report of the American Historical Association for the Year 1896,* 2 vols. (Washington: Government Printing Office, 1896) 1:294–295.

19. Raymond C. Miller, "James Ford Rhodes," in William T. Hutchinson, ed., *The Marcus W. Jernegan Essays in American Historiography* (Chicago: University of Chicago Press, 1937), 175; J. Franklin Jameson to Rhodes, May 7, 1908, Rhodes Papers; Rhodes to Carl Schurz, October 15, 1893, Carl Schurz Papers, Manuscript Division, Library of Congress; Rhodes, "Newspapers as Historical Sources," *Atlantic Monthly* 103 (May 1909): 651, 656.

20. In these years graduate students at Johns Hopkins completed eleven dissertations on slavery. See John David Smith, "The Formative Period of American Slave Historiography" (Ph.D. diss., University of Kentucky, 1977), 85–108.

21. Rhodes sometimes hired research assistants, notably Edward G. Bourne, to perform valuable spade work in primary materials. See Rhodes to Bourne, August 2, 1890, Rhodes Papers.

22. The best known exception is Edward Channing's *History of the United States,* 6 vols. (New York: Macmillan, 1905–1925).

23. Wilson to Scudder, August 14, 1893, in Link, ed., *The Papers of Woodrow Wilson,* 8:310.

Notes to Chapter 3

1. W.E.B. Du Bois, *Darkwater—Voices from Within the Veil* (1920; reprint, New York: AMS Press, 1969), 9.

2. On Du Bois's contributions to the study of slavery and race, see John David Smith, "A Different View of Slavery—W.E.B. Du Bois' Critique," in "The Formative Period of American Slave Historiography, 1890–1920" (Ph.D. diss., University of Kentucky, 1977), chapter 8.

3. See Herbert Aptheker's valuable *Annotated Bibliography of the Published Writings of W.E.B. Du Bois* (Millwood, NY: Kraus-Thomson, 1973).

4. Rawick, "Toward a New History of Slavery in the U.S.," *Speak Out,* n.d., 2, copy in Robert S. Starobin Papers, in possession of the Starobin family, Hancock, Massachusetts.

5. For views of Du Bois in this period contrary to the tone of this sketch, see review of Du Bois, *Darkwater,* in *Journal of Negro History* 5 (April 1920): 257–258, and "W.E.B. Du Bois," *Messenger* 11 (March 1919): 21–22. Both attack Du Bois's basic conservatism and avoidance of substantive economic and political issues. Another critic, a white Tennessean, accused Du Bois of "blind[ing] himself to all that the negro owes to the white man by looking at the injustices the negro has suffered. . . . [Du Bois] is a man with a brilliant mind, but a diseased soul." E.E. Miller, "We and Our Colored Neighbors," *Southern Agriculturist* 50 (April 15, 1920): 5.

6. Fred Landon and Everett E. Edwards, "A Bibliography of the Writings of Professor Ulrich Bonnell Phillips," *Agricultural History* 8 (October 1934): 196–218.

7. Smith, "Ulrich B. Phillips—Scientific Apologist for Slavery" and "Ulrich B. Phillips—Disciple of the Color Line and . . . Defender of the Faith of the South," in "The Formative Period of American Slave Historiography, 1890–1920," chapters 9 and 10.

8. Du Bois, "The Study of the Negro Problems," *Annals of the American Academy of Political and Social Science* 11 (January 1898): 14.

9. Gutman, "The World Two Cliometricians Made," *Journal of Negro History* 60 (January 1975): 58–59, 220, 219, and *The Black Family in Slavery and Freedom* (New York: Pantheon Books, 1976), 31, 32, 259, 554.

10. Du Bois, however, wavered on the question of the equality of the races. On numerous occasions, he urged blacks to challenge statements branding their race inferior to the whites. But in other instances, Du Bois characterized Negroes as backward, childlike, and underdeveloped. He accepted inherent racial and cultural differences between the races. In 1897, Du Bois wrote that blacks and whites were separated by "spiritual, psychical, differences—undoubtedly based on the physical, but infinitely transcending them." Du Bois, "The Conservation of Races," *American Negro Academy Occasional Papers, No. 2* (Washington: American Negro Academy, 1897), 8. Invaluable on this theme is August Meier, *Negro Thought in America, 1880–1915* (1963; reprint, Ann Arbor: University of Michigan Press, 1971), 190–206.

11. Du Bois, "Credo," *Independent* 57 (October 6, 1904): 787; Phillips to Yates Snowden, January 13, 1905, Yates Snowden Papers, South Caroliniana Library, University of South Carolina.

12. Gerald M. Capers to John David Smith, January 2, 1976, in possession of the author.

13. Du Bois, "The Storm and Stress in the Black World," *Dial* 30 (April 16, 1901): 262, 263; "The Southerner's Problem," *Dial* 38 (May 1, 1905): 316.

14. Phillips, "Early Railroads in Alabama," *Gulf States Historical Magazine* 1 (March 1903): 345; review of N. Dwight Harris, *History of Negro Servitude in Illinois*, in *American Historical Review* 10 (April 1905): 697; review of James C. McGregor, *The Disruption of Virginia*, in *Mississippi Valley Historical Review* 10 (December 1923): 332.

15. Phillips, ed., *Plantation and Frontier Documents: 1649–1863*, 2 vols. (Cleveland: A.H. Clark, 1909) 1:103.

16. Hart, *Slavery and Abolition, 1831–1841* (New York: Harper & Brothers, 1906), xv and passim.

17. Phillips to George J. Baldwin, May 2, 1903, Ulrich B. Phillips Papers, Southern Historical Collection, University of North Carolina at Chapel Hill.

18. Du Bois's *Black Reconstruction in America, 1860–1880* (1935; reprint, New York: Atheneum, 1973), is a notable exception.

19. Du Bois, *The Negro* (New York: H. Holt, 1915), 150; Du Bois, "Serfdom," *Voice of the Negro* 2 (July 1905): 481; "The Southerner's Problem," 316; "The Negro, as He Really Is," *World's Work* 11 (June 1901): 863.

20. Phillips, "The Plantation as a Civilizing Factor," *Sewanee Review* 12 (July 1904): 264; "The Southern Situation in 1903," unpublished manuscript, Ulrich Bonnell Phillips Collection, Yale University.

21. Phillips, "The Southern Situation in 1903"; Phillips, *American Negro Slavery: A Survey of the Supply, Employment and Control of Negro Labor as Determined by the Plantation Régime* (New York: D. Appleton, 1918), 343, 8, 117, 342, 450, 504, and passim.

22. Du Bois, *Crisis* 5 (March 1913): 239–240.

23. Bruce to Phillips, March 11, 1919, Phillips Collection; *Baltimore Sun*, August 3, 1918, U.B. Phillips Scrapbook, Phillips Collection.

24. Review in *American Political Science Review* 12 (November 1918): 722, 723, 724, 725, 726.

25. Du Bois, *Black Reconstruction in America*, 720, 731, 732; *Dusk of Dawn* (1940; reprint, New York: Schocken Books, 1968), 318.

26. Phillips, *American Negro Slavery*, 147, 148, 454.

27. Du Bois, "The Relation of the Negroes to the Whites in the South," *Annals of the American Academy of Political and Social Science* 18 (July 1901): 132.

28. Phillips, *American Negro Slavery*, 327.

29. Wendell Holmes Stephenson, "Ulrich B. Phillips: Newspaper Correspondent," unpublished manuscript, Wendell Holmes Stephenson Papers, Duke University; John Herbert Roper, "A Case of Forgotten Identity: Ulrich B. Phillips as a Young Progressive," *Georgia Historical Quarterly* 60 (Summer 1976): 165–175.

30. Phillips to Bancroft, April 1, 1915, Frederic Bancroft Papers, Columbia University. Phillips later broke with Bancroft when the latter's criticisms of other historians became acerbic and irrational. See Phillips to Bancroft, October 20, November 15, 1915, Bancroft Papers.

31. John David Smith, "Ulrich B. Phillips and Academic Freedom at the University of Michigan," *Michigan History* 62 (May/June 1978): 11–15.

32. Phillips, "The Historic Civilization of the South," *Agricultural History* 12 (April 1938): 148, 149.

33. In *American Negro Slavery*, 432, Phillips recognized Du Bois along with Booker T. Washington and Paul Laurence Dunbar as exceptional blacks.

Notes to Chapter 4

1. Bancroft, *Slave Trading in the Old South* (1931; reprint, New York: Frederick Ungar, 1959).

2. See John David Smith, "The Formative Period of American Slave Historiography, 1890–1920" (Ph.D. diss., University of Kentucky, 1977), passim.

3. Bancroft, *Slave Trading in the Old South,* 406, 340.

4. Ibid., 368, 378, 376.

5. Ibid., 282 and passim.

6. Woodson review in *Journal of Negro History* 16 (April 1931): 240, 241.

7. Brown review in *Opportunity; A Journal of Negro Life* 10 (January 1932): 24.

8. Woodson review, 240–241.

9. Cowley review in *New Republic* 49 (December 9, 1931): 107.

10. Stephenson review in *Southwestern Social Science Quarterly* 12 (June 1931): 88.

11. Bancroft, *Slave Trading in the Old South,* 24, 69, 86, 208, 234n, 283n, 235n.

12. Nevins, *The Gateway to History* (1938; reprint, Garden City, NY: Anchor Books, 1962), 55.

13. Jacob E. Cooke, *Frederic Bancroft: Historian* (Norman: University of Oklahoma Press, 1957), 7–8, 13–15.

14. Gerald W. McFarland, "The New York Mugwumps of 1884: A Profile," *Political Science Quarterly* 78 (March 1963): 46.

15. Bancroft made three other "long trips as far as New Orleans," in 1902, 1905, and 1912. Bancroft to Charles S. Sydnor, April 20, 1931, Charles S. Sydnor Papers, Duke University Archives.

16. Bancroft, *New York Evening Post,* January 16, February 10, 18, 1885.

17. He was especially proud of having nearly forty years of experience "getting historical evidence out of ex-slaves." Bancroft to Theodore D. Jervey, January 19, 1922, Frederic Bancroft Papers, Columbia University.

18. Bancroft's multi-volume history of the South was divided into four books. These are deposited along with his papers at Columbia University.

19. Bancroft's older brother, Edgar, was one of the nation's foremost corporation lawyers. He supported Frederic's historical work and made him financially independent. See Cooke, *Frederic Bancroft: Historian,* 52–56.

20. Bancroft to André Beydon, July 10, 1909, Bancroft Papers; Bancroft to John P. Cushing, October 23, 1931, Bancroft Papers; Bancroft to Charles S. Sydnor, April 26, 1931, Sydnor Papers.

21. Dunning in *Critic* 36 (May 1900): 394.

22. Cooke, *Frederic Bancroft: Historian,* 139, 9.

23. Smith, "The Formative Period of American Slave Historiography, 1890–1920," chapter 9.

24. Phillips to J. Franklin Jameson, August 24, 1906, *American Historical Review* Editorial Correspondence, Manuscript Division, Library of Congress; Bell I. Wiley, "Ulrich Bonnell Phillips—The Man and the Historian" [notes for speech, 1963], 1–12, copy in possession of the author.

25. Phillips, "Wisconsin University Object Lesson for Georgia," *Atlanta Constitution,* December 4, 1904; John Herbert Roper, "A Case of Forgotten Identity: Ulrich B. Phillips as a Young Progressive," *Georgia Historical Quarterly* 60 (Summer 1975): 165–175.

26. Phillips to William W. Ball, November 28, 1923, W.W. Ball Papers, Duke University.

27. Gabriel to Admissions Committee, Graduate's Club, September 27, 1929, Ralph Henry Gabriel Papers, Yale University.

28. Kellar, "The Historian and Life," *Mississippi Valley Historical Review* 34 (June 1947): 12.

29. Smith, "The Formative Period of American Slave Historiography, 1890–1920," chapters 9 and 10.

30. John David Smith, " 'Keep 'Em in a Fire-Proof Vault'—Pioneer Southern Historians Discover Plantation Records," *South Atlantic Quarterly* 78 (Summer 1979): 376–391; Phillips, "The Plantation Product of Men," *Proceedings of the Second Annual Session of the Georgia Historical Association* (Atlanta: Georgia Historical Association, 1918), 14.

31. Phillips, "The Master Touch," *New York Times,* March 29, 1931.

32. J. Franklin Jameson to Phillips, November 25, 1905, *American Historical Review* Editorial Correspondence.

33. Gerald M. Capers to John David Smith, January 2, 1976, in possession of the author.

34. Phillips to Fairfax Harrison, July 3, 1926, Fairfax Harrison Papers, Virginia Historical Society.

35. Bancroft to J. Franklin Jameson, November 28, 1905, J. Franklin Jameson Papers, Manuscript Division, Library of Congress; Bancroft to Dunbar Rowland, April 30, 1908, Dunbar Rowland Papers, Mississippi Department of Archives and History.

36. Bancroft to William E. Dodd, January 10, 1914, William E. Dodd Papers, Manuscript Division, Library of Congress.

37. See, for example, *The Government of the American Historical Association* [n.p., n.d.], and Frederic Bancroft, John H. Latané, and Dunbar Rowland, *Why the American Historical Association Needs Thorough Reorganization* (Washington: National Capital Press, 1915).

38. Billington, "Tempest in Clio's Teapot: The AHA Rebellion of 1915," *American Historical Review* 77 (April 1973): 349, 350, 351, 359, 361.

39. Phillips to Bancroft, April 1, 6, 1915, Bancroft Papers; Phillips, "The American Historical Association," *Nation* 101 (September 16, 1915): 356.

40. Bancroft to Dunbar Rowland, July 18, August 11, 1915, Rowland to Bancroft, July 28, 1915, Rowland Papers; Bancroft to Oswald Garrison Villard, July 27, 1915, Oswald Garrison Villard Papers, Houghton Library, Harvard University; Phillips to Bancroft, July 15, October 20, 1915, Bancroft to Villard, July 29, 1915, Bancroft Papers.

41. Jameson to H. Morse Stephens, October 11, 1915, in *An Historian's World—Selections from the Correspondence of John Franklin Jameson,* ed. Elizabeth Donnan and Leo F. Stock (Philadelphia: American Philosophical Society, 1956), 185.

42. Ford to John Spencer Bassett, September 21, 1915, copy in Wendell Holmes Stephenson Papers, Duke University; Ford to Phillips, September 30, 1915, *American Historical Review* Editorial Correspondence.

43. Phillips to Ford, October 9, 1915, *American Historical Review* Editorial Correspondence; Phillips to Andrew C. McLaughlin, October 14, 1915, Phillips to Ford [draft], n.d., Stephenson Papers; Ford to Jameson, October 13, 1915, *American Historical Review* Editorial Correspondence; Jameson to Herbert Putnam, July 26, 1927, in *An Historian's World,* ed. Donnan and Stock, 325.

44. Phillips, "The American Historical Association," *Nation* 101 (October 21, 1915): 495.

45. Phillips to Bancroft, October 20, 23, November 15, 20, 1915, Bancroft Papers. On November 9, Bancroft informed Dunbar Rowland that he was amused by his correspondence with Phillips: "It is not worth while to take him seriously any longer." Rowland Papers.

46. Bancroft to Rhodes, December 14, 1918, Bancroft to Du Bois, September 25, December 11, 1918, Bancroft Papers. Du Bois's review appeared in *American Political Science Review* 12 (November 1918): 722–726.

47. Bancroft to Theodore D. Jervey, July 15, 1918, January 8, 1924, Bancroft to Harrison A. Trexler, October 23, 1929, Bancroft to Allan Nevins, March 13, 1932, Bancroft Papers. For Phillips's early comment, see "The Economic Cost of Slaveholding in the Cotton Belt," *Political Science Quarterly* 20 (June 1905): 257.

48. Bancroft to Theodore D. Jervey, October 10, 1931, Bancroft to Trexler, October 17, 1931, Bancroft Papers.

49. Phillips to J. Franklin Jameson, November 26, 1925, Jameson to Phillips, December 1, 1925, Phillips to Henry E. Bourne, February 19, 1931, *American Historical Review* Editorial Correspondence.

50. Bancroft to Yates Snowden, June 14, 1915, Yates Snowden Papers, South Caroliniana Library, University of South Carolina.

51. Charles P. Whittemore, "Frederic Bancroft, 1860–1945" (master's thesis, Columbia University, 1947), 76.

Notes to Chapter 5

1. Blassingame, "Redefining *The Slave Community:* A Response to the Critics," in *Revisiting Blassingame's The Slave Community,* ed. Al-Tony Gilmore (Westport, CT: Greenwood Press, 1978), 158.

2. See, for example, Bruce E. Steiner, "A Planter's Troubled Conscience," *Journal of Southern History* 28 (August 1962): 343; Sterling Stuckey, "Remembering Denmark Vesey," *Negro Digest* 15 (February 1966): 33; John Henrik Clark, ed., *William Styron's Nat Turner: Ten Black Writers Respond* (Boston: Beacon Press, 1968), 7, 10, 16, 57; Edward F. Sweat, review of Ralph B. Flanders, *Slavery in Georgia,* in *Journal of Negro History* 53 (January 1968): 82; Jane H. Pease, "A Note on Patterns of Conspicuous Consumption Among Seaboard Planters, 1820–1860," *Journal of Southern History* 35 (August 1969): 381–382; Herbert Aptheker, *Afro-American History: The Modern Era* (New York: Citadel Press, 1971), 9, 21, 81–83, 94, 175; William W. Nichols, "Slave Narratives: Dismissed Evidence in the Writing of Southern History," *Phylon* 32 (Winter 1971): 403; Charles Crowe, "Historians and 'Benign Neglect': Conservative Trends in Southern History and Black Studies," *Reviews in American History* 2 (June 1974): 164–168; Brenda L. Jones, " 'Time on the Cross': A Rallying Cry for Racists!" *Freedomways* 15 (1975): 30–31; Melvin Drimmer, "Thoughts on the Study of Slavery in the Americas and the Writing of Black History," *Phylon* 36 (June 1975): 127–128, 136–137; A. Leon Higginbotham, Jr., "To the Scale and Standing of Men," *Journal of Negro History* 60 (July 1975): 350; Randall M. Miller, "When Lions Write History: Slave Testimony and the History of American Slavery," *Washington State University Research Studies* 44 (March 1976): 14–15; Peter Kolchin, "The Sociologist as Southern Historian," *Reviews in American History* 5 (March 1977): 22; Aptheker, "Commentary," in *Comparative Perspectives in New World Plantation Societies,* ed. Vera Rubin and Arthur Tuden (New York: New York Academy of Sciences, 1977), 493; Earl E. Thorpe, "The Slave Community: Studies of Slavery Need Freud and Marx," in Gilmore, ed., *Revisiting Blassingame's The Slave Community,* 42; William L. Van Deburg, *The Slave Drivers* (Westport, CT: Greenwood Press, 1979), 32–35.

3. See Fred Landon and Everett E. Edwards, "A Bibliography of the Writings of Professor Ulrich B. Phillips," *Agricultural History* 8 (October 1934): 196–218, and David M. Potter, Jr., "A Bibliography of the Printed Writings of Ulrich Bonnell Phillips," *Georgia Historical Quarterly* 18 (September 1934): 270–282. Neither bibliography is complete.

4. These articles are analyzed in John David Smith, "The Formative Period of American Slave Historiography, 1890–1920" (Ph.D. diss., University of Kentucky, 1977), 269–283.

5. Phillips, "The Economics of the Plantation," *South Atlantic Quarterly* 2 (July

1903): 233, 235, 236; Phillips, "Making Cotton Pay," *World's Work* 8 (May 1904): 4792; Phillips, "The Plantation as a Civilizing Factor," *Sewanee Review* 12 (July 1904): 264; Phillips, "Conservatism and Progress in the Cotton Belt," *South Atlantic Quarterly* 3 (January 1904): 7, 8, 3.

6. Phillips, "The Slave Labor Problem in the Charleston District," *Political Science Quarterly* 22 (September 1907): 437; Phillips, "Black-Belt Labor, Slave and Free," University of Virginia, Phelps-Stokes Fellowship Papers, *Lectures and Addresses on the Negro in the South* (Charlottesville: Michie, 1915), 130; Phillips, "Racial Problems, Adjustments and Disturbances," in *The South in the Building of the Nation,* ed. Julian A.C. Chandler and others, 12 vols. (Richmond: Southern Historical Publication Society, 1909), 4:200; Phillips, "The Economics of the Plantation," 231; Phillips, "Racial Problems, Adjustments and Disturbances," 226, 223; Phillips, "The Origin and Growth of the Southern Black Belts," *American Historical Review* 11 (July 1906): 805.

7. Phillips, "Conservatism and Progress in the Cotton Belt," 8; Phillips, "The Economic Cost of Slaveholding in the Cotton Belt," *Political Science Quarterly* 20 (June 1905): 261.

8. Phillips, "The Economic Cost of Slaveholding in the Cotton Belt," 260.

9. Phillips, *American Negro Slavery: A Survey of the Supply, Employment and Control of Negro Labor as Determined by the Plantation Régime* (New York: D. Appleton, 1918).

10. For an analysis of these themes and others, see Smith, "The Formative Period of American Slave Historiography, 1890–1920," 283–295.

11. Phillips, *American Negro Slavery,* 296, 327, 322, 327.

12. Phillips, *Life and Labor in the Old South* (Boston: Little, Brown, 1929).

13. Ibid., 199–200. In 1929, Phillips's book was selected as the best nonfiction work from among those submitted in a competition sponsored by Little, Brown and Company. His manuscript was published, and he received a large cash prize.

14. For a differing opinion, see C. Vann Woodward's introduction to the paperback edition of *Life and Labor in the Old South* (1929; reprint, Boston: Little, Brown, 1963), v.

15. Bruce to Phillips, March 11, 1919, Ulrich Bonnell Phillips Collection, Yale University.

16. Hamilton, "Interpreting the Old South," *Virginia Quarterly Review* 5 (October 1929): 631; Allen Tate in *New Republic* 59 (July 10, 1929): 211.

17. Commager in *New York Herald Tribune,* May 19, 1929.

18. Stanley M. Elkins and Bennett H. Wall identify nine state studies on slavery (1924–1963) that bear the Phillips stamp. See Elkins, *Slavery: A Problem in American Institutional and Intellectual Life* (1959; reprint, New York: Grosset & Dunlap, 1963), 15, and Wall, "African Slavery," in *Writing Southern History: Essays in Historiography in Honor of Fletcher M. Green,* ed. Arthur S. Link and Rembert W. Patrick (Baton Rouge: Louisiana State University Press, 1965), 185n.

19. Gutman, "The World Two Cliometricians Made," *Journal of Negro History* 60 (January 1975): 58–59, 220, 219, and *The Black Family in Slavery and Freedom* (New York: Pantheon Books, 1976), 21, 32, 259, 554.

20. Du Bois, "The Experts," *Crisis* 5 (March 1913): 239–240, and in *American Political Science Review* 12 (November 1918): 722–726.

21. Woodson in *Journal of Negro History* 4 (January 1919): 102–103; in *Mississippi Valley Historical Review* 5 (March 1919): 480–482; Bancroft to James Ford Rhodes, December 14, 1918, Frederic Bancroft Papers, Columbia University.

22. *Detroit Saturday Night,* April 19, 1919; Ovington in *Survey* 40 (September 28, 1918): 718.

23. Brewer in *Journal of Negro History* 14 (October 1929): 535–536; Bancroft to Harrison A. Trexler, October 17, 1931, Bancroft Papers; Bancroft, *Slave Trading in the*

Old South (1931; reprint, New York: Ungar, 1969), 24, 80, 208, 234n, 235n, 283. Also see Charles H. Wesley's review in *Opportunity* 7 (December 1929): 385.

24. Gray, *History of Agriculture in the Southern United States to 1860*, 2 vols. (1932; reprint, Gloucester, MA: Peter Smith, 1970), 2:476 and passim.

25. Russel, "The Economic History of Negro Slavery in the United States," *Agricultural History* 11 (October 1937): 308–321; Govan, "Was Plantation Slavery Profitable?" *Journal of Southern History* 8 (November 1942): 513–535; Smith, "Was Slavery Unprofitable in the Ante-Bellum South?" *Agricultural History* 20 (January 1946): 62–64.

26. Eugene D. Genovese is a notable exception.

27. Hofstadter, "U.B. Phillips and the Plantation Legend," *Journal of Negro History* 29 (April 1944): 109–124; Hofstadter to Frank L. Owsley, May 18, 1944, Frank L. Owsley Papers, Joint University Libraries, Nashville.

28. Ruben F. Kugler, "U.B. Phillips' Use of Sources," *Journal of Negro History* 47 (July 1962): 167.

29. Robert W. Fogel and Stanley L. Engerman, draft of manuscript on Phillips's slave price data, 1973–74, unpublished paper in possession of the author; Anne W. Chapman, "Inadequacies of the 1848 Charleston Census," *South Carolina Historical Magazine* 81 (January 1980): 25.

30. Aptheker, *American Negro Slave Revolts* (1943; reprint, New York: International Publishers, 1970), 13. In his preface to the 1969 edition, Aptheker described Phillips as "a devout white supremacist who was as incapable of writing truthfully of what it meant to be a Negro slave ... as it would have been for Joseph Goebbels to have written truthfully of what it meant to be a Jew." Reprinted in 1970 edition, 2.

31. This resulted in part from the many sympathetic appraisals of Phillips and his work. See, for example, Wood Gray, "Ulrich Bonnell Phillips," in *The Marcus W. Jernegan Essays in American Historiography*, ed. William T. Hutchinson (Chicago: University of Chicago Press, 1937), 354–373; Fred Landon, "Ulrich Bonnell Phillips: Historian of the South," *Journal of Southern History* 5 (August 1939): 364–371; Philip C. Newman, "Ulrich Bonnell Phillips—The South's Foremost Historian," *Georgia Historical Quarterly* 25 (September 1941): 244–261; Wendell Holmes Stephenson, *The South Lives in History* (Baton Rouge: Louisiana State University Press, 1955), 58–94; Sam E. Salem, "U.B. Phillips and the Scientific Tradition," *Georgia Historical Quarterly* 44 (June 1960): 172–185.

32. Stampp, "The Historian and Southern Negro Slavery," *American Historical Review* 57 (April 1952): 615–620.

33. Stampp, *The Peculiar Institution: Slavery in the Ante-Bellum South* (New York: Knopf, 1956), vii.

34. For an exhaustive critique of Stampp's book, see Fogel and Engerman, *Time on the Cross: Evidence and Methods* (Boston: Little, Brown, 1974), 218–246.

35. On the theories of "scapegoating" and "projection," see Irving L. Janis and others, *Personality: Dynamics, Development, and Assessment* (New York: Harcourt, Brace & World, 1969), 165–166, 376–377.

36. Dew, review of Genovese, ed., *The Slave Economy of the Old South*, in *Louisiana History* 10 (Spring 1969): 183.

37. Genovese, "Ulrich Bonnell Phillips and His Critics," *American Negro Slavery* (1918; reprint, Baton Rouge: Louisiana State University Press, 1966), vii–ix.

38. Genovese, "Race and Class in Southern History: An Appraisal of the Work of Ulrich Bonnell Phillips," *Agricultural History* 41 (October 1967): 354.

39. Genovese, *Roll, Jordan, Roll: The World the Slaves Made* (New York: Pantheon, 1974), 7. Responding to this criticism, Genovese insists that "Phillips' notion of paternalism was radically different from my own." Genovese to John David Smith, June 28, 1978, in possession of the author.

40. G. Ray Mathis, ed., "Ulrich Bonnell Phillips and the Universities of Georgia and Wisconsin," *Georgia Historical Quarterly* 53 (June 1969): 241–243; William L. Van Deburg, "Ulrich B. Phillips: Progress and the Conservative Historian," *Georgia Historical Quarterly* 55 (Fall 1971): 406–416; James D. Wilson, "The Role of Slavery in the Agrarian Myth," *Recherches Anglaises et Américaines* 4 (1971): 12–22; Allan M. Winkler, "Ulrich Bonnell Phillips: A Reappraisal," *South Atlantic Quarterly* 71 (Spring 1972): 234–245; Ruth H. Crocker, "Ulrich Phillips: A Southern Historian Reconsidered," *Louisiana Studies* 15 (Summer 1976): 113–130; John H. Roper, "A Case of Forgotten Identity: Ulrich B. Phillips as a Young Progressive," *Georgia Historical Quarterly* 60 (Summer 1976): 165–175; Roper, "Ulrich Bonnell Phillips: His Life and Thought" (Ph.D. diss., University of North Carolina at Chapel Hill, 1977); Daniel J. Singal, "Ulrich B. Phillips: The Old South as the New," *Journal of American History* 63 (March 1977): 871–891; John David Smith, "Ulrich Bonnell Phillips and Academic Freedom at the University of Michigan," *Michigan History* 62 (Spring 1978): 11–15; Smith, "An Old Creed for the New South—Southern Historians and the Revival of the Proslavery Argument, 1890–1920," *Southern Studies: An Interdisciplinary Journal of the South* 18 (Spring 1979): 75–87; Smith, "'Keep 'Em in a Fire-Proof Vault'—Pioneer Southern Historians Discover Plantation Records," *South Atlantic Quarterly* 78 (Summer 1979): 376–391; Smith, "Du Bois and Phillips—Symbolic Antagonists of the Progressive Era," *Centennial Review* 24 (Winter 1980): 88–102; Smith, "Historical or Personal Criticism? Frederic Bancroft Versus Ulrich B. Phillips," *Washington State University Research Studies* 49 (June 1981): 73–86.

41. Stampp, "Slavery—The Historian's Burden," in *Perspectives and Irony in American Slavery,* ed. Harry P. Owens (Jackson, MS: University Press of Mississippi, 1976), 160, and *The Imperiled Union: Essays on the Background of the Civil War* (New York: Oxford University Press, 1980), 200.

42. See Smith, "Du Bois and Phillips—Symbolic Antagonists of the Progressive Era," 100–102.

43. Eaton to John David Smith, January 28, 1976, in possession of the author.

44. Phillips, ed., *Plantation and Frontier Documents: 1649–1863,* 2 vols. (Cleveland: A.H. Clark, 1909), 1:98–99.

45. Phillips, *Life and Labor,* 251; "Plantations with Slave Labor and Free," *American Historical Review* 30 (July 1925): 743.

46. Phillips, *American Negro Slavery,* 436.

47. See I.A. Newby, *Jim Crow's Defense: Anti-Negro Thought in America, 1900–1930* (Baton Rouge: Louisiana State University Press, 1965), 52–82.

Notes to Chapter 6

1. See John David Smith, "The Formative Period of American Slave Historiography, 1890–1920" (Ph.D. diss., University of Kentucky, 1977), 461.

2. Walter F. Willcox, "Introduction," in Alfred Holt Stone, *Studies in the American Race Problem* (New York: Doubleday, Page, 1908), xv.

3. "Some Recent Race Problem Literature," *Publications of the Southern History Association* 8 (November 1904): 451–461; "More Race Problem Literature," *Publications of the Southern History Association* 10 (July 1906): 218–227; "More Race Problem Discussion," *Publications of the Southern History Association* 11 (January 1907): 20–37; "Negro Labor and the Boll Weevil," *Annals of the American Academy of Political and Social Science* 33 (March 1909): 391–398; "A Plantation Experiment," *Quarterly Journal of Economics* 19 (February 1905): 270–287; "The Italian Cotton Grower: The Negro's Problem," *South Atlantic Quarterly* 4 (January 1905): 42–47.

4. "The Negro in the Yazoo-Mississippi Delta," *Publications of the American Economic Association,* 3rd ser., 3 (1902), 235–272.

5. "Some Problems of Southern Economic History," *American Historical Review* 13 (July 1908): 779–797.

6. Merton L. Dillon, "Ulrich B. Phillips: An Assessment of an Historian's Debts" (unpublished paper delivered at the meeting of the Southern Historical Association, November 5, 1982, Memphis, Tennessee).

7. Sydnor, *Slavery in Mississippi* (Washington: American Historical Association, 1933).

8. Wharton, *The Negro in Mississippi, 1865–1890* (Chapel Hill: University of North Carolina Press, 1947), 282, 291.

9. Kirwan, *Revolt of the Rednecks: Mississippi Politics: 1876–1926* (Lexington: University of Kentucky Press, 1951), 319.

10. Genovese, *Roll, Jordan, Roll: The World the Slaves Made* (New York: Pantheon, 1974), 309.

11. See John David Smith, "'Keep 'Em in a Fire-Proof Vault'—Pioneer Southern Historians Discover Plantation Records," *South Atlantic Quarterly* 78 (Summer 1979): 376–391.

12. Stone to Dodd, July 10, 1907, William E. Dodd Papers, Manuscript Division, Library of Congress.

13. Stone, *Material Wanted for an Economic History of the Negro* (Washington: n.p., n.d.). A copy of Stone's sixteen-page pamphlet/questionnaire is located in the Pamphlet Collection, Perkins Library, Duke University. Unless otherwise noted, all remaining references to Stone, quoted and paraphrased, are drawn from this work.

14. William H. Kilpatrick, *Preserving Southern History Material: An Address Before the Southern Club of Columbia University, July 31, 1923* (New York: Columbia University Press, 1923).

15. Stone, "The Cotton Factorage System of the Southern States," *American Historical Review* 25 (April 1915), 557–565.

16. Starobin, *Industrial Slavery in the Old South* (New York: Oxford University Press, 1970).

17. Although he mentioned slavery in many of his writings, Stone rarely focused directly on the subject. See, for example, the articles published in his *Studies in the American Race Problem*. Stone's most detailed treatment of slavery was "The Early Slave Laws of Mississippi," *Publications of the Mississippi Historical Society* 2 (1899): 133–146.

Notes to Chapter 7

1. See David Brion Davis, "Slavery and the Post–World War II Historians," *Daedalus* 103 (Spring 1974), 1–16; Orlando Patterson, "Slavery," *Annual Review of Sociology* 3 (1977): 407–449; Peter H. Wood, "'I Did the Best I Could For My Day': The Study of Early Black History During the Second Reconstruction, 1960–1976," *William and Mary Quarterly* 35 (April 1978): 185–225.

2. See John David Smith, "The Formative Period of American Slave Historiography 1890–1920" (Ph.D. diss., University of Kentucky, 1977).

3. See, for example, William J. Strong, "Blacklisting: The New Slavery," *Arena* 21 (March 1899), 273–292; "Slavery in Alabama," *Independent* 55 (June 11, 1903): 1416–1417; Theodore Roosevelt to James Ford Rhodes, November 29, 1904, Theodore Roosevelt Papers, Manuscript Division, Library of Congress; William E. Dodd to Oswald Garrison Villard, July 3, 1906, Oswald Garrison Villard Papers, Harvard University; Raymond, "Slave Laws Halt South's Progress," *Chicago Tribune,* January 5, 1908; "What Is Slavery?" *Independent* 74 (February 20, 1913): 389; Herbert J. Seligman, "Slavery in Georgia, A.D., 1921," *Nation* 112 (April 20, 1921): 591.

4. See Smith, "The Formative Period of American Slave Historiography, 1890–1920," chapter 4.

5. Review of Joel Chandler Harris, *Uncle Remus: His Songs and His Sayings,* in *Nation* 31 (December 2, 1880): 398.

6. See John David Smith, "An Old Creed for the New South: Southern Historians and the Revival of the Proslavery Argument, 1890–1920," *Southern Studies: An Interdisciplinary Journal of the South* 18 (Spring 1979): 75–88.

7. Roger L. Ransom and Richard Sutch, *One Kind of Freedom: The Economic Consequences of Emancipation* (New York: Cambridge University Press, 1977), 303.

8. This information is drawn from the Tenth Census of the United States, Agriculture Schedules, 1880, Newberry County, South Carolina, roll 13, page 18, and South Carolina Will Transcripts, 1782–1868, Newberry County, South Carolina, volume 4, book 1, roll 20, page 158, South Carolina Department of Archives and History.

9. Report Book (1855–1908), Newberry College, Newberry, South Carolina, page 223, manuscript in Registrar's Office, Newberry College; *Catalogue of Newberry College, Newberry, South Carolina, 1898–99* (Newberry: Lutheran Publications Board, 1899), 18.

10. Official transcript of Howell M. Henry, Registrar's Office, Vanderbilt University, Nashville, Tennessee; Warren F. Kuehl, *Dissertations in History* (Lexington: University of Kentucky Press, 1965), v. For useful biographical information, see Howell M. Henry Alumni Correspondence File, Vanderbilt University Archives.

11. Henry to Salley, January 28, 1909, Alexander S. Salley Papers, South Caroliniana Library, University of South Carolina.

12. Henry's dissertation was published in Emory, Virginia, in 1914. Negro University Press reprinted it in 1968. The book has been omitted entirely from two of the most influential historiographical essays on slavery. See Stanley M. Elkins, "An Introduction: Slavery as a Problem in Historiography," *Slavery: A Problem in American Institutional & Intellectual Life* (1959; reprint, New York: Grosset & Dunlap, 1963), 1–26, and Bennett H. Wall, "African Slavery," in *Writing Southern History: Essays in Historiography in Honor of Fletcher M. Green,* ed. Arthur S. Link and Rembert W. Patrick (Baton Rouge: Louisiana State University Press, 1965), 175–197. In "The Literature of Slavery: A Re-Evaluation," *Indiana Magazine of History* 47 (September 1951): 255, 258n, Chase C. Mooney all but ignored Henry's book.

13. See Henry, "The Slave Laws of Tennessee," *Tennessee Historical Magazine* 2 (March 1916): 175–203. In the early 1940s, however, Henry did publish two articles expressing his fear of the spread of Nazism into Latin America. See "The Nazi Threat to the Western Hemisphere," *South Atlantic Quarterly* 39 (October 1940): 367–384, and "Western Hemisphere Accord," *South Atlantic Quarterly* (July 1942): 239–253.

14. Stevenson to John David Smith, June 29, 1976, in possession of the author.

15. Stevenson, *Increase in Excellence: A History of Emory and Henry College* (New York: Appleton-Century Crofts, 1963), 137–138.

16. Stevenson to John David Smith, October 17, 1979, May 31, June 29, 1976, in possession of the author.

17. John B. Walters, Jr., to John David Smith, August 11, 1976, in possession of the author.

18. Stevenson to John David Smith, October 17, 1979.

19. Henry, *The Police Control of the Slave in South Carolina* (Emory, VA: n.p., 1914), 6, 30, 28, 15, 21.

20. Ibid., 29n, 209, 214–215, and passim.

21. Ibid., 6, 7, 79, 20.

22. Ibid., 57, 154–155.

23. Ibid., 145–154. "As early as 1793," however, Charlestonians "formulated a series of extralegal measures concerning the reception of blacks in the harbor remarkably similar to those enacted thirty years later." See George D. Terry, "A Study of the Impact of the French Revolution and the Insurrections in Saint-Domingue upon South Carolina: 1790–1805" (master's thesis, University of South Carolina, 1975), 6, 61–62.

24. Henry, *The Police Control of the Slave in South Carolina,* 30–32, 28, 38, 39, 40.

25. Ibid., 108, 99, 79, 145, 141, 119, 48, 74. Henry maintained, however, that many of the regulations mentioned in this paragraph were enforced at times of fear of slave revolt. Henry sought to be scrupulously fair and impartial in his assessment of slave punishments. See Henry to Yates Snowden, March 10, 1913, Yates Snowden Papers, South Caroliniana Library, University of South Carolina.

26. Henry, *The Police Control of the Slave in South Carolina,* 125, 108, 113, 114, 108.

27. Ibid., 44–45, 46, 50.

28. Ibid., 21, 18, 22.

29. Ibid., 22.

30. Carson in *Mississippi Valley Historical Review* 2 (June 1915): 145–146.

31. C.B. Walter in *Journal of Negro History* 1 (April 1916): 219–221.

32. Phillips in *American Historical Review* 20 (April 1915): 672.

33. Carson in *Mississippi Valley Historical Review,* 146; Phillips in *American Historical Review,* 672.

34. Phillips, *American Negro Slavery: A Survey of the Supply, Employment and Control of Negro Labor as Determined by the Plantation Régime* (New York: D. Appleton, 1918), 477n, 502n, 509n, and *Life and Labor in the Old South* (Boston: Little, Brown, 1929), 162n (quote), 171n.

35. This analysis is based on the examination of thirty-eight books, articles, and theses that cite *The Police Control of the Slave in South Carolina.* Excluded have been bibliographical references to Henry's volume lacking either page numbers or comment. In addition to Phillips's works cited above, see Anthony G. Albanese, "The Plantation as a School: The Sea Islands of Georgia and South Carolina, a Test Case, 1800–1860" (Ed.D. diss., Rutgers University, 1970), 198n, 281; Herbert Aptheker, *American Negro Slave Revolts* (1942; reprint, New York: International, 1970), 63n, 136n, 168n, 189n, 268n, and *Nat Turner's Slave Rebellion* (1966; reprint, New York: Grove Press, 1968), 69n, 77n; John L. Bradley, "Slave Manumission in South Carolina, 1820–1860" (master's thesis, University of South Carolina, 1964), 2n, 42n, 64n, 67n, 86n, 98n, 99n, 101n, 105n; Carl H. Brown, "The Reopening of the Foreign Slave Trade in South Carolina, 1803–1807" (master's thesis, University of South Carolina, 1968), 10n, 20n; Alfloyd Butler, "The Blacks' Contribution of Elements of African Religion to Christianity in America: A Case Study of the Great Awakening in South Carolina" (Ph.D. diss., Northwestern University, 1975), 20; Steven A. Channing, *Crisis of Fear: Secession in South Carolina* (New York: Simon and Schuster, 1970), 33n; Jimmy G. Cobb, "A Study of White Protestants' Attitudes Toward Negroes in Charleston, South Carolina, 1790–1845" (Ph.D. diss., Baylor University, 1976), 81n; David W. Cole, "The Organization and Administration of the South Carolina Militia System, 1670–1783" (Ph.D. diss., University of South Carolina, 1953), iiin, 65n, 66n; John D. Duncan, "Servitude and Slavery in Colonial South Carolina, 1670–1776" (Ph.D. diss., Emory University, 1972), 541n; M. Foster Farley, "A History of Negro Slave Revolts in South Carolina," and "The Fear of Negro Slave Revolts in South Carolina, 1690–1865," *Afro-American Studies* 3 (1972): 100n, 102n, 207; Daniel J. Flanigan, "Criminal Procedures in Slave Trials in the Antebellum South," *Journal of Southern History* 40 (November 1974): 541n, 542n, 543n, 547n; Eugene D. Genovese, *Roll Jordan Roll: The World the Slaves Made* (New York: Pantheon Books, 1974), 685,

722, 745, 763, 794; Lewis Cecil Gray, *History of Agriculture in the Southern United States to 1860,* 2 vols. (1933; reprint, Gloucester, MA: Peter Smith, 1958), 1:559n; Phillip M. Hamer, "Great Britain, the United States, and the Negro Seamen Acts, 1822–1848," *Journal of Southern History* 1 (February 1935): 3n; William C. Henderson, "The Slave Court System in Spartanburg County," *Proceedings of the South Carolina Historical Association* (1976): 38n; A. Leon Higginbotham, Jr., *In the Matter of Color: Race and the American Legal Process: The Colonial Period* (New York: Oxford University Press, 1978), 169, 184, 199, 201; Michael S. Hindus, "Prison and Plantation: Criminal Justice in Nineteenth-Century Massachusetts and South Carolina" (Ph.D. diss., University of California, Berkeley, 1975), 82, 206, 209, 169; Alan F. January, "The First Nullification: The Negro Seamen Acts Controversy in South Carolina, 1822–1860" (Ph.D. diss., University of Iowa, 1976), 64, 105, 109, 110, 113, 223; Charles Joyner, "Slave Folklife on the Waccamaw Neck: Antebellum Black Culture in the South Carolina Lowcountry" (Ph.D. diss., University of Pennsylvania, 1977), 280; John Lofton, *Insurrection in South Carolina: The Turbulent World of Denmark Vesey* (Yellow Springs, OH: Antioch Press, 1964), 248, 251, 253, 254, 255, 256, 265; Marjorie S. Mendenhall, "A History of Agriculture in South Carolina, 1790–1860" (Ph.D. diss., University of North Carolina, 1940), 86n, 116n; George C. Rogers, Jr., *History of Georgetown County, South Carolina* (Columbia: University of South Carolina Press, 1970), 344n, 345, 346n; M. Eugene Sirmans, "The Legal Status of the Slave in South Carolina, 1670–1740," *Journal of Southern History* 28 (November 1962): 469n; Yates Snowden, ed., *History of South Carolina,* 5 vols. (New York: Lewis, 1920), 1:233; 2:1144, 1155; Kenneth M. Stampp, *The Peculiar Institution: Slavery in the Ante-Bellum South* (New York: Knopf, 1956), 117n, 159n, 187n, 209n, 210n, 222n, 226, 233n; Leonard P. Stavisky, "The Negro Artisan in the South Atlantic States, 1800–1860: A Study of Status and Economic Opportunity with Special Reference to Charleston" (Ph.D diss., Columbia University, 1958), 85n; Rosser H. Taylor, *Ante-Bellum South Carolina: A Social and Cultural History* (Chapel Hill: University of North Carolina Press, 1942), 172n, 174n, 177n, 178n, 179n, 184n, 185n, 186n; Richard C. Wade, "The Vesey Plot: A Reconsideration," *Journal of Southern History* 30 (May 1964): 144–161; David D. Wallace, *The History of South Carolina,* 4 vols. (New York: American Historical Society, 1934), 2:499n, 507n, 415n, 416n; Marina Wikramanayake, "The Free Negro in Ante-Bellum South Carolina" (Ph.D. diss., University of Wisconsin, 1966), 34, 121, 229; Jack K. Williams, "Crime and Punishment in South Carolina, 1801–1861" (Ph.D. diss., Emory University, 1953), iv; Latham A. Windley, "A Profile of Runaway Slaves in Virginia and South Carolina from 1730 Through 1787" (Ph.D. diss., University of Iowa, 1974), 16n, 26n, 168; Harvey Wish, "American Slave Insurrections Before 1861," *Journal of Negro History* 22 (July 1937): 310n, 316n, 317n; Peter H. Wood, *Black Majority: Negroes in Colonial South Carolina from 1670 Through the Stono Rebellion* (New York: W.W. Norton, 1975), 274n.

36. Wallace, *The History of South Carolina,* 2:499n.

37. Wood, *Black Majority,* 274n.

38. Aptheker, *American Negro Slave Revolts,* 189n.

39. Hindus, "Black Justice Under White Law: Criminal Prosecutions of Blacks in Antebellum South Carolina," *Journal of American History* 63 (December 1976): 596.

40. January, "The First Nullification," 223; Higginbotham, *In the Matter of Color,* 201; Cole, "The Organization and Administration of the South Carolina Militia System," 66n.

41. Fogel and Engerman, *Time on the Cross: Evidence and Methods* (Boston: Little, Brown, 1974), 178.

42. See, for example, John V. Denson, "Slavery Laws in Alabama," *Alabama Polytechnic Institute Historical Studies,* Third Series (1908), 1–55; Jacob Trieber, "Legal

Status of Negroes in Arkansas Before the Civil War," *Publications of the Arkansas Historical Association* 3 (1911): 175–183; E.M. Violette, "The Black Code in Missouri," *Proceedings of the Mississippi Valley Historical Association for the Year 1912–1913* 6 (1913): 287–316.

43. Laprade, "Some Problems in Writing the History of American Slavery," *South Atlantic Quarterly* 10 (April 1911): 134–137.

44. West, "The Status of the Negro in Virginia During the Colonial Period."

45. See Wade, "The Vesey Plot: A Reconsideration," 143–161, and *Slavery in the Cities: The South, 1820–1860* (1964; reprint, New York: Oxford University Press, 1970). Wade's argument—that no conspiracy actually existed—has been thoroughly revised by Robert S. Starobin's "Denmark Vesey's Slave Conspiracy of 1822: A Study in Rebellion and Repression," in *American Slavery: The Question of Resistance,* ed. John H. Bracey et al. (Belmont, CA: Wadsworth Publishing, 1971), 142–157; Sterling Stuckey, "Remembering Denmark Vesey," *Negro Digest* 15 (February 1966): 28–41; and Eugene D. Genovese, *From Rebellion to Revolution: Afro-American Slave Revolts in the Making of the Modern World* (Baton Rouge: Louisiana State University Press, 1979), 14, 26, 44–50.

46. See Flisch, "The Common People of the Old South," *Annual Report of the American Historical Association for the Year 1908,* 2 vols. (Washington: Government Printing Office, 1909), 2:139–140, and Starobin, *Industrial Slavery in the Old South* (1970; reprint, New York: Oxford University Press, 1971).

Notes to Chapter 8

1. Idus A. Newby, *Jim Crow's Defense: Anti-Negro Thought in America, 1900–1930* (Baton Rouge: Louisiana State University Press, 1965), 70–71, 98, 125; Claude H. Nolen, *The Negro's Image in the South: The Anatomy of White Supremacy* (Lexington: University of Kentucky Press, 1968), xvii, 3, 19, 28, 155, 161, 201; Lawrence J. Friedman, *The White Savage: Racial Fantasies in the Postbellum South* (Englewood Cliffs, NJ: Prentice-Hall, 1970), 23–27 and passim; George M. Fredrickson, *The Black Image in the White Mind: The Debate on Afro-American Character and Destiny, 1817–1914* (New York: Harper & Row, 1971), 204–213; John S. Haller, Jr., *Outcasts from Evolution: Scientific Attitudes of Racial Inferiority, 1859–1900* (Urbana: University of Illinois Press, 1971), 209; Paul M. Gaston, *The New South Creed: A Study in Southern Mythmaking* (New York: Knopf, 1971), 123–128; Jack Temple Kirby, *Darkness at the Dawning: Race and Reform in the Progressive South* (Philadelphia: Lippincott, 1972), 91–93; Bruce Clayton, *The Savage Ideal: Intolerance and Intellectual Leadership in the South, 1890–1914* (Baltimore: Johns Hopkins University Press, 1972), 5, 40, 138, 188; Pete Daniel, *The Shadow of Slavery: Peonage in the South, 1901–1969* (Urbana: University of Illinois Press, 1972), 11, 23, 29, 58, 96, 127, 138. These authors recognize proslavery thought in the white supremacist ideology of the Progressive era. But its pervasiveness in the literature has not been systematically examined.

2. See John David Smith, "The Formative Period of American Slave Historiography, 1890–1920" (Ph.D. diss., University of Kentucky, 1977).

3. Cooper, *A Voice from the South by a Black Woman of the South* (Xenia, OH: Aldine Printing House, 1892), 179.

4. Editorial, "Feudalism or Slavery," *Independent* 55 (April 2, 1903): 805–806; "Slavery in Alabama," *Independent* 55 (June 11, 1903), 1416–1417; Theodore Roosevelt to James Ford Rhodes, November 29, 1904, Theodore Roosevelt Papers, Manuscript Division, Library of Congress; Richard Barry, "Slavery in the South To-Day," *Cosmopolitan Magazine* 42 (March 1907): 481–491; Raymond, "Slave Laws Halt South's Progress," *Chicago Tribune,* January 5, 1908; Herbert J. Seligmann, "Slavery in Georgia, A.D. 1921," *Nation* 112 (April 20, 1921): 591.

5. William J. Strong, "Blacklisting: The New Slavery," *Arena* 21 (March 1899): 273–292; William E. Dodd to Oswald Garrison Villard, July 3, 1906, Oswald Garrison Villard Papers, Houghton Library, Harvard University; Dodd to Edwin Mims, September 15, 1906, Edwin Mims Papers, Joint University Libraries, Nashville; David Y. Thomas, "Social Aspects of the Slavery Question," *Dial* 51 (November 1, 1911): 330; editorial, "What Is Slavery?" *Independent* 74 (February 20, 1913): 389.

6. Smith, "The Formative Period of American Slave Historiography," 62–75.

7. John David Smith, "An Old Creed for the New South: Southern Historians and the Revival of the Proslavery Argument, 1890–1920," *Southern Studies: An Interdisciplinary Journal of the South* 18 (Spring 1979): 75–88.

8. Smith, "The Formative Period of American Slave Historiography," chapters 7 and 8.

9. Earlie Endris Thorpe, "Negro Historiography in the United States" (Ph.D. diss., Ohio State University, 1953), chapters 1–4; *Black Historians: A Critique* (New York: Morrow, 1971), 65–142; Robert William Fogel and Stanley L. Engerman, *Time on the Cross: Evidence and Methods* (Boston: Little, Brown, 1974), 170–171, 192–213.

10. Alexander Crummell, "The Need of New Ideas and New Aims for a New Era," *Africa and America: Addresses and Discourses* (1891; reprint, Miami: Mnemosyne, 1969), 14–19; editorial, "Emancipation Celebration," *Indianapolis Freeman,* December 4, 1897; editorial, "Emancipation Celebration," *New York Age,* August 13, 1908.

11. Booker T. Washington, "The Influence of the Negroes' Citizenship" (speech delivered on July 10, 1896), in *The Booker T. Washington Papers,* ed. Louis R. Harlan, 14 vols. (Urbana: University of Illinois Press, 1972–1989) 4:191, 193; Kelly Miller, "The Race Problem in the South—A Negro's View," *Outlook* 60 (December 31, 1898): 1059; William H. Council, *Lamp of Wisdom: Or, Race History Illuminated* (Nashville: Haley, 1898), 16.

12. Booker T. Washington, "The Economic Development of the Negro in Slavery," in Washington and W.E.B. Du Bois, *The Negro in the South* (Philadelphia: G.W. Jacobs, 1907), 16; Kelly Miller, "The Negro's Part," *Radicals and Conservatives and Other Essays on the Negro in America* (1908; reprint, New York: Schocken Books, 1968), 107–108; William H. Council, "The Future of the Negro," *Forum* 27 (July 1899): 575. Other examples of the proslavery argument in black thought during these years include C.H.J. Taylor, *Whites and Blacks* (Atlanta: J.P. Harrison, 1889), 5–9; H.M. Turner, "The American Negro and the Fatherland," in *Africa and the American Negro,* ed. John W.E. Bowen (Atlanta: Gammon Theological Seminary, 1896), 195; Theophilus G. Steward, "The American Freedman," *Indianapolis Freeman,* April 17, 1897; C.H. Turner, "New Year Thoughts About the Negro," *Southwestern Christian Advocate* 34 (January 26, 1899): 3; Irving E. Lowery, *Life on the Old Plantation in Ante-Bellum Days* (Columbia, SC: State, 1911); John Wesley Gilbert, "A Voice from the Negro Race," *Methodist Quarterly Review* 60 (October 1911): 717–718.

13. J.G. Robinson, "Africa, and the Educated Wealthy Negroes of America," *A.M.E. Church Review* 10 (July 1893): 159; E.W. Lampton, "The Material Progress of the Race," in *The United Negro: His Problems and His Progress,* ed. I. Garland Penn and J.W.E. Bowen (Atlanta: D.E. Luther, 1902), 311; William Pickens, "Grounds of Hope for the American Negro," *American Missionary* 65 (January 1911): 661; Work, "The Songs of the Southland," *Voice of the Negro* 4 (January–February 1907): 51.

14. Benjamin T. Tanner, review of James H.W. Howard, *Bond and Free,* in *A.M.E. Church Review* 3 (October 1886): 207; "Ante-Bellum Echoes," *Richmond Planet,* n.d., reprinted in *Indianapolis Freeman,* February 11, 1893; editorial, "Forgotten History," *Washington Bee,* December 23, 1899.

15. Kelly Miller, "The National Bird—Eagle or Jim Crow?" unpublished manuscript, n.d., Kelly Miller Papers, Howard University; W.H. Crogman, "Twenty-Sixth Anniversary of the Emancipation Proclamation," *Talks for the Times* (South Atlanta: Franklin

Printing and Publishing, 1896), 204; Charles B. Purvis to Jonathan P. Dolliver, February 14, 1909, Whitefield McKinlay Papers, Manuscript Division, Library of Congress; Archibald H. Grimké, "Reaction and Danger," unpublished manuscript [1916?], Archibald H. Grimké Papers, Howard University; A Georgia Negro Peon, "The New Slavery in the South," *Independent* 56 (February 25, 1904): 409–414; Charles W. Chesnutt, "Peonage, or the New Slavery," *Voice of the Negro* 1 (September 1904): 394–397; editorial, "New Southern Slavery," *New York Age*, December 19, 1907; "'Negro Is Still Slave,' Declares Prof. Du Bois," *Cincinnati Times-Star*, December 5, 1910; A Negro Nurse, "More Slavery at the South," *Independent* 72 (January 25, 1912): 196–200; editorial, "Slavery Not Dead," *Washington Bee*, February 28, 1914; Lafayette M. Hershaw, "Peonage," *The American Negro Academy Occasional Papers No. 15* (Washington: American Negro Academy, 1915), 5, 11. Ex-slave Ida B. Wells considered lynching to be the "last relic of barbarism and slavery"—the ultimate form of intimidation of the freedmen. See *Southern Horrors: Lynch Law in All Its Phases* (New York: New York Age Print, 1892), 24, and *A Red Record: Tabulated Statistics and Alleged Causes of Lynchings in the United States* (Chicago: Donohue & Henneberry, 1895), 8.

16. Booker T. Washington to George Washington Cable, October 8, 1889, Booker T. Washington Collection, Howard University; Washington to Emily Howland, December 27, 1894, Miscellaneous American Letters and Papers, Schomburg Center, New York Public Library; R.L. Smith, "The Elevation of Negro Farm Life," *Independent* 52 (August 30, 1900): 2104; editorials, "Slavery in the South" and "Slave Pen Abolished," *Washington Bee*, March 9, 16, 1901; James Weldon Johnson, "The Hour of Opportunity," *New York Age*, October 18, 1917; D.E. Tobias, "A Negro on the Position of the Negro in America," *Nineteenth Century* 46 (December 1899): 959, 961; W.E.B. Du Bois, "The Spawn of Slavery: The Convict-Lease System in the South," *Missionary Review of the World* n.s. 14 (October 1901): 737, 740; editorial, "The New Slave System of the South," *Colored American Magazine* 6 (August 1903): 618; cartoon, "The New Southern Slavery," *New York Age*, December 13, 1906; editorial, "Portuguese and American Slavery," *Cleveland Gazette*, April 10, 1909.

17. T. Thomas Fortune, *Black and White: Land, Labor and Politics in the South* (1884; reprint, New York: Arno Press, 1968), 235–236; Fortune, "The Negro's Place in American Life at the Present Day," in Washington et al., *The Negro Problem: A Series of Articles by Representative Negroes of To-Day* (1903; reprint, Miami: Mnemosyne, 1969), 227, 229; Washington to Francis J. Garrison, August 31, 1903, Miscellaneous American Letters and Papers, Schomburg Center; Benjamin T. Tanner, "The Afro American and the Three R's," *Independent* 47 (October 17, 1895): 1387; Alexander Crummell, "The Prime Need of the Negro Race," *Independent* 49 (August 19, 1897): 1065; Kittredge Wheeler to W.E.B. Du Bois, July 20, 1903, in *The Correspondence of W.E.B. Du Bois*, ed. Herbert Aptheker, 3 vols. (Amherst: University of Massachusetts Press, 1973–1978) 1:59.

18. "Choose Ye . . . Whom Ye Will Serve!" *Howard's American Magazine* 4 (April 1900): 388; Frederick L. McGhee, "Another View," *Howard's American Magazine* 5 (October 1900): 95–96; W.E.B. Du Bois, "Of the Culture of White Folk," *Journal of Race Development* 7 (April 1917): 445–446.

19. Charles B. Purvis to Francis J. Grimké, November 16, 1912, in *The Works of Francis J. Grimké*, ed. Carter G. Woodson, 4 vols. (Washington: Associated, 1942), 4:128; Robert Graves to the editor, *New York Age*, October 26, 1916; Francis J. Grimké to U.S. Employment Service of the Department of Labor, September 24, 1917, in Woodson, ed., *The Works of Francis J. Grimké*, 4:197; F.H. Miller to William Pickens, March 15, 1918, Pickens to Miller, March 20, 1918, William Pickens Papers, Schomburg Center. The latter two references discuss the virtual enslavement of blacks in service battalions and stevedore regiments serving in the U.S. Army during World War I.

20. "Let My People Go," *Indianapolis Freeman,* September 24, 1892. Numerous blacks remarked that despite the Thirteenth Amendment, their race remained enslaved by caste and color. See, for example, Archibald H. Grimké, "John Brown and the New Slavery," unpublished manuscript, n.d., Archibald H. Grimké Papers; editorial, "The South Hysterical on the Negro Problem," *Alexander's Magazine* 3 (March 15, 1907): 223–226; Mary Church Terrell to the editor, *Charleston News and Courier* [1907], Mary Church Terrell Papers, Manuscript Division, Library of Congress.

21. Du Bois, "The Study of the Negro Problems," *Annals of the American Academy of Political and Social Science* 11 (January 1898): 14. Surveying the literature twenty-one years later, Carter G. Woodson found little improvement. Woodson, "Negro Life and History in Our Schools," *Journal of Negro History* 4 (July 1919): 273, 275–277.

22. Baker, "The Negro Woman," *Alexander's Magazine* 3 (December 15, 1906): 76, 77.

23. Woodson, review of Reuter, *The Mulatto in the United States,* in *Journal of Negro History* 4 (January 1919): 106. Other critical reviews of Reuter's book by blacks include Jessie Fauset in *Survey* 41 (March 8, 1919): 842–843; Kelly Miller in *American Journal of Sociology* 25 (September 1919): 218–224; and Woodson in *Mississippi Valley Historical Review* 7 (September 1920): 175–176.

24. W.E.B. Du Bois, "The Experts," *Crisis* 5 (March 1919): 239–240; Du Bois, review of Phillips, *American Negro Slavery,* in *American Political Science Review* 7 (November 1918): 722, 725; Woodson reviews in *Mississippi Valley Historical Review* 5 (March 1919): 480, and in *Journal of Negro History* 4 (January 1919): 103.

25. T. Thomas Fortune, "The Race Problem: The Negro Will Solve It," *Belford's Magazine* 5 (September 1890): 493; R.C.O. Benjamin, "The Equality Myth," *Indianapolis Freeman,* October 29, 1892; Frederick Douglass, "Lessons of the Hour," *A.M.E. Church Review* 11 (July 1894): 135; Fauset to Joel E. Spingarn, February 12, 1913, Joel E. Spingarn Papers, Howard University; James Oppenheim, "The Slave" [poem], *A.M.E. Church Review* 31 (April 1915): 377.

26. Boas, "Human Faculty as Determined by Race," *Proceedings of the American Association for the Advancement of Science* 43 (1894): 308, 317, 325, 327; "Race Problems in America," *Science,* n.s. 29 (May 28, 1909): 843, 847–848; "Psychological Problems in Anthropology," *American Journal of Psychology* 21 (July 1910): 371–384; *The Mind of Primitive Man* (New York: Macmillan, 1911), 268–271 and passim.

27. Boas, "The Real Race Problem," *Crisis* 1 (December 1910): 22.

28. William H. Ferris, "Typical Negro Traits," *American Missionary* 62 (April 1908): 99–100; Charles H. Wesley, "Interest in a Neglected Phase of History," *A.M.E. Church Review* 32 (April 1916): 265; Wesley to John David Smith, July 25, 1978, in possession of the author; James M. Boddy, "The Ethnic Unity of the Negro and Anglo-Saxon Race," *Colored American Magazine* 9 (March 1905): 124–128; George W. Forbes, "Afro-American Folk-Songs Only Bases for a National Music," *A.M.E. Church Review* 31 (July 1914): 87; J.M. Henderson, "Effects of Environments," *Indianapolis Freeman,* March 5, 1898; C.V. Roman, *American Civilization and the Negro* (1916; reprint, Philadelphia: F.A. Davis, 1921), v, vii.

29. Fortune, "The Nationalization of Africa," in Bowen, ed., *Africa and the American Negro,* 199.

30. William H. Dawley, Jr., "The Mind of Primitive Man," *A.M.E. Church Review* 28 (April 1911): 778. Ex-slave George William Cook noted ironically that masters "maintained that the Negro could not become intelligent, yet much time and money were spent to remove him from the opportunity." Cook, "Is There a Problem?" unpublished manuscript [1905?], George William Cook Papers, Howard University.

31. Boas, "The Negro and the Demands of Modern Life: Ethnic and Anatomical Considerations," *Charities* 15 (October 7, 1905): 86, 87; "Commencement Address at

Atlanta University, May 31, 1906," *Atlanta University Leaflet—No. 19* [n.p., n.d.], 3–7, 8, 9; "The Anthropological Position of the Negro," *Van Norden Magazine* 2 (April 1907): 45–47; "Industries of the African Negroes," *Southern Workman* 38 (April 1909): 224–225 and passim.

32. Johnson, *A School History of the Negro Race in America* (1911; reprint, New York: AMS Press, 1969), 9.

33. Washington, *The Story of the Negro*, 2 vols. (1909; reprint, New York: Peter Smith, 1940) 1:13–14, 23, 27–28, 29, 31, 54, 65, 2:11, 265; Du Bois, ed., *The Health and Physique of the Negro American* (Atlanta: Atlanta University Press, 1906), 13–38; *The Negro* (New York: H. Holt, 1915), passim. Du Bois acknowledged his great debt to Boas in "Forum of Fact and Opinion," *Pittsburgh Courier,* December 4, 1937.

34. Work, "Some Parallelisms in the Development of Africans and Other Races," *Southern Workman* 35 (November 1906), 614–621 and 36 (January, February, March 1907): 37–43, 105–111, 166–175; "The African Medicine Man," *Southern Workman* 36 (October 1907), 561–564; "An African System of Writing," *Southern Workman* 37 (October 1908): 518–526; "The African Family as an Institution," *Southern Workman* 38 (June, July, August 1909): 343–352, 391–396, 433–441; "African Agriculture," *Southern Workman* 39 (November, December 1910): 613–618, 681–687; "The Passing Tradition and the African Civilization," *Journal of Negro History* 1 (January 1916): 34–41.

35. Du Bois, "Marrying of Black Folk," *Independent* 69 (October 13, 1910): 813. In 1907, Dihdwo Twe, an African studying in America, attacked slavery on similar grounds. According to Twe, the slaves suffered irreparable harm under the degrading influences of the Anglo-Saxon. He noted, for example, how the masters took from the slave his African name, his standards of morality, "the lofty traditions and sweet legends of his native land," and even his language. "A Message from Africa," *American Journal of Religious Psychology and Education* 11 (1906–1907): 298, 300, 302.

36. Greener, "The White Problem," *Indianapolis Freeman,* September 1, 8, 1894.

37. Bowen, "The Comparative Status of the Negro at the Close of the War and of Today," *Africa and the American Negro,* 166, 167, 168.

38. Francis J. Grimké, "Pride: A High Look and a Proud Heart," n.d., in Woodson, ed., *The Works of Francis J. Grimké,* 11, 541; Frederick Douglass, "Introduction," *The Reason Why the Colored American Is Not in the World's Columbian Exposition* (1892), reprinted in *The Life and Writings of Frederick Douglass,* ed. Philip S. Foner, 4 vols. (New York: International, 1955), 4:471–473; Crogman, "The Negro's Needs," *Talks for the Times,* 144; Nathan B. Young, "A Race Without an Ideal," *A.M.E. Church Review,* 15 (October 1898): 606; Louis F. Post, "The National Afro-American Council," *Howard's American Magazine* 4 (November 1899): 39; T.W. Jones, "The Negro as a Business Man," in *Twentieth Century Negro Literature,* ed. D.W. Culp (1902; reprint, New York: Arno Press, 1969), 371; Forbes, "Colored Slave Owners and Traders in the Old Days," *A.M.E. Church Review* 29 (January 1913): 300, 301.

39. Joseph C. Price, "The Race Problem Stated," unpublished manuscript, n.d., Carter G. Woodson Collection, Manuscript Division, Library of Congress; Fortune, *Black and White,* 33, 52, 59, 62, 98, 198–199; "Missouri Former Slaves," *Philadelphia Sunday Item,* July 24, 1892, and "Stories of Runaway Slaves," *Detroit News-Tribune,* July 22, 1894, reprinted in *Slave Testimony: Two Centuries of Letters, Speeches, Interviews, and Autobiographies,* ed. John W. Blassingame (Baton Rouge: Louisiana State University Press, 1977), 501–511, 513–533; Wesley J. Gaines, "The Evils of African Slavery," *The Negro and the White Man* (Philadelphia: A.M.E. Publishing House, 1897), 22–31; Mary White Ovington, comp., "Slaves' Reminiscences of Slavery," *Independent* 68 (May 26, 1910): 1131–1136.

40. Douglass, "Slavery," unpublished manuscript [1895?], 13, Frederick Douglass Papers, Manuscript Division, Library of Congress.

41. Washington, *Up from Slavery* (1901; reprint, Airmont, 1967), 15, 19, 21; Washington, *The Story of My Life and Work* (Naperville, IL: J.L. Nichols, 1900), 30, 32, 34; Sinclair, *The Aftermath of Slavery: A Study of the Condition and Environment of the American Negro* (Boston: Small, Maynard, 1905), 3, 6, 7, 9, 11, 14, 15, 17; Woodson, *The Negro in Our History* (1922; reprint, Washington: Associated, 1924), 107 and chapter 3. Woodson's textbook was written in 1917 but not published until 1922.

42. T. Thomas Fortune, "The Afro-American," *Arena* 3 (December 1890): 116; Alexander Crummell, "The Black Woman of the South," *Africa and America,* 63–66; Katherine Davis Tillman, "Afro-American Women and Their Work," *A.M.E. Church Review* 11 (April 1895): 479–484; Mary Church Terrell, "A Reply to a Statement Recently Made," *A.M.E. Church Review* 17 (January 1901): 217; "Refutation of Charges Against Colored Women," *Howard's American Magazine* 6 (April 1901): 350; Virginia W. Broughton, "The Social Status of the Colored Women and Its Betterment," in Penn and Bowen, eds., *The United Negro,* 449.

43. Woodson, "The Beginnings of the Miscegenation of the Whites and Blacks," *Journal of Negro History* 3 (October 1918): 351.

44. James C. Matthews, "Henry Highland Garnet," unpublished manuscript, April 17, 1882, John Edward Bruce Papers, Schomburg Center; editorial, "Why the Young Negro Steals," *Birmingham Wide-Awake,* January 24, 1900; S.C. Cross, "The Negro and the Sunny South," *Colored American Magazine* 5 (July 1902): 195; Kealing, "The Characteristics of the Negro People," in Washington et al., *The Negro Problem,* 174–180. W.E.B. Du Bois identified similar deficiencies in "Social Effects of Emancipation," *Survey* 29 (February 1, 1911): 571.

45. Francis J. Grimké, "A True Pride and Race Development," unpublished manuscript, n.d., Francis J. Grimké Papers, Howard University; T. Thomas Fortune, "'Good Indians' and 'Good Niggers,'" *Independent* 51 (June 22, 1899): 1689–1690; Dihdwo Twe, "A Message From Africa," 303; W.E.B. Du Bois, "The Social Evolution of the Black South," *American Negro Monographs* 1 (March 1911): 5; Robert R. Moton, "Status of the Negro in America," *Current History* 16 (May 1922): 226.

46. Brawley, *A Short History of the American Negro* (New York: Macmillan, 1913), 60; Washington, *Working with the Hands* (New York: Doubleday, Page, 1904), 16.

47. Du Bois, *The Philadelphia Negro* (Philadelphia: University of Pennsylvania, 1899), 67, 71, 74–75, 147, 161, 178; "The Negro as He Really Is," *World's Work* 11 (June 1901): 853–854, 863.

48. Du Bois, "The Negro and Crime," *Independent* 51 (May 18, 1899): 1355; Washington, "Education Will Solve the Negro Problem, A Reply," *North American Review* 171 (August, 1900): 223, 225; Alexander Walters, "Negro Progress," *Independent* 58 (March 14, 1901): 652; John Henry Smyth, "Negro Creativity," in Culp, ed., *Twentieth Century Negro Literature,* 436; George Edmund Haynes, "After Emancipation—What?" *A.M.E. Church Review* 29 (January 1913): 284; Fortune, "Movement of the Afro-American Population from the Southern States," *A.M.E. Church Review* 33 (January 1917): 128, 129.

49. Du Bois, "The Training of Negroes for Social Power," *Outlook* 75 (October 17, 1903): 413; *The Philadelphia Negro,* 71; ed., *The Negro American Family* (Atlanta: Atlanta University Press, 1908), 17, 21–22; *The Negro,* 187–188.

50. Du Bois, "The Problem of Housing the Negro—The Home of the Slave," *Southern Workman* 30 (September 1901): 486, 490, 491, 492, 493.

51. Joseph T. Wilson, *The Black Phalanx* (1890; reprint, New York: Arno Press, 1968), 96; Washington, "The American Negro and His Economic Value," *International Monthly* 11 (December 1900): 672–674; Hightower H. Kealing, "The Negro's Contribution to His Own Development," in Penn and Bowen, eds., *The United Negro,* 207; H.H. Proctor, "From the Address of Dr. Proctor," *American Missionary* 59 (November 1905):

284; editorial, "Afro-American Womanhood," *New York Age,* February 22, 1906; Archibald H. Grimké, "Modern Industrialism and the Negroes of the United States," *The American Negro Academy Occasional Papers No. 12* (Washington: American Negro Academy, 1908), 5; C.V. Roman, "An Impending Crisis," *Journal of the National Medical Association,* n.d., reprinted in *A.M.E. Church Review* 36 (January 1910): 228.

52. W.S. Scarborough, "The Negro and the Trades," *Southern Workman* 36 (February 1897): 26–27; John S. Durham, *To Teach the Negro History: A Suggestion* (Philadelphia: McKay, 1897), 17, 33, 47; Du Bois, ed., *The Negro Artisan* (Atlanta: Atlanta University Press, 1902), 13–21; Thomas J. Calloway, "The American Negro Artisan," *Cassier's Magazine* 25 (March 1904): 435, 440, 445; Wilson, "Some Negro Poets," *A.M.E. Church Review* 4 (January 1888): 237; Monroe N. Work, "The Spirit of Negro Poetry," *Southern Workman* 37 (February 1908): 73–77; Arthur A. Schomburg, *Racial Integrity* [1913], copy in Arthur A. Schomburg Papers, Schomburg Center; Benjamin Brawley, "Three Negro Poets: Horton, Mrs. Harper and Whitman," *Journal of Negro History* 2 (October 1917): 384–392; Leonora Herron, "Conjuring and Conjure-Doctors," *Southern Workman* 24 (July 1895): 117–118; Alice M. Bacon, "Conjuring and Conjure-Doctors," *Southern Workman* (November, December 1895): 193–194, 209–210; Robert R. Moton, "Sickness in Slavery Days," *Southern Workman* 28 (February 1899): 74–75; W.E.B. Du Bois, "The Religion of the American Negro," *New World* 9 (December 1900): 615, 618; Clement Richardson, "Some Slave Superstitions," *Southern Workman* 41 (April 1912): 246–248; Kelly Miller, "The Historic Background of the Negro Physician," *Journal of Negro History* 1 (April 1916): 101.

53. R.R. Wright, "The Negro as an Inventor," *A.M.E. Church Review* 11 (April 1886): 398, 410; Brawley, "The Negro Genius," *Southern Workman* 44 (May 1915): 306, 307; Woodson, *The Education of the Negro Prior to 1861* (Washington: Association for the Study of Negro Life and History, 1919).

54. Alexander Crummell, "Comments on a Lecture Delivered by Mr. J.W. Cromwell," unpublished manuscript, July 21, 1890, Alexander Crummell Papers, Schomburg Center; Frederick Douglass, "Slavery," 21; B.F. Lee, Jr., "Negro Organizations," *Annals of the American Academy of Political and Social Science* 49 (September 1913): 129; Kelly Miller, "Negro's Musical Gift," *Washington Post,* May 10, 1903, clipping in Miller Papers; "The Artistic Gifts of the Negro," *Voice of the Negro* 3 (April 1906): 253; Frederick Douglass, *The Life and Times of Frederick Douglass from 1817 to 1882* (London: Christian Age Office, 1882), 28–29; Daniel Webster Davis, "Echoes from a Plantation Party," *Southern Workman* 28 (February 1899): 59. Also see: W.E.B. Du Bois, *The Souls of Black Folk: Essays and Sketches* (1903; reprint, Greenwich, CT: Fawcett, 1961), 181–183, 185–190; anon., "The Plantation Melody," *Colored American Magazine* 11 (July 1906): 59–61; H.H. Proctor, "The Theology of the Songs of the Southern Slave," *Southern Workman* 36 (November, December 1907): 588, 655, 656.

55. William Hannibal Thomas, "Religious Characteristics of the Negro," *A.M.E. Church Review* 9 (April 1893): 392–393; Harris Barrett, "Negro Folk Songs," *Southern Workman* 41 (April 1912): 238–245; Sinclair, *The Aftermath of Slavery,* 15; Du Bois, "The Religion of the American Negro," 619–620; Du Bois, *Souls of Black Folk,* 183; Du Bois, ed., *The Negro Church* (Atlanta: Atlanta University Press, 1903), 23 -24; Francis J. Grimké, "God and Prayer as Factors in the Struggle," n.d., in Woodson, ed., *The Works of Francis J. Grimké,* 1:279.

56. Robert R. Moton, "A Negro's Uphill Climb," *World's Work* 13 (April 1907): 8740; John W. Cromwell, "The Early Negro Convention Movement," *The American Negro Academy Occasional Papers No. 9* (Washington: American Negro Academy, 1904); Monroe N. Work, "Secret Societies as Factors in the Economical Life of the Negro," in *Democracy in Earnest,* ed. James E. McCulloch (Washington: Southern Socio-

logical Congress, 1918), 344–345; Gaines, "The Negro in Slavery Days," *Alexander's Magazine* 6 (September 15, 1908): 203; P.M. Lewis to the editor, *Indianapolis Freeman,* August 25, 1894; anon., "White Slavery: A Fragment of American History," *A.M.E. Church Review* 17 (October 1900): 132–133; Du Bois, ed., *Economic Co-Operation Among Negro Americans* (Atlanta: Atlanta University Press, 1907), 20, 24, 25; Du Bois, *John Brown* (1909; reprint, New York: International, 1962), 79, 81, 82, 84; Du Bois, *The Negro,*196.

57. Williams, *History of the Negro Race in America from 1619–1880,* 2 vols. (1883; reprint, New York: Arno Press, 1968), 1:305, 299; 2:82, 545, 547, 548.

58. T. Thomas Fortune, *The Negro in Politics* (New York: Ogilvie & Rowntree, 1885), 6; Cromwell, *The Negro in American History* (Washington: American Negro Academy, 1914), 12; Grimké, "Right on the Scaffold, or the Martyrs of 1822," *The American Negro Academy Occasional Papers No. 7* (Washington: American Negro Academy, 1901), 5, 8, 9; Grimké, "Prejudice, Preparing, Eruption," *New York Age,* November 30, 1905; Cromwell, "The Aftermath of Nat Turner's Insurrection," *Journal of Negro History* 5 (April 1920): 233.

59. Grimké, "The Ultimate Criminal," unpublished manuscript, n.d., Archibald H. Grimké Papers.

60. See, for example, Alexander Crummell's unpublished sermons. Though he was an unflagging critic of slavery, Crummell's contradictory statements nonetheless are apt to confuse. In "The American Negro, Before the War, and Now" (1891), Crummell condemned slavery for denying the bondsmen education. But in "The Discipline of Freedom" (n.d.), he praised slavery for the discipline that it instilled in the blacks—a trait that Crummell found drastically wanting in the race. Crummell Papers.

61. S.P. Fullinwider notes similar tensions and contradictions in the black thought of these years in *The Mind and Mood of Black America* (Homewood, IL: Dorsey Press, 1969), chapters 1–4.

62. See Woodson to Archibald H. Grimké, July 29, 1921, and enclosed "Questionnaire on Negro History," Archibald H. Grimké Papers. More than half of the questions concerned such aspects of slavery as the bondsmen's meetings, their garden truck patches, preachers, and teachers.

63. Fleming, "The American Negro Academy," *Publications of the Southern History Association* 9 (January 1905): 50.

Notes to Chapter 9

1. Most notably: John W. Blassingame, *The Slave Community: Plantation Life in the Antebellum South* (New York: Oxford University Press, 1972); Eugene D. Genovese, *Roll, Jordan, Roll: The World the Slaves Made* (New York: Pantheon, 1974); Peter H. Wood, *Black Majority: Negroes in Colonial South Carolina from 1670 Through the Stono Rebellion* (New York: Alfred A. Knopf, 1974); Herbert G. Gutman, *The Black Family in Slavery and Freedom, 1750–1925* (New York: Pantheon, 1976); Lawrence W. Levine, *Black Culture and Black Consciousness: Afro-American Folk Thought from Slavery to Freedom* (New York: Oxford University Press, 1977); Charles W. Joyner, "Slave Folklife on the Waccamaw Neck: Antebellum Black Culture in the South Carolina Lowcountry" (Ph.D. diss., University of Pennsylvania, 1977); and Joyner, *Down by the Riverside: A South Carolina Slave Community* (Urbana: University of Illinois Press, 1984).

2. Meier review of Herbert G. Gutman, *The Black Family in Slavery and Freedom,* in *Civil War History* 24 (March 1978): 84.

3. My definition of "folk culture" is deliberately broad. It encompasses the traditional, "tangible products of the folk, . . . the totality of folklife." See Richard M. Dorson,

"Introduction," *Folklore and Folklife: An Introduction* (Chicago: University of Chicago Press, 1972), 40. For similar usage, see Stith Thompson, "Folklore," in *Standard Dictionary of Folklore, Mythology, and Legend*, ed. Maria Leach, 2 vols. (New York: Funk and Wagnalls, 1949), 1:403, and John F. Szwed and Roger D. Abrahams, *Afro-American Folk Culture: An Annotated Bibliography of Materials from North, Central and South America and the West Indies*, 2 vols. (Philadelphia: Institute for the Study of Human Issues, 1978), 1:xiii.

4. See John David Smith, *Black Slavery in the Americas: An Interdisciplinary Bibliography, 1865–1980*, 2 vols. (Westport, CT: Greenwood Press, 1982), 2:1339–1368.

5. See John David Smith, "The Formative Period of American Slave Historiography, 1890–1920" (Ph.D. diss., University of Kentucky, 1977), 62–84, and William L. Van Deburg, *Slavery and Race in American Popular Culture* (Madison: University of Wisconsin Press, 1984), 69–86. There are two useful anthologies on the black folk culture of these years. See Bruce Jackson, ed., *The Negro and His Folklore in Nineteenth-Century Periodicals* (1967; reprint, Austin: University of Texas Press, 1977), and Bernard Katz, ed., *The Social Implications of Early Negro Music in the United States* (New York: Arno Press, 1969).

6. Higginson, "Negro Spirituals," *Atlantic Monthly* 19 (June 1867): 685–694.

7. Ibid., 694; *Army Life in a Black Regiment* (1869; reprint, Boston: Beacon Press, 1962), 221, 222.

8. For an excellent appraisal of the work of Allen, Ware, and Garrison, see Dena J. Epstein, *Sinful Tunes and Spirituals: Black Folk Music to the Civil War* (Urbana: University of Illinois Press, 1977), 303–320, and Gerald Robbins, "William F. Allen: Classical Scholar Among the Slaves," *History of Education Quarterly* 5 (December 1965): 211–223.

9. Allen, Ware, and Garrison, *Slave Songs of the United States* (New York: A. Simpson, 1867), i, iv–viii.

10. Ibid., xii; Epstein, *Sinful Tunes and Spirituals*, 327, 328; Allen, Ware, and Garrison, *Slave Songs of the United States*, xxx–xxxii; Epstein, *Sinful Tunes and Spirituals*, 348.

11. W.E.B. Du Bois, "Of the Sorrow Songs," *The Souls of Black Folk* (1903; reprint, Greenwich, CT: Fawcett, 1961), 186–188, 189.

12. Du Bois review of Edward Krehbiel, *Afro-American Folksongs*, in *Crisis* 7 (April 1914): 300; Edward Krehbiel, *Afro-American Folksongs: A Study in Racial and National Music* (New York: G. Schirmer, 1914), vi, ix, 14, 22, 35, 43–46, 56. Krehbiel's work has outlasted that of his critics, especially Richard Wallaschek and Louise Pound. See John Lovell, Jr., *Black Song: The Forge and the Flame: The Story How the Afro-American Spiritual Was Hammered Out* (New York: Macmillan, 1972), 105. In addition to the works on slave music cited above, I based my analysis on: John M. Brown, "Songs of the Slave," *Lippincott's Magazine* 2 (December 1868): 617–623; James M. Trotter, *Music and Some Highly Musical People* (Boston: Lee and Shepherd, 1881); Joel Chandler Harris, "Plantation Music," *Critic* 3 (December 15, 1883): 505–506; J.A. Macon, *Uncle Gabe Tucker: Or, Reflection, Song, and Sentiment in the Quarters* (Philadelphia: J.B. Lippincott, 1883); C.J. Ryder, "The Theology of the Plantation Songs," *American Missionary* 46 (January 1892): 9–16; Henry C. Wood, "Negro Camp-Meeting Melodies," *New England Magazine*, n.s. 6 (March 1892): 60–64; William E. Barton, "Old Plantation Hymns," *New England Magazine*, n.s. 19 (December 1898): 443–455; Barton, "Recent Negro Melodies," *New England Magazine*, n.s. 19 (February 1899): 707–719; Barton, *Old Plantation Hymns: A Collection of Hitherto Unpublished Melodies of the Slave and Freedman* (Boston: Lamson, Wolffe, 1899); Daniel W. Davis, "Echoes from a Plantation Party," *Southern Workman* 28 (February 1899): 54–59; Jeanette Robinson Murphy, "The Survival of African Music in America," *Popular Science Monthly* 55 (September 1899): 660–672; Marion A. Haskell, "Negro Spirituals," *Century* 58 (August 1899): 577–581; Barton, "Hymns of the Slave and the Freedman," *New England Magazine*, n.s. 19 (Janu-

ary 1899): 609–624; Emily Hallowell, *Calhoun Plantation Songs* (Boston: C.W. Thompson, 1901); Charles Peabody, "Notes on Negro Music," *Journal of American Folk-Lore* 16 (July–September 1903): 148–152; Kelly Miller, "The Artistic Gifts of the Negro," *Voice of the Negro* 3 (April 1906): 252–257; anon., "The Plantation Melody," *Colored American Magazine* 11 (July 1906): 59–61; Henry H. Proctor, "The Theology of the Songs of the Slave," *Southern Workman* 36 (November, December 1907): 584–592, 652–656; John W. Work, "The Songs of the Southland," *Voice of the Negro* 4 (January–February 1907): 51–54; Monroe N. Work, "The Spirit of Negro Poetry," *Southern Workman* 37 (February 1908): 73–77; Howard W. Odum, "Religious Folk-Songs of the Southern Negroes," *American Journal of Religious Psychology and Education* 3 (July 1909): 265–365; Odum, "Folk-Song and Folk Poetry as Found in the Secular Songs of the Southern Negroes," *Journal of American Folk-Lore* 24 (July–September, October–December 1911): 255–294, 351–396; Harris Barrett, "Negro Folk Songs," *Southern Workman* 41 (April 1912): 238–245; John W. Work, *Folk Song of the American Negro* (Nashville: Fisk University, 1915); Robert R. Moton, "Negro Folk Music," *Southern Workman* 44 (June 1915): 329–330; John A. Lomax, "Self-Pity in Negro Folk-Songs," *Nation* 105 (August 9, 1917): 141–145; Natalie C. Burlin, *Hampton Series Negro Folk-Songs,* 4 vols. (New York: G. Schirmer, 1918–1919); Burlin, "Negro Music at Birth," *Musical Quarterly* 5 (January 1919): 86–89; Burlin, "Black Singers and Players," *Musical Quarterly* 5 (October 1919): 499–504; Burlin, *Songs and Tales from the Dark Continent* (New York: G. Schirmer, 1920).

13. See Richard A. Waterman, "On Flogging a Dead Horse: Lessons Learned from the Africanisms Controversy," *Ethnomusicology* 7 (May 1963): 83–87.

14. Thaddeus Norris, "Negro Superstitions," *Lippincott's Magazine* 6 (July 1870): 92.

15. Cable, "Creole Slave Dances: The Dance in Place Congo," *Century* 31 (February 1886): 517–532, and "Creole Slave Songs," *Century* 31 (April 1886): 807–828.

16. Cable, "Creole Slave Dances," 519–526; Cable, "Creole Slave Songs," 813–815.

17. Jeanette Robinson Murphy, "The Survival of African Music in America," *Popular Science Monthly* 55 (September 1899), 661. In addition to the writings on Africanisms cited above, I based my analysis on: A.F. Chamberlain, "Negro Dialect," *Science* 12 (July 13, 1888): 23–24; H. Carrington Bolton, "Decoration of Graves of Negroes in South Carolina," *Journal of American Folk-Lore* 4 (July–September 1891): 214; Octave Thanet, "Folk-Lore in Arkansas," *Journal of American Folk-Lore* 5 (April–June 1892): 121–125; Alcée Fortier, *Louisiana Folk-Tales* (Boston: Houghton Mifflin, 1895); W.S. Scarborough, "Notes on the Function of Modern Languages in Africa," *Proceedings of the American Philological Association* 27 (July 1896): xlviii; J.N. Calloway, "African Sketches," *Southern Workman* 31 (1902): 618–621; R.H. Nassau, *Fetichism in West Africa* (New York: Charles Scribner's Sons, 1904); L.C. Van Panhuys, "About the Ornamentation in Use by Savage Tribes in Dutch Guiana and Its Meaning," *Proceedings of the Thirteenth International Congress of Americanists, 1902* (1905): 209–212; G. Stanley Hall, "The Negro in Africa and America," *Pedagogical Seminary* 12 (1905): 350–368; Hubert H.S. Aimes, "African Institutions in America," *Journal of American Folk-Lore* 18 (January–March 1905): 15–32; Monroe N. Work, "Some Parallelisms in the Development of Africans and Other Races," *Southern Workman* 35 (November 1906): 614–621, and 36 (January, February, March 1907): 37–43, 105–111, 166–175; Work, "The African Medicine Man," *Southern Workman* 36 (October 1907): 561–564; John Bennett, "Gullah: A Negro Patois," *South Atlantic Quarterly* 7 (October 1908): 332–347; Chamberlain, "Brazil," *Journal of American Folk-Lore* 21 (1908): 263; Franz Boas, "Industries of the African Negroes," *Southern Workman* 38 (April 1909): 217–229; Calvin D. Wilson, "Negroes Who Owned Slaves," *Popular Science Monthly* 86 (November 1912): 483–494.

18. Owens, "Folk-Lore of the Southern Negroes," *Lippincott's Magazine* 20 (Decem-

ber 1877): 748, 749. For a recent inquiry into this question, see William D. Piersen, "An African Background for American Negro Folktales?" *Journal of American Folklore* 84 (April–June 1971): 204–214.

19. See, for example, Crane, "Plantation Folk-Lore," *Popular Science Monthly* 18 (April 1881): 824–833; Charles C. Jones, Jr., *Negro Myths from the Georgia Coast Told in the Vernacular* (Boston: Houghton, Mifflin, 1888); Hanns Oertel, "Notes on Six Negro Myths from the Georgia Coast," *Journal of American Folk-Lore* 2 (October–December 1889): 309; Louis Pendleton, "Notes on Negro Folklore and Witchcraft in the South," *Journal of American Folk-Lore* 3 (July–September 1890): 201–207; A.M.H. Christensen, *Afro-American Folk Lore Told Round Cabin Fires on the Sea Islands of South Carolina* (Boston: J.G. Cupples, 1892); A. Gerber, "Uncle Remus Traced to the Old World," *Journal of American Folk-Lore* 6 (October–December 1893): 245–257; A.B. Ellis, "Evolution in Folklore: Some West African Prototypes of the 'Uncle Remus' Stories," *Popular Science Monthly* 48 (November 1895): 93–104; John G. Williams, *"De Old Plantation"* (Charleston: Walker, Evans & Cogswell, 1895); W.S. Scarborough, "Negro Folk-Lore and Dialect," *Arena* 86 (January 1897): 186–192; Annie W. Whitney, "Negro American Dialects," *Independent* 53 (August 22, 29, 1901): 1079–1081, 2039–2042; Anne V. Culbertson, *At the Big House: Where Nancy and Aunt 'Phrony Held Forth on the Animal Tales* (Indianapolis: Bobbs-Merrill, 1904); Henry C. Davis, "Negro Folk-Lore in South Carolina," *Journal of American Folk-Lore* 27 (July–September 1914): 241–254; A.O. Stafford, "Folk Literature of the Negro," *Crisis* 10 (October 1915): 296–299; John M. McBryde, "Brer Rabbit in the Folk Tales of Other Races," *Sewanee Review* 19 (April 1919): 185–206; Elsie Clews Parsons, "Joel Chandler Harris and Negro Folklore," *Dial* 66 (May 17, 1919): 491–493.

20. The most balanced analysis of Harris and his writings is R. Bruce Bickley, Jr., *Joel Chandler Harris* (Boston: Twayne, 1978). My discussion of Harris's folktales is limited to his first book, *Uncle Remus: His Songs and His Sayings* (New York: D. Appleton, 1880).

21. See, for example, Darwin T. Turner, "Daddy Joel Harris and His Old-Time Darkies," *Southern Literary Journal* 1 (December 1968): 20–41, and Alice Walker, "Uncle Remus, No Friend of Mine," *Southern Exposure* 9 (Summer 1981): 29–31.

22. Robert A. Bone, *Down Home: A History of Afro-American Short Fiction from Its Beginnings to the End of the Harlem Renaissance* (New York: G.P. Putnam's Sons, 1975), 19.

23. Harris to G. Laurence Gomme, June 9, 1883, Harris to Clemens, August 4, 1881, in Julia Collier Harris, *The Life and Letters of Joel Chandler Harris* (Boston: Houghton, Mifflin, 1918), 157–158, 168.

24. Richard A. Long, "The Uncle Remus Dialect: A Preliminary Linguistic View" (paper presented at meeting of Southeastern Conference on Linguistics, 1969), abstracted in *Abstracts in Anthropology* 2 (February 1971): 68.

25. Sterling Brown, *The Negro in American Fiction* (Washington: Associates in Negro Folk Education, 1937), 53, 54.

26. See Bernard Wolfe, "Uncle Remus and the Malevolent Rabbit," in *Mother Wit from the Laughing Barrel: Readings in the Interpretation of Afro-American Folklore*, ed. Alan Dundes (Englewood Cliffs, NJ: Prentice-Hall, 1973), 527–528. This essay appeared originally in *Commentary* 8 (July 1949): 31–41. Michael Flusche poses a viable alternative interpretation of the Uncle Remus tales. He notes, for example, that adversary relationships within the weak animal group are not explained by the weak/strong/slave/master paradigm. See "Joel Chandler Harris and the Folklore of Slavery," *Journal of American Studies* 9 (December 1975): 347–363.

27. See Bone, *Down Home,* 79–80, and William L. Andrews, *The Literary Career of*

NOTES TO CHAPTER 9   193

Charles W. Chesnutt (Baton Rouge: Louisiana State University Press, 1980). My interpretation of Chesnutt's folk tales is limited to his first book, *The Conjure Woman* (Boston: Houghton, Mifflin, 1899).

28. Writing in 1901, Chesnutt referred to the conjure stories as remnants of his "childish recollection," admitting that he "took . . . considerable liability with my subject." See "Superstitions and Folklore of the South," in Dundes, ed., *Mother Wit from the Laughing Barrel,* 370, 372. This essay appeared originally in *Modern Culture* 13 (May 1901): 231–235.

29. Bone, *Down Home,* 81–89. Also see Eugene Terry, "The Shadow of Slavery in Charles Chesnutt's *The Conjure Woman,*" *Ethnic Groups* 4 (May 1982): 103–125.

30. David D. Britt, "Chesnutt's Conjure Tales: What You See Is What You Get," *College Language Association Journal* 15 (March 1972): 269–279.

31. Melvin Dixon, "The Teller as Folk Trickster in Chesnutt's *The Conjure Woman,*" *College Language Association Journal* 18 (December 1974): 186–187; Joel Taxel, "Charles Waddell Chesnutt's Sambo: Myth and Reality," *Negro American Literature Forum* 9 (Winter 1975): 105–108.

32. Gloria C. Oden, "Chesnutt's Conjure as African Survival," *MELUS* 5 (Spring 1978): 38–48. To place Chesnutt's tales within the context of their day, I benefited from William W. Brown, *My Southern Home: Or, the South and Its People* (New York: A.G. Brown, 1880); W. William Newell, "Myths of Voodoo Worship and Child Sacrifices in Hayti," *Journal of American Folk-Lore* 1 (April–June 1888): 16–30; anon., "Negro Dances in Arkansas," *Journal of American Folk-Lore* 1 (April–June 1888): 83; Sara M. Handy, "Negro Superstitions," *Lippincott's Magazine* 48 (December 1891): 735–739; Joseph A. Haskell, "Sacrificial Offerings Among North Carolina Negroes," *Journal of American Folk-Lore* 4 (July–September 1891): 267–269; anon., "Negro Superstition Concerning the Violin," *Journal of American Folk-Lore* 5 (October–December 1892): 329–330; Frank D. Banks, "Plantation Courtship," *Journal of American Folk-Lore* 7 (January–March 1894): 147–149; Alice M. Bacon, "Conjuring and Conjure-Doctors," *Southern Workman* 24 (November, December 1895): 193–194, 209–211; Leonora Herron, "Conjuring and Conjure Doctors," *Southern Workman* 24 (July 1895): 117–118; Ada W. Trowbridge, "Negro Customs and Folk-Stories of Jamaica," *Journal of American Folk-Lore* 9 (October–December 1896): 279–287; Julien A. Hall, "Negro Conjuring and Tricking," *Journal of American Folk-Lore* 10 (July–September 1897): 241–243; Robert R. Moton, "Sickness in Slavery Days," *Southern Workman* 28 (February 1899): 74–75; F. Julian Carroll, "Mysticism Among the Negroes," *New York Medical Journal* 71 (April 21, 1900): 594–596; Roland Steiner, "Observations on the Practice of Conjuring in Georgia," *Journal of American Folk-Lore* 14 (July–September 1901): 173–180; John R.L. Diggs, "Negro Church Life," *Voice of the Negro* 1 (February 1904): 46–50; Marvin Dana, "Voodoo, Its Effects on the Negro Race," *Metropolitan Magazine* 28 (August 1908): 529–538; Samuel B. Jones, "The British West Indian Negro—Customs, Manners, and Superstitions," *Southern Workman* 40 (October 1911): 580–589; Clement Richardson, "Some Slave Superstitions," *Southern Workman* 41 (April 1912): 246–248; Kelly Miller, "The Historic Background of the Negro Physician," *Journal of Negro History* 1 (April 1916): 99–109.

33. Hiram K. Moderwell, "The Epic of the Black Man," *American Missionary* 72 (April 1918): 44.

34. Du Bois, "The Religion of the American Negro," *New World* 9 (December 1900): 618.

35. Ibid., 619–620.

36. Du Bois, *The Philadelphia Negro* (Philadelphia: University of Pennsylvania, 1899), 71; *The Negro American Family* (Atlanta: Atlanta University, 1908), 21–22; *The Negro* (1915; reprint, New York: Oxford University Press, 1970), 188.

37. Du Bois, *"The Problem of Housing the Negro—The Home of the Slave,"* Southern *Workman* 30 (September 1901): 486.

38. Ibid., 488–491.

39. Ibid., 491–493.

40. See, for example, *Roll, Jordan, Roll,* 356, 451; Gutman, *The Black Family in Slavery and Freedom,* 3–44, 190, 260–262, and passim; Elliott Rudwick, "W.E.B. Du Bois as Sociologist" in *Black Sociologists: Historical and Contemporary Perspectives,* ed. James E. Blackwell and Morris Janowitz (Chicago: University of Chicago Press, 1974), 25–55.

41. See anonymous review of Joel Chandler Harris, *Uncle Remus: His Songs and His Sayings,* in *Nation* 31 (December 2, 1880): 398.

42. On this theme, see Raymond Hedin, "Muffled Voices: The American Slave Narrative," *Clio* 10 (Winter 1981): 129.

43. See, for example, Du Bois, "The Conservation of Races," *American Negro Academy Occasional Papers, No. 2* (Washington: The Academy, 1897), 8, and "The Problem of Housing the Negro."

44. Odum, "Religious Folk-Songs of the Southern Negroes," 22, 11, 15; *The Social and Mental Traits of the Negro* (New York: Columbia University, 1910), 66–67; "Folk-Song and Folk-Poetry as Found in the Secular Songs of the Southern Negroes," 255–294, 351–396. Another example of racism in a treatment of slave music is Henry C. Wood, "Negro Camp-Meeting Melodies," 61.

45. Parsons, *Folk-Lore of the Sea Islands, South Carolina* (Cambridge: American Folk-Lore Society, 1923), xxi, 61, 62, 111, 149. Parsons completed her field work in 1919, but her book did not appear until 1923.

Notes to Chapter 10

1. See Michael Vaughan Woodward, "The Publications of Ellis Merton Coulter to 1 July 1977," *Georgia Historical Quarterly* 61 (Fall 1977): 268–278; Woodward, "Ellis Merton Coulter and the Southern Historiographic Tradition" (Ph.D. diss., University of Georgia, 1982), chapter 1; Woodward, "E. Merton Coulter and the Art of Biography," *Georgia Historical Quarterly* 64 (Summer 1980): 159–171; Kenneth Coleman, "Ellis Merton Coulter," *Proceedings and Papers of the Georgia Association of Historians* (1981), 46–50; B. Phinizy Spalding, "Ellis Merton Coulter," *Georgia Historical Quarterly* 65 (Spring 1981): [i-iii]; Albert B. Saye, "A Tribute to Ellis Merton Coulter," *Georgia Historical Quarterly* 65 (Fall 1981): 183–188; Valeria Gennaro Lerda, "Ellis Merton Coulter: A Personal Tribute," *Georgia Historical Quarterly* 65 (Winter 1981): 307–315; Barry Saunders, "E. Merton Coulter Dies; Historian, UGA Legend," *Atlanta Constitution,* July 6, 1981.

2. Franklin, "Whither Reconstruction Historiography?" *Journal of Negro Education* 17 (Fall 1948): 454–455, 460.

3. Weisberger, "The Dark and Bloody Ground of Reconstruction Historiography," *Journal of Southern History* 25 (November 1959): 434.

4. Taylor, "The White South from Secession to Redemption," in *Interpreting Southern History: Historiographical Essays in Honor of Sanford W. Higginbotham,* ed. John B. Boles and Evelyn Thomas Nolen (Baton Rouge: Louisiana State University Press, 1987), 182; Cox, "From Emancipation to Segregation: National Policy and Southern Blacks," in Boles and Nolen, eds., *Interpreting Southern History,* 200n.

5. Woodward, "Ellis Merton Coulter and the Southern Historiographic Tradition," 3–4.

6. J.O. Van Meter to Coulter, September 13, 1946, Coulter to Van Meter, September 16, 1946, Ellis Merton Coulter Papers, University of Georgia.

7. Woodward, "Ellis Merton Coulter and the Southern Historiographic Tradition," 4–7.

8. Warren F. Kuehl, *Dissertations in History: An Index to Dissertations Completed in History Departments of United States and Canadian Universities, 1873–1960* (Lexington: University of Kentucky Press, 1965), 38.

9. Coulter, "Effects of Secession Upon the Commerce of the Mississippi Valley," *Mississippi Valley Historical Review* 3 (December 1916): 275–300, and "Commercial Intercourse with the Confederacy in the Mississippi Valley, 1861–1865," *Mississippi Valley Historical Review* 5 (March 1919): 377–395.

10. John David Smith to Coulter, January 3, 1978, Coulter to Smith, January 13, 1978, in possession of the author.

11. Coulter, *The Civil War and Readjustment in Kentucky* (Chapel Hill: University of North Carolina Press, 1926), 455. This source will hereafter be cited as Coulter, *CWRK,* with the appropriate page numbers.

12. Coulter to Smith, January 13, 1978.

13. Coulter, *The Cincinnati Southern Railroad and the Struggle for Southern Commerce, 1865–1872* (Chicago: American Historical Society, 1922); Coulter to Smith, January 13, 1978; Connelley and Coulter, *History of Kentucky,* ed. Charles Kerr, 5 vols. (Chicago: American Historical Society, 1922), 1:iv. Coulter obtained much of his primary material on Kentucky—on the Civil War and other eras as well—while researching *History of Kentucky.* See, for example, Coulter's "Early Frontier Democracy in the First Kentucky Constitution," *Political Science Quarterly* 39 (December 1924): 665–677.

14. Coulter to Van Meter, September 16, 1946, Coulter Papers.

15. Coulter to Louis R. Wilson, January 10, 1925, Coulter to Wilson, February 10, 1925, University of North Carolina Press Records, University of North Carolina Archives.

16. Coulter, *CWRK,* 80, 100.

17. Ibid., 151, 439.

18. Ibid., 274, 286, 329.

19. Marion A. Green, "A Few Minutes with the Authors," *Louisville Times,* August 14, 1926; [Edward Tuthill?] in *Lexington Herald,* December 6, 1926, clipping in Coulter Papers; [R.S. Cotterill?] in *Filson Club History Quarterly* 1 (October 1926): 38; anon. in *Register of the Kentucky State Historical Society* 25 (January 1927): 107.

20. Cotterill in *Mississippi Valley Historical Review* 13 (December 1926): 439; Owsley in *American Historical Review* 32 (January 1927): 345; Boyd in *South Atlantic Quarterly* 26 (July 1927): 306; B.B. Kendrick in *Political Science Quarterly* 42 (June 1927): 288; John A. Krout in *Historical Outlook* 18 (December 1927): 392. The last three clippings are located in the University of North Carolina Press Records.

21. Hamilton in *North Carolina Historical Review* 5 (January 1928): 123–124. Significantly, Hamilton served as the reader who advised the University of North Carolina Press to publish Coulter's book. See Coulter to Louis R. Wilson, May 9, 1925, University of North Carolina Press Records.

22. Cotterill in *Mississippi Valley Historical Review,* 438–439.

23. Franklin, "Whither Reconstruction Historiography?" 446; *Reconstruction After the Civil War* (Chicago: University of Chicago Press, 1961), 236.

24. Connelly, "Neo-Confederatism or Power Vacuum: Post-War Kentucky Politics Reappraised," *Register of the Kentucky Historical Society* 64 (October 1966): 257–258; Webb, "Kentucky: 'Pariah Among the Elect,'" in *Radicalism, Racism, and Party Realignment: The Border States During Reconstruction,* ed. Richard O. Curry (Baltimore: Johns Hopkins University Press, 1969), 105, 144–145; Webb, *Kentucky in the Reconstruction Era* (Lexington: University Press of Kentucky, 1979), 97.

25. Lowell H. Harrison, "Significant Books in Kentucky History," *Filson Club His-*

tory Quarterly 51 (July 1977): 276; Klotter, "Clio in the Commonwealth: The Status of Kentucky History," *Register of the Kentucky Historical Society* 80 (Winter 1982): 76.

26. Woodward, "Ellis Merton Coulter: A Case Study in the Development of Conservative Racism in the New South," *Midwest Quarterly* 20 (Spring 1979): 274, 276; Woodward, "Ellis Merton Coulter and the Southern Historiographic Tradition," 173–174; Coulter, *CWRK,* 432.

27. Coulter, *CWRK,* 340, 247, 205, 164, 263, 265, 341, 265, 268, 362, 347, 344, 343.

28. Ibid., 260–261, 283, 285, 423.

29. Franklin, "Whither Reconstruction Historiography?" 449.

30. These published Columbia University dissertations include W.W. Davis, *The Civil War and Reconstruction in Florida* (1913); Walter L. Fleming, *The Civil War and Reconstruction in Alabama* (1905); J.W. Garner, *Reconstruction in Mississippi* (1901); J.G. de Roulhac Hamilton, *Reconstruction in North Carolina* (1914); Charles W. Ramsdell, *Reconstruction in Texas* (1910); Thomas S. Staples, *Reconstruction in Arkansas* (1923); and C. Mildred Thompson, *Reconstruction in Georgia* (1915).

31. Donald, "Introduction to the Torchbook Edition," in *Essays on the Civil War and Reconstruction,* ed. William Archibald Dunning (1898; reprint, New York: Harper & Row, 1965), x; Weisberger, "The Dark and Bloody Ground of Reconstruction Historiography," 446.

32. Du Bois, *Black Reconstruction in America, 1860–1880* (1935; reprint, New York, Atheneum, 1973), 731. For Du Bois's specific criticisms of the "Dunning school," see pages 719–721. For the perspective of a contemporary white revisionist historian, see Francis B. Simkins, "New Viewpoints of Southern Reconstruction," *Journal of Southern History* 5 (February 1939): 49–61.

33. Philip R. Muller, "Look Back Without Anger: A Reappraisal of William A. Dunning," *Journal of American History* 61 (September 1974): 334.

34. Coulter, *CWRK,* 289, 312, 358, 351, 362, 356.

35. Ibid., 347, 356, 410.

36. Scrugham, *The Peaceable Americans of 1860–61: A Study in Public Opinion* (1921; reprint, New York: Octagon Books, 1976), 105n. Edward Conrad Smith's *The Borderland in the Civil War* (New York: Macmillan, 1927) appeared a year after the publication of Coulter's book. Smith focused broadly, including in his study Kentucky, Missouri, western Virginia, southern Ohio, southern Indiana, and southern Illinois. He excluded the postwar years from his consideration. Though more moderate than Coulter in describing the "excesses" of the U.S. Army in Kentucky, Smith's overall treatment of Kentucky and the Civil War largely mirrored Coulter's. See 279, 372–375.

37. On Progressive historiography, see Lee Benson, *Turner & Beard: American Historical Writing Reconsidered* (New York: Free Press, 1960), 96–101, 107–109; Richard Hofstadter, *The Progressive Historians: Turner, Beard, Parrington* (New York: Knopf, 1968), 41–43, 190–200, 437–443; Gene Wise, *American Historical Explanations: A Strategy for Grounded Inquiry* (Homewood, IL: Dorsey Press, 1973), 97–100. In 1900, Turner hired Coulter's mentor, Carl Russell Fish, to develop a course in the "History of New England." Two years later, Turner recruited Ulrich Bonnell Phillips to teach southern history. Turner specialized in the history of the West. With these colleagues in place, Turner established Wisconsin's School of History, where "Particular attention is given to the study of the evolution of the various sectional groupings—social, economic, and political—in the history of the United States, and to the physiographic factors in American development." See Ray Allen Billington, *Frederick Jackson Turner: Historian, Scholar, Teacher* (New York: Oxford University Press, 1973), 243, 244.

38. Coulter, *CWRK,* 229, 250.

Notes to Chapter 11

1. Ulrich B. Phillips, holograph copy of "Plantations East and South of Suez," n.d., Ulrich Bonnell Phillips Collection, Yale University.

2. Phillips to Yates Snowden, May 26, 1929, Yates Snowden Papers, South Caroliniana Library, University of South Carolina; Wallace Notestein to Phillips, June 5, 1929, Ulrich B. Phillips Papers, Southern Historical Collection, University of North Carolina at Chapel Hill; Phillips to Notestein, June 14, 1929, Wallace Notestein Papers, Yale University; Phillips to Fairfax Harrison, June 17, 1929, Fairfax Harrison Papers, Virginia Historical Society; Phillips to Snowden, June 23, 1929, Snowden Papers; Phillips to Herbert A. Kellar, July 4, 1929, Herbert A. Kellar Papers, State Historical Society of Wisconsin; Frank D. Fackenthal to Phillips, April 26, 1929, [telegram] Phillips Papers; "Wins Kahn Fellowship. Prof. U.B. Phillips of Michigan to Make World Tour," *New York Times,* May 4, 1929; Phillips, "Nilotics and Azande," *Albert Kahn Foundation for the Foreign Travel of American Teachers Reports* 9 (1930), [11]; Phillips to Notestein, June 14, 1929, Notestein Papers. On the Kahn Foundation Fellowship, see "Globe Trotter Fellowship," *New York Times,* May 18, 1911. The appointment was designed for "a professor of one of the smaller colleges in the South or West who has little opportunity to see men and things abroad, but has a mental equipment equal to that of the majority of his colleagues in the larger institutions."

3. Phillips to Notestein, May 5, 1929, Notestein Papers; Phillips to Dana C. Munro, May 19, 1929, *American Historical Review* Editorial Correspondence, Manuscript Division, Library of Congress; Phillips to Notestein, August 30, 1929, Notestein Papers; untitled memorandum, September 24, 1929, Kyoto, Japan, Phillips Collection; "Report No. 2, October 22, 1929, From Professor Ulrich B. Phillips on Board S.S. President Adams," John H.T. McPherson Papers, University of Georgia.

4. Phillips to Claude H. Van Tyne, November 14, 1929, Claude H. Van Tyne Papers, University of Michigan; Phillips, "Plantations East and South of Suez," *Agricultural History* 5 (July 1931): 93, 94; Phillips to Kellar, November 4, 1929, Kellar Papers.

5. Phillips, "Plantations East and South of Suez," 94, 96, 95; Phillips to Kellar, November 4, 1929, Kellar Papers.

6. Phillips, "Plantations East and South of Suez," 96, 97; Phillips, *American Negro Slavery: A Survey of the Supply, Employment and Control of Negro Labor as Determined by the Plantation Régime* (New York: Appleton-Century-Crofts, 1918), 304.

7. Phillips to Notestein, November 14, 1929, Notestein Papers; Phillips, "Plantations East and South of Suez," 97, 98.

8. Phillips, "Plantations East and South of Suez," 100, 99, 100.

9. Ibid., 100–105.

10. Ibid., 105–107.

11. Ibid., 108; Phillips, "Nilotics and Azande," 11; Phillips to Notestein, December 18, 1929, Notestein Papers; Phillips, "Negroes of the Sudan," unpublished typescript, page 1, Phillips Collection.

12. Phillips, "Nilotics and Azande," 11, 17, 18. Phillips published an emended version of "Nilotics and Azande" as "Azandeland," *Yale Review* 20 (December 1930): 293–313.

13. Phillips, "Nilotics and Azande," 17, 18, 11, 12.

14. Ibid., 19, 34, 20.

15. Ibid., 20–21, 25, 21–22, 28–29, 25, 24, 22, 23.

16. Ibid., 29, 31, 32, 34, 35, 36; Phillips to Notestein, January 15, 1930, Notestein Papers; Phillips to Ralph Henry Gabriel, January 20, 1930, Ralph Henry Gabriel Papers, Yale University; Phillips to Kellar, June 18, 1930, Kellar Papers.

17. Phillips to Notestein, January 15, 1930, Notestein Papers; Phillips, "Nilotics and Azande," 36, 45, 37, 38, 43.

18. Phillips, "Nilotics and Azande," 43, 44, 45.

19. Genovese, "Race and Class in Southern History: An Appraisal of the Work of Ulrich Bonnell Phillips," in *Ulrich Bonnell Phillips: A Southern Historian and His Critics,* ed. John David Smith and John C. Inscoe (1990; reprint, Athens: University of Georgia Press, 1993), 126n.

20. Dillon, *Ulrich Bonnell Phillips: Historian of the Old South* (Baton Rouge: Louisiana State University Press, 1985), 148; Phillips, "The Historic Civilization of the South," *Agricultural History* 12 (April 1938): 143, 149. Phillips delivered his paper, "The Historic Civilization of the South," in Blacksburg, Virginia, in July 1931. See "Rural Institute Opens Tonight," *Roanoke Times* (Virginia), July 27, 1931. The paper was published posthumously.

21. Edward W. Said, *Orientalism* (1978; reprint, New York: Random House, 1979), 95; Phillips to Notestein, December 18, 1929, Notestein Papers; H.G. Kidd to Phillips, August 31, 1930, Phillips Papers.

22. Phillips, "The Historic Civilization of the South," 144.

23. Phillips, "Negroes of the Sudan," 60–61, Phillips Collection. On the continuity of Phillips's racism between 1918 and 1929, see John David Smith, *An Old Creed for the New South: Proslavery Ideology and Historiography, 1865–1918* (1985; reprint, Athens: University of Georgia Press, 1991), 273–274.

24. Phillips, "The Historic Civilization of the South," 149.

25. Phillips, "Report of Impressions," October 1931, page 2, General Education Board Papers, Rockefeller Archives Center; Phillips, "The Historic Civilization of the South," 149.

26. Phillips to Donald Davidson, June 20, 1929, Donald Davidson Papers, Vanderbilt University.

Notes to Chapter 12

1. Review of Joel Williamson, *After Slavery: The Negro in South Carolina During Reconstruction, 1861–1877,* in *Civil War History* 12 (March 1966): 93.

2. Eaton died in Lexington, Kentucky, on August 12, 1980. See his obituaries in *Lexington Herald,* August 13, 1980, and *Louisville Courier-Journal,* August 15, 1980. On Eaton's personality and scholarship, see Thomas D. Clark, "Clement Eaton," *Register of the Kentucky Historical Society* 80 (Spring 1982): 140–150.

3. Eaton to John David Smith, March 19, 1979, in possession of the author.

4. Ibid.

5. Ibid.

6. Albert D. Kirwan, "Introduction," *The Civilization of the Old South: Writings of Clement Eaton* (Lexington: University of Kentucky Press, 1968), ix.

7. Ibid.

8. Eaton to John David Smith, March 19, 1979.

9. Clement Eaton interview, Lexington, Kentucky, May 9, 1977; Eaton to John David Smith, March 19, 1979.

10. Eaton to John David Smith, March 19, 1979.

11. Eaton to John David Smith, January 28, 1976, in possession of the author.

12. Kirwan, *The Civilization of the Old South,* viii.

13. Eaton to John David Smith, March 19, 1979.

14. Eaton, *Freedom of Thought in the Old South* (Durham: Duke University Press, 1940). In an enlarged and revised form, this book was published under the title *The Freedom-of-Thought Struggle in the Old South* (New York: Harper & Row, 1964).

15. Eaton to John David Smith, March 19, 1979.

16. Eaton to John David Smith, January 25, 1979, in possession of the author.

17. Eaton, "James Woodrow and the Freedom of Teaching in the South," reprinted in *The Pursuit of Southern History: Presidential Addresses of the Southern Historical Association, 1935–1963*, ed. George Brown Tindall (Baton Rouge: Louisiana State University Press, 1964), 449.

18. Eaton to John David Smith, March 19, 1979.

19. Eaton, *The Civilization of the Old South*, x.

20. Eaton, "Student Days with Thomas Wolfe," *Georgia Review* 17 (Summer 1963): 146.

21. See Paul Buck, ed., *Social Sciences at Harvard, 1860–1920* (Cambridge: Harvard University Press, 1965), 129–174 and passim.

22. Eaton, "Student Days with Thomas Wolfe," 151.

23. Ibid., 153–154.

24. Clement Eaton to Mama, May 24, 1925, Clement Eaton Papers, Margaret I. King Library, University of Kentucky.

25. Eaton to John David Smith, March 19, 1979.

26. Merk to Eaton, July 13, 1925, Eaton Papers.

27. Eaton, *The Civilization of the Old South*, xi.

28. Merk to Eaton, April 10, 1931, Eaton Papers.

29. Merk to Eaton, December 14, 1928, Eaton Papers.

30. Merk to Eaton, June 11, 1934, Eaton Papers.

31. Eaton's revised dissertation received the Duke University Press prize for 1939.

32. Clement Eaton interview, Lexington, Kentucky, November 5, 1975, Alumni-Faculty Oral History Project, Margaret I. King Library, University of Kentucky. I wish to thank Terry L. Birdwhistell for providing me with a copy of the Eaton interview.

33. The Eaton interview includes penetrating, critical observations of his years at Kentucky.

34. Eaton, *A History of the Old South* (New York: Macmillan, 1949, 1966, 1975).

35. (New York: Macmillan, 1954).

36. Eaton, *Henry Clay and the Art of American Politics* (Boston: Little, Brown, 1957).

37. Joseph G. Tregle, Jr., in *Mississippi Valley Historical Review* 44 (September 1957): 357.

38. (New York: Harper, 1961).

39. (1964; reprint Baton Rouge: Louisiana State University Press, 1967).

40. *Pennsylvania Magazine of History and Biography* 88 (October 1964): 502.

41. Eaton to John David Smith, January 28, 1976; Wendell H. Stephenson, review of *The Growth of Southern Civilization*, in *American Historical Review* 67 (July 1962): 1058–1059. In 1978 and 1979, Eaton was gathering material on immigrants and urban dwellers in the South to broaden the scope of *A History of the Old South*, which he was revising at the time of his death. See, for example, Eaton to Randall M. Miller, December, 1978, in possession of Miller.

42. Eaton, *The Leaven of Democracy: The Growth of the Democratic Spirit in the Time of Jackson* (New York: G. Braziller, 1963); *The Waning of the Old South Civilization* (New York: Pegasus, 1969); *Jefferson Davis* (New York: Free Press, 1977).

43. His last publication was "Charles Darwin and Catherine Hopley: Victorian Views of Plantation Societies," *Plantation Society in the Americas* 1 (February 1979): 16–27.

44. For a listing of Eaton's awards and honors, see the program, "Clement Eaton— Distinguished Professor of the Year [1955–1956]," College of Arts and Sciences, University of Kentucky, copy in Eaton Papers.

45. "James Woodrow and the Freedom of Teaching in the South," 449.

46. Ibid.

47. Ibid.

48. *Chattanooga News-Free Press,* November 10, 1961, clipping in Eaton Papers.

49. *Charleston News and Courier,* November 14, 1961, clipping in Eaton Papers.

50. Ibid.

51. Ibid.

52. In a related manuscript, "Diary of a Day in Columbia, S.C., July 15, 1960," Eaton wrote: "Read the Columbia *State* and disagreed with the conservative political and social views—doubtless the editor would call me a "pinko," as I overheard some politicians refer to liberals in regard to the treatment of Negroes." Eaton Papers.

53. On the origins of this question, see "Communism and the Negro Tenant Farmer," *Opportunity: A Journal of Negro Life* 9 (August 1931): 234–235; and Wilson Record, *The Negro and the Communist Party* (Chapel Hill: University of North Carolina Press, 1951).

54. Frances Mathews Hails (c. 1882–1968) served for more than thirty years as chief clerk and archivist at the Alabama Department of Archives and History. See "Miss Frances Hails Credited With Finding Flag of Republic," *Montgomery Advertiser,* March 8, 1939, and "Historic Earth Beneath State Capitol Is Laden with Fabulous Treasure," *Birmingham News,* April 23, 1939.

55. John Allan Wyeth (1845–1922) organized the first American postgraduate medical school, New York Polyclinic Hospital and Medical School, in 1881. During the Civil War he served in the Confederate cavalry and spent fifteen months in a Federal prison. A medical graduate of the University of Louisville (1869), Wyeth introduced several new surgical procedures and wrote numerous medical/surgical treatises. See *National Cyclopaedia of American Biography,* 59 vols. to date (New York and Clifton Heights, NJ: James T. White, 1893–), 41:55–56.

56. Thomas Edward Watson (1856–1922) championed the cause of southern farmers in the late nineteenth century. Opposed to the New South rhetoric of Henry Grady and others, Watson charged that southern agrarians would profit little from the northern and southern industrialists. Elected to Congress on a Farmers' Alliance platform in 1890, Watson came to symbolize the Populist revolt in the South. He opposed Populist fusion with the Democrats, but ran unsuccessfully for vice president on the Bryan (Democratic) ticket. In 1904 and 1908, Watson was the presidential candidate of the Populists. By 1910, Watson, consumed by frustration, turned away from attacking capitalists to assailing blacks, Jews, and Catholics. See C. Vann Woodward, *Tom Watson, Agrarian Rebel* (New York: Rinehart, 1938).

57. Joseph Emerson Brown (1821–1894) was elected governor of Georgia in 1857, 1859, 1861, and 1863. Devoted to the principle of state rights, he fought incessantly with Jefferson Davis when the Confederate president moved sharply toward centralization. After the Civil War, Brown became a Republican and worked to minimize the length of military rule in Georgia. In 1871, he rejoined the Democrats and served his party in the United States Senate (1880–1891). According to historian C. Mildred Thompson, Brown was an uncommonly astute politician: "He was first in secession, first in reconstruction, and very nearly first in the restoration of Democratic home rule. Consequently, he came up on top at every revolution of the wheel of destiny." See Thompson, *Reconstruction in Georgia: Economic, Social, Political* (New York: Columbia University Press, 1915), 223, and Joseph Parks, *Joseph E. Brown of Georgia* (Baton Rouge: Louisiana State University Press, 1977).

58. See, for example, Marie Bankhead Owen to J.G. de Roulhac Hamilton, July 23, 1930, J.G. de Roulhac Hamilton Papers, Southern Historical Collection, University of North Carolina at Chapel Hill. Mrs. Owen, director of the Alabama Department of Archives and History, was "very much perturbed by" the visits to her state by archivists and historians in search of manuscript materials. North Carolina, under Hamilton's guidance,

and Duke University, led by William K. Boyd, were the national leaders in the acquisition of such materials. See John David Smith, " 'Keep 'Em in a Fireproof Vault'—Pioneer Southern Historians Discover Plantation Records," *South Atlantic Quarterly* 78 (Summer 1979): 376–391.

59. Clement Claiborne Clay (1816–1882) graduated from the University of Alabama in 1834. After serving in the state legislature in the 1840s, he was elected to the United States Senate in 1853. Clay was an articulate spokesman for state sovereignty and southern independence. During the Civil War, he served in the Confederate Senate and, in 1864, traveled on a secret mission to Canada to negotiate peace terms with agents of the Lincoln administration. See Ezra J. Warner and Wilfred Buck Yearns, *Biographical Register of the Confederate Congress* (Baton Rouge: Louisiana State University Press, 1975), 52–53.

60. Carl Lamson Carmer (1893–1976) was a New York native educated at Hamilton College and Harvard University. He taught English at several colleges, including the University of Alabama, and wrote numerous books. He is best known for his regional history and folklore pertaining to Alabama and New York. His *Stars Fell on Alabama* was published in 1934. See Carmer's obituary published in the *New York Times,* September 12, 1976.

61. Nathan Bryan Whitfield (1799–1868) descended from North Carolinians Bryan Whitfield and Winifred Bryan. See Whitfield Family File, Alabama Department of Archives and History, Montgomery.

62. Clarence Kirven (1879–1974) was a prominent lumber manufacturer in both Alabama and North Carolina. See "Pioneers of Marengo County," in *Demopolis Times* (Alabama), June 6, 1974.

63. William Lowndes Yancey (1814–1863) has been described as the "strongest and most single-minded defender of southern rights." A native Georgian, he married into a wealthy South Carolina family and, after settling in Alabama, became one of the state's most influential politicians, serving in the Alabama legislature in the 1840s and in the United States House of Representatives from 1844 to 1845. Yancey introduced Alabama's secession ordinance. During the Civil War he served as a diplomat and, later, as a member of the Confederate Senate, where Yancey broke with the Davis administration over the issue of state rights in the Confederacy. See Warner and Yearns, *Biographical Register of the Confederate Congress,* 264–265.

64. Richmond Pearson Hobson (1870–1937) graduated from the United States Naval Academy in 1889 and served in the Navy's construction department until 1903. During the Spanish-American War he led the expedition that sank the collier *Merrimac* at the entrance of Santiago harbor, effectively impeding the Spanish fleet's escape from the harbor. Hobson was captured and imprisoned by the Spanish during the war. He later served in the United States Congress (1907–1913) and in his many speeches, lectures, and writings advocated American naval superiority. See Thomas McA. Owen, ed., *History of Alabama and Dictionary of Alabama Biography,* 4 vols. (Chicago: S.J. Clarke, 1921), 3:821–822.

65. Dixon Hall Lewis (1802–1848) ranked among Alabama's foremost state rights Democrats in the antebellum period. Whether serving in the United States House of Representatives (1829–1844) or in the Senate (1844–1848), he consistently opposed the Bank of the United States, federally sponsored internal improvements programs, and the protective tariff. He played a key role in passing the Walker Tariff of 1846, which significantly reduced tariff rates. See Thomas P. Abernethy, *The Formative Period in Alabama, 1815–1828* (1922; reprint, University: University of Alabama Press, 1965), 135, 136, 147–149.

66. William Holcombe Thomas (1867–1945) graduated from Emory University in 1887 and, after reading law for one year, was admitted to the Alabama bar. He practiced

law for thirteen years before being elected associate judge of the City Court of Montgomery in 1901. Seven years later, he was appointed judge of the City Court. Thomas returned to private practice in 1911, but in 1915 he was elected associate justice of the Alabama Supreme Court, where he served until his death. See *Alabama Official and Statistical Register* (Wetumpka: State of Alabama, Department of Archives and History, 1935), 101–102.

67. On February 17, 1865, Union soldiers under the command of General William Tecumseh Sherman entered Columbia. During the night, one-third of the city was destroyed by fire. According to Marion B. Lucas (*Sherman and the Burning of Columbia* [College Station: Texas A&M University Press, 1976]), the fire was probably started by southern troops who ignited cotton bales before evacuating the city, but, he adds, the physical condition of the city, poor relief by both Union and Confederate forces, general confusion, and a strong wind combined to spread the fire. For this and other references to South Carolina subjects, I wish to acknowledge the generous and useful suggestions of Allen H. Stokes of the South Caroliniana Library.

68. Camp Jackson was established in Columbia in 1917 as a training facility for American soldiers. During World War I, Columbia became an important military concentration center, and the soldier population doubled that of the city. After the war the camp survived as a National Guard training center. During World War II the camp again served as a training center and concentration point for American soldiers.

69. Narciso G. Gonzales (1858–1903), the son of a Cuban revolutionary general, who himself fought with the Cuban rebels in the Spanish-American War, established the *Columbia State* and made it a reform paper. He was an outspoken critic of child labor in South Carolina's factories, of the state's political machines, and of its poor record of progressive reform. The vitriolic editor and publisher was assassinated by Lt. Governor James Tillman, the nephew of "Pitchfork" Ben Tillman and the victim of some of Gonzales's barbs. See Lewis P. Jones, *Stormy Petrel: N.G. Gonzales and His State* (Columbia: Published for the South Carolina Tricentennial Commission by the University of South Carolina Press, 1973).

70. Benjamin Ryan Tillman (1847–1918) was elected governor of South Carolina in 1890. He championed the cause of the small upland farmers against the Bourbon regime of Wade Hampton. An agrarian reformer, Tillman established the state agricultural college at Clemson and the female normal school (Winthrop College). He standardized state railroad rates, instituted the state primary, and established a state monopoly over liquor sales. According to historian William J. Cooper, Jr., Tillman's radicalism in power "amounted to little more than strident Negrophobism. He initiated no programs to better the lot of hard-pressed agrarians, nor did he ever appeal to landless whites or blacks." See John A. Garraty, ed., *Encyclopedia of American Biography* (New York: Harper & Row, 1974), 1102; and also Francis Butler Simkins, *Pitchfork Ben Tillman, South Carolinian* (Baton Rouge: Louisiana State University Press, 1944).

71. Maxcy Gregg (1814–1862) espoused state rights and secession in the 1850s. A lawyer and veteran of the Mexican War, he objected to the Compromise of 1850, especially the admission of California as a free state. In 1857–1858, Gregg favored the reopening of the African slave trade as a means to force the South's withdrawal from the Union. Gregg helped to frame South Carolina's secession ordinance. As a Confederate general during the Civil War, he served with distinction in the peninsular campaign of 1862. He was killed at Fredericksburg. See Robert E. Krick, "Maxcy Gregg: Political Extremist and Confederate General," *Civil War History* 19 (December 1973): 293–313.

72. On the evolution of the University of South Carolina, see Daniel W. Hollis, *The University of South Carolina*, 2 vols. (Columbia: University of South Carolina Press, 1951–1956).

73. Preston Smith Brooks (1819–1857), planter, lawyer, veteran of the Mexican War, and member of the United States House of Representatives (1852–1857), attained a dubious fame by caning Senator Charles Sumner in the Senate in 1856. Sumner had delivered a strong, and coarse, speech on the Kansas issue, in which he denigrated Brooks's uncle, Senator A.P. Butler of South Carolina, among others. Of unstable mind, Brooks waited two days before he sneaked up on Sumner, who was working at his Senate seat, and then rained blows upon him. The act intensified sectional tensions greatly, for northerners deemed it proof of the slaveholders' corruption and southerners delighted in the suffering of the antislavery senator. Brooks resigned his House seat after being investigated by a congressional committee, but he was unanimously re-elected by his constituents. He spent much of 1856 and 1857 being feted by southerners for his act, while privately agonizing over the dangerous political implications of his rashness. See James E. Waimsley, "Brooks, Preston Smith," in *Dictionary of American Biography,* 20 vols. (New York: Charles Scribner's Sons, 1928–1936), 3:88.

74. Charles Sumner (1811–1874) was one of the most prominent public figures of his day. Educated at Harvard, Sumner became a distinguished lawyer, a professor at Harvard Law School, and a popular orator. He entered the United States Senate as a "Free Soiler" in 1851, but became an architect of the Republican party. Sumner's antislavery arguments and his sometimes overly abusive speeches against the Fugitive Slave Act and the Kansas-Nebraska Act earned him the enmity of many southerners. After his beating at the hands of Brooks, Sumner left his Senate seat vacant for two years as silent testimony to southern barbarity. During the Civil War, he pushed for emancipation and for a strong, prolonged military occupation of the South after the war. He was a leader among Radical Republicans, sponsor of civil rights bills, and a supporter of the Freedmen's Bureau and an amendment to insure black suffrage. See David H. Donald, *Charles Sumner and the Coming of the Civil War* (New York: Knopf, 1967) and *Charles Sumner and the Rights of Man* (New York: Knopf, 1970).

75. Robert Mills (1781–1855), born in Charleston, became one of America's most respected architects and engineers. As a young man, he came under the influence of Thomas Jefferson, Charles Bulfinch, and especially Benjamin H. Latrobe. He designed the Congregational Church (the "Circular Church") in Charleston in 1804, introducing there the auditorium principle for seating. From 1808 to 1817, he worked successfully in Philadelphia, designing and building churches and reconstructing the old state house (Independence Hall). In 1817, Mills moved to Baltimore where he designed several important churches and public buildings. In 1820, he returned to Charleston as state engineer and architect. Under his direction, South Carolina improved its water system and constructed many public buildings. In Charleston, he is chiefly remembered for his design of the Fireproof Building (now the South Carolina Historical Society), but he earned a national reputation for his work after 1830, when he had removed to Washington. Among his legacies were the Treasury building, the Patent Office, the Post Office, and the Washington Monument. See Fiske Kimball, "Mills, Robert," *Dictionary of American Biography,* 13:9–13.

76. Henry Campbell Davis (1879–1951) graduated from South Carolina College in 1898 and received his master's degree from the University of South Carolina in 1907. A specialist on Edgar Allan Poe, black folklore in South Carolina, and historical syntax, Davis had taught at various high schools and at the University of Washington before coming to the University of South Carolina in 1904. Davis was never head of the department of English, but he did serve as head of the English language division of the department from 1935 until his retirement from the university in 1949. See *Directory of American Scholars: A Biographical Directory* (Lancaster, PA: Science Press, 1942), 198–199; "University of South Carolina Instructional Staff Survey of 1948," University Ar-

chives, University of South Carolina, 104–105; and John R. Heiting (Assistant Archivist, McKissick Museums of the University of South Carolina) to Randall M. Miller, August 6, 1981, in possession of Miller.

77. Joseph LeConte (1823–1901) graduated from the University of Georgia in 1841, studied and practiced medicine for several years, and then went to Harvard University to study zoology and geology under Louis Agassiz in 1850. LeConte taught at various colleges, including the University of South Carolina, before accepting an appointment as professor of geology and natural history at the University of California in 1869. He became the first president of the University of California soon after. LeConte established an international reputation for his many publications on geology, optics, physiology, and evolution. See H. Lewis McKinney, "Joseph LeConte," in *Dictionary of Scientific Biography*, ed. Charles C. Gillispie, 16 vols. (New York: Scribner, 1970–1980), 8:122–123.

78. James Woodrow (1828–1907), the uncle of Woodrow Wilson, was born in England but educated in the United States. He graduated from Jefferson College in Pennsylvania, studied under Louis Agassiz at Harvard, and earned his Ph.D. from Heidelberg University in Germany. Woodrow taught at several schools in Alabama and at Oglethorpe University in Milledgeville, Georgia. In 1860, he was ordained a Presbyterian minister, and in 1861 he accepted the chair of natural sciences at the Presbyterian Seminary at Columbia, South Carolina. He held his professorship there until 1886, even while serving as chief of the Confederate chemical laboratory at Columbia during the Civil War, as treasurer of foreign missions of the Southern Presbyterian General Assembly (1861–1872), as editor of the quarterly *Southern Presbyterian Review* (1861–1885), as publisher of the weekly *Southern Presbyterian* (1865–1893), and as professor of science at the University of South Carolina. From 1891 to 1897, Woodrow was president of the university. Woodrow got into trouble with his co-religionists in 1884, when he argued that no fundamental conflict existed between the Bible and science because the Bible did not teach science. In trying to adapt evolution as a deeper revelation of God's majesty, and by suggesting that Adam had evolved from a lower animal form, Woodrow ran afoul of fundamentalists who insisted on the infallibility of the Bible, even as science. Although Woodrow defended his arguments ably, his opponents forced his removal from his chair at the seminary and from his positions in the Southern Presbyterian church. Eaton presented his research on Woodrow, "Professor James Woodrow and the Freedom of Teaching in the South," as his presidential address, delivered in Chattanooga to the Southern Historical Association in 1961. His address was subsequently published in the *Journal of Southern History* 28 (February 1962): 3–17. On Woodrow's life see John E. Pomfret, "Woodrow, James," *Dictionary of American Biography*, 20:495–496.

79. Rockwell Kent (1882–1971) was one of America's foremost painters and book illustrators, famous for his stark and rugged landscapes and his advocacy of left-wing causes. Kent's popularity declined in the late 1940s and 1950s because of his politics and his links to Communism. Kent received the Lenin Peace Prize in 1967 for his support of the Soviet Union. He gave the Soviet Union eighty of his paintings and hundreds of his drawings. As an architect, illustrator, cartoonist, painter, trade unionist, author, and "political controversialist," he believed he could change society through art. See his obituary in the *New York Times,* March 14, 1971, and David Traxel, *An American Saga: The Life and Times of Rockwell Kent* (New York: Harper & Row, 1980).

80. Tolliver C. Callison (1884–1966) received his LL.B. from the University of South Carolina in 1909 and first practiced law in Charleston (1910–1911). He served as solicitor with the Eleventh Judicial Circuit of South Carolina from 1921 to 1936, as assistant attorney general of South Carolina from 1940 to 1950, and as attorney general of the state from 1951 to 1959. See Louise J. Dubose, ed., *South Carolina Lives: The Palmetto Who's Who* (Hopkinsville, KY: Historical Records Association, 1963), 91.

81. John Mobley Daniel (1883–1951) graduated from Furman University in 1904 and, after reading law for several months, was admitted to the South Carolina bar in 1904. Daniel first practiced law and published a newspaper in Saluda, but in 1907, he moved to Greenville, where he maintained his law practice until his death. Daniel served as a magistrate for Greenville Township (1916–1920), as a member of the state House of Representatives (1911–1912), as assistant attorney general of South Carolina (1920–1925), and from 1925 to 1950 as attorney general of South Carolina. *National Cyclopaedia of American Biography,* 43:196.

82. Margaret Woods Babcock Meriwether (1895–1968) graduated from Wellesley College in 1917 and married Robert L. Meriwether (1890–1958), who was head of the history department at the University of South Carolina for many years and was also the first director of the South Caroliniana Library at the University. Mrs. Meriwether was an archivist at the South Caroliniana Library until her retirement in 1960 and a writer. She was also a founding member of the League of Women Voters in South Carolina. See Dubose, *South Carolina Lives,* 413, and Eleanor M. Richardson (Reference Librarian, South Caroliniana Library) to Randall M. Miller, August 17, 1981, (in possession of Miller).

83. Wade Hampton II (1791–1858) was the eldest son and namesake of the Revolutionary War soldier, congressman, and planter Wade Hampton (1751?–1835). After a brief stint in the army during the War of 1812 and a short stay at South Carolina College, Hampton devoted himself to managing "Millwood," the family plantation near Columbia. There Hampton entertained many of America's prominent political and literary figures, bred blooded horses, and extended the family fortune by planting and by shrewd purchases of Mississippi lands. See the obituary in *Charleston Daily Courier,* February 12, 15, 1858.

84. Wade Hampton III (1818–1902) was the eldest son of Wade Hampton II. He graduated from South Carolina College and read law, but lived and worked as a planter, managing both the South Carolina estates and the Mississippi property. Hampton served in the state legislature from 1853 to 1861. During the Civil War, he won fame as a cavalry officer with J.E.B. Stuart, commanding the cavalry serving with Lee's army after Stuart's death. After the war, Hampton tried to restore his South Carolina and Mississippi lands, but he slowly became involved in politics, opposing Radical Reconstruction and, in 1876, accepting the nomination for governor by the "straight-out" Democrats. The 1876 gubernatorial campaign was marked by "Red shirt" parades, bullyragging, and Hampton's pledges of an end to Republican political corruption and fairness to blacks under a conservative regime. Hampton was elected in 1876, and re-elected in 1878, but he was never able to carry out his pledges of establishing racial harmony and good government. Hampton became identified with white-rule government and Bourbon politics as governor and as a United States senator from 1879 to 1891. See Hampton M. Jarrell, *Wade Hampton and the Negro: The Road Not Taken* (Columbia: University of South Carolina Press, 1949), and Manly W. Wellman, *Giant in Gray: A Biography of Wade Hampton of South Carolina* (New York: Scribner, 1949).

85. Mary Martin Rucker was the second wife of Elbert Marion Rucker, Jr. (1866–1926), who came to the University of South Carolina in 1910 as a professor of law.

86. Thomas Cooper (1759–1839) of England early won attention in America for his attacks on the British political establishment and his support for the French Revolution. He emigrated to the United States in 1794 and attached himself to the Jeffersonians. He suffered under the Alien and Sedition Acts in 1800, but was rewarded by Jefferson with an appointment as a judge in Pennsylvania. He later taught at Dickinson College and the University of Pennsylvania and was Jefferson's choice as principal professor at the University of Virginia, but clerical opposition prevented his appointment there. In 1820, he

became a professor at South Carolina College and soon after its president—a post he retained until 1834. Although his materialistic philosophy and contempt for the clergy generated opposition to his tenure there, his ardent defense of slavery and state rights, and his recanting of much of his earlier Jeffersonian liberalism, gained him support from the conservative political establishment in South Carolina. See Dumas Malone, *The Public Life of Thomas Cooper, 1783–1839* (New Haven: Yale University Press, 1926). Cooper's volte-face both fascinated and angered Eaton in his study of southern "liberalism."

87. Henry Timrod (1828–1867) lived on the edge of poverty much of his life. He tutored privately and, in 1864, became the editor of the *Columbia South Carolinian*. He published many poems in southern newspapers and magazines, but the Civil War occasioned his most important, and noticed, work. Although celebrated as the "Laureate of the Confederacy," Timrod was hardly bellicose or militant in his works. A few of his poems favoring war made his reputation, but most of his work expressed the sorrows and losses of war. See Edd W. Parks, *Henry Timrod* (New York: Twayne, 1964), and Guy A. Cardwell, "Henry Timrod," in *Southern Writers: A Biographical Dictionary,* ed. Robert Bain, Joseph M. Flora, and Louis D. Rubin (Baton Rouge: Louisiana State University Press, 1979), 455–457.

88. John Smith Preston (1809–1881) was born in Virginia but moved to South Carolina in 1840 to join his brother, William Campbell Preston (1794–1860), and his wife's family. He acquired a large sugar plantation in Louisiana, which gave him sufficient wealth to become a patron of the arts. A secessionist, he served with distinction in the southern army, but he made his most important contribution to the Confederacy as superintendent of the Confederate Bureau of Conscription. He remained an "unreconstructed rebel" until his death. His brother, a native of Philadelphia, graduated from South Carolina College and became an eminent lawyer and statesman in South Carolina. A state rights man, he served in the state legislature for several terms and, in 1836, was elected to the United States Senate. Preston resigned his Senate seat in a dispute with Martin Van Buren's supporters in South Carolina. In 1846, he became president of South Carolina College, but he stepped down in 1851 because of poor health. See J.G. de R. Hamilton, "Preston, John Smith," *Dictionary of American Biography* 15:202–203, and "Preston, William Campbell," *Dictionary of American Biography* 15:207–208.

89. Beginning with Laurence Manning, a Revolutionary War hero and planter in the Santee River region of South Carolina, the Manning family produced prominent planters and politicians for 100 years in South Carolina. They included Richard I. Manning I (1789–1836), who served in the United States House of Representatives and also as governor of his state during the Nullification Crisis; his son John Laurence Manning (1816–1889), who was elected governor of South Carolina in 1852 and extended the family properties significantly; Richard I. Manning II (d. 1861), who devoted himself to planting; and Richard I. Manning III (1859–1931), who was a banker, legislator, and in 1914 a Progressive reform governor of South Carolina. See Robert Milton Burts, *Richard Irvine Manning and the Progressive Movement in South Carolina* (Columbia: University of South Carolina Press, 1974), 1–13 and passim.

90. See n. 67.

91. Alexander S. Salley, Jr. (1871–1961) was a lawyer, historian, and bibliophile who gathered a considerable collection of writings by southerners, particularly those of William Gilmore Simms. Salley graduated from The Citadel in 1892 and was admitted to the South Carolina bar in 1899. As secretary and treasurer of the South Carolina Historical Society from 1899 to 1905, he quadrupled the society's membership. He revived the Historical Commission of South Carolina in 1905 and served as its secretary from that date to his retirement in 1949. The Commission (now the South Carolina Department of Archives and History) changed his title to director in 1946, and he held that title in an

honorary capacity after his retirement. Salley wrote, compiled, or edited several works on South Carolina history. See Clifford K. Shipton, "Alexander Samuel Salley," *Proceedings of the American Antiquarian Society* 71 (1962): 13–14.

92. The Battle of King's Mountain was fought on October 7, 1780, at King's Mountain, now in York County, South Carolina, just south of the North Carolina border. It was fought between American irregulars and a force of 1,000 British troops—all Loyalists save for their commander, who had a British commission. The Americans defeated the British in a bitter contest, killing, wounding, or capturing almost all the Loyalists.

93. Eaton derived his view of Graniteville, no doubt, from Broadus Mitchell's works: *The Rise of Cotton Mills in the South* (Baltimore: Johns Hopkins University Press, 1921) and *William Gregg, Factory Master of the Old South* (Chapel Hill: University of North Carolina Press, 1928). Eaton did not significantly alter his view of Graniteville and manufacturing in the South. See for example his interpretation in *A History of the Old South: The Emergence of a Reluctant Nation,* 3rd ed. (New York: Macmillan, 1975), 422–427.

94. Eaton refers to the Delaware River at Easton, Pennsylvania, where Lafayette College is located. He was teaching at Lafayette at the time.

95. Eugene Talmadge (1884–1946) was a lawyer and farmer who became one of Georgia's most powerful and controversial political figures. He served as governor of the state from 1933 to 1937 and again from 1941 to 1943, and was elected governor again in 1946 in a campaign that killed him. Throughout his career Talmadge advocated white supremacy, religious fundamentalism, and individualism. He prospered politically because of his easy rapport with country folk, even as he preached a doctrine of hard work and self-denial, rather than public assistance, as the basic prescription for ending Georgia's rural poverty. Talmadge opposed many New Deal measures and broke with the Roosevelt administration in 1935. He tried unsuccessfully to win election to the United States Senate in 1936 and 1938, but otherwise fought Roosevelt successfully in the state. His administrations were marked by special favors to business—such as the establishment of uniform license tags—and the growing strength of his political machine. He also engaged in purges of the university system (see n. 100). See William Anderson, *The Wild Man from Sugar Creek: The Political Career of Eugene Talmadge* (Baton Rouge: Louisiana State University Press, 1975).

96. Helen Douglas Mankin (1896–1956) graduated from Rockford College in Illinois and from the Atlanta Law School. She practiced law in Atlanta and also served five terms (1937–1946) in the General Assembly of Georgia. In February 1946 she was elected to the 79th Congress to fill the vacancy left by the resignation of Robert Ramspeck. She was not returned to Congress in the regular election of 1946. See *Official Congressional Directory, 79th Congress, 2d Session, Beginning January 14, 1946,* 2d ed., corrected to June 29, 1946 (Washington: Government Printing Office, 1946), 22, and *Biographical Directory of the American Congress, 1774–1971* (Washington: United States Government Printing Office, 1971), 1333.

97. Robert A. Toombs (1810–1885) graduated from Union College in New York in 1828 and attended the law school at the University of Virginia. He rapidly rose in law and politics in Georgia. After several terms in the state legislature he entered Congress as a Whig Congressman (1845–1853) and became a prominent Whig and Unionist Senator (1853–1861). Toombs joined the secessionist movement late in 1860. He served as the Confederacy's first secretary of state and then as a brigadier general, seeing action in the Virginia theater. He was often at odds with the Davis government, however. He fled America after the war, but returned in 1867. See Ulrich B. Phillips, *The Life of Robert Toombs* (New York: Macmillan, 1913), and William Y. Thompson, *Robert Toombs of Georgia* (Baton Rouge: Louisiana State University Press, 1966).

98. On the role of literary societies, and on college life generally, see E. Merton Coulter, *College Life in the Old South* (1928; reprint, Athens: University of Georgia Press, 1951), 103–133 and passim.

99. Ellis Merton Coulter (1890–1981) graduated from the University of North Carolina and took his doctorate at the University of Wisconsin. After a brief stint at Marietta College in Ohio, he came to the University of Georgia in 1919, where, except for a few brief absences, he remained until his retirement in 1958. Coulter wrote or edited thirty-six books and more than 100 articles dealing with the South, especially with Georgia. From 1924 until 1973, he edited the *Georgia Historical Quarterly*. See Horace Montgomery, "A Few Words About Ellis Merton Coulter," *Georgia Historical Quarterly* 58 (Spring 1974): 6–14; Michael V. Woodward, "Ellis Merton Coulter: A Case Study in the Development of Conservative Racism in the New South," *Midwest Quarterly* 20 (Spring 1979): 269–280. For the most complete list of Coulter's books and articles, see Woodward, "The Publications of Ellis Merton Coulter to 1 July 1977," *Georgia Historical Quarterly* 61 (Fall 1977): 268–278.

100. Chester M. Destler (1904–) earned his Ph.D. in history from the University of Chicago in 1932. His teaching career spanned almost three decades, first at the College of the Ozarks in Missouri and later at Albion College in Michigan, Elmira College in New York, and Connecticut College. His best-known work is *American Radicalism, 1865–1901* (New London: Connecticut College, 1946). In 1941, Destler was fired from Georgia Teachers College at Statesboro (now Georgia Southern University) as part of Governor Eugene Talmadge's purge of the Georgia University System. Talmadge was convinced that the Georgia University System spawned too many liberal and integrationist teachers, and in 1941, he struck at the system by demanding that the Board of Regents fire Walter D. Cocking, dean of the University of Georgia College of Education, and Marvin S. Pittman, president of Georgia Teachers College. Talmadge distrusted their loyalties to the South because they had been educated in New York and endorsed programs to provide education to black children. When the regents balked, Talmadge packed the board, who subsequently voted to fire both educators. The purge was under way. Talmadge forced the dismissal of eight other employees of the University System (Destler among them) and began a search for "subversive" texts and materials in the Georgia schools. A special committee identified twenty-three such texts—books that "harbored unwelcome assumptions about such things as the humanity of black people and the scientific inadequacy of the Biblical explanation of the creation." The Southern Association of College and Secondary Schools investigated Talmadge's activities and voted to remove accreditation from white colleges in the University System. Accrediting agencies of professional schools followed suit. The purge became the principal issue in the 1942 gubernatorial primary election, and Talmadge lost the election partly because of his high-handed actions. Upon taking office, Governor Ellis G. Arnall, who had defeated Talmadge in the Democratic primary, reorganized the Board of Regents to prevent further political manipulation and, thereby, restored the University System to good standing with the accrediting agencies.

Destler insists that Coulter was wrong in assuming that he was dismissed because he used a book about blacks. He recalls using Arthur Raper's *Preface to Peasantry* and E. Rupert Vance's *Human Geography of the South* in one course, but doubts Talmadge or his supporters knew about them. Destler speculates that his dismissal grew out of personal conflicts between himself and Talmadge. Destler had chaired an editorial committee for the University System that produced a syllabus and readings for the compulsory freshmen course in social studies. Talmadge objected to the requirement that students read from the magazine *Survey Graphic,* which included a portrait of an enslaved black in chains. Talmadge blamed Pittman for this and moved to fire Pittman. Destler had written and signed the first essay in the readings. It discussed the comparative intelligence of humans.

Drawing upon the "most recent" anthropological research of the times, Destler concluded that "there was no measurable difference in intelligence between the races." This argument flew in the face of Talmadge's racist assumptions about black intelligence. Destler doubts that Talmadge actually read the essay, but Pittman tried to protect Destler anyway.

Destler had also served on a committee that produced a revised version of *Georgia Problems* for the required sophomore social studies course on that theme. He also chaired the library committee of the faculty council of the University System and thus was identified with the introduction of "subversive" books. Destler had a cousin of the governor enrolled in his class on "Georgia Problems" during the semester preceding the purge. The young man "repeatedly rebelled vocally against the candid treatment that the text gave to the state's problems, so vocal as to disrupt the class" and to cause Destler to "reprimand him repeatedly."

Destler's non-academic activities also were such as to assure Talmadge's outrage, "if he knew of them." Destler had staged a conference on the state's problems, had led in the organization of a library for blacks in Bulloch County, and had acquired a bookmobile with a white driver and black assistant who "carried books to every white and black family in Bulloch and two other counties" and brought "sets of supplemental readers to all white and black schools."

Destler was treated shabbily in the purge, not even being informed of the specific reasons for his dismissal. Pittman tried to defend his faculty member, but only fell victim to the purge himself. Destler went to Elmira College in 1941. See Anderson, *Wild Man from Sugar Creek,* 195–204; William F. Holmes, "Society and Culture in an Urban Age," in *A History of Georgia,* ed. Kenneth Coleman (Athens: University of Georgia Press, 1977), 377–379 (quote taken from p. 378); Marvin S. Pittman, "Political Interference of Governor Eugene Talmadge with the Georgia Teacher's College," typescript in Special Collections, University of Georgia; Chester M. Destler to Randall M. Miller, August 9, 1981, in possession of Miller.

101. Sidney Walter Martin (1911–), a native Georgian, joined the University at Athens in 1935. He received his Ph.D. from the University of North Carolina in 1942. A specialist in southern history, Martin served as Dean of the College of Liberal Arts at the University of Georgia and, in 1966, was appointed president of Valdosta State College. He retired in 1978. *Directory of American Scholars,* 7th ed., 4 vols. (New York: Bowker, 1978), 1:442.

102. Henry Morrison Flagler (1830–1913), a longtime vice president and director of Standard Oil Company, became attracted to Florida in the 1880s. He built railroads and hotels to develop Florida's farming and tourist industries. See Martin, *Florida's Flagler* (Athens: University of Georgia Press, 1949).

103. Joel Chandler Harris (1848–1908) was born in Eatonton. He suffered a "sad and unfortunate" childhood and left Eatonton at an early age to become a typesetter. Harris lived in the world of newspapers thereafter. He worked for several papers, including the *Savannah Morning News,* for which he wrote a popular humor column. In 1873, Harris joined Henry Grady's *Atlanta Constitution,* where he remained until his retirement in 1900. There he urged sectional reconciliation and southern economic revitalization. He also developed the character Uncle Remus as his narrator, eventually transforming the character into a shrewd teller of folktales. When Harris gathered his Uncle Remus columns into a book in 1880, he was immediately recognized as an "expert" on the Old South. Harris produced other collections of Uncle Remus tales, among other works, but later in life he devoted himself to works out of the Uncle Remus mode. See Paul M. Cousins, *Joel Chandler Harris: A Biography* (Baton Rouge: Louisiana State University Press, 1968); Wayne Mixon, *Southern Writers and the New South Movement, 1865–1913* (Chapel Hill: University of North Carolina Press, 1980), 73–84.

104. Frederick Law Olmsted (1822–1903) was America's foremost landscape architect in the nineteenth century. Olmsted also wrote several influential travel books about the South. Prompted by abolitionist William Lloyd Garrison, Olmsted embarked on his first southern tour in 1852. He was commissioned by the *New York Times* to provide an account of his travels. His letters to the paper reached a large audience. After some significant revisions by Olmsted, who gave his account a distinctly more antislavery cast than it had in its original form, Olmsted published his travel account in 1856 under the title *A Journey in the Seaboard Slave States*. He also published accounts of other trips to the South: *A Journey Through Texas* (1857) and *A Journey in the Back Country* (1860). Olmsted's three books about the South were widely quoted in his own day, and subsequently by historians, and found a large following in the North. In 1861, a condensed version of the books appeared as *The Cotton Kingdom*. Recent research has demonstrated that Olmsted edited his accounts severely and was not the objective observer many northerners and later readers thought him to be. See Broadus Mitchell, *Frederick Law Olmsted: A Critic of the Old South* (Baltimore: Johns Hopkins University Press, 1924); Laura W. Roper, *FLO: A Biography of Frederick Law Olmsted* (Baltimore: Johns Hopkins University Press, 1973); and Charles C. McLaughlin, ed., *The Papers of Frederick Law Olmsted,* 4 vols. (Baltimore: Johns Hopkins University Press, 1977–1997).

105. James C. Bonner (1904–) graduated from the University of Georgia in 1926 and received his Ph.D. from the University of North Carolina in 1943. He taught at West Georgia College and Randolph-Macon College in Virginia before joining the faculty of Georgia College in 1944, where he remained until his retirement in 1969. A specialist in southern agricultural history and local history, Bonner has written several books and many articles. He is best known for his books *A History of Georgia Agriculture, 1732–1860* (Athens: University of Georgia Press, 1964) and *Georgia's Last Frontier: The Development of Carroll County* (Athens: University of Georgia Press, 1971). See *Directory of American Scholars*, 1:63.

106. David Brydie Mitchell (1766–1837) was twice governor of Georgia (1809–1813 and 1815–1817). A staunch Democratic-Republican and Jacksonian, Mitchell still pushed for internal improvements in the state, improved the banking facilities, and strengthened the militia. He vigorously prosecuted the War of 1812. In 1817, Mitchell resigned his office to become a Federal Indian agent to the Creeks. He negotiated a treaty (1818) that garnered 1.5 million acres of land from the Creeks, but his tenure was marred by charges of corruption. See Robert Sobel and John Raimo, eds., *Biographical Dictionary of the Governors of the United States, 1789–1978,* 4 vols. (Westport, CT: Meckler Books, 1978), 1:285.

107. Sir Charles Lyell (1797–1875), a product of Oxford University in England, conducted many important geological investigations in England, Sicily, and North America, among other places, and wrote several of the standard texts on geology used in the nineteenth century. In his work, he demonstrated the relationship between the physical changes of the past and the development of organisms, thereby helping to lay the scientific foundation for the theory of evolution. His geological observations in the United States were widely consulted by American geologists, engineers, and scientists. He also commented on slavery and social life in the United States in his books *Travels in North America* (1845) and *A Second Visit to the United States of North America* (1849). See Grenville A.J. Cole, "Lyell, Sir Charles," *Dictionary of National Biography*, 63 vols. (New York: Oxford University Press, 1885–1903), 34:319–324.

108. Sidney Lanier (1842–1881), "The Poet of the South," attended Oglethorpe University where he came under the influence of James Woodrow (see n. 78). Imprisonment during the Civil War impaired Lanier's health thereafter, and he struggled with pain and tuberculosis his entire life. Lanier worked as a musician, lecturer, university professor,

and lawyer—mostly in Baltimore—but he gained fame, if little money, from his poetry. Much of his poetry was highly spiritual. Edd W. Parks, *Sidney Lanier: The Man, the Poet, the Critic* (Athens: University of Georgia Press, 1968); Thomas D. Young, "Sidney Lanier," in *American Writers: A Collection of Literary Biographies*, ed. Leonard Unger (New York: Scribner, 1979), supplement 1, part 1, 349–373.

109. Herschel V. Johnson (1812–1880) was a prominent political figure in Georgia and the nation during the 1840s and 1850s. Trained as a lawyer, Johnson entered state politics and prospered. He served several terms in the state legislature, served as governor (1853–1857), and sat in the United States Senate (1848–1849). As a Unionist, he joined the Stephen A. Douglas ticket in 1860 as the regular Democratic vice-presidential candidate. Although he opposed secession in Georgia, Johnson supported the Confederacy. His state rights position, however, placed him at odds with the Davis administration. Johnson was elected to the United States Senate in 1865, but he was denied his seat by Congress. Percy S. Flippin, *Herschel V. Johnson of Georgia: State Rights Unionist* (Richmond, VA: Dietz, 1931).

110. John Carter Matthews (1909–) received his Ph.D. from the University of Virginia in 1939. A specialist in colonial and Revolutionary America, he taught at Virginia, King College in Tennessee, Stephens College in Missouri, Towson State College in Maryland, and Mercer University. See Spright Dowell, *A History of Mercer University, 1833–1953* (Macon, GA: Mercer University, 1958), 397.

111. David M. Feild (1902–) received his law degree from the University of North Carolina in 1929. Before joining the Mercer faculty in 1935, Feild taught at Furman University in South Carolina and practiced law in Greenville, South Carolina. He served as an attorney on the staff of the Criminal Division, United States Department of Justice, 1944–1945. See *Mercer University Bulletin* 32 (February 1946), 13.

112. Charles Tait (1768–1835) was a United States senator in his native Georgia who played an important role in securing the admission of Alabama as a state in 1819. Settling in Alabama in that year, he became a district judge and acquired and ran plantations in Monroe and Wilcox counties. Tait also received notice for his discovery of the "Claiborne beds"—Ecocene deposits—at his Claiborne home plantation. His son, James A. Tait (1791–1855), had served as an Indian agent and fought the Creeks during the War of 1812 before settling in Alabama to become a prosperous planter. James Tait built "Dry Forks" plantation in 1835 and resided there until his death. See Charles H. Moffat, "Charles Tait, Planter, Politician, and Scientist of the Old South," *Journal of Southern History* 14 (May 1948): 206–233, and James Tait Books, Letters, and Tait Family folder, Alabama Department of Archives and History.

113. There is no record at Tuskegee of a Professor Coe. Eaton probably refers here to Oliver C. Cox who in 1945 chaired Tuskegee's social studies division. Cox held a Ph.D. from the University of Chicago. See *Bulletin of Tuskegee Institute, 1945–1946* (Tuskegee, 1946?), 11, and Daniel T. Williams (Archivist of Tuskegee Institute) to John David Smith, February 16, 1979, in the possession of the author.

114. Robert D. Reid (1914–1980), a native of Alabama and a graduate of Talladega College, earned his Ph.D. at the University of Minnesota in 1945. A specialist in the history of blacks, he served on the editorial board of the *Journal of Negro History* for many years. In 1972 he came to Auburn University as a professor of history, after having taught at Tuskegee Institute from 1937 to 1969, except for two years at Savannah State University, and having been vice president of Alabama State University from 1969 to 1972. See his obituary in the *Journal of Southern History* 46 (November 1980): 644.

115. Frederick Douglass Patterson was a graduate of Prairie View A&M College. He received his D.V.M. from Iowa State College in 1923 and his Ph.D. from Cornell University nine years later. Patterson came to Tuskegee in 1928 to head the school's veterinary

division. From 1933 to 1935, he directed the Institute's School of Agriculture. In 1935, he became president of the Institute, and in 1953, he assumed the duties of Educational Director of the Phelps Stokes Fund. See *In Appreciation of President Frederick D. Patterson* (Tuskegee: Tuskegee Institute, 1953), and "Patterson Quits at Tuskegee," unidentified clipping, Tuskegee Institute Archives.

116. Booker T. Washington (1856–1915) was born a slave but rose to become the most powerful black figure of his day. A graduate of Hampton Institute, Washington favored industrial education rather than liberal arts training for blacks. He achieved influence among and financial support from white benefactors by espousing a policy of public accommodation with whites and not contesting too vigorously the emergence of Jim Crowism and the disfranchisement of blacks in the South. He worked covertly to attack segregation and the unfair treatment of blacks, but his public stance perhaps contributed to the rapid rise of antiblack forces in southern politics. Washington built Tuskegee Institute as a model for black education and there trained many of the black teachers who would bring rudimentary education to southern blacks during an era of Jim Crowism and proscription. See Louis R. Harlan, *Booker T. Washington: The Making of a Black Leader, 1856–1901* (New York: Oxford University Press, 1972); and Harlan, "The Secret Life of Booker T. Washington," *Journal of Southern History* 37 (August 1971): 393–416.

117. Richard Nathaniel Wright (1908–1960) was born on a cotton plantation near Natchez, Mississippi. As a boy, Wright suffered the desertion of his father and the paralyzing illness of his mother, which left him to fend for himself. At age fifteen, Wright left Memphis, where he had earlier removed, to settle in Chicago. There he worked at several menial jobs and subsisted on relief. Wright also began to write and to participate in Republican party campaigns. By 1933, Wright had joined the Communist party, largely because of its vocal support for oppressed peoples. His early writing bore the stamp of Communist influence, and much of it appeared in left-wing journals. Wright moved to New York City in the 1930s, working with the Federal Writers Project and finally prospering from the sales and attention from his classic *Native Son* (1940). In 1945, he wrote his "autobiographical" novel *Black Boy,* which also received critical acclaim and enjoyed good sales. In 1946, Wright settled in Paris, France, where he lived until his death. Wright wrote other novels and several travel books. See Michael Fabre, "Wright, Richard Nathaniel," *Dictionary of American Biography, Supplement Six, 1956–1960* (1980), 715–717, and Keneth Kinnamon, *The Emergence of Richard Wright: A Study in Literature and Society* (Urbana: University of Illinois Press, 1972).

118. Walter Duncan Bellingrath (1869–1955) moved from his native Georgia to Alabama in 1886 as an employee of the Louisville and Nashville Railroad. He settled in Mobile in 1903 and founded the Coca-Cola Bottling Company there. Bellingrath and his wife Bessie Morse Bellingrath (1878–1943) devoted their fortune to the creation of Bellingrath Gardens on the Isle-aux-Oies River near Mobile. The gardens were opened to the public after Bellingrath's death. See Henry S. Marks, comp., *Who Was Who in Alabama* (Huntsville: Strode, 1972), 27.

119. Ashmead Pringle (1908–) is a native of Charleston who graduated from the College of Charleston in 1927 and the Harvard Business School in 1929. Pringle ran a fertilizer plant in Charleston for many years. Now retired from the business, he spends much of his time studying local history and working in local civil and philanthropic causes. Pringle never became a member of the Carolina Plantation Society, although his father, Ashmead Pringle, Sr., became a member by 1947. The Carolina Plantation Society was organized in 1932 and was an exclusive club reserved for men who were bona fide owners of, "and part time resident upon, a plantation in the coastal section of the State of South Carolina." Ownership of such a plantation by one's wife was sufficient qualification for membership. Members were also drawn from prominent citizens of South Caro-

lina who were residents of Charleston. See "Notes from a Telephone Conversation with Ashmead Pringle," August 28, 1981, in possession of Randall M. Miller, and *Carolina Plantation Society Yearbook, 1947,* copy at Charleston Library Society.

120. Owen Wister (1860–1938) had strong ties to the South. His mother was the daughter of Pierce Butler and Fanny Kemble (see n. 124). Wister graduated from Harvard in 1882 and Harvard Law School in 1885 and was admitted to the Pennsylvania bar, but early on in his career he inclined toward writing about the American West. Most of Wister's important works related to his western subjects, and he is remembered today largely for his last western novel, *The Virginian* (1902). A prolific writer, Wister also produced farces and satires, books on education and politics, and biographies. His novel, *Lady Baltimore* (1906), was set in Charleston. Although "gingerly admired in its day," the book is now "deservedly forgotten." See Wallace Stegner, "Wister, Owen," *Dictionary of American Biography, Supplement Two, 1936–1940* (1958), 728–730.

121. John Berkely Grimball (1800–1892) owned six rice and cotton plantations in the Colleton district and South Carolina low country. Like many low-country planters, he spent his summers in Charleston and also engaged in mercantile pursuits. Grimball was one of the wealthiest and most astute planters of his day. During the Civil War, Grimball fled his plantations, but he regained most of his property after the war. See Grimball's "Diary," 1832–1883, Southern Historical Collection, University of North Carolina at Chapel Hill. Grimball's "Diary," which runs to seventeen volumes, is a rich source on South Carolina political, social, and economic life. Eaton referred to it often in his own work.

122. Samuel Gilman (1791–1858) was born in Massachusetts and graduated from Harvard College in 1811. After teaching several years in Boston, Gilman removed to Charleston in 1819, where he was ordained as minister of the Second Independent Church of Charleston. The church had recently embraced Unitarianism. Gilman was a capable minister and the author of numerous religious tracts, but he earned his reputation for his poetry. In his day he reigned, along with his wife Caroline Howard Gilman (1794–1888), as one of Charleston's leading literary figures. His most famous work was the ode "Fair Harvard" (1836). See Scott H. Paradise, "Gilman, Samuel," *Dictionary of American Biography,* 7:305–306; and William Stanley Hoole, "The Gilmans and the Southern Rose," *North Carolina Historical Review* 11 (April 1934): 116–128.

123. Major Stede Bonnet (d. 1718) served with distinction in the British army in Barbados before embarking on a career as a pirate. Marauding off the coast from Maine to the Carolinas, he was a major menace until the British captured him on the Cape Fear River. The British hung him. See Yates Snowden, *History of South Carolina,* 5 vols. (Chicago: Lewis, 1920), 1:174–182, and Frank R. Stockton, *Buccaneers and Pirates of Our Coasts* (New York: Macmillan, 1960), 237–263.

124. Frances Anne Kemble (1809–1893) was born into a theatrical family in England and enjoyed a much-acclaimed stage career of her own. In 1832, she accompanied her father on his American tour. In 1834, she retired from the stage because she had married Pierce Butler, heir to a large cotton and rice plantation on the Sea Islands of Georgia. Kemble admired America but angered many Americans by her criticisms of some American social habits and institutions. In 1835, she published a two-volume work, *Journal of a Residence in America,* describing her American tour, but American critics saw only her few jibes at American customs. In 1838–1839, Kemble joined her husband on his Georgia plantation. There she witnessed slavery for the first time. The experience shocked her, and she recorded her impressions of plantation life in her diary, which she published in 1863 as *A Journal of a Residence on a Georgian Plantation in 1838–1839.* Its criticisms of slavery and the South reflected the rifts that led to her divorce of Butler after her stay in Georgia. Kemble returned to England and the stage in 1846. See Winifred E. Wise, *Fanny Kemble: Actress, Author, Abolitionist* (New York: Putnam, 1967), and John A.

Scott, ed., *Journal of a Residence on a Georgian Plantation in 1838–1839* (New York: Alfred A. Knopf, 1961), ix-lix and passim.

125. James Edward Oglethorpe (1696–1785) was instrumental in securing the charter for the colony of Georgia in 1732 and led the colonists to the "debtor-province" in 1733. Oglethorpe laid out Savannah, defended the colony against the Spanish during the War of Jenkins' Ear (see n. 127), and organized the colony's political and economic life during his tenure as trustee and governor. Oglethorpe returned to England in 1743, although he retained an interest in Georgia until his death. B. Phinizy Spalding, *Oglethorpe in America* (Chicago: University of Chicago Press, 1977).

126. John Wesley (1703–1791) and Charles Wesley (1707–1788) were raised in the High Church Anglicanism of their minister father Samuel Wesley, but because of their experiences at Oxford and their missionary ventures, they became evangelicals and founders of the Methodist religious movement. John Wesley came to Georgia in 1735. The German Moravians much influenced his work there, and subsequent contact with them in Georgia and in England contributed to his definition of conversion. In Georgia, Wesley fared poorly in his mission. He did not "convert" many Indians, and he fell to squabbling with his white congregations in Savannah. He left the colony in 1737 rather than face a civil suit arising from his administration of his church and a failed courtship. In England, Wesley moved rapidly to become the great itinerant minister of the British Isles, preaching to thousands. Wesley also wrote hymns and numerous religious tracts and sermons. Charles Wesley spent six months in Georgia in 1736 as secretary to Governor James Oglethorpe. After his return to England, he devoted himself to writing hymns. Wesley published over 6,000 hymns, many of them still in use today, and lent a powerful spiritual feeling to Methodism by his hymns. During the 1850s, he accompanied his brother in their missions. See Alexander Gordon, "Wesley, Charles," *Dictionary of National Biography* 20:1209–1213, and Gordon, "Wesley, John," *Dictionary of National Biography* 20:1214–1225.

127. The Battle of Bloody Marsh occurred on July 7, 1742, during the War of Jenkins' Ear, on St. Simon's Island in Georgia. It was the decisive contest of the war in the Georgia theater. James Oglethorpe led the British troops who repelled a Spanish invasion. The British victory ended Spain's efforts thereafter to mount a full-scale military expedition to drive the English from the southern colonies. See Phinizy Spalding, "The Vision of Georgia and the Challenge of Spain," in Coleman, ed., *A History of Georgia*, 25–33.

Notes to Chapter 13

1. Laprade, "Newspapers as a Source for the History of American Slavery," *South Atlantic Quarterly* 9 (July 1910): 230–238, and "Some Problems in Writing the History of American Slavery," *South Atlantic Quarterly* 10 (April 1911): 134–141.

2. Laprade, "Some Problems in Writing the History of American Slavery," 134. Laprade's interest in slavery is evident in his unpublished manuscript, "The Legal Status of the Negroes in the District of Columbia Previous to the Abolition of Slavery, 1800–1862" [1911], William Thomas Laprade Papers, Duke University Archives.

3. See John David Smith, "The Formative Period of American Slave Historiography, 1890–1920" (Ph.D. diss., University of Kentucky, 1977).

4. Hamilton, "Three Centuries of Southern Records, 1607–1907," *Journal of Southern History* 10 (February 1944): 23–25; Mrs. Granville T. Prior to John David Smith, February 13, 1975, in possession of the author.

5. *Southern Historical Society Papers* 1 (January 1876): 41; "Historical Sketch of the Association," *Publications of the Southern History Association* 1 (January 1897): 5–6; E. Merton Coulter, "What the South Has Done About Its History," *Journal of Southern History* 2 (February 1936): 27; George P. Garrison to Franklin L. Riley, December 26, 1907,

Franklin L. Riley Papers, Southern Historical Collection, University of North Carolina at Chapel Hill.

6. Justin Winsor, "Manuscript Sources of American History—The Conspicuous Collections Extant," *Papers of the American Historical Association* 3 (May 1887): 19, 22, 27; Wendell Holmes Stephenson, "The South Lives in History: A Decade of Historical Investigation," *Historical Outlook* 23 (April 1932): 153; William P. Trent, *William Gilmore Simms* (Boston: Houghton, Mifflin, 1892), v; Trent, "The Study of Southern History," *Publications of the Vanderbilt Southern History Society* 1 (1895): 16; Weeks to Thomas M. Pittman, December 24, 1899, Thomas Merritt Pittman Papers, Southern Historical Collection, University of North Carolina at Chapel Hill.

7. Alfred Holt Stone to Dodd, July 10, 1907, Baker to Dodd, June 23, 1909, William E. Dodd Papers, Manuscript Division, Library of Congress.

8. Review of Thomas Nelson Page, *The Old South: Essays Social and Political,* in *Sewanee Review* 1 (November 1892): 90; Lynn R. Meekins to Herbert Baxter Adams, April 10, 1893, Herbert Baxter Adams Papers, Johns Hopkins University Library.

9. Stephenson, "The South Lives in History," 153; Jameson to Thomas M. Owen, January 14, 1905, Jameson to Hart, January 12, 1905, Hart to Jameson, January 23, 1905, J. Franklin Jameson Papers, Manuscript Division, Library of Congress; Hamilton, "History in the South—A Retrospect of Half a Century," *North Carolina Historical Review* 31 (April 1954): 177; Hamer, "The Records of Southern History," *Journal of Southern History* 5 (February 1939): 9; Hamilton, "Three Centuries of Southern Records, 1607–1907," 16; Coulter, "What the South Has Done About Its History," 6.

10. William E. Dodd, "Some Difficulties of the History Teacher in the South," *South Atlantic Quarterly* 3 (April 1904): 121; Charles H. Haskins, "Report of the Proceedings of the Nineteenth Annual Meeting of the American Historical Association," *Annual Report of the American Historical Association for the Year 1903,* 2 vols. (Washington: Government Printing Office, 1904), 1:29; Ford, "Manuscripts and Historical Archives," *Annual Report of the American Historical Association for the Year 1913,* 2 vols. (Washington: Government Printing Office, 1915), 1:78; Barker, letter to the editor, *Nation* 99 (July 2, 1914): 15; Fleming to Barker, December 30, 1912, copy in Wendell Holmes Stephenson Papers, Duke University Library; *New York Times,* September 7, 1924, clipping in Dodd Papers; Kilpatrick, *Preserving Southern History Material: An Address Before the Southern Club of Columbia University, July 31, 1923* (New York: Columbia University Press, 1923).

11. "Report of the Mississippi Historical Commission," *Publications of the Mississippi Historical Society* 5 (1902): 75; Phillips to Yates Snowden, January 13, 1905, Yates Snowden Papers, South Caroliniana Library, University of South Carolina; Owen to William K. Boyd, November 22, 1907, William K. Boyd Papers, Duke University Archives; *Montgomery Journal* (Alabama), December 23, 1903, clipping in Thomas M. Owen Papers, Alabama Department of Archives and History; Owen, ed., "Report of the Alabama History Commission to the Governor of Alabama," *Publications of the Alabama Historical Society* 1 (1900), passim; Owen to W.G. Leland, September 1, 1906, Jameson Papers.

12. Bancroft to Rowland, March 22, 1912, Frederic Bancroft Papers, Columbia University Library; Carl A. Ray to John David Smith, February 6, 1975, in possession of the author; Hamer, "The Records of Southern History," 12; Connor, "The North Carolina Historical Commission," *Publications of the North Carolina Historical Commission* 1 (1907): 9–10; Paul P. Hoffman to John David Smith, February 7, 1975, in possession of the author; J.D. Rodeffer, "The South's Interest in the Library of Congress," *South Atlantic Quarterly* 4 (October 1905): 319, 322; John C. Broderick to John David Smith, February 27, 1975, in possession of the author; John McDonough, "Manuscript Resources for the Study of Negro Life and History," *Quarterly Journal of the Library of Congress* 26 (July 1969): 136; Bancroft to Theodore D. Jervey, December 8, 1914, Bancroft Papers.

13. Smith, "The Formative Period of American Slave Historiography, 1890–1920," chapters 9 and 10.

14. Ibid.

15. Ibid.; Phillips to Andrew C. McLaughlin, December 10, 1904, Jameson Papers.

16. Phillips, unpublished and untitled manuscript beginning, "The field of Southern history is so rich" [1904?], Ulrich B. Phillips Collection, Yale University Library; "The South Carolina Federalists, I," *American Historical Review* 14 (April 1909): 529.

17. Phillips to George J. Baldwin, May 5, 1903, Phillips to Lucien H. Boggs, February 23, 1903, Ulrich B. Phillips Papers, Southern Historical Collection, University of North Carolina at Chapel Hill; Phillips, "The Public Archives of Georgia," *Annual Report of the American Historical Association for the Year 1903*, 2 vols. (Washington: Government Printing Office, 1904) 1:467; Phillips to Snowden, March 31, 1906, Snowden Papers; Phillips, "Plantation Records in General," in *Florida Plantation Records from the Papers of George Noble Jones,* ed. Phillips and James David Glunt (St. Louis: Missouri Historical Society, 1927), 1–5.

18. Phillips, *The Life of Robert Toombs* (New York: Macmillan, 1913).

19. Phillips to J. Franklin Jameson, November 20, 1905, Jameson Papers; Phillips to Jameson, October 10, 1907, *American Historical Review* Editorial Correspondence, Manuscript Division, Library of Congress; Phillips to Frederick Jackson Turner, July 12, 1903, Frederick Jackson Turner Correspondence, University of Wisconsin Archives; Phillips to Jameson, December 24, 1912, Phillips to Waldo G. Leland, January 16, 1905, Phillips to Andrew C. McLaughlin, February 17, April 27, 1904, Jameson Papers.

20. Phillips to J. Franklin Jameson, July 8, 1905, *American Historical Review* Editorial Correspondence; Phillips to Yates Snowden, September 26, 1909, Snowden Papers; *Galveston News* (Texas), January 31, 1929, clipping in Phillips Scrapbook, Phillips Collection.

21. Phillips, "The Public Archives of Georgia," 439–474, and "Georgia Local Archives," *Annual Report of the American Historical Association for the Year 1904* (Washington: Government Printing Office, 1905): 555–596.

22. Phillips, "The Public Archives of Georgia," 464; "Documentary Collections and Publications in the Older States of the South," *Annual Report of the American Historical Association for the Year 1905,* 2 vols. (Washington: Government Printing Office, 1906), 1:203–204.

23. Craven, "Some Historians I Have Known," *Maryland Historian* 1 (Spring 1970): 11.

24. Landon, "Ulrich Bonnell Phillips: Historian of the South," *Journal of Southern History* 5 (August 1939): 367; Hamilton to Phillips, October 27, 1928, Dexter Perkins to Hamilton, January 7, 1929, J.G. de Roulhac Hamilton Papers, Southern Historical Collection, University of North Carolina at Chapel Hill.

25. On Kellar, see Margaret C. Norton, "Herbert Anthony Kellar, 1887–1955," *American Archivist* 19 (April 1956): 151–153, and William B. Hesseltine and Donald R. McNeil, eds., *In Support of Clio: Essays in Memory of Herbert A. Kellar* (Madison: State Historical Society of Wisconsin, 1958), iii–viii, 41–43, 140.

26. Phillips to Kellar, February 15, March 1, 9, 24, 1926, Kellar to Phillips, March 17, 1926, Herbert Anthony Kellar Papers, State Historical Society of Wisconsin.

27. Kellar, "Notes on Trips to Virginia with Ulrich B. Phillips in Search of Manuscripts," pages 1–4, Kellar Papers.

28. Ibid., 4–9.

29. James P. Hendrix, Jr., "From Romance to Scholarship: Southern History at the Take-Off Point," *Mississippi Quarterly* 30 (Spring 1977): 193–211.

Notes to Chapter 14

1. See Robert Reynolds Simpson, "The Origin of State Departments of Archives and History in the South" (Ph.D. diss., University of Mississippi, 1971).

2. Dunbar Rowland, "The Importance of Preserving Local Records, Illustrated by the Spanish Archives of the Natchez District," *Annual Report of the American Historical Association for the Year 1905*, 2 vols. (Washington: Government Printing Office, 1906), 1:205.

3. See John David Smith, "The Formative Period of American Slave Historiography, 1890–1920" (Ph.D. diss., University of Kentucky, 1977), 5–11.

4. John David Smith, *An Old Creed for the New South: Proslavery Ideology and Historiography, 1865–1918* (1985; reprint, Athens: University of Georgia Press, 1991), 239–284.

5. Phillips to George J. Baldwin, May 2, 1903, Ulrich B. Phillips Papers, Southern Historical Collection, University of North Carolina at Chapel Hill; Phillips to Snowden, March 31, 1906, Yates Snowden Papers, South Caroliniana Library, University of South Carolina.

6. Phillips, unpublished and untitled manuscript beginning, "The field of Southern history is so rich" [1904?], Ulrich B. Phillips Collection, Yale University Library; Phillips, "Documentary Collections and Publication in the Older States of the South," *Annual Report of the American Historical Association for the Year 1905*, 2 vols. (Washington: Government Printing Office, 1906), 1:203–204. For a critique of Phillips as "scientific" historian, see W.K. Wood, "U.B. Phillips, Unscientific Historian: A Further Note on His Methodology and Use of Sources," *Southern Studies: An Interdisciplinary Journal of the South* 21 (Summer 1982): 146–162.

7. Phillips, "Historical Notes of Milledgeville, Ga.," *Gulf States Historical Magazine* 2 (November 1903): 170.

8. *Report of the Chancellor of the University of Georgia* (1901), 11–12, Phillips Collection; Wendell H. Stephenson, "Ulrich B. Phillips, the University of Georgia, and the Georgia Historical Society," *Georgia Historical Quarterly* 41 (June 1957): 118–125.

9. Phillips to Frederick Jackson Turner, July 12, 1903, Frederick Jackson Turner Correspondence, University of Wisconsin Archives; Phillips to Lucien H. Boggs, February 23, 1903, Phillips Papers.

10. Phillips to George J. Baldwin, April 17, 1903, Phillips Papers.

11. Phillips, "The Public Archives of Georgia," *Annual Report of the American Historical Association for the Year 1903*, 2 vols. (Washington: Government Printing Office, 1904), 1:439; Phillips to George J. Baldwin, April 17, September, 26, 1903, Phillips Papers. In spite of Phillips's negative assessment, between 1904 and 1916, Candler edited thirty-five volumes of Georgia Colonial, Revolutionary, and Confederate Records. See Theodore H. Jack, "The Preservation of Georgia History," *North Carolina Historical Review* 4 (July 1927): 245–246.

12. Phillips, "The Public Archives of Georgia," 440, 459–460, 455; Phillips, "Georgia Local Archives," *Annual Report of the American Historical Association for the Year 1904* (Washington: Government Printing Office, 1905), 592.

13. Phillips, "The Public Archives of Georgia," 441, 444, 449, 454.

14. Ibid., 454, 451.

15. Ibid., 440, 444, 461, 467.

16. Phillips, "Georgia Local Archives," 555, 568, 569, 581.

17. Ibid., 582, 583, 584.

18. Phillips, "The Public Archives of Georgia," 456, 457.

19. Ibid., 458.

20. Ibid., 464.

21. Phillips, "Georgia Local Archives," 560, 566, 567.

22. Phillips, "Documentary Collections and Publication in the Older States of the South," 203, 201, 202, 202–203.

23. Ibid., 201, 202.

24. Ibid., 203, 204.

25. J. Carlyle Sitterson, "The Southern Historical Collection, 1930–1980: The Pursuit of History," *Bookmark* (Chapel Hill: Friends of the Library and the Southern Historical Collection at the University of North Carolina at Chapel Hill, 1981), 46–59; Mattie U. Russell, "Brief History of the Manuscript Department and the Flowers Collection," *Duke University Library Newsletter*, n.s. 24 (April 1980): 4–5; Hamilton to Phillips, October 27, 1928, Dexter Perkins to Hamilton, January 7, 1929, J.G. de Roulhac Hamilton Papers, Southern Historical Collection, University of North Carolina at Chapel Hill.

26. John David Smith, " 'Keep 'Em in a Fireproof Vault'—Pioneer Southern Historians Discover Plantation Records," *South Atlantic Quarterly* 78 (Summer 1979): 387–391; Dillon, *Ulrich Bonnell Phillips: Historian of the Old South* (Baton Rouge: Louisiana State University Press, 1975), 125, 126. Dillon argues that "Phillips' large reputation as a discoverer and user of" private manuscripts "rests in great measure upon the materials Kellar helped him acquire from 1925 to 1929."

27. John Herbert Roper, *U.B. Phillips: A Southern Mind* (Macon, GA: Mercer University Press, 1984), 67–89.

28. Commenting on Phillips's assessment of Georgia's public records, as well as Maud Barker Cobb's 1917 survey, Mary Givens Bryan remarked, "Some items they reported missing have turned up in the assembling of the archives, while others reported on file are today missing." See Bryan, "Recent Archival Developments in Georgia," *American Archivist* 16 (January 1953): 56.

Notes to Chapter 15

1. See John David Smith and John C. Inscoe, eds., *Ulrich Bonnell Phillips: A Southern Historian and His Critics* (1990; reprint, Athens: University of Georgia Press, 1993).

2. Phillips is the subject of two biographies: John Herbert Roper, *U.B. Phillips: A Southern Mind* (Macon, GA: Mercer University Press, 1984), and Merton L. Dillon, *Ulrich Bonnell Phillips: Historian of the Old South* (Baton Rouge: Louisiana State University Press, 1985).

3. See Brooks Simpson, "Editors, Editing and the Historical Profession," *OAH Newsletter* (May 1989), 8–9.

4. In addition to these three documentaries and the edited articles mentioned in this article, Phillips also edited "South Carolina Federalist Correspondence, 1789–1797," *American Historical Review* 14 (July 1909): 776–790, and "Some Letters of Joseph Habersham," *Georgia Historical Quarterly* 10 (June 1926): 144–163.

5. *Annual Report of the American Historical Association for the Year, 1903*, 2 vols. (Washington: Government Printing Office, 1904), 1:409 [hereinafter cited as *AHA Annual Report*]; *AHA Annual Report, 1908* (2 vols., 1909), 1:19; *AHA Annual Report, 1913* (2 vols., 1915), 19. On Phillips's long and persistent interest in archives and manuscripts, see John David Smith, " 'Keep 'Em in a Fire-Proof Vault'—Pioneer Southern Historians Discover Plantation Records," *South Atlantic Quarterly* 78 (Summer 1979): 376–391, and Smith, "The Historian as Archival Advocate: Ulrich Bonnell Phillips and the Records of Georgia and the South," *American Archivist* 52 (Summer 1989): 320–331.

6. Phillips, "Documentary Collections and Publication in the Older States of the South," *AHA Annual Report, 1905* (2 vols., 1906), 1: 200–204.

7. Phillips to Richard T. Ely, October 28, 1907, Richard T. Ely Papers, State Historical Society of Wisconsin.

8. Jameson to Phillips, December 12, 1905, *American Historical Review* Editorial Correspondence, Manuscript Division, Library of Congress; Jameson to H. Morse Ste-

phens, October 11, 1915, in *An Historian's World: Selections from the Correspondence of John Franklin Jameson,* ed. Elizabeth Donnan and Leo F. Stock (Philadelphia: American Philosophical Society, 1956), 185.

9. See Fred Landon and Everett E. Edwards, "A Bibliography of the Writings of Professor Ulrich Bonnell Phillips," *Agricultural History* 8 (October 1934): 196–218.

10. Worthington Chauncey Ford, "The Editorial Function in United States History," *American Historical Review* 23 (January 1918): 280–281; Clarence E. Carter, "Historical Editing," *Bulletins of the National Archives,* no. 7 (August 1952): 5–7.

11. "Report of the Historical Manuscripts Commission of the American Historical Association," *AHA Annual Report, 1896* (2 vols., 1897), 1:478–479; "Organization and Activities," *AHA Annual Report, 1911,* 21.

12. Mary-Jo Kline, *A Guide to Documentary Editing* (Baltimore: Johns Hopkins University Press, 1987), 2–4.

13. Phillips, "Early Railroads in Alabama," *Gulf States Historical Magazine* 1 (March 1903): 345; Phillips, "Documentary Collections and Publication in the Older States of the South," 1:202; Phillips's review of Theodore D. Jervey, *The Slave Trade, Slavery, and Color,* in *American Historical Review* 32 (October 1926): 169; Phillips to the editor, February 27, 1922, Phillips to Henry E. Bourne, June 7, 1931, *American Historical Review* Editorial Correspondence; Phillips's review of Catterall, *Judicial Cases Concerning American Slavery and the Negro,* in *American Historical Review* 32 (January 1927): 332; Phillips to J. H. Easterby, April 17, 1931, J.H. Easterby Papers, South Caroliniana Library, University of South Carolina.

14. See "The Public Archives of Georgia," *AHA Annual Report, 1903* (2 vols., 1904), 1:439–474; and "Georgia Local Archives," *AHA Annual Report, 1904* (1905), 555–596.

15. Phillips, "Documents," *Gulf States Historical Magazine* 2 (July 1903): 58–60; Phillips, "Documents," *Gulf States Historical Magazine* 2 (March–May 1904): 412, 419n; Phillips, "The Draper Collection of Manuscripts," *Gulf States Historical Magazine* 2 (March–May 1904): 421–422; Phillips, "Historical Notes of Milledgeville, Ga.," *Gulf States Historical Magazine* 2 (November 1903): 171.

16. Harold L. Miller, "The American Bureau of Industrial Research and the Origins of the 'Wisconsin School' of Labor History," *Labor History* 25 (Spring 1984): 174, 184–185; Ely to Phillips, December 16, 1908, Phillips to Ely, December 17, 1908, Ulrich B. Phillips Papers, Southern Historical Collection, University of North Carolina at Chapel Hill.

17. Phillips to Robert Preston Brooks, February 11, 1908, Ulrich B. Phillips Letters, University of Georgia; Dillon, *Ulrich Bonnell Phillips,* 73–74; Benjamin G. Rader, *The Academic Mind and Reform: The Influence of Richard T. Ely in American Life* (Lexington: University of Kentucky Press, 1966), 169–170; Phillips to Ely, December 11, 1908, Phillips Papers.

18. Phillips to J.B. Adams, December 15, 1908, Phillips Papers; Phillips to Ely, December 12, 17, 18, 1908, Ely Papers.

19. Ely, "Preface," in Phillips, ed., *Plantation and Frontier Documents: 1649–1863,* 2 vols. (Cleveland: A.H. Clark, 1909) [published separately as *A Documentary History of American Industrial Society,* Volumes 1 and 2 (1910)], 1:31–32.

20. Commons to Phillips, January 13, 1908, John R. Commons Papers, State Historical Society of Wisconsin.

21. Phillips, "Introduction," *Plantation and Frontier Documents,* 1:103, 97, 69; Phillips to A.L. McLoughlin, May 16, 1904, *American Historical Review* Editorial Correspondence; Ely, "Preface," in Phillips, ed., *Plantation and Frontier Documents,* 1:30–31.

22. Miller, "The American Bureau of Industrial Research," 174; Carnegie Institution of Washington, *Yearbook No. 3, 1904* (Washington: Carnegie Institution of Washington, 1905), 146; Carnegie Institution of Washington, *Yearbook No. 4, 1905* (Washington:

Carnegie Institution of Washington, 1906), 41, 238; Phillips to Ely, December 11, 1908, Phillips Papers; McCarthy to John Franklin Jameson, October 1, 1903, in "Letters: Charles McCarthy to J. Franklin Jameson," ed. Elizabeth Donnan and Leo F. Stock, *Wisconsin Magazine of History* 33 (September 1949): 78; Edward A. Fitzpatrick, *McCarthy of Wisconsin* (New York: Columbia University Press, 1944), 23. McCarthy coached football at the University of Georgia, 1897–1898, when Phillips was a student there.

23. Phillips, "Industrial Society in the Ante-Bellum South: An Outline of the Field," unpublished manuscript, n.d., page 14, Ely Papers; Phillips to Ely, June 23, July 8, 1904, June 26, 1906, Ely Papers; Phillips to E.B. Craighead, August 23, 1907, Ulrich B. Phillips Personnel File, Tulane University Archives; Phillips, *Plantation and Frontier Documents*, 1:23, 95.

24. Phillips, *Plantation and Frontier Documents*, 1:95, 96, 97, 98.

25. Ibid., 1:23, 95, 97, 95, 103.

26. Ibid., 1:98.

27. Ibid., 1:100, 101.

28. Ibid., 1:214–215, 259–260; 2:89; 1:102.

29. Ibid., 1:186–193, 98, 99.

30. Ibid., 1:72, 73, 72, 71; Phillips, "The Black Belt," *Sewanee Review* 12 (January 1904): 76; Phillips, "The Plantation as a Civilizing Factor," *Sewanee Review* 12 (July 1904): 263; Phillips, "Conservatism and Progress in the Cotton Belt," *South Atlantic Quarterly* 3 (January 1904): 8.

31. Shepherd's review of *Plantation and Frontier Documents*, in *Political Science Quarterly* 25 (September 1910): 526–527; Winthrop More Daniels, "The Slave Plantation in Retrospect," *Atlantic Monthly* 107 (March 1911): 363, 365; Matthew B. Hammond, "A History of Labor in America," *Dial* 49 (October 1, 1910): 237; Stone's review of *Plantation and Frontier Documents*, in *American Historical Review* 16 (October 1910): 138–139; "Preface" in Green, ed., *Ferry Hill Plantation Journal, January 4, 1838–January 15, 1839* (Chapel Hill: University of North Carolina Press, 1961), vii.

32. Farrand's review of *Plantation and Frontier Documents*, in *Yale Review* 19 (August 1910): 190, 192, 189, 190, 191; anon. review of *Plantation and Frontier Documents*, in *Nation* 91 (October 13, 1910): 342.

33. Phillips, *Plantation and Frontier Documents*, 1:71; 2:161–164, 162.

34. Phillips to Ely, December 12, 1908, Ely Papers. Arthur H. Clark also published Fleming's documentary. See Fleming, ed., *Documentary History of Reconstruction: Political, Military, Social, Religious, Educational and Industrial, 1865 to 1906*, 2 vols. (Cleveland: A.H. Clark, 1906–1907).

35. Phillips to Jameson, July 8, 1905, *American Historical Review* Editorial Correspondence. Mrs. Erwin's letters figured prominently in Phillips's later edition of the papers of Toombs, Stephens, and Cobb. See *AHA Annual Report, 1911* (2 vols., 1913), 2:9.

36. John David Smith, *An Old Creed for the New South: Proslavery Ideology and Historiography, 1865–1918* (1985; reprint, Athens: University of Georgia Press, 1991).

37. Phillips's review of Elizabeth Donnan, ed., *Documents Illustrative of the History of the Slave Trade to America, Vol. 1*, in *American Historical Review* 36 (January 1931): 407–408. Phillips noted that in Donnan's edition, "the planters, in a sense, [also] have no hearing." See p. 408.

38. See Phillips, *Plantation and Frontier Documents*, 2:92–93, 75, 79; 1:330, 214–230, 319–320; 2:75–98, 99–126, 41–42; 2:41–42. Phillips left no record of the corpus of documents available to him in 1909. Consequently there is no way to determine which, if any, documents pertaining to African Americans he omitted from publication.

39. Ibid., 1:97.

40. Phillips, *American Negro Slavery: A Survey of the Supply, Employment and Control of Negro Labor as Determined by the Plantation Régime* (New York: D. Appleton and Company, 1918), i.

41. See Phillips to Ely, August 26, 1904, September 13, 1905, June 26, 1906, April 19, 1909, Ely Papers; Phillips to Rowland, February 6, 1907, Dunbar Rowland Papers, Mississippi Department of Archives and History.

42. Dillon, *Ulrich Bonnell Phillips*, 125, 126.

43. Ibid., 52, 53; Roper, *U.B. Phillips: A Southern Mind*, 59.

Select Bibliography

Books and Dissertations

Aptheker, Herbert. *American Negro Slave Revolts.* 1943. Reprint, New York: International, 1970.

————. *Annotated Bibliography of the Published Writings of W.E.B. Du Bois.* Millwood, NY: Kraus-Thomson Organization, 1973.

Bailey, Fred Arthur. *William Edward Dodd: The South's Yeoman Scholar.* Charlottesville: University Press of Virginia, 1997.

Bancroft, Frederic. *Slave Trading in the Old South.* 1931. Reprint, New York: Frederick Ungar, 1959.

Blassingame, John W. *The Slave Community: Plantation Life in the Antebellum South.* New York: Oxford University Press, 1972.

Boles, John B., and Evelyn Thomas Nolen, eds. *Interpreting Southern History: Historiographical Essays in Honor of Sanford W. Higginbotham.* Baton Rouge: Louisiana State University Press, 1987.

Brown, Joseph E. *Slavery in Massachusetts and Georgia Contrasted. Mulattoes Accounted For.* Washington: n.p., 1884.

Bruce, Dickson D. *Archibald Grimké: Portrait of a Black Independent.* Baton Rouge: Louisiana State University Press, 1993.

Cimbala, Paul A., and Robert F. Himmelberg, eds. *Historians and Race: Autobiography and the Writing of History.* Bloomington: Indiana University Press, 1996.

Cooke, Jacob E. *Frederic Bancroft: Historian.* Norman: University of Oklahoma Press, 1957.

Coulter, E. Merton. *The Civil War and Readjustment in Kentucky.* Chapel Hill: University of North Carolina Press, 1926.

Cruden, Robert. *James Ford Rhodes: The Man, the Historian, and His Work.* Cleveland: Western Reserve University, 1961.

Dillon, Merton L. *Ulrich Bonnell Phillips: Historian of the Old South.* Baton Rouge: Louisiana State University Press, 1985.

Du Bois, W.E.B. *Black Reconstruction in America, 1860–1880.* 1935. Reprint, New York: Atheneum, 1975.

————. *Darkwater—Voices from Within the Veil.* 1920. Reprint, New York: AMS Press, 1969.

Eaton, Clement. *Freedom of Thought in the Old South*. Durham: Duke University Press, 1940.

Epstein, Dena J. *Sinful Tunes and Spirituals: Black Folk Music to the Civil War*. Urbana: University of Illinois Press, 1977.

Fogel, Robert William, and Stanley L. Engerman. *Time on the Cross: Evidence and Methods*. Boston: Little, Brown, 1974.

Franklin, John Hope. *George Washington Williams: A Biography*. Chicago: University of Chicago Press, 1985.

Genovese, Eugene D. *Roll, Jordan, Roll: The World the Slaves Made*. New York: Pantheon Books, 1974.

———, ed. *The Slave Economy of the Old South: Selected Essays in Economic and Social History*. Baton Rouge: Louisiana State University Press, 1968.

Gilmore, Al-Tony, ed. *Revisiting Blassingame's The Slave Community*. Westport, CT: Greenwood Press, 1978.

Goggin, Jacqueline. *Carter G. Woodson: A Life in Black History*. Baton Rouge: Louisiana State University Press, 1993.

Green, Fletcher M. *Writing and Research in Southern History*. Spartanburg, SC: Band & White, 1942.

Gutman, Herbert G. *The Black Family in Slavery and Freedom, 1750–1925*. New York: Pantheon Books, 1976.

Hale, Grace Elizabeth. *Making White: The Culture of Segregation in the South, 1890–1940*. New York: Pantheon, 1998.

Harlan, Louis R. *Booker T. Washington: The Making of a Black Leader, 1856–1901*. New York: Oxford University Press, 1972.

Henry, Howell M. *The Police Control of the Slave in South Carolina*. Emory, VA: n.p., 1914.

Howe, M.A. DeWolfe. *James Ford Rhodes: American Historian*. New York: D. Appleton, 1929.

Jones, Norrece T., Jr. *Born a Child of Freedom Yet a Slave: Mechanisms of Control and Strategies of Resistance in Antebellum South Carolina*. Hanover: Wesleyan University Press, 1990.

Joyner, Charles. *Down by the Riverside: A South Carolina Slave Community*. Urbana: University of Illinois Press, 1984.

Kilpatrick, William H. *Preserving Southern History Material: An Address Before the Southern Club of Columbia University*. New York: Columbia University Press, 1923.

Kirwan, Albert D., ed. *The Civilization of the Old South: Writings of Clement Eaton*. Lexington: University of Kentucky Press, 1968.

Levine, Lawrence W. *Black Culture and Black Consciousness: Afro-American Folk Thought from Slavery to Freedom*. New York: Oxford University Press, 1977.

Lewis, David Levering. *W.E.B. Du Bois: Biography of a Race*. New York: Henry Holt, 1993.

Link, Arthur S., and Rembert W. Patrick, eds. *Writing Southern History: Essays in Historiography in Honor of Fletcher M. Green*. 1965. Reprint, Baton Rouge: Louisiana State University Press, 1967.

Litwack, Leon F. *Trouble in Mind: Black Southerners in the Age of Jim Crow*. New York: Alfred A. Knopf, 1998.

Mahan, Harold E. *Benson J. Lossing and Historical Writing in the United States, 1830–1890*. Westport, CT: Greenwood Press, 1996.

McMurry, Linda O. *Recorder of the Black Experience: A Biography of Monroe Nathan Work*. Baton Rouge: Louisiana State University Press, 1985.

Meier, August. *Negro Thought in America, 1880–1915*. 1963. Reprint, Ann Arbor: University of Michigan Press, 1970.

Mier, August, and Elliott Rudwick. *Black History and the Historical Profession, 1915–1980*. Urbana: University of Illinois Press, 1986.

Moore, George H. *Notes on the History of Slavery in Massachusetts.* New York: D. Appleton, 1866.

Mulder, John M. *Woodrow Wilson: The Years of Preparation.* Princeton: Princeton University Press, 1978.

Nevins, Allan. *The Gateway to History.* 1938. Reprint, Garden City, NY: Anchor Books, 1962.

Novick, Peter. *That Noble Dream: The "Objectivity Question" and the American Historical Profession.* Cambridge: Cambridge University Press, 1988.

Parish, Peter J. *Slavery: History and Historians.* New York: Harper & Row, 1989.

————, ed. *Reader's Guide to American History.* London: Fitzroy Dearborn, 1997.

Phillips, Ulrich Bonnell. *American Negro Slavery: A Survey of the Supply, Employment and Control of Negro Labor as Determined by the Plantation Régime.* New York: D. Appleton, 1918.

————. *Life and Labor in the Old South.* Boston: Little, Brown, 1929.

————, ed. *Plantation and Frontier Documents: 1649–1863.* 2 vols. Cleveland: A.H. Clark, 1909.

Phillips, Ulrich Bonnell, and James David Glunt, eds. *Florida Plantation Records.* St. Louis: Missouri Historical Society, 1927.

Rhodes, James Ford. *History of the United States from the Compromise of 1850.* Vol. 1, *1850–1854.* New York: Macmillan, 1892.

Roper, John Herbert. *U.B. Phillips: A Southern Mind.* Macon, GA: Mercer University Press, 1984.

Rothberg, Morey, ed. *John Franklin Jameson and the Development of Humanistic Scholarship in America*: Vol. 2, *The Years of Growth, 1859–1905.* Athens: University of Georgia Press, 1996.

Rothberg, Morey, and Jacqueline Goggin, eds. *John Franklin Jameson and the Development of Humanistic Scholarship in America*: Vol. 1, *Selected Essays.* Athens: University of Georgia Press, 1993.

Smith, John David. *An Old Creed for the New South: Proslavery Ideology and Historiography, 1865–1918.* 1985. Reprint, Athens: University of Georgia Press, 1991.

————. *Black Slavery in the Americas: An Interdisciplinary Bibliography, 1865–1980.* 2 vols. Westport, CT: Greenwood Press, 1982.

————. "The Formative Period of American Slave Historiography, 1890–1920." Ph.D. diss., University of Kentucky, 1977.

————. ed. *Anti-Black Thought, 1863–1925: "The Negro Problem."* 11 vols. New York: Garland, 1993.

Smith, John David, and John C. Inscoe, eds. *Ulrich Bonnell Phillips: A Southern Historian and His Critics.* 1990. Reprint, Athens: University of Georgia Press, 1993.

Stampp, Kenneth M. *The Peculiar Institution: Slavery in the Ante-Bellum South.* New York: Knopf, 1956.

Stephenson, Wendell Holmes. *The South Lives in History: Southern Historians and Their Legacy.* Baton Rouge: Louisiana State University Press, 1955.

————. *Southern History in the Making: Pioneer Historians of the South.* Baton Rouge: Louisiana State University Press, 1964.

Stone, Alfred Holt. *Materials Wanted for an Economic History of the Negro.* Washington: n.p, n.d.

————. *Studies in the American Race Problem.* New York: Doubleday, Page, 1908.

Stuckey, Sterling. *Slave Culture: Nationalist Theory and the Foundations of Black America.* New York: Oxford University Press, 1987.

Van Deburg, William L. *Slavery and Race in American Popular Culture.* Madison: University of Wisconsin Press, 1984.

Walker, Clarence E. *Deromanticizing Black History: Critical Essays and Reappraisals.* Knoxville: University of Tennessee Press, 1991.

Warren, Kenneth W. *Black and White Strangers: Race and American Literary Realism.* Chicago: University of Chicago Press, 1993.

White, Shane, and Graham White. *Stylin': African American Expressive Culture from Its Beginnings to the Zoot Suit.* Ithaca: Cornell University Press, 1998.

Williams, George Washington. *History of the Negro Race in America.* 2 vols. New York: G.P. Putnam's Sons, 1882.

Williamson, Joel. *The Crucible of Race: Black-White Relations in the American South Since Emancipation.* New York: Oxford University Press, 1984.

Articles

Adams, Michael C.C. "Clement Eaton: Scholar and Gentleman." *Filson Club History Quarterly* 60 (July 1986): 319–346.

Clark, Thomas D. "Clement Eaton." *Register of the Kentucky Historical Society* 80 (Spring 1982): 140–150.

Davis, David Brion. "Slavery and the Post–World War II Historians." *Daedalus* (Spring 1974): 1–16.

Du Bois, W.E.B. "The Experts." *Crisis* 5 (March 1913): 102–103.

———. "The Study of the Negro Problems." *The Annals of the American Academy of Political and Social Science* 11 (January 1898): 1–23.

Eaton, Clement. "The Forward Lookers of the New South." In *Americana-Austriaca: Festschrift des Amerika-Instituts der Universität Innsbruck, anläblich seines zehnjährigen Bestehens.* 35–50. Vienna: Wilhelm Braumüller, 1966.

———. "James Woodrow and the Freedom of Teaching in the South." In *The Pursuit of Southern History: Presidential Addresses of the Southern Historical Association, 1935–1963,* 438–450. ed. George Brown Tindall. Baton Rouge: Louisiana State University Press, 1964.

Franklin, John Hope. "Whither Reconstruction Historiography?" *Journal of Negro Education* 17 (Fall 1948): 446–461.

Genovese, Eugene D. "Race and Class in Southern History: An Appraisal of the Work of Ulrich Bonnell Phillips." *Agricultural History* 41 (October 1967): 345–358.

Gutman, Herbert. "The World Two Cliometricians Made." *Journal of Negro History* 60 (January 1975): 53–227.

Hamilton, J.G. de Roulhac. "History in the South—A Retrospect of Half a Century." *North Carolina Historical Review* 31 (April 1954): 173–181.

———. "On the Importance of Unimportant Documents." *Library Quarterly* 12 (July 1942): 511–518.

Hendrix, James P., Jr. "From Romance to Scholarship: Southern History at the Take-Off Point." *Mississippi Quarterly* 30 (Spring 1977): 193–211.

Henry, Howell M. "The Slave Laws of Tennessee." *Tennessee Historical Magazine* 2 (March 1916): 175–203.

Hofstadter, Richard. "U.B. Phillips and the Plantation Legend." *Journal of Negro History* 29 (April 1944): 109–124.

Landon, Fred, and Everett E. Edwards. "A Bibliography of the Writings of Professor Ulrich Bonnell Phillips." *Agricultural History* 8 (October 1934): 196–218.

Lewis, Bernard. "The Historical Roots of Racism." *American Scholar* 67 (Winter 1998): 17–25.

Mooney, Chase C. "The Literature of Slavery: A Re-Evaluation." *Indiana Magazine of History* 47 (September 1951): 251–260.

Moore, Frederick W. "The Recent Revival of Interest in Historical Teaching and Investigation in the South." *American Historical Magazine* 9 (July 1904): 201–210.

Muller, Philip R. "Look Back Without Anger: A Reappraisal of William A. Dunning." *Journal of American History* 61 (September 1974): 325–338.

Phillips, Ulrich Bonnell. "Documentary Collections and Publication in the Older States of the South." In *Annual Report of the American Historical Association for the Year 1905.* 1:200–204. 2 vols. Washington: Government Printing Office, 1906.

———. "Georgia Local Archives." In *Annual Report of the American Historical Association for the Year 1904.* 555–596. Washington: Government Printing Office, 1905.

———. "The Historic Civilization of the South." *Agricultural History* 12 (April 1938): 142–150.

———. "The Plantation as a Civilizing Factor." *Sewanee Review* 12 (July 1904): 257–267.

Roper, John Herbert. "A Case of Forgotten Identity: Ulrich Bonnell Phillips as a Young Progressive." *Georgia Historical Quarterly* 60 (Summer 1976): 165–175.

———. "The Public Archives of Georgia." In *Annual Report of the American Historical Association for the Year 1903.* 1:439–474. 2 vols. Washington: Government Printing Office, 1904.

Simpson, Brooks. "Editors, Editing and the Historical Profession." *OAH Newsletter* (May 1989): 8–9.

Smith, John David. "Black Intellectuals as Activists in the Age of Jim Crow." *Reviews in American History* 22 (June 1994): 328–334.

———. "Caroline H. Pemberton: Critic of the New Proslavery Argument." *Negro History Bulletin* 45 (October–December, 1982): 113–114.

———. "Essay Review: 'Scientific History' at The Johns Hopkins University." *Pennsylvania Magazine of History and Biography* 115 (July 1991): 421–426.

———. "An Old Creed for the New South: Southern Historians and the Revival of the Proslavery Argument, 1890–1920." *Southern Studies: An Interdisciplinary Journal of the South* 18 (Spring 1979): 75–87.

———. "Review Essay: The Life and Labor of Ulrich Bonnell Phillips." *Georgia Historical Quarterly* 70 (Summer 1986): 257–272.

———. "Review Essay: 'The Work It Did Not Do Because It Could Not': Georgia and the 'New' Freedmen's Bureau Historiography." *Georgia Historical Quarterly* 82 (Summer 1998): 331–349.

———. "Ulrich B. Phillips and Academic Freedom at the University of Michigan." *Michigan History* 62 (May–June 1978): 11–15.

———. "Ulrich Bonnell Phillips: The Southern Progressive as Racist." *Yale University Library Gazette* 56 (April 1982): 70–75.

Stampp, Kenneth M. "The Historian and Southern Negro Slavery." *American Historical Review* 57 (April 1952): 613–624.

Stephenson, Wendell Holmes. "The South Lives in History: A Decade of Historical Investigation." *Historical Outlook* 23 (April 1932): 153–163.

Stone, Alfred Holt. "The Mulatto Factor in the Race Problem." *Atlantic Monthly* 91 (May 1903): 658–662.

Wiley, Bell I. "The Role of the Archivist in the Civil War Centennial." *American Archivist* 23 (April 1960): 131–142.

Wood, Peter H. " 'I Did the Best I Could for My Day': The Study of Early Black History During the Second Reconstruction, 1960 to 1976." *William and Mary Quarterly* 35 (April 1978): 185–225.

Woodward, Michael Vaughan. "Ellis Merton Coulter: A Case Study in the Development of Conservative Racism in the New South." *Midwest Quarterly* 20 (Spring 1979): 269–280.

Index

About the Author

John David Smith is Graduate Alumni Distinguished Professor of History at North Carolina State University. In 1998–1999, he served as Fulbright Professor of American Studies at the Amerika-Institut, Ludwig-Maximilians-Universität, Munich. Dr. Smith is the author or editor of eleven books, including *An Old Creed for the New South: Proslavery Ideology and Historiography, 1865–1918* (1985, 1991), *Dictionary of Afro-American Slavery* (1988, 1997, with Randall M. Miller), *Ulrich Bonnell Phillips: A Southern Historian and His Critics* (1990, 1993, with John C. Inscoe), *Black Voices from Reconstruction* (1996, 1997), and an edition of W.E.B. Du Bois's *John Brown* (M.E. Sharpe, 1997). Professor Smith received the Myers Center Award for the Study of Human Rights in North America for his eleven-volume documentary, *Anti-Black Thought, 1863–1925: "The Negro Problem"* (1993).